Y0-AAD-750

The Imperial University

The Imperial University

Academic Repression and Scholarly Dissent

Piya Chatterjee and Sunaina Maira, Editors

University of Minnesota Press
Minneapolis
London

An earlier version of chapter 2, by Roberto J. González, was published in *Militarizing Culture: Essays on the Warfare State* (Walnut Creek, Calif.: Left Coast Press, 2010).

An earlier version of chapter 11, by Jasbir Puar, previously appeared as "Citation and Censorship: The Politics of Talking about the Sexual Politics of Israel," *Feminist Legal Studies* 13, no. 2. Published online, July 15, 2011.

An earlier version of chapter 13, by Vijay Prashad, previously appeared as "Teaching by Candlelight," *Social Text* 90, vol. 25, no. 1 (Spring 2007): 105–15.

Copyright 2014 by the Regents of the University of Minnesota

All rights reserved. No part of this publication may be reproduced, stored in a retrieval system, or transmitted, in any form or by any means, electronic, mechanical, photocopying, recording, or otherwise, without the prior written permission of the publisher.

Published by the University of Minnesota Press
111 Third Avenue South, Suite 290
Minneapolis, MN 55401-2520
http://www.upress.umn.edu

Library of Congress Cataloging-in-Publication Data
The Imperial University : academic repression and scholarly dissent / Piya Chatterjee and Sunaina Maira, editors.
Includes bibliographical references and index.
ISBN 978-0-8166-8089-4 (hc : alk. paper)—ISBN 978-0-8166-8090-0 (pb : alk. paper)
1. Education. 2. Public schools—United States—Finance. I. Chatterjee, Piya. II. Maira, Sunaina.

LB2825.I47 2014
371.010973—dc23   2013038691

Printed in the United States of America on acid-free paper

The University of Minnesota is an equal-opportunity educator and employer.

20 19 18 17 16 15 14   10 9 8 7 6 5 4 3 2 1

Dedicated to Sri Rama Prasad Chatterjee—beloved baba, teacher, and friend. With deepest respect and gratitude.

And to the Irvine 11, the Davis Dozen, and all those scholars and students who paid the price.

Contents

Introduction
The Imperial University: Race, War, and the Nation-State   1
Piya Chatterjee and Sunaina Maira

I. Imperial Cartographies

1. New Empire, Same Old University? Education
   in the American Tropics after 1898   53
   Victor Bascara

2. Militarizing Education: The Intelligence
   Community's Spy Camps   79
   Roberto J. González

3. Challenging Complicity: The Neoliberal University
   and the Prison-Industrial Complex   99
   Julia C. Oparah

II. Academic Containment

4. Neoliberalism, Militarization, and the Price of Dissent:
   Policing Protest at the University of California   125
   Farah Godrej

5. Faculty Governance at the University of
   Southern California   145
   Laura Pulido

6. The Boycott, Divestment, and Sanctions Movement and
   Violations of Academic Freedom at Wayne State University   169
   Thomas Abowd

7. Decolonizing Chicano Studies in the Shadows
   of the University's "Heteropatriracial" Order   187
   Ana Clarissa Rojas Durazo

III. Manifest Knowledges

8. Normatizing State Power: Uncritical
   Ethical Praxis and Zionism   217
   Steven Salaita

9. Nobody Mean More: Black Feminist
   Pedagogy and Solidarity   237
   Alexis Pauline Gumbs

10. Teaching outside Liberal-Imperial Discourse:
    A Critical Dialogue about Antiracist Feminisms   261
    Sylvanna Falcón, Sharmila Lodhia,
    Molly Talcott, and Dana Collins

11. Citation and Censure: Pinkwashing and the
    Sexual Politics of Talking about Israel   281
    Jasbir Puar

IV. Heresies and Freedoms

12. Within and Against the Imperial University:
    Reflections on Crossing the Line   301
    Nicholas De Genova

13. Teaching by Candlelight   329
    Vijay Prashad

14. UCOP versus R. Dominguez: The FBI Interview.
    A One-Act Play *à la* Jean Genet   343
    Ricardo Dominguez

Acknowledgments   355

Contributors   357

Index   361

The Imperial University

Race, War, and the Nation-State

Piya Chatterjee and Sunaina Maira

Storm Troopers and Students

Piya: January 19, 2012. It is midafternoon on a brisk and beautiful winter day in the Inland Empire of Southern California. I enter my second floor office in the Department of Women's Studies at the University of California, Riverside. The hallway is silent. It reminds me, sadly, of any colorless and functional corporate office building. I wish for sound, some sign of collective social life. This alienating silence is particularly acute today given the noisy scenes of protest (including some Rabelaisian revelries with drumming and chants) taking place just a few hundred feet away in the student commons. The Board of Regents of the University of California (UC) is meeting on campus to address the budget crisis that has, for some years now, imperiled this great public university system and led to severe tuition hikes. Students know that their fees will be raised again. Contingent faculty and other workers know they will be plunged into further precarity. For some years now, the alliances forged among student, faculty, and labor unions in response to the public education crisis have meant that any high-level UC administrators' gathering is met with well-planned protests and resistance. But it also means that police officers and other law enforcement agents are in full gear and out in full force.

Earlier in the day, I join other protestors who throng the site of the meeting and whose mood is quite upbeat. "Whose university?" someone chants. "Our university!" replies the crowd. Plainclothes men mingle with protesters, lots of cameras are out. A friend, familiar with surveillance techniques, nudges me: "No need to get paranoid," she says, "but you do realize we are all being photographed?" A police officer repeatedly asks us to clear the commons. "*Our* university!" chants the crowd in response. In that micromoment of regulation around who should people "the commons," I sense that a fence is being

1

built—and reinforced—around who can inhabit this public space of higher education and what it means for them to do so. *Whose* university, indeed?

Later, sitting in my quiet office, I suddenly hear a loud buzzing sound outside my window. A police helicopter is circling over the empty sports field adjacent to the building. It might be an optical illusion (because from that lofty mobile panopticon, it can see much more than I can), but it seems to be circling an empty expanse of green. I watch as the helicopter's circles become smaller, tighter—it begins to resemble a psychotic bee. It seems utterly mad: the silence within, the angry buzzing outside. Suddenly, a small troop of khaki-clad youth march around the corner to my right. They have little bandanas around their neck, they are in perfect formation—they pass by quickly. I blink hard because it seems so unreal—the quick, youthful military march whose steps I cannot hear. Later, I am told that they were deployed by the Riverside sheriff's department.

This tableau feels surreal and I decide to move back to the noise and action near the student commons. The scene has now turned tense. Police in full riot gear are nose-to-nose with students who are pushing them back. Protestors want the police out of their commons. I learn from someone that some protestors have been arrested. The Riverside Police Department's SWAT team is already here and the regents have been escorted to their meeting in what looked like a secret service mission and military cavalcade, fit for royalty: regents, indeed. By late evening, the protestors have dispersed, but some of us, witnesses and participants, remain—talking about the various registers of militarized presence: the sheriff's scouts, the campus police in full riot gear, the SWAT team. The disruption of this collective protest seems to have hardly caused a ripple as we stand there in the now-quiet bucolic green expanse. But as if to remind us of the hyperreal qualities of this landscape of power, we hear the thump of marching steps. Twenty men in light green khaki march by in platoon formation. They make no sound except for the quiet thud of their steps. They are young, not much older than some of the students I teach. The SWAT team is going home.

What can we make of this strange coupling of the bucolic and the brutal, of storm troopers and students? How can we make sense of a corporatized alienation and silence alongside the visible regulation of the "public" and contours of permissible protest? How can we understand more deeply this militarized performance of state university power and its "normalization" within the quiet green peace of a public university campus? What is being "secured" in this performance of power?

Occupy the Occupation

Sunaina: November 2011. Just a few months prior to the events witnessed by Piya at UC Riverside, I had watched the pepper spraying of students by police on my campus, UC Davis. I was actually halfway across the world at the time, in Ramallah, Palestine. Pondering the question of U.S. public university students' right to protest from contexts such as the occupied West Bank, where the basic freedom of mobility let alone right to education is highly restricted, underscores the ways in which higher education is firmly embedded in global structures of repression, militarism, and neoliberalism. In fact, that November morning while I was working in Zamn cafe, one of the many upscale coffee shops that have burgeoned in the new neoliberal economy of Ramallah, I looked up from my laptop and saw the image of Lt. John Pike, spraying UC Davis students with chemical weapons, on the large-screen television that was broadcasting Al Jazeera news. It was a slightly surreal moment.

The video of the attack on the student protesters, seated on the ground, quickly went viral and drew national and global condemnation of this stark staging of state violence against the 99 percent, renaming the campus "Pepper Spray University." Not all who watched the video of the police attack on the student protesters, however, were aware that this dramatic event was the culmination of a long history of UC student protests, including at UC Davis, against tuition hikes as the burden of the UC and state's budget crisis was increasingly placed on UC students. In the months leading up to the infamous incident of November 18, 2011, UC Davis students had joined the growing Occupy movement, inspired by the revolutionary uprisings in Tunisia and Egypt. In fact, they had protested just a few days earlier against the fee hikes and also the violent assaults by police on UC Berkeley students and faculty. Student protesters, some of whom belonged to Occupy/Decolonize UC Davis (UCD), occupied the administration building and erected tents on the campus Quad. The administration refused to allow Tahrir Square to be brought to the Quad, but the protesters insisted on their right to remain—in defense of the right to education. Then the pepper spray.

In fall 2009, UC Davis students had also occupied the administration building, and fifty-two protesters were arrested. In March 2010, three hundred protesters had shut down the campus bus service and marched to the freeway to attempt to block traffic; they were beaten by police with batons. Many of these students were youth of color, some were from immigrant and working- or lower-middle-class families. When the Occupy/Decolonize UCD movement was launched in the wake of the Tahrir Square uprising, some began to also critique the ways in which neoliberal multiculturalism effectively masked the racialized politics of exclusion from higher education.[1] In spring 2012, Occupy protesters began doing a regular sit-in at the U.S. Bank branch on campus, protesting the bank's contract with the campus and the complicity of both institutions with mounting student debt and the privatization of higher education. On March 29, the bank was shut down, but eleven students and one faculty member were charged by the Yolo County district attorney with a slew of misdemeanors, facing up to eleven years in prison. Among the "Davis Dozen" were students who had been pepper sprayed and who were part of a lawsuit brought by the ACLU against the university. In fact, given that it was the university who had asked the district attorney to file criminal charges against the Davis Dozen, it was apparent that this much-less publicized case was an opportunity for the administration to clamp down on the campus Occupy movement after having been unable to do so in the fall, given the national and international outcry over the pepper spraying. Some student activists were also brought up individually for investigation by Student Judicial Affairs for issues apparently related to involvement in other campus activism. In other words, this was a tactic of legal pepper spraying.

One of the issues that had rocked the campus earlier in spring 2012, and in which some Occupy activists had been involved, was the attack on the Palestine solidarity movement at UC Davis in the wake of the controversial interruption of an Israeli soldier's talk on campus by a student. Off-campus, pro-Israel groups began issuing vitriolic statements of condemnation, and UC president Mark Yudof sent a strident letter to the entire UC community condemning the disruption. The UC Davis Students for Justice in Palestine had actually staged a silent walkout at the event in order to avoid criminal charges similar to those that had harshly penalized the UC Irvine and UC Riverside students, known as the Irvine 11. These eleven students had disrupted the speech of the Israeli ambassador at UC Irvine after the 2009 massacre in Gaza and had been prosecuted by the Orange County district attorney for their civil disobedience. The criminalization of the Irvine 11 sent a chilling message to Palestine solidarity activists that free speech in the case of critique of the Israeli state was not free, even in the academy, and came with the price of possible felony charges by the state. But the case also sparked creative organizing strategies as student activists nationwide began

walking out of pro-Israel events with their mouths taped, silently performing a critique of censorship and the exceptional repression of open debate
on this issue. It became apparent that Israeli government officials and soldiers of a foreign (occupying) military—supported and funded heavily by
the United States—had more freedom of political speech on U.S. public university campuses than college students (not to mention the fact that many
Arab and Muslim American youth have been subjected to FBI surveillance
and entrapment since 9/11).

In Ramallah, as the Arab revolutions swept across the region in 2011, Palestinian youth, too, protested against military occupation as well as internal
repression. Palestinian students continue to be abducted and incarcerated
by Israel, which restricts their access to schools and colleges, as highlighted by
the Right to Education campaign at Birzeit University. Young activists began
stenciling graffiti on the walls of Ramallah with slogans such as "Occupy
Wall Street, Not Palestine" and "#Un-Occupy." Student activists at UC Davis
were simultaneously rethinking the vocabulary of "occupy," which signifies a
tactic of protest and also a colonial practice, and adopted the label "decolonize" to indicate their solidarity with indigenous peoples. "Decolonize the
university" is their demand—occupy the banks and occupy the occupation
of other lands, other universities, and other societies transformed and devastated by settler colonialism, militarism, and neoliberal capitalism.

The Imperial University

In a post-9/11 world, the U.S. university has become a particularly charged
site for debates about nationalism, patriotism, citizenship, and democracy.
The "crisis" of academic freedom emerges from events such as the ones we
witnessed in Riverside and Davis but also in many other campuses where
administrative policing flexes its muscles along with the batons, chemical
weapons, and riot gear of police and SWAT teams and where containment
and censorship of political critique is enacted through the collusion of the
university, partisan off-campus groups and networks, and the state. After
9/11, we have witnessed a calamitously repressive series of well-coordinated
attacks against scholars who have dared to challenge the national consensus on U.S. wars and overseas occupations. Yet there has been stunningly
little scholarly attention paid to this policing of knowledge, especially
against academics who have dared to challenge the national consensus on
U.S. wars and overseas occupations and U.S. foreign policy in the Middle

East. Simultaneously, the growing privatization of the public university, as in California, has demonstrated the ways in which the gates of access to public higher education are increasingly closed and the more subtle ways in which dissident scholarly and pedagogical work (and their institutional locations) is delegitimized and—in particularly telling instances—censored at both public and private institutions. The 9/11 attacks and the crises of late capitalism in the global North have intensified the crisis of repression in the United States and also the ongoing restructuring of the academy—as well as resistance to that process—here as well as in the global South.[2]

What does it mean, then, to challenge the collusion of the university with militarism and occupation, the privatization of higher education, and economies of knowledge from within the U.S. university? When scholars and students who openly connect U.S. state formation to imperialism, war, and racial violence are disciplined, then how are we to understand freedom, academic and otherwise? How is post-9/11 policing and surveillance linked to racial, gendered, and class practices in the neoliberal academy? Has the War on Terror simply deepened a much longer historical pattern of wartime censorship and monitoring of intellectual work or is this something new?

This edited volume offers reports from the trenches of a war on scholarly dissent that has raged for two or three decades now and has intensified since 9/11, analyzed by some of the very scholars who have been targeted or have directly engaged in these battles. The stakes here are high. These dissenting scholars and the knowledges they produce are constructed by right-wing critics as a threat to U.S. power and global hegemony, as has been the case in earlier moments in U.S. history, particularly during the Cold War. Much discussion of incidents where academics have been denied tenure or publicly attacked for their critique of U.S. foreign or domestic policies, as in earlier moments, has centered on the important question of academic freedom. However, the chapters in this book break new ground by demonstrating that what is really at work in these attacks are the logics of racism, warfare, and nationalism that undergird U.S. imperialism and also the architecture of the U.S. academy. Our argument here is that these logics shape a systemic structure of repression of academic knowledge that counters the imperial, nation-building project.

The premise of this book is that the U.S. academy is an "imperial university." As in all imperial and colonial nations, intellectuals and scholarship play an important role—directly or indirectly, willingly or unwittingly—in legitimizing American exceptionalism and rationalizing U.S. expansionism and repression, domestically and globally. The title of this book, then, is not a rhetorical flourish but offers a concept that is grounded in the particular imperial formation of the United States, one that is in many ways ambiguous and shape-shifting.[3] It is important to note that U.S. imperialism is characterized by deterritorialized, flexible, and covert practices of subjugation and violence and as such does not resemble historical forms of European colonialism that depended on territorial colonialism.[4] As a settler-colonial nation, it has over time developed various strategies of control that include proxy wars, secret interventions, and client regimes aimed at maintaining its political, economic, and military dominance around the globe, as well as cultural interventions and "soft power." The chapters here help to illuminate and historicize the role of the U.S. university in legitimizing notions of Manifest Destiny and foundational mythologies of settler colonialism and exceptional democracy as well as the attempts by scholars and students to challenge and subvert them.

This book demonstrates the ways in which the academy's role in supporting state policies is crucial, even—and *especially*—as a presumably liberal institution. Indeed, it is precisely the support of a liberal class that is always critical for the maintenance of "benevolent empire."[5] As U.S. military and overseas interventions are increasingly framed as humanitarian wars—to save oppressed others and rescue victimized women—it is liberal ideologies of gender, sexuality, religion, pluralism, and democracy that are key to uphold.[6] The university is a key battleground in these culture wars and in producing as well as contesting knowledges about the state of the nation.

We argue that the state of permanent war that is core to U.S. imperialism and racial statecraft has three fronts: military, cultural, and academic. Our conceptualization of the imperial university links these fronts of war, for the academic battleground is part of the culture wars that emerge in a militarized nation, one that is always presumably under threat, externally or internally. Debates about national identity and national culture shape the battles over academic freedom and the role of the university in defining the racial boundaries of the nation and its "proper" subjects and "proper" politics. Furthermore, pedagogies of nationhood, race, gender, sexuality, class, and culture within the imperial nation are fundamentally intertwined with the interests of neoliberal capital and the possibilities of economic dominance.

The chapters here link the critique of the university to the contemporary as well as historical workings of race, warfare, and the nation-state. They demonstrate that an analysis of the foundational linkages between the U.S.

academy and the imperial nation-state need to be critically scrutinized, especially in the post-9/11 moment, and that overseas imperial interventions are linked to domestic repression, policing, and containment that penetrate the university. In drawing attention to the core issue of U.S. imperialism, this volume goes beyond a liberal discourse of academic freedom, one that is generally bounded by the nation and individual rights. Shifting the focus from notions of freedom of expression, the chapters here link the battles over knowledge production and the policing of critical scholarship to the geopolitics of U.S. imperialism across historical time and space. The contributors to this book bring together seemingly disparate geographic areas and historical moments that are key sites of U.S. expansionism and U.S.-backed occupation (such as the Philippines, Palestine, Hawaii, and Puerto Rico) as well as varied fields of scholarship (such as American studies, cultural studies, Middle East studies, feminist studies, queer studies, and ethnic studies) precisely to show how knowledge building is central to the imperial project.

The chapters speak to one another across self-evident areas, themes, disciplines, and historical periods. Through multidisciplinary research, autobiographical reflection, and writing in theoretical as well as personal registers, the book offers an intellectual and political intervention that we have imagined as a project of solidarity. As scholars who spend long hours sitting in our quiet offices—occasionally interrupted by the buzz of a helicopter—or in cafes in zones of differential occupation, wondering what acts of violence are *not* being televised, we began working on this book in order to engage in a conversation that often only happens in university hallways or over cocktails at academic conferences but not enough in public and in print. The contributors to this book raise crucial questions about the imperial university that we hope will generate and contribute to an important, unfolding conversation with scholars, intellectuals, and students and also activists, policymakers, and interested readers in the United States and beyond.

Insiders/Outsiders/Solidarities

Our geopolitical positions—of our immediate workplaces as well as transnational work circuits—underscore the complex contradictions of our locations within the U.S. academy. These paradoxes of positionality and employment have seeded this project in important ways. We have both taught at the University of California for many years—in addition to other U.S. universities—and have been members of the privileged upper caste of

THE IMPERIAL UNIVERSITY · 9

U.S. higher education: the tenured professoriate. We have each used these privileges of class, education, and cultural capital to live and work transnationally and have organized around and written about issues of warfare, colonialism, occupation, immigration, racism, gender rights, youth culture, and labor politics, within and outside the United States. In fact, we first began working together when we collaborated in 2008 on a collective statement of feminist solidarity with women suffering from the violence of U.S. wars and occupation, during the invasions of Iraq and Afghanistan and the Israeli siege of Gaza.[7] Yet our privileges of entry, of inclusion, *and* of outside-ness are also always marked by the "dangerous complicities" of imperial privilege and neoliberal capital, as the chapters by Julia Oparah; Sylvanna Falcón, Sharmila Lodhia, Molly Talcott, and Dana Collins; Vijay Prashad; and Laura Pulido powerfully remind us. Even as we have recognized the institutional privileges and complicities through which we can do this work, we have experienced at various moments and in different ways—as the chapters by Alexis Gumbs, Clarissa Rojas, Thomas Abowd, and Nicholas De Genova suggest—a keen sense of being "outsiders" within—in the university, in academic disciplines, in different nations.[8]

As scholars and teachers located within "critical ethnic studies" and "women and gender studies," we are also well aware of a certain politics of value, legitimacy, and marginality at play, especially as the dismantling of the public higher education system and attacks on ethnic studies around the nation accelerate. The struggles to build ethnic studies and women/gender/sexuality studies as legitimate scholarly endeavors within the academy, emerging from several strands of the civil rights and antiwar movements, are well chronicled and keenly debated. The precarious positions as well as increasing professionalization and policing of these interdisciplinary fields within the current restructuring of the university is a matter of deep concern; for example, in the wake of the assault on ethnic studies in Arizona, the dismantling of women's studies programs, and in a climate of policing and criminalizing immigrant "others" across the nation.

The pressure on academics to fund one's own research—following the dominant grant-writing models of science and technology—is now even more explicit in a time of fiscal crisis and deepening fissures between faculty in the humanities, social sciences, physical sciences, education, and business who occupy very different positions in an increasingly privatized university.[9] Prashad reminds us in his chapter of the consequences of the fiscal crisis for college students who bear a massive and growing burden of debt. We recognize these pressures on faculty and students as stemming from neoliberal capitalism and the university's capitulation to a global "structural adjustment" policy that is now coming "home" to roost in the United States, as astutely argued by Farah Godrej in her analysis linking the neoliberal university to militarism and violence. The academy has also tried to market the notion of "public scholarship," transforming activist scholarship into a commodifiable form of knowledge production and dissemination that can affirm the university's civic engagement—confined by the parameters of permissible politics, as incisively critiqued by Salaita, Rojas, and Abowd. If we cannot—*or choose not to*—market our scholarship and pedagogies through these programs of funding and institutionalization, we find our work further devalued within the dominant terms of privatization in the academy. Given that neoliberal market ideologies now underwrite the "value" of our research and intellectual work, what happens to scholars whose writing directly tackles the questions of U.S. state violence, logics of settler colonialism, and global political and economic dominance?

We know from stories about campaigns related to tenure or defamation of scholars, often shared in hallways during conferences and sometimes through e-mail listservs and the media, that there are serious costs to writing and speaking about these matters. For far too many colleagues who confront the most taboo of topics, such as indigenous critiques of genocide and settler colonialism or especially the question of Palestine, the price paid has been extraordinarily high. It has included the denial of promotion to tenure, being de-tenured, not having employment contracts renewed, or never being hired and being blacklisted, as this book poignantly illustrates. Coupled with the loss of livelihood or exile from the U.S. academy, many scholars have been stigmatized, harassed, and penalized in overt and covert ways. There are numerous such cases, sadly way too many to recount here—most famously those of Ward Churchill, Norman Finkelstein, David Graeber, Joel Kovel, Terri Ginsberg, Marc Ellis, Margo Nanlal-Rankoe, Wadie Said, and Sami Al-Arian—but it is generally only the handful that generate public campaigns that receive attention while many others remain unknown, not to mention innumerable cases of students who have been surveilled or harassed, such as Syed Fahad Hashmi from Brooklyn College, while again there are countless other untold stories.[10] These are the scandals and open secrets, we argue, that need to be revealed and placed in broader frames of analysis of labor and survival within the U.S. university system.[11]

As some of the chapters powerfully demonstrate, struggles against censure, self-censorship, and institutional silencing are connected to longer genealogies in which the alliance between the academy and state power is abundantly clear. We consider this gathering of chapters an act of collective and collaborative solidarity between authors and editors, who in different ways have engaged and challenged the dominant codes of belonging and citizenship within the academic nation. Indeed, as the chapters suggest, these critiques also offer the possibility of a decolonized university—one in which we can both imagine and enact our pedagogies and scholarship through a postcarceral and nonimperial institutional lens, as suggested by Oparah and Falcón et al. and as gestured to by several other authors. Such a process of decolonization is possible through the work of solidarity. The collection joins a growing archive of urgent conversations about the future of critique and dissent in the U.S. university that we will continue to engage with through a web archive that accompanies the book. We hope this digital project will allow this conversation to spill over from the pages of the book and continue in the years to come.

Crises and Continuities

While the heightened patriotism in the wake of 9/11 and a decade of U.S. wars and occupation overseas have amplified the role of the academy in shaping our understanding of U.S. global dominance and simultaneously intensified attacks on "anti-American" views—particularly in relation to the Middle East and to Islam—there is nothing "new" about this state of emergency. Ongoing debates about the role of the imperial university are indicative of the "state of exception"; that is, the exclusion of some from liberal democracy and eviction from political rights is not a sudden break but is constitutive of the imperial state and the state of permanent war.[12] The notion of the "imperial university" suggests that the War on Terror and the post-9/11 culture wars made hypervisible the *persistent* role of higher education in shaping the discourses of nationalism, patriotism, citizenship, and democracy. This is a key premise of our framework and one that underlies many of the chapters here.

Indeed, in the immediate aftermath of 9/11, Lynne Cheney and Joseph Lieberman's American Council of Trustees and Alumni (ACTA) and other neoconservative groups sounded a clarion call for an intensified scrutiny of scholarship that challenged U.S. dominance.[13] These campaigns underscored the frontlines of the culture wars through robust deployment of notions of patriotism and national security considered key to defending "Western civilization" in a nation presumably facing an existential threat. Animating this powerful sense of danger to U.S. dominance are specific kinds of "anti-American" scholarship and the dangerous knowledges they impart. Furthermore, the specter unleashed by unruly student protestors and the repression that they elicit can be viewed as one important aspect of this end game of cultural and imperial supremacy—and its pepper spraying and paranoias.

The post-9/11 policing of knowledge and the neoliberal restructuring of the university create pressure points that reveal the forces of political imperialism and the economic matrix within which they are embedded, as argued by Godrej and Prashad, among others. This is a matrix that is historically formed: an imperial "knowledge complex" is fed by the profitable business of militarism, incarceration, and war. A decade after 9/11, the crises of late capitalism in the global North (and the dismantling of public education) unravel the "safety nets" for many university students and employees; this is a process that Gumbs points out has a much longer genealogy that is intertwined with the racial management of populations within and beyond the campus. The "downsizing" of the university unmasks an ideological "precarity" even for critically engaged tenured or tenure-track faculty, among the most elite and "protected" of academic workers, as suggested by Pulido's reflection on tenure battles in an elite, private institution. In fact, Oparah points out that private, liberal arts institutions are crucial to the corporate logics of the "global knowledge marketplace," so that the neoliberal restructuring of the public university is clearly at work at private institutions as well, as wittily observed in Prashad's account of his own college. Furthermore, Oparah argues that liberal arts colleges provide the corporate sector and the military-prison-industrial complex with "moral capital" precisely because of their supposed liberalism. As Prashad's analysis suggests, the crises of "academic freedom" or student debt allow us to dig more deeply into the ways in which neoliberal practices and their geopolitics intersect—and how this informs the consolidation of the corporate university.

The bursts of dissent (both within scholarly production and in student protests and the Occupy movement) suggest that "business as usual" is being disrupted in the U.S. university. However, this dissent—and the modes of repression it provokes—begs the question of what sustains "business as usual." Our introductory vignette, juxtaposing the bucolic green of a "peaceful" campus with the performance of militarized power, offers our unease with the normalized terms of "peace" in our elysian surroundings, not to mention with the complicity of the U.S. state with military occupations elsewhere and the lockdown on open critique of particular foreign states. The police in riot gear do not signal something exceptional; rather, their presence unmasks the codes of "the normal" in academic discourse and practice. It is a normalization that we see routinely in the grants that we are encouraged to apply for and in Department of Defense funding that many scientists, social scientists, and technologists receive for their research, as discussed in Roberto González's chapter. The capital provided by these grants has built the foundations of some of the most powerful and preeminent universities in the world: MIT, Stanford, UC Berkeley, California Institute of Technology (Caltech), and many others. The alliance between military research and science, which is well known, builds the deepest strata of connection and complicity between imperial statecraft and the knowledge complex of the U.S. academy. This, also, is nothing new, as González and Oparah demonstrate in analyzing the historical, global economies within which U.S. intelligence and prison systems enact violent logics of incapacitation and counterinsurgency.

The contributors to this book seek to illuminate the historical continuities of crisis and the boundaries of regulation and containment, especially in the current moment, because they reveal the threshold of academic repression. This involves connecting analyses of localized domestic dissent (e.g., in student protests) to the censorship of scholarship and pedagogies of critique of U.S. state projects (especially related to support for Israel and the domestic and global frontlines of the War on Terror). Many of the chapters highlight that the regulation and repression of various forms of dissent share core ideologies—about corporate and militarized capitalism as the means and ends of state power as well as the deeper codes of cultural, racial, and national supremacy that they enable. When the University of California debates the purchase of an army tank, as it did in Berkeley in 2012, it crudely reveals the profound strategic confluence of military science and militarized praxis in fortifying the citadels of higher learning.

There are four overlapping arenas central to this complex field of engagement and debate that undergird the conceptual framework of our book: *imperial cartographies*, *academic containment*, *manifest knowledges*, and *heresies and freedoms*. These arenas provide a rubric for understanding the intersecting fronts of the academic, cultural, and military wars, and they also provide the scaffolding for the chapters that follow in this book.

Imperial Cartographies

Empires of knowledge rest on the foundation of racial statecraft, militarized science, and enduring notions of civilizational superiority. What we call "imperial cartographies" can be traced through the meshed contours of research methods and scholarly theories as they are staked out in the pragmatic mappings of conquest, settlement, and administration of U.S. empire.[14] It is important to note that expert knowledge on "other" cultures and civilizations has been a cornerstone of the development of academic disciplines and used in the management of "difference" within the nation as well as the conquest and management of native populations by the United States, here and overseas.

For example, Victor Bascara examines an early iteration (and a model, perhaps) of what Bill Readings has called the "Americanization" of the university.[15] Bascara's chapter on the imperial universities founded in the U.S.-controlled territories of Hawaii, Puerto Rico, and the Philippines after 1898 demonstrates how educational discourse and practices in the colonies exemplified a complex colonizing mission. Cultural "difference" was mapped within the classroom through a distinct racial and gendered lens, one that, however benevolently, consistently tracked the ideologies of U.S. military, cultural, and economic supremacy. The educational mission for inclusion and civilization "there," on the periphery, became a laboratory for new regimes of governmentality "here," within the immediate territorial borders of the United States.

If universities of the imperial periphery introduced a new governmentality and constructed mobile, but unequal, racial/gendered and national subjects, then these processes must also be understood within the epistemologies of "othering" being constructed by disciplines such as anthropology. Late nineteenth-century anthropology emerged through centuries-old scientific curiosity (and debates) about human difference as well as the administrative imperatives of other imperial powers, such as Britain.[16] Theoretical constructions of categories such as "savage" and "primitive" were not mere reflections of ivory tower ruminations about human origins and human science or "cultural" essences but helped create the very scaffoldings of European and later U.S. imperial cartographies.[17]

If these constructions of racial hierarchy shaped the curricular and disciplinary consensus about difference in the imperial university, then what can we say about institutional research practices that explicitly furthered state projects, especially during times of internal and external crises, such as war? In other words, what happens when professional scholars use their disciplinary tools and training to further military projects to defend the "national interest"? Academic knowledges about others have been significant as both information and "intelligence" for the subjugation and administration of indigenous and minoritized communities, within and beyond the United States, as demonstrated by González's fascinating research on the contemporary Intelligence Community Center of Academic Excellence programs that target students of color. While this volume does not explore the fuller histories of the relationship between the U.S. academy and war efforts throughout the twentieth century, we gesture to some historical "plottings" that signal an enduring coimplication between the institutionalized practices of the military and the academy. It is this deep *historicized* process of normalization that has created the dominant "consensus" and "silence" in the imperial university in the post-9/11 period.

During World War I, for instance, some archaeologists worked as spies to literally offer "on ground geographical knowledges" that, as David Price argues, were "highly valued in wartime intelligence circles."[18] This involvement, however, created controversy when Franz Boas, the preeminent anthropologist, protested the involvement of anthropologists with U.S. military intelligence.[19] Though Boas was not supported by a majority of his colleagues, the controversy has shaped the debates about the politics and ethics of anthropologists' relationship to military intelligence to this day, as addressed in González's chapter and by the Network of Concerned Anthropologists within the American Anthropological Association.

The imperial university was deeply embroiled in issues of war, labor, and protest throughout the first half of the twentieth century and during the earlier Red Scare. World War I and its aftermath saw the targeting and deportation of anarchists and antiwar socialists during the infamous Palmer Raids in a period of heightened nationalism and repression. The American Association of University Professors (AAUP) was cofounded in 1915 by John Dewey and Arthur Lovejoy; the latter resigned from Stanford University over a controversy regarding the abuse of immigrant labor by the industrialist Stanford family.[20] In 1940, the Rapp-Coudert Committee was established to "investigate 'subversive activities' at public and private colleges in New York."[21] Faculty and students at the City College of New York were protesting fascism and capitalism through the 1930s, with progressive student groups staging mass protests and sit-ins. The committee actually subpoenaed and questioned more than a hundred faculty, students, and staff; denounced more than eight hundred public school teachers and college faculty; and fired over sixty CCNY faculty.[22]

It is, of course, World War II and the ascendance of the United States as a global superpower that propelled the alliance between the U.S. state and the academy to new heights. The Manhattan Project and the development of the atom bomb sealed this intimate and soon inextricable link between scientific research and militarism. As R. C. Lewontin powerfully suggests, "It is not General Groves at his desk in the Los Alamos labs that has provided the symbolic image of the atom bomb project's iconography but an Italian professor building an atomic pile under the spectator's stands of the University of Chicago's athletic field. It is there, not in the Nevada desert, that Henry Moore's ambiguous fusion of a mushroom cloud and a death's head memorializes the Bomb."[23] As U.S. and Allied forces launched themselves into the global theatre of war, they recognized that they needed condensed, accelerated training about the geographies and peoples they were encountering. Ironically, it was the Boasian commitment to field-based linguistic anthropology that created the capacity for "quickly learning and teaching the languages of the new theatres of warfare."[24] Further, Army Specialized Training Programs (ASTPs) were established on 227 college and university campuses,[25] and some anthropologists helped create "pocket guides" for Army Special Forces. These booklets summarized a region's geographical history and included gems of "cultural advice" such as "not approaching Egyptian women" and "not concluding that East Indian men holding hands are homosexuals,"[26] early predecessors to the post-9/11 manuals on understanding "the Arab mind" or Islam used to train U.S. military interrogators and FBI agents in the War on Terror.

If the distilled study of "other cultures," enabled by academic expertise, became important for warcraft in external theaters, other sets of research skills were used for the surveillance and containment of "others" *within* the nation-state. For instance, anthropologists at the Bureau of Indian Affairs monitored and influenced war-related opinion on Native American reservations.[27] Some anthropologists were involved in studying Japanese American communities as they "adapted" to their lives in the concentration camps set up by the War Relocation Authority, "one of the most publicly visible and volatile topics relating to anthropology's war time contributions."[28] Between 1945 and 1948, this rapid and intense distillation of "method" and "information" about world cultures consolidated in area studies, arguably a paradigm shift in U.S. scholarship, and one that was based on an interdisciplinary approach that would literally carve out—and map—"regions" of the world.

By the end of World War II and the onset of the Cold War, the state-university compact to ensure that scientific knowledges would continue to serve U.S. global power was well assured. Noam Chomsky has argued that by 1945, U.S. wealth and power in the "international sphere probably had no counterpart in history."[29] Out of this mesh of forces of capital and super-power politics and supremacy emerged a consensus that state (and corporate) funding for "research and development" in science and technology in the service of military development was vital for the growth of universities.[30]

Warnings about the dangers of this deep alliance between the U.S. military and intelligence, civil society, and the academy came not only from the margins but also from the Oval Office itself. Dwight Eisenhower prophetically warned about consequences of the immense power inhered in what he called the "military-industrial complex." Interestingly, in an earlier draft of this famous speech, he had apparently inserted the word "academic" in the now famous mantra of power, but it was deleted.[31] It was another politician, William Fulbright, who issued a clear warning of the dangers of academic collusion with the militarized state when he stated, "In lending itself too much for the purpose of government, a university fails its higher purpose."[32] These concerns about the narrowing of the sphere of democratic debate were also being raised by distinguished scholars (such as Hannah Arendt and John Dewey[33]) but McCarthyism and a new wave of political repression ensured that questions were not asked about the business of war—or the reasons that the business of war was also becoming an academic business.[34]

This intersection of Department of Defense, Pentagon, and research university interests resulted in massive amounts of funding and shifted the fiscal nature of universities' state patronage from land-grant, agricultural resources to the huge war chest of the defense establishment. This fiscal patronage was both overt and covert, involving individual academics and departments across the disciplines, not just the sciences, with support from military grants. Chomsky, for example, remembers that in 1960 the political science department at MIT was funded by the CIA; closed seminars were held and "they had a villa in Saigon where students were working on pacification projects for doctoral dissertations."[35] As González points out in his chapter, "the CIA supported social science research throughout the 1950s and 1960s to perfect psychological torture techniques that were outsourced to Vietnam, Argentina, and other countries." World War II and the Cold War had created, without a doubt, the prime "condition for the socialization of research and education."[36] At the height of the Cold War, social scientists were recruited to serve in military intelligence operations—whether gathering more "benign" forms of information, serving with the army in Vietnam, or teaching in the School of the Americas—and after 9/11, became "embedded" with the military in Afghanistan and Iraq.[37]

It is important also to note the countervailing forces that exposed some of these practices of imperial cartography and research to critical scrutiny and engaged in social protest and academic dissent. The combined pressures of decolonization, the U.S. civil rights movement, and the anti–Vietnam War protests in the 1960s unmasked the collusion between knowledge production and U.S. warcraft at significant moments. For instance, a scandal erupted about Project Camelot, initiated by the Special Operations Research Office (SORO) in 1964 and aimed at Latin America, with the stated goal to "devise procedures for assessing the potential for internal wars within national societies."[38] When exposed in Chile, it drew "unwelcome attention" to the clear geopolitical, Cold War imperatives of area studies.[39]

If area studies constituted a certain kind of imperial cartography, its design also had "unintended consequences," as argued by Immanuel Wallerstein. Most importantly, it opened up "interdisciplinary studies" in new ways and dislodged traditional ethnography and Oriental studies, the dominant approaches for the study of "Others." These shifts created space for more "radical" visions of interdisciplinarity and curricular formation in the 1970s—namely, in the demand for, and establishment of, both ethnic studies and women's studies. Decolonizing and radical social movements (within and outside the United States), especially the antiwar movement, were profoundly important in carving out some space for alternative cartographies of knowledge—albeit marginal ones—within the university.

If the protest movements of the 1960s interrupted the hegemonic workings of the military-academy nexus, the post-9/11 historical moment, according to many, is a retrenchment and intensification of this matrix of power. It is important to recognize the paradox cohering within the processes of collusion and protest at work in the academic-military-industrial complex. On the one hand, if it were not for the ruptures of the 1960s, however short-lived, we as scholars in ethnic studies and women's studies would not be employed in the very institutional sites that were created by those interventions. On the other hand, as Roderick Ferguson has argued and as Rojas and Gumbs suggest here, ethnic studies is increasingly part of an institutional incorporation and recuperation of protest movements and dissenting scholarship that can reproduce the deeply imperial logics of management and violence.[40] This recomposition and absorption rests in the very paradox of the material realities that greatly expanded the U.S. academy and historically allowed it to prosper—military funding and military science. It was a prosperity that meant, and continues to mean, the normalization and acceptance of great repression within the academy and beyond, as evoked by Godrej and De Genova. Both repression and protest, then, might be viewed as part of the Janus-faced coin of the imperial university as engendered by U.S. economic power, especially in the immediate postwar period: a global supremacy intimately connected to the state-military alliance that protected its global capitalist interests.

What, then, are the "new" avatars of this imperial cartography? There are powerful historical continuities in the academy of the alliances among the natural and technological sciences, the social sciences, and the military-prison-industrial complex (MPIC), or the academic-MPIC. It is important to theorize, and map, the international political economies that underwrite the immensely powerful alliances among transnational corporate capital (especially in the business of war and prisons), the military industry, and the state. González draws attention to the $60 million Department of Defense–funded Minerva Consortium, which continues to provide funding to social science research projects connected to "national security." The role of the academy in these alliances consolidates what Oparah calls "dangerous complicities," which inform the politics of institutional—and disciplinary—survival in difficult economic times.

Certainly, there has also been resistance to the consolidation of the academic-military-industrial complex, for example, by the Network of Concerned Anthropologists and academics opposed to the Human Terrain System[41] and by some scholars in the American Psychological Association during the heated debate about the role of psychological experts in torture practiced by the U.S. military in the War on Terror.[42] There is also a long history of scientists who challenged the military imperatives of defense research—for example, offering an alternative definition of national security during the era of the Cold War and the nuclear arms race—and who were themselves regarded as "national security threats."[43]

But the question remains, is scholarly dissent simply the other face of the coin of academic repression—that is, are expressions of protest doomed to be incorporated into the imperial cartographies they resist or it possible for them to create alternative mappings that resist recuperation? The chapters in this book allude to this enduring dilemma about resistance from within, directly and indirectly; some authors suggest that what is needed is a new paradigm that reframes the architecture of repression. For example, across distinctly different sites of (neo)colonialism and global capitalism, Oparah argues for an unmasking of a transnational carceral logic of "new" empire that traffics between the imperial core and its peripheries. She argues that it is not *more,* "countercarceral" knowledge that scholars resisting the "militarization and prisonization of academia" must produce in order to realize a postcarceral academy. Rather, academics must use their privilege to challenge the complicity of the academy with, and call for divestment from, prison and military industries. As Oparah and also Prashad eloquently suggest, the university must be reimagined as a site of solidarity with those engaged in struggles against neoliberal capitalism and organizing for the abolition of the academic-MPIC.

The chapters in this book provide analyses of imperial cartographies that can undergird this solidarity from within the academic-MPIC, uncovering the role of the carceral academy and exposing the hidden links between prison regimes in Iraq and Afghanistan as well as within the United States, not to mention secret prisons or "black sites" overseas. Orientalist constructions of terrorists or religious "fanatics" underwrite military interventions in Iraq, Afghanistan, and Pakistan as well as counterterrorism programs in the United States. As scholars such as González have observed, counterinsurgency has a cultural front that rests on racialized understandings and management of populations, an argument that is extended in his chapter on intelligence training through new programs recruiting students of color for new, presumably cosmopolitan careers.[44] Indeed, González argues that the new intelligence centers are predicated on a transnational, racial mapping where the "emphasis is on the importance of building an ethnically and culturally diverse pool of intelligence agents who might blend in more easily abroad"[45] and on the need for "FBI agents who can speak to Muslim women that might be intimidated by men." Curricular development in these new, multicultural sites of imperial knowledge production reproduce enduring racial/gendered stereotypes and old Orientalist binaries of the "East and West" necessary for new fronts of war.

This external Orientalized mapping is intimately coupled with racialized disciplinary regimes within the United States. If students of color in public universities are being targeted for intelligence training in more systematic ways since 2001, then Oparah and Gumbs remind us of the historical presence of military recruitment and the prison industry at these same institutions. Oparah's chapter remaps the indelible connections between U.S. militarization (abroad) and logics of carcerality (at home) through academic institutions that invest in and produce the capital, workers, *and* knowledges for an immensely profitable MPIC, one increasingly linked to foreign zones of occupation, such as in Palestine-Israel. These racialized, gendered, and classed mappings of an "empire within" are intimately linked to the subjugation of "foreign," racialized others beyond U.S. borders—a simultaneous logic, and process, that is then used to contain, and target, dissent from within the imperial university.

Academic Containment

State warfare and militarism have shored up deeply powerful notions of patriotism, intertwined with a politics of race, class, gender, sexuality, and religion, through the culture wars that have embroiled the U.S. academy. The fronts of "hot" and "cold" wars—military, cultural, and academic—have rested on an ideological framework that has defined the "enemy" as a threat to U.S. freedom and democracy. This enemy produced and propped up in the shifting culture wars—earlier the Communist, now the (Muslim) terrorist— has always been both external and internal. The overt policing of knowledge production, exemplified by right-wing groups such as ACTA, reveals an ideological battle cry in the "culture wars" that have burgeoned in the wake of the civil rights movement—and the containment and policing demanded within the academy. Defending the civilizational integrity of the nation requires producing a national subject and citizen by regulating the boundaries of what is permissible and desirable to express in national culture—and in the university. As Readings observed, "In modernity, the University becomes the model of the social bond that ties individuals in a common relation to the idea of the nation-state."[46] Belonging is figured through the metaphor of patriotic citizenship, in the nation and in the academy, through displays of what Henry Giroux has also called "patriotic correctness": "an ideology that privileges conformity over critical learning and that represents dissent as something akin to a terrorist act."[47]

This is where the recent culture wars have shaped the politics of what we call academic containment. For right-wing activists, the nation must be fortified by an educational foundation that upholds, at its core, the singular superiority of Western civilization. A nation-state construed as being under attack is in a state of cultural crisis where any sign of disloyalty to the nation is an act of treachery, including acts perceived as intellectual betrayal. The culture wars have worked to uphold a powerful mythology about American democracy and the American Dream and a potent fiction about freedom of expression that in actuality contains academic dissent. This exceptionalist mythology has historically represented the U.S. nation as a beacon of individual liberty and a bulwark against the Evil Empire or Communist bloc; Third Worldist and left insurgent movements, including uprisings within the United States in the 1960s and 1970s and in Central America in the 1980s; Islamist militancy and anti-imperial movements since the 1980s; and the threat posed by all of these to the American "way of life." The battle against Communism, anti-imperial Third Worldism, and so-called Islamofascism entailed regulating and containing movements sympathetic to these forces at home, including intellectuals with left-leaning tendencies and radical scholars or students—all those likely to contaminate young minds and indoctrinate students in "subversive" or "anti-American" ideologies.

What does it mean, then, to contain scholars who "cross the line" in their academic work or public engagement? Academic containment can take on many modalities: stigmatizing an academic as too "political," devaluing and marginalizing scholarship, unleashing an FBI investigation, blacklisting, or not granting scholars the final passport into elite citizenship in the academic nation—that is, tenure. These various modalities of containment, which are discussed by Thomas Abowd, Laura Pulido, and Steven Salaita, among others, narrow the universe of discourse around what is really permissible, acceptable, and tolerable for scholars in the imperial university. All these modes are at work in the three important moments of ideological policing that we touch on here: World War I and the McCarthy era of the 1940s–1950s, the COINTELPRO era from the late 1950s to early 1970s, and the post-9/11 era or "new Cold War," which is the major focus of this book.

Moments of social stress and open dissent about class politics in the United States during World War I and the first decades of the twentieth century make clear that containment worked in tandem with emerging definitions of "academic freedom." As the U.S. professoriate began to build its ranks at the end of the nineteenth century and a few scholars[48] challenged the status quo, "academic freedom" emerged as a way to deal with these dissenters as well as the "relative insecurity" felt by many in this new profession.[49] Indeed, the tumult of the turn of the century led to a pattern within the academy that has persisted—the exclusion of ideas as well as behavior that the majority did not like and an increasingly internalized notion that "advocacy for social change" was a professional risk for academics.

The AAUP's Seligman Report of 1915 reveals that the notion of academic freedom was, in fact, "deeply enmeshed" with the "overall status, security, and prestige of the academic profession."[50] Setting up procedural safeguards was important, but its language regarding "appropriate scholarly behavior" and cautiousness about responding to controversial matters in the academy (by ensuring that all sides of the case were presented) suggested the limits of dissent. Academic freedom, then, is a notion that is deeply bound up with academic containment—a paradox suggested in our earlier discussion of protest and inclusion/incorporation in the academy and one that has become increasingly institutionalized since the formation of the AAUP.

The academic repression of the McCarthy era received its impetus from President Truman's March 22, 1947, executive order that "established a new loyalty secrecy program for federal employees." However, the roots of institutional capitulation—by both administrators and faculty—when the state targeted academics who were communists or viewed as "sympathizers" are much deeper. It is also significant that the notion of "appropriate behavior" for faculty rested on a majoritarian academic "consensus" about "civil" and "collegial" comportment. For example, Ellen Schechter notes cases prior to the Cold War where scholars were fired *not* necessarily for their political affiliations per se but due to "their outspoken-ness."[51] This repression from within—not just beyond—the academy reveals the cultures of academic containment where, as Pulido, Gumbs, and Rojas remind us, certain kinds of "unruliness" must be managed or excised.

The logic of academic containment was dramatically staged during the civil rights and antiwar struggles, when the FBI surveilled and arrested Black Power, anti-imperialist, and radical scholar-activists during the era of COINTELPRO (1956–1971). Angela Davis, most famously, was fired from UCLA by then California governor Ronald Reagan for being a member of the Communist Party. Some of these radical intellectuals went on to develop and establish programs in ethnic studies, critical race studies, and women's studies, fields that later became embroiled in the conservative attacks that unfolded in the 1980s and 1990s against the specter of an "un-American" and "divisive" multiculturalism. Works such as Allan Bloom's *The Closing of the American Mind,* Roger Kimball's *Tenured Radicals: How Politics has Corrupted Our Higher Education,* and in some ways also David Hollinger's

Postethnic America: Beyond Multiculturalism generated anxieties about the presumed failure of university education to transmit an essential set of knowledges and a contentious debate about the divisiveness of multiculturalism and movements for group rights.[52]

Right-wing hysteria and neoconservative moral panics in the culture wars were accompanied by liberal concerns that ethnic studies, and to some extent women's studies and queer studies, were devolving into "identity politics." Liberal-left intellectuals, such as Todd Gitlin, worried that ethnic and racial studies asserted an identitarianism that was an abandonment of a "proper" left politics. Salaita points out that Gitlin also criticized as irresponsible scholars who challenged the policies of the Israeli state, as have other progressive scholars open to critiques of militarism or colonialism—except in the case of Israel. In other words, the culture wars were fought not just between the right and left but within the liberal-progressive left as well.

In her painful—and politically revealing—experience with Chicana/o studies in California public institutions over the past twenty years, Rojas offers a glimpse "of the ways imperial projects order gender/sexual/racial politics at the public university" and the "resulting devastating violence deployed on subjects deemed dangerous to the colonial imaginary of a colonial, heteropatriarchal Chicano studies." The difficult question that Rojas's "testimonio" addresses is how to connect this hetero-masculinist logic and violence—what she calls heteropatriracialities—to the "incorporation" of ostensibly liberatory, decolonizing projects such as Chicano/a studies that were birthed through the antiwar and antiracist movements of the 1960s. We view this perverse "incorporation" of ethnic studies as the result of a dangerous "internalization" of the imperial project of the university and also as meshing well with the hetero-masculinist and classed cultures that shape the dominant, everyday practices of the imperial academy. Containment is not abstract at all—it is marked decisively, and often violently, on specific kinds of bodies whose presence is definitively marked as "Other," as evident in Abowd's and Godrej's chapters. If one speaks from already dangerous embodiments, structured historically, then that speech risks always being seen as a threat. The "natives" within the academy must be most careful and most civilized in their speech, as Rojas and Abowd suggest. Their queer/sexed/raced bodies mark always-possible threats. There are enough natives who perform the terms of civilization and capitulation and contain themselves: that is how empires have always ruled—through tokenism, exceptionalism, and divide-and-rule. When it comes from "within," containment and silencing—as Rojas shows us—can be the most devastating of all.

These stories of academic containment must be situated within the culture wars and also within the context of what Christopher Newfield, among other critics, calls a "long counterrevolution" against the gains of the civil rights and left movements of previous decades.[53] Newfield argues that rightwing movements waged a cultural offensive that targeted "progressive trends in the public universities" as an important front of "roundabout wars" on the middle class, waged through the "culture wars on higher education": "The culture wars were economic wars" against the new, increasingly racially integrated middle class, "discrediting the cultural framework that had been empowering that group."[54] In other words, the culture wars were also class wars staged on a racial battlefield, for the corporatization and privatization of the public university, as in California, occurred as it was becoming more racially integrated.[55]

Several chapters illustrate the ways in which academic containment emerges with and though the containment of economic, racial, and cultural struggles. In Gumbs's chapter, the class wars are situated in the racial management of student of color and immigrant populations in the CUNY system in the post–civil rights era of open admissions and campus occupations by students; violent policing to enforce "law and order" accompanied rising incarceration rates of people of color. Similarly, Godrej's chapter illuminates the ways in which protests of university privatization and nonviolent civil disobedience by students and faculty during the current budget crisis in the University of California have been met with police brutality by increasingly militarized campuses; casting these movements as a threat evades the structural violence of tuition hikes, exclusion, impoverishment, home foreclosures, and the "neoliberal disinvestment in the concept of education as a public good."

In effect, the neoliberal structuring of the university is also a racial strategy of management of an increasingly diverse student population, as increasing numbers of minority and immigrant students have entered public higher education. Well-funded, neoconservative organizations and partisan groups, such as ACTA, David Horowitz's Freedom Center, and Campus Watch, have placed ethnic studies, feminist and queer studies, and critical cultural studies in their bull's-eye as the political project of leftist professors running amok in the academy and teaching biased curricula. In addition, campaigns such as Horowitz's Academic Bill of Rights and Student Bill of Rights constructed the figure of a new victim in the culture wars: the "American student" whose freedom to challenge these partisan faculty had been suppressed.[56] According to these right-wing campaigns, "radical" scholars were force-feeding U.S. college students with anti-American views, and right-wing students were being marginalized and "discriminated" against due to their political ideology and affirmative action programs. Thus the language of marginalization and exclusion was turned on its head, as the discourse of right-wing victimhood and ideological discrimination was unleashed against the political movements and intellectual projects that opposed racial and class inequality.

In addition, the right appropriated the language of "diversity," a key point of contradiction in the academic culture wars. For example, the "Students for Academic Freedom" campaign launched by Horowitz used the notion of "intellectual pluralism" to mask its well-orchestrated attack on the left.[57] The cultural right manufactured a portrait of itself as the true advocate of intellectual pluralism and freedom, remaking diversity through a "free market" model based on the right to choice in the marketplace of ideas.[58] The notion of choice, central to models of flexible accumulation and global economic competitiveness for proponents of neoliberal capitalism, underlies the tenet of intellectual choice. A "weak" multiculturalism and liberal notion of tolerance thus served the right well, for they used it to argue that the problem was not simply that of "diversity," which they apparently embraced, but that there wasn't enough "intellectual diversity" on college campuses. Teaching, and also research, was becoming one-sided, to the detriment of those upholding "true" American values, who were increasingly marginalized in hotbeds of left indoctrination into anti-Americanism on college campuses. In addition, as Pulido's case study demonstrates, as faculty and administrators of color—not to mention women—have made their way into the ranks of university management, academic institutions can hide behind the language of racial (and gender) representativeness and tokenist inclusion to deflect critiques of systemic problems with faculty governance.

The strategic co-optation of the language of pluralism for academic containment is nowhere more evident than in the assault on progressive scholarship in Middle East studies and postcolonial studies and in the intense culture wars over Islam, the War on Terror, and Israel-Palestine. The 9/11 attacks and the heightened Islamophobia they generated allowed Zionist and neoconservative groups to intensify accusations that progressive Middle East studies scholars and scholars critical of U.S. foreign policy were guilty of bias and "one-sided" partisanship, as observed in accounts of censure, suspicion, and vilification by Abowd, De Genova, and Salaita. The post-9/11 culture wars conjured up new and not-so-new phantoms of enemies—in particular, the racialized specter of the "terrorist." This figure, and the racial panic associated with it, has been sedimented in the national imaginary as synonymous with the "Muslim" and the "Arab" since the Iranian Revolution of 1978–1979 and the First Intifada against Israeli occupation in the late 1980s. The War on Terror consolidated Orientalist caricatures of Muslim fanatics and Arab militants, but it is important to note that these also dredged up avatars of a historical logic of containment and annihilation of indigenous others.[59] The native, the barbarian, and the foreigner converge in this cultural imaginary that legitimizes violence against anti-Western, uncivilized regions incapable of democratic self-governance and that is produced by expert knowledge of other peoples and regions. The wars in Iraq and "Af-Pak" and the global hunt for terrorists entailed an intensified suspicion and scrutiny of ideologies that supported militant resistance or "anti-American" sentiments and necessitated academic research on communities that were supposedly "breeding grounds" for terrorism.

The post-9/11 panic about Muslim terrorists and enemy aliens increasingly focused on the threat of "homegrown terrorism" as the War on Terror shifted its focus to "radicalized" communities within the United States, especially Muslim American youth. At the same time, as Godrej observes, the criminalization of those considered threats to national security has included the violent repression of Occupy activists and student protesters and indefinite detention authorized by the PATRIOT (Provide Appropriate Tools Required to Intercept and Obstruct Terrorism) Act and the National Defense Authorization Act. Protests focused on higher education thus blur into dissent against U.S. warfare and the homeland security state in a climate of heightened campus securitization and university collaboration with the FBI in the interest of "public safety." Anarchists are considered domestic terror threats to be contained, and Muslim or Arab American students (or faculty) who are *also* anarchists are subjected to multiple levels of containment and scrutiny, as suggested in the chapter by Falcón et al. Academic containment is clearly part of a larger politics of repression and policing in the national security state that affects faculty and students as well as the campus climate in general.

While the FBI has interviewed unknown numbers of Muslim and Arab American college students and infiltrated and monitored Muslim student organizations since 9/11, counterterrorism experts have generated models of "radicalization" of Muslim youth, especially males, invoking cultural pathologies of "hate" and alienation. Regimes of surveillance, detention, and deportation of terrorists, or terrorist sympathizers lurking within the nation, are underwritten by a gendered and racialized logic: the imperative to save women, particularly Muslim and Middle Eastern women, from inherently misogynistic Muslim and Middle Eastern men. Cultural knowledge and academic expertise are needed to refine policies of humanitarian intervention in these imperial cartographies of nations or cultures whose women are in need of rescue and nations or civilizations in need of saving, as brilliantly argued by Jasbir Puar in her work on U.S. and Israeli homonationalisms. While it is easy to critique overtly racist commentators in the culture wars, we must note that it is not just right wing but also liberal critics and scholars who worry that a new "political correctness" is supposedly silencing critiques of cultures and religious communities whose social norms are inherently antithetical to Western secular modernity (that is, Muslims and Arabs). This allegation ignores the deafening silences in many quarters—including in the academy—about ongoing state terror against particular, racialized populations.[60]

Indeed, the antiwar movement has been dismally weak on most college campuses since 2003–2004 and there have barely been any campus protests against the wars and drone attacks in Afghanistan and Pakistan that continue to be waged by Obama or against the prison at Guantanamo. A troubling trend since 9/11 is that U.S. liberal feminism concerned about the oppression of Muslim women—but not about the occupation, colonization, and devastation of their societies by warfare or neoliberal capitalism—has found perhaps unlikely allies in neocon activists in the culture wars, from Irshad Manji and Ayaan Hirsi Ali to Horowitz.[61] And equally significantly, these external attacks on critical scholarship have occurred in a context where the neoliberal privatization of the university has accelerated and where attacks on women's and gender studies, queer studies, and also ethnic studies programs have intensified.

In addition, we see a gendered and racial logic in academic containment where the figure of the "angry Arab" (or Muslim) male scholar is often subjected to policing by a deeply politicized notion of academic "civility." There is a general uneasiness about male scholars of color as inappropriately aggressive if they challenge the status quo, especially in the context of U.S. nationalisms and nationalisms allied with U.S. hegemony—that is, American Zionist movements. This is evident from the string of campaigns targeting

Arab and Palestinian male academics in the United States, such as Sami Al-Arian, Joseph Massad, Rashid Khalidi, and Abowd, who alludes to the racial logic in the allegations drummed up against him by Zionist activists and the dismal, and in some cases hostile, response of the university administration.

So while there are indeed Arab and Muslim female academics who have been targeted by Zionist campaigns, notably the Palestinian academic Nadia Abu El Haj, it is evident that Arab and Muslim masculinities are framed in the culture wars as inherently violent and potentially perverse. At the minimum, they are insufficiently conforming to or excessively threatening to white American masculinity, and, at worst, they are an existential threat to the nation, but in either case they must be contained. On the other hand, Arab and Muslim femininities are viewed by this same Orientalist logic as inherently victimized and in need of protection, but it is generally difficult to view the Arab or Muslim male scholar as in need of saving and support within the framework of liberal white "civility."

Abowd pinpoints the unease with "uppity" Arab male academics who challenge the powerful status quo in the academy in a climate in which Arabophobia, not to mention Islamophobia, has consolidated the conflation of critiques of Israel with sympathy for terrorism. This is a moment in which even campus boycott and divestment movements focused on Israel are attacked as "anti-Semitic," as evident in the firestorm over the panel on boycott at Brooklyn College in 2013;[62] there is a complex conflation of racialization, racism, gendering, and right-wing nationalism that is at work here, one that Puar and Salaita address.[63] Furthermore, as Abowd notes, overtly racialized constructions and suspicion of Muslim male academics—or academics who *might* be Muslim—as inherently anti-Semitic and militant and who must be disciplined, emerge in unexpected moments and in academic spaces where one would assume this kind of blatant racial suspicion is impermissible. Falcón et al.'s chapter cites the poignant case of an Arab/Muslim American male student who was removed from the classroom by police and was considered a "threat" due to his radical, anti-imperialist critiques, which, not surprisingly, he felt increasingly fearful of expressing in class. Their chapter reminds us that we need to think more deeply about how the post-9/11 apparatus of policing and surveillance has affected students who feel the most vulnerable and has transformed the classroom environment.

The racial and gendered logic of academic containment is powerfully evident in De Genova's autobiographical chapter, which suggests that the critique of white male scholars who directly challenge dominant ideologies of militarism and U.S. foreign policy, if expressed in terms that unsettle the acceptable academic consensus in elite institutions, is also deeply troubling and compels other academics to distance themselves from dissent considered beyond the pale. Processes of racialization and gendering—the building of consensus around war and nation making—are intertwined with the daily work and lived experience of scholars within the university, making it a highly charged site in debates about the mission of higher education and the future of the nation-state.

Manifest Knowledges

The U.S. academy has been built, historically, on a set of conceptual and political foundations about what it means to educate people about freedom, democracy, and citizenship. The university is an institution that has roots in an Enlightenment project of liberal Western modernity and was founded as a space historically open only to male, propertied subjects. In addition, as we have argued and as the chapters demonstrate, the U.S. university has been a space where foundational histories of settler colonialism and Manifest Destiny have been buttressed, exposed, and contested. The linkages between the university and the global expansionism of the United States are thus crucial to explore if we understand the academy as an imperial university that produces what we call "manifest knowledges"—what is, and what can be, known about histories of genocide, warfare, enslavement, and social death and what are manifestly insurgent truths.

All the chapters in this book speak to this issue, some more directly than others. Gumbs brilliantly excavates pedagogies of both disciplining and subalternity in the teaching of English composition, which she describes as a tool for making expendable, minority student populations "composed" in the context of imperial racism and genocidal violence—manifest knowledges are enacted in both police brutality and overseas invasions, from New York to Grenada and Palestine. Black feminist poets June Jordan and Audre Lorde subverted the dictates of what Gumbs describes as "police English" in criminology programs that supported the pedagogy of police brutality, insisting instead on teaching black English and exploring how imperialism, in the United States and elsewhere, defined who was human.

There is by now a robust body of scholarship in several fields such as American studies, Native American studies, indigenous studies, ethnic studies, queer studies, and feminist studies that has challenged canonical tenets of U.S. history and Manifest Destiny. Yet it is also very apparent that manifest knowledges about state violence and imperialism continue to be contested in the settler colony and its academy—including knowledge about U.S. support for *other* states' violence and settler colonial policies, as pointed out by Salaita, Gumbs, Falcón et al., and Puar, as well as by Abowd and Oparah. Manifest knowledges thus involve the production, and policing, of foundational truths about a global apparatus of settler colonialism that extends beyond the United States to other imperial and colonial sites. Scholarship and critical teaching of U.S. foreign (imperial) policy in Iraq and Afghanistan and, in particular, of U.S. support for the Israeli state and its colonial and apartheid policies have long come under fire from a constellation of right-wing and pro-Israel think tanks and groups. Critiques of the contradictions between a state practicing discrimination based on religion and race and its self-professed image as an exemplar of "liberal democracy," in a sea of backward and antidemocratic Arab and Muslim nations, began to mount around the world and, gradually, in the United States, particularly on college campuses. There has been growing condemnation of Israel's illegal occupation, especially in the wake of the massacre of civilians in Gaza in 2008–2009, the murder of international solidarity activists aboard the humanitarian aid flotilla trying to break the siege of Gaza in 2010, and the second war on Gaza in fall 2012. As Abowd notes, the Boycott, Divestment, and Sanctions (BDS) movement in the United States has grown since 2008–2009, but this has also led to an unprecedented demonization of Palestine solidarity and Muslim American student groups, who became increasingly engaged with antiwar activism and progressive-left alliances after 9/11. American Zionists rejected the possibility that there could be "human rights" for Palestinians—a population synonymous with "Islamic Jihad."[64]

For instance, in 2010, the Anti-Defamation League (ADL) blacklisted Students for Justice in Palestine (SJP), a Palestine solidarity organization with autonomous campus chapters across the nation, as one of the top ten anti-Israel organizations in the United States—along with the Muslim Student Association, the leftist antiwar coalition ANSWER, and Jewish Voice for Peace—for daring to "accuse Israel of racism, oppression and human rights violations."[65] The ADL was outraged that "SJP chapters regularly organize activities presenting a biased view of the Israeli-Palestinian conflict, including mock 'apartheid walls' and 'checkpoint' displays, presentations by sensationalistic anti-Israel speakers and longer programs like Palestine Awareness and Israeli Apartheid weeks," featuring "speakers who described Israel as an 'ethnocentric racist society' and Zionism as 'inherently undemocratic.'" The report, and the scare quotes therein, revealed precisely what was so effective about these student protests but so threatening to a group such as the ADL, which has long masqueraded as an antiracist organization advocating for civil rights—except in the case of Israel-Palestine, where it supports racial discrimination and the suspension of civil rights.[66] Salaita astutely observes that this contradiction arises from a situation in which "support for Israel is actually necessitous of proper multicultural consciousness" for academics and so considered normative and apolitical, while support for Palestinian rights is considered indecently "political." The academic battle over the permissibility and boundaries of knowledge production about Israel-Palestine has thus become one of the most charged sites of manifest knowledges in the imperial university today.

As SJP activists began using creative protest strategies, erecting mock checkpoints and simulacra of the Israeli "security wall" in the middle of campuses, the racial politics of Israeli state technologies of policing, segregation, encampment, collective punishment, and displacement of Arabs and Muslims suddenly erupted into plain sight in the U.S. academy. This provoked a vicious backlash from those who had long sought to suppress these "facts on the ground" and support the Israeli state's exceptionalism, including in the academy, as noted by Salaita and Puar. The ADL, for example, has a long history of blacklisting and harassment of faculty who are critical of Israel, such as Noam Chomsky and William Robinson, a sociologist at UC Santa Barbara who was accused of anti-Semitism for his critique of Israel's war on Gaza in 2009.[67] The threat of "deportation" from the academic nation—which can and has resulted in the loss of livelihood—creates a stifling climate of repression in which many faculty and doctoral students engage in self-censorship, altering their research agendas and teaching for fear of threats to their careers.

The ADL is just one of many prominent, off-campus groups active in the culture wars related to Israel-Palestine that regularly intervenes in college campuses and documents cases of anti-Semitism conflated with "anti-Israelism" and, consequently—as Puar notes in her chapter and Salaita has observed elsewhere—promotes the indivisibility of Israel and Jewishness.[68] This tactic has been taken to new levels in campaigns to define campus activism critical of Israel as racist and anti-Semitic and hence in violation of Title VI of the Civil Rights Act, as well as in the California State Assembly resolution HR 35, mentioned by Prashad, which makes a similarly stunning move.[69]

But the point is also, as Salaita has argued, that groups such as the ADL have used the language of liberal humanism and tolerance, civil rights, and antiracism to promote and consolidate the commonsense that "support for Israel is a prerequisite of responsible multicultural citizenship," nowhere more evident than in the U.S. academy.[70] Furthermore, Puar's groundbreaking work on homonationalism incisively critiques the ways in which the production of Israel as gay friendly and thus liberal and modern has made Israeli "pinkwashing" of its repression and violence against Palestinians, including queer Palestinians, an effective strategy for recruiting liberal gays and lesbians worldwide. This liberal, "multicultural conviviality" conflates American and Israeli exceptionalisms and produces a commonsensical pro-Israelism that defines acceptable national belonging and multicultural citizenship here in the United States—not simply in Israel or only for Jewish Americans.[71] This manifest knowledge has become a cornerstone of notions of "civility" and of academic freedom in the U.S. academy, as indicated by Abowd's chapter as well as De Genova's observations of the fliers attacking him as betraying Israel, not just the United States, after 9/11. This is because, as Salaita points out, allegiance to U.S. state power is conflated with loyalty to Israel.

At the same time, the book is unique in situating an analysis of the Palestine issue, which often seems "exceptional" in the U.S. academy, in relation to a longer genealogy of settler colonialism and a broader structure of McCarthyism that extends beyond Middle East studies and implicates fields such as feminist, queer, and ethnic studies. It in this regard that Gumbs's eloquent chapter on the poetics of solidarity offers a different window into the writing and pedagogy of June Jordan and Audre Lorde, situating it in relation to their anti-imperialist critiques of the Israeli assault on Palestine and also the U.S. invasion of Grenada in the 1980s. Puar also interrogates the ways in which Israeli homonationalism is entangled with the politics of global gay and lesbian organizing and anti-Muslim racism in Europe and the United States and undermines transnational queer and feminist solidarity through regimes of censure within and beyond the academy. Manifest knowledges are, thus, produced and regulated in multiple sites, and these chapters offer alternative archives of composition and citation, censure and solidarity.

As the normative commonsense and also the censorship of the Palestine question has begun to dissolve somewhat in the academy in recent years and the Arab uprisings shifted the dominant narrative about the "Arab and Muslim world," if ever so slightly, a new front of the culture wars has shifted its focus to solidarity with Palestinian, Arab, and Muslim queers and women who must be rescued by the West from homophobia, honor killings, or other "cultural crimes." Puar points out that the "woman question," as a rationale for colonial domination, has increasingly been replaced by the "homosexual question," harnessing sexual rights to a discourse of racial and cultural superiority and buttressed by academic knowledge circuits. As Gumbs argues, in an earlier moment, black feminist writers developed a queer poetics of survival and insurgent knowledge production in the context of racial panics over saving white femininity from the threat of minority and immigrant males and in an era of assaults on the self-determination of Third World nations. Manifest knowledges of gender and sexuality are thus intimately bound with colonialist and racial logics of rescue and freedom in modernity that infuse the culture wars.[72]

Falcón et al. bring the question of manifest knowledges as a queer and feminist question into the classroom and into the context of transnational feminist pedagogy and collaboration as part of their Collective of Antiracist Scholar Activists. They grapple collectively with what it means to teach antiracist, feminist critiques of capitalism, imperialism, and heteronormativity while not falling prey to the university's demand for "superserviceable feminism" and "competitive individualist" scholarly production as women scholars with and without tenure-track positions. The form of their coauthored chapter/dialogue creatively expresses their desire for challenging the demands for neoliberal productivity while being cognizant of their complex institutional positions and the opportunities available as academics to teach feminist, critical race, and postcolonial theory. As scholar-activists, their pedagogy and collaboration become a method for resisting manifest knowledges, not just about U.S. imperial culture, but about what it means to be a "proper," productive academic. As hinted at in our opening reflections on the Occupy student movement, Falcón et al.'s chapter calls on us to create anti-imperialist spaces of knowledge production and pedagogy within our classrooms and "occupy" the imperial university.

Heresies and Freedoms

Following from the production of manifest knowledges and logic of academic containment in the imperial university, the chapters in this section explore how liberal codes of academic freedom are undermined or consolidated as neoliberal privatization weakens spaces of critique in the academy. The chapters by De Genova, Prashad, and Dominguez in the concluding section of the book, as well as other chapters, critique what could be described as the "holy grail" of academic freedom, one of the pillars upon which academic liberalism builds its edifice and which is central to the academic wars. We argue that there is a narrowing of the field of possible dissent in the U.S. academy precisely because of the ways in which the repression of knowledge production and the resistance to academic repression are both constituted through notions of academic freedom and academic heresies.

We gestured earlier to how the development of "academic freedom" took place against the backdrop of World War I and the early twentieth century precisely because of the nonconformity of individual scholars in class and wartime politics. Academic freedom emerged as a way to both negotiate a sense of professional insecurity as well as construct a measured response to matters of "national interest" (such as anticapitalist or antiwar protest). This was a critical time for establishing the protocols of professionalism for academia. Ellen W. Shrecker, in her magisterial study of McCarthyism's effects on the academy, argues that the pivotal Seligman Report by the AAUP in 1915 "reveals how deeply enmeshed the notion of academic freedom was with the overall status, security and prestige of the academic profession."[73] It is apparent that academic freedom continues to be fragile given the increasing professionalization of the academy and hypercompetitiveness of the academic job market.

Indeed, De Genova's experience of "crossing the line" at Columbia University, in the post-9/11 climate of hypernationalism, is part of a genealogy that he traces to 1917, when Columbia penalized two faculty members for their public opposition to World War I. A controversy arose at the time about the distinguished historian, Charles Beard, who remarked in 1916 (during debates about U.S. "neutrality") that the "world's strongest republic could certainly withstand the inconsequential effort of a single 'To Hell with the Flag' comment."[74] Outraged trustees at Columbia interrogated Beard about his comment and political views in an unpleasant echo of De Genova's own account of academic repression. Though Beard was eventually "exonerated," he resigned when his two colleagues at Columbia were terminated due to their political views. A powerful precedent about the boundaries of political—especially antistate—speech was set into motion.

Where were "academic freedom" and the AAUP during this ferment? The newly created organization kept a distance from the unrest enveloping the Columbia campus and was "unwilling to offer its limited assistance to those being driven off campuses."[75] Schecter argues that the AAUP's early discussions of academic freedom sought primarily to protect faculty from outsiders' "meddling" with scholar's teaching and research by setting up "procedural safeguards." But these safeguards could not adequately address political dissidence or any political positions that were considered "unsympathetic" by the majority of academics. What appeared to be "protection" was really about perceptions, and evaluations, of institutional loyalty and "appropriate" behavior that would not jeopardize the professionalism and status of academia.

When the litmus test of the AAUP's politics and "academic freedom" arrived four decades later, in the form of McCarthyite repression, the academy's capitulation to state imperatives and the subsequent destruction of many individual careers and lives should not come as a surprise. Prashad points out that faculty were expelled for their relationship to the Communist Party under the guise of defending academic freedom, for to be a Communist was to be enslaved by dogma and to be unfree. Academic freedom was constructed through a negative and reactive polarity to create the narrow boundaries for "permissible dissent" rather than a positive protection in support of dissent. Clyde Barrow observes, "It created an intellectually defensible zone of political autonomy for the professoriate, which . . . sufficiently circumscribed as to exclude as unscholarly whatever political behavior the leading member of the academic community feared might trigger outside intervention."[76] Even when university presidents could have protected their faculty, most did not, as in the case at the University of Washington discussed by Prashad. The fact that some university administrators could, and did, resist assaults on academic freedom showed that universities could have defied state repression—but most chose not to.

Loyalty to the institution and profession was built on a hegemonic consensus (including among "liberal" faculty) of protecting economic security, most importantly for the majority. Indeed, adherence to this "corporate ideal" was premised on the artificial bifurcation of "politics" and "administration" so that the (administrative) protection of tenure (and other procedural safeguards) could be seen as outside of the realms of the "political."[77] As the chapters by De Genova, Prashad, and Salaita suggest, this ideologically constructed bifurcation continues to haunt radical and progressive scholars in battles over tenure, employment, and teaching today, even if the particular definition of what constitutes the threshold of the "political" shifts over time in the imperial university.

Clearly, if academic freedom is invoked as a "holy grail" in regulating and containing the proper subjects of the imperial nation, the "bad" citizen of the academy is considered heretical. As Ricardo Dominguez and Pulido, Abowd, and De Genova eloquently discuss, acts of transgression of the boundaries of belonging to the academic nation illuminate how narrow, and fragile, the universe of dissent is. While it is perhaps easy to pinpoint, if not always to counter, the campaigns of right-wing and conservative scholars and activists against academic dissent, these chapters highlight an important point—that for academics, censorship and repression generally comes wrapped in a liberal mantle, and it is waged through the language of diversity, dialogue, and, often, academic freedom *itself*. Right-wing and neoconservative activists—or what Prashad calls "cultural vigilantes"—in the culture wars have not only strategically reshaped the discourse of diversity and feminism, as alluded to earlier, but also appropriated the language of "academic freedom." Indeed, right-wing groups such as Horowitz's Students for Academic Freedom have used the notion of "intellectual pluralism" to police teaching and invoked academic freedom as a new ideological battle cry for the right. So the following are the crucial questions: How is it possible to transform academic freedom into a justification for the closing down, rather than opening up, of intellectual and political debates? What inheres in the principle of academic freedom that allows it to be appropriated, apparently seamlessly, by those who align themselves with the political and economic status quo?

The answers lie, to a large extent, in the definition and utilization of academic freedom as a liberal principle and in the paradoxes that this liberal politics generates in the academy and beyond. Prashad argues that the liberal precept of academic freedom draws on John Stuart Mills's conception of the necessity of "contrary opinions" for providing checks and balances for social norms but not for enabling a "transformative political agenda." A Eurocentric genealogy of academic freedom would trace it to notions of critical pedagogy in German universities in the eighteenth and nineteenth centuries, intertwined with notions of economic and political liberalism embedded in Enlightenment modernity.

Cary Nelson, the renowned president of the American Association for University Professors (AAUP), who for many U.S. academics represents the face of institutionalized academic freedom, writes, "Academic freedom thus embodies Enlightenment commitments to the pursuit of knowledge and their adaption to different political and social realities."[78] The AAUP issued the Declaration of Principles on Academic Freedom and Academic Tenure in 1915,[79] and for some scholars, such as Robert Post, this declaration is the "greatest articulation of the logic and structure of academic freedom."[80] According to Post, this is because it conceptualizes academic freedom as based on "compliance with professional norms" specific to academic labor and on the safeguarding of scholarly expertise that produces "professional self-regulation" and "professional autonomy" for faculty.[81] Yet even Post acknowledges that there is a paradox inherent in this conceptualization based on academic labor, for these professional norms are not so easily defined and so academic freedom is "simultaneously limited by, and independent of, professional norms."[82] A critic of the AAUP's unwillingness to protect scholars targeted by McCarthyism suggests the AAUP upholds procedural freedom without an understanding of the importance of expanding its understanding of political freedom: "Stripped of its rhetoric, academic freedom thus turns out to be an essentially corporate protection. And as we trace its development during the Cold War, we should not be surprised to find that it was involved more often to defend the well-being of an institution rather than the political rights of an individual."[83]

Other scholars, such as Judith Butler, also point out that the AAUP's formulation of academic freedom intended to "institutionalize a set of employer-employee relationships in an academic setting," not to guarantee academic freedom as an individual right.[84] While she agrees with Post that academic freedom should not be rooted in "individual freedom" or simply in First Amendment rights of freedom of expression, she goes further to point to the collusion between the university and the state in defining professional norms and professional freedom in scholarship and to emphasize that expectations of what is permissible for academics are always historically evolving and often politically motivated. So these professional constraints are contingent and contested, not fixed; Butler argues, "As faculty members, we are constrained to be free, and in the exercise of our freedom, we continue to operate within the constraints that made our freedom possible in the first place."[85]

We take these critiques of an individually based, constrained, and "weak" notion of academic freedom further, arguing that academic freedom is perhaps not tenable as a basis for a just struggle for "freedom," if that struggle needs to be defined by affirmative principles rooted in progressive or left conceptions of freedom, justice, and equality, as suggested by Prashad. In other words, academic freedom is not, and should not be, the holy grail of dissent. Academic freedom is generally understood—and operationalized in the U.S. academy today—as an ideologically neutral principle of freedom of expression and First Amendment rights. It is thus a libertarian, not just liberal, notion of individual freedom, and it is framed as a core principle of Western modernity and democracy, serving both the liberal-left and the conservative-right. In this model, neo-Nazis or antiabortion advocates have the same rights to academic freedom in the university as do queer activists or antiwar proponents. There is no progressive ethos built into the principle of academic freedom, and this is what makes it easily available for recuperation and resort by the right as much as the left. Prashad makes the important observation that even the academic left often tends to take refuge in the "safe harbor" of academic freedom rather than engaging in a struggle for "genuine campus democracy" and labor rights for workers on campuses and for the right to education as a public good and for a "culture of solidarity," as evoked by Dominguez.

Perhaps one of the most ironic examples of what could be described as the use of academic freedom as a smoke screen for larger struggles over other kinds of freedoms was the cancellation of the AAUP's own conference on academic boycotts, slated to be held in 2006 at the Rockefeller Conference Center in Bellagio, Italy. The conference featured a diverse group of scholars with a range of views on the strategy of academic boycott—some in favor, some opposed—within the context of the emerging, global debate about the Palestinian call for an academic boycott of Israeli academic institutions, inspired by the boycott of South African institutions in the apartheid era. However, under mounting pressure from Israeli and pro-Israel academics, the meeting was cancelled.

The AAUP, instead, published online many of the papers intended for presentation at the conference, but it also issued a report strongly condemning the academic boycott. Joan Scott and Harold Linder, who had helped organize the conference and later edited the online publication, expressed dismay that the conference was canceled, but they also concluded that the AAUP's "principled opposition to academic boycott" was an expression of its commitment to academic freedom.[86] While Joan Scott later revised her position in an eloquent essay,[87] this seemingly contradictory position is an argument that is often used in opposition to the academic boycott, in the case of Israel, and it expresses a deeper paradox that illuminates the fault line at the core of academic freedom—as does the entire saga of the failed conference. Is it possible that closing off the possibility of a boycott of academic institutions—in the context of their complicity with military occupation and apartheid policies—is an expression of academic freedom, or is it a denial of that academic freedom? *And whose* academic freedom is being upheld?

Lisa Taraki, a sociologist at Birzeit University in the West Bank who was scheduled to present at Bellagio, noted in her paper, "I think that the abstract ideas of academic freedom and the free exchange of ideas cannot be the only norms influencing the political engagement of academics. Often, when oppression characterizes all social and political relations and structures, as in the case of apartheid South Africa or indeed Palestine, there are equally important and sometimes more important freedoms that must be fought for, even—or I would say especially—by academics and intellectuals."[88] Omar Barghouti, a Palestinian intellectual who is, like Tarakai, a cofounder of the Palestinian Academic and Cultural Boycott of Israel (PACBI), argued that the AAUP was "privileging academic freedom as above all other freedoms." Citing Judith Butler, he argued that this position excluded the freedom of "academics in contexts of colonialism, military occupation, and other forms of national oppression where 'material and institutional foreclosures . . . make it impossible for certain historical subjects to lay claim to the discourse of rights itself'. . . . Academic freedom, from this angle, becomes the exclusive privilege of some academics but not others."[89]

Barghouti and Taraki make two crucial points: First, they state that academic freedom cannot trump other rights to freedom (and other freedoms)—the right to freedom of mobility for students and scholars to attend college, to travel to conferences, and to do research; the collective right to self-determination; the freedom from occupation and racial segregation; and, in essence, the freedom to live in peace, dignity, and equality. As suggested by our introductory vignettes, the freedom and right to education of students living in zones of occupation and war overseas must be linked to the freedom of students and scholars working—and protesting—within the imperial university. Proponents of the academic boycott of Israeli institutions argued that the campaign is, thus, in *support* of and produces academic freedom, and also supports human rights for *all*—as it was in the boycott of South African institutions. Second, they allude to the selectivity of the principle of academic freedom—why South Africa and not Palestine?—and the ways in which the U.S. academy (like the Israeli academy) and professional associations such as the AAUP are firmly embedded in a political context while pretending to be outside or above it.[90]

This adjudication of neutrality and self-professed impartiality is, in fact, a political stance, as argued by Salaita and illustrated by De Genova's reflections on the limits of academic solidarity with radical critiques of U.S. imperialism. The holy grail of academic freedom shores up the political commitments and investments—not to mention the intellectual freedoms—of powerful academics and constituencies and fails to protect the commitments and interventions of the heretics who are less powerful or far outside the status quo. This is powerfully illustrated by the intense political campaign targeting De Genova for his "blasphemous" criticism of U.S. military violence and Dominguez's farcical play about his experience of being investigated by the FBI and UC San Diego due to the Electronic Disturbance Theater's "virtual sit-in" protesting the UC fee hikes and the Transborder Immigrant Tool project.[91] We must ask, why is it that some cases of academic "blasphemy" provoke an outpouring of sympathy and support from colleagues while other cases are considered too heretical to warrant (ready) solidarity?

Nelson's own writing on academic freedom is instructive in revealing the AAUP president's political position on academic freedom and its limits—just one instance of exceptionalisms in the intense debate about academic freedoms and heresies among distinguished, progressive scholar-activists. In *No University Is an Island: Saving Academic Freedom,* Nelson denounces "major fractions of the Left," especially academics, who have apparently "grown increasingly hostile and unforgiving toward Israel."[92] Nelson's sweeping statements include anecdotal observations of departments (unnamed) that have apparently refused to consider job candidates who do not support the two-state solution or who support Israel, proclaiming without any specific evidence that there is a hostile academic environment for "faculty and students with sympathies for Israel."[93] One wonders if Nelson is speaking of the same U.S. academy that the authors in this book and so many other scholars—inhabit and work in or whether he is, indeed, living on "an island."

We discuss the Bellagio train wreck and Nelson's position here because of the prominent role of the AAUP in adjudicating and defining the boundaries of academic freedom—and academic heresies—as evident in more recent controversies.[94] Despite the AAUP's otherwise impressive record on issues related to academic labor, the issue of Palestine-Israel seems to be a sticking point for the organization, as is the case in so many other liberal-progressive spaces, including academic ones—precisely because it is obfuscated through a discourse of academic freedom. This illustrates the fault lines in a principle of academic freedom that evacuates politics, in selective instances, or circumscribes and contains what is proper politics for academics, shaping the stance that scholars can or should take in response to twenty-first-century occupation, settler colonialism, wars, apartheid, and encampment.

Steven Best, Anthony Nocella II, and Peter McLaren, in their edited volume on academic repression, incisively observe that academic freedom, in fact, functions as an "alibi for the machinery of academic repression and control" and ends up justifying the "absorption of higher education into the larger constellation of corporate-military power."[95] Academic repression, they argue, is constitutive of the academic-military-industrial complex, a framework that situates the university squarely within, and not outside of, the network of state apparatuses of control, discipline, surveillance, carcerality, and violence, as alluded to by Dominguez and as argued by Godrej, Oparah, and Gumbs. In other words, as Taraki and Barghouti also suggest, it does not make sense (for progressives-leftists) to fight for academic freedom outside of the struggle against neoliberal capitalism, racism, sexism, homophobia, warfare, and imperialism. To state it more clearly, there can be no true "freedom" in the academy if there is no such freedom in society at large.[96]

The holy grail of academic freedom, defined within the liberal parameters critiqued by Prashad, has been institutionalized as a limited and problematic horizon for progressive academic mobilization. Academic freedom maintains the illusion of an autonomous university space in a militarized and corporate society such as the United States and in a "surveillance society and post-Constitutional garrison state" that continues to be consolidated under Obama, as suggested by Dominguez and other authors.[97] This does not mean giving up entirely on invoking academic freedom, for it can be, and is, often strategically used as a minimal line of defense to introduce critical ideas and broaden public debates within the academy. However, progressive campaigns organized around the principle of academic freedom often run into a profound fault line in their mobilization, if not also organized around larger political principles. In our experience, campaigns focused on organizing in defense of scholars targeted since 9/11, especially those working in Middle East and Palestine studies, often end up struggling with these same contradictions if they attempt to cohere simply around "academic freedom" rather than a more rigorous (progressive) political consensus, given how fractured the academic left is when it comes to Middle East politics and Israel-Palestine.

Critics of the academy, such as Readings, make a fundamental point: "The University is not going to save the world by making the world more true," and it must be viewed as all institutions are, not as an exceptional space or site of radicalism and "redemption" but as a site where "academics must work without alibis, which is what the best of them have intended to do."[98] In other words, the university is an institution within an imperial nation-state—a point understated by Readings—and so any struggle waged within or against it must not romanticize its progressive possibilities and must be squarely situated within a struggle that extends beyond its hallowed walls. This is what the Occupy movement, discussed at the outset, attempted to do on many campuses, and this is also why it was so brutally suppressed—because it made a linkage between the university and larger structures of power, as in earlier movements of student uprising, that was fundamentally threatening to the imperial university.

Conclusion: Decolonizing the University

Scholars working in zones of occupation, militarism, settler colonialism, and imperialism, here and there, call on us to recraft our notion of "academic freedom" by focusing unflinchingly on the larger structural forces and deeper alliances between the MPIC and the academy. If we heed this call seriously, we are moved to think about the question of freedom—academic and otherwise—in a much deeper way. Ultimately, our project is to decolonize the imperial university, and the chapters here help us understand how imperial cartographies produce manifest knowledges and logics of academic containment that structure the U.S. academy and its repression. Academic heresies and insurgencies are constitutive of this critique of the holy grail of academic freedom and of the spaces that we can create in our pedagogies and academic work through forms of intellectual guerilla warfare and theaters of dissent, as suggested by Rojas and Dominguez, among others. This involves not shying away from forms of speech and scholarship that compel unease, as De Genova courageously suggests—challenging genocide, "death," and the many forms of violence under white supremacy and in the settler colonial state. We can build on Gramsci's critical work on hegemony in thinking of insurgent spaces within the academy that must be fostered in alliance and direct engagement with those "organic intellectuals" or movements beyond the university, even as those alliances are surveilled or censured. If this book is a project of solidarity—one we hope will continue to evolve through our web archive—it aims to help support and build dissent focused on dismantling empire, and thinking freedom otherwise.

Notes

1. See Sunaina Maira and Julie Sze, "Dispatches from Pepper-Spray University: Privatization, Repression, and Revolts," *American Quarterly* 64, no. 2 (June 2012): 315–30.

2. Mahmood Mamdani, "The Importance of Research in a University," *Pambazuka News* 526 (April 21, 2011), http://www.pambazuka.org/en/issue/526.

3. Ann L. Stoler and Carole McGranahan, "Introduction: Refiguring Imperial Terrains," in *Imperial Formations*, ed. Ann L. Stoler, Carole McGranahan, and Peter Perdue (Santa Fe, N.Mex.: School for Advanced Research, 2007), 3–44.

4. Amy Kaplan, "Where Is Guantánamo?," in *Legal Borderlands: Law and the Construction of American Borders*, special issue of *American Quarterly*, ed. Mary L. Dudziak and Leti Volpp, 57, no. 3 (2005): 831–58; Amy Kaplan and Donald Pease, eds., *Cultures of United States Imperialism* (Durham: Duke University Press, 1993).

5. Uday S. Mehta, *Liberalism and Empire: A Study in Nineteenth-Century British Liberal Thought* (Chicago: University of Chicago Press, 1999).

6. Sunaina Maira, "'Good' and 'Bad' Muslim Citizens: Feminists, Terrorists, and U.S. Orientalisms," *Feminist Studies* 35, no. 3 (2009): 631–56; Randall Williams, *The Divided World: Human Rights and Its Violence* (Minneapolis: University of Minnesota Press, 2010).

7. Piya Chatterjee and Sunaina Maira, "An Open Letter to All Feminists: Statement of Solidarity with Palestinian, Arab, and Muslim Women Facing War and Occupation," *Monthly Review Zine*, March 13, 2008, http://mrzine.monthlyreview.org/2008/cm130308.html.

8. For an incisive exploration of some of these contradictions, see Mary E. John, "Postcolonial Feminists in the Western Intellectual Field: Anthropologists and Native Informants?," *Inscriptions* 5, no. 6 (1989): 49–74.

9. See Christopher Newfield, *Unmaking the Public University: The Forty-Year Assault on the Middle Class* (Cambridge, Mass.: Harvard University Press, 2008); Christopher Newfield, *Ivy and Industry: Business and the Making of the American University* (Durham: Duke University, 2003); Sheila Slaughter, *Academic Capitalism and the New Economy: Markets, States and Higher Education* (Baltimore: Johns Hopkins University Press, 2004).

10. Jeanine Theoharis, "My Student, the 'Terrorist,'" *Chronicle Review*, April 3, 2011, http://chronicle.com/article/My-Student-the-Terrorist/126937/.

11. See also Rosalind Gill, "Breaking the Silence: The Hidden Injuries of Neoliberal Academia," in *Secrecy and Silence in the Research Process: Feminist Reflections*, ed. R. Gill and R. Flood (London: Routledge, 2009).

12. Giorgio Agamben, *State of Exception*, trans. Kevin Attell (Chicago: University of Chicago Press, 2005).

13. See, for example, Erin O'Connor and Maurice Black, "Academic Freedom and

Middle East Studies," American Council of Trustees and Alumni, winter 2008, http://www.goacta.org/news/academic_freedom_and_middle_east_studies, and numerous other analysis produced by ACTA on www.goacta.org; Kenton R. Bird and Elizabeth Barker, "Academic Freedom and 9/11: How the War on Terrorism Threatens Free Speech on Campus," *Communication Law and Policy* 7 (Autumn 2002): 431–60.

14. The scholarly critique about the relationship between Anthropology and colonial administration is considerable. For a sampling, see Talal Asad, ed., *Anthropology and the Colonial Encounter* (Atlantic Highlands, N.J.: Humanities Press, 1973); Jan van Breman and Akitoshi Shimizu, *Anthropology and Colonialism in Asia and Oceania* (Richmond, Surrey: Curzon, 1999); Diane Lewis, "Anthropology and Colonialism," *Current Anthropology* 14, no. 4 (December 1973): 581–602.

15. Bill Readings, *The University in Ruins* (Cambridge, Mass.: Harvard University Press, 1996), 2. It is important to note here, though, that Readings's argument about "Americanization" of the university is embedded within his subtle readings of globalization in the current period and not a wholesale argument about U.S. hegemonic expansion. We use his term to signal this early twentieth-century model that is certainly about the latter, especially in epistemological and curricular formations as Bascara outlines.

16. For the most comprehensive study of the emergence of these ideas in the history of anthropology, see George Stocking, *Race, Culture and Evolution: Essays in the History of Anthropology* (Chicago: University of Chicago Press, 1982).

17. For example, some of the earliest British ethnologists were also colonial administrators—who became experts on the languages and "customs and manners" of the natives whom they tried to both understand and control. See Peter Pels, "From Texts to Bodies: Brian Houghton Hodgson and the Emergence of Ethnology in India," in *Anthropology and Colonialism in Asia and Oceania*, ed. Jan van Bremen and Akitoshi Shimuzu (Richmond, Surrey: Curzon, 1999), 66; Sita Venkateswar, *Development and Ethnocide: Colonial Practices in the Andaman Islands* (Copenhagen: International Work Group for Indigenous Affairs, 2004).

18. David Price, *Anthropological Intelligence: The Deployment and Neglect of American Anthropology in the Second World War* (Durham: Duke University Press, 2008), 8.

19. For more specific, and longitudinal, studies of anthropologists' involvement in various forms of military intelligence, see John D. Kelly, Beatrice Jauregui, Sean T. Mitchell, and Jeremy Walton, eds., *Anthropology and Global Counterinsurgency* (Chicago: University of Chicago Press, 2010); Eric Wakin, *Anthropology Goes to War: Professional Ethics and Counterinsurgency in Thailand* (Madison: University of Wisconsin Press, 1992); Montgomery McFate, "Anthropology and Counterinsurgency: The Strange Story of Their Curious Relationship," *Military Review* (March/April 2005),

24–38. McFate's article provides a fascinating and detailed analysis of the Boas controversy.

20. Steven Best, Anthony J. Nocella II, and Peter McLaren, "The Rise of the Academic-Industrial Complex and the Crisis in Free Speech," in *Academic Repression: Reflections from the Academic-Industrial Complex*, ed. Anthony J. Nocella II, Steven Best, and Peter McLaren (Oakland, Calif.: AK Press, 2010), 17.

21. Ibid., 22.

22. Ibid., 21.

23. R. C. Lewontin, "The Cold War and the Transformation of the Academy," in *The Cold War and the University: Toward an Intellectual History of the Postwar Years*, ed. Noam Chomsky et al. (New York: New Press, 1977), 13.

24. Price, *Anthropological Intelligence*, 74. The 1942 Intensive Language Program was "designed to plug American campuses directly into war prepared-ness" (Price, *Anthropological Intelligence*, 75).

25. For a detailed analysis, see Immanuel Wallerstein, "The Unintended Consequences of Cold War Area Studies," in *The Cold War and the University: Toward an Intellectual History of the Postwar Years*, ed. Noam Chomsky et al. (New York: New Press, 1977), 199.

26. Price, *Anthropological Intelligence*, 43.

27. Ibid., 27.

28. Ibid., 165.

29. Noam Chomsky, "The Cold War and the University," in *The Cold War and the University: Toward an Intellectual History of the Postwar Years*, ed. Noam Chomsky et al. (New York: New Press, 1977), 176.

30. David Meireran and Amy Goodman Interview, "Carnegie Military University: How the Pentagon Funds Universities to Contribute to War," *Democracy Now!*, November 19, 2004, http://www.democracynow.org/2004/11/19/carnegie_military _university_how_the_pentagon; Stuart Leslie, *The Cold War and American Science: The Military-Industrial-Academic Complex at MIT and Stanford* (New York: Columbia University Press, 1993).

31. Henry Giroux, *The University in Chains: Confronting the Military-Industrial-Academic Complex* (Boulder, Colo.: Paradigm Publishers: 2007), 11. Giroux argues that he deleted the phrase before he delivered the address on January 17, 1961.

32. Ibid. The full speech can be found in William J. Fulbright, "The War and Its Effects: The Military-Academic Industrial Complex," in *Super-State: Readings in the Military Industrial Complex*, ed. Herbert I. Schiller and Joseph D. Phillips (Urbana: University of Illinois Press, 1970), 173–78.

33. Giroux, *The University in Chains,* 161. He notes, "ACTA is not a friend of the principle of academic freedom, nor is it comfortable with John Dewey's notion that education should be responsive to the deepest conflicts of our time, or Hannah

Arendt's insistence that debate and a commitment to persuasion are the essence of a democratically oriented politics."

34. Jonathan Feldman, *Universities in the Business of Repression: The Academic-Military-Industrial Complex and Central America* (Boston: South End, 1989). Feldman offers a comprehensive accounting with copious statistics and naming of persons and amounts of funding. See, especially, his appendix, 245–308.

35. Chomsky, "The Cold War and the University," 181. Half of MIT's $200 million budget in 1969 was funded by the military (Ibid., 182); see also Feldman, *Universities in the Business of Repression*, 208, for a table on 1983 DOD Contracts at MIT.

36. See Lewontin, "The Cold War and the Transformation of the Academy," 10–12.

37. For the role of anthropological expertise and training in war, see Price, *Anthropological Intelligence*, and also Roberto González's chapter. For more contemporary analysis, see John D. Kelly et al., *Anthropology and Global Counterinsurgency*

38. For a detailed discussion of Project Camelot and the Chilean exposé, see Wallerstein, "The Unintended Consequences of Cold War Area Studies," 220–23.

39. Mark Solovey, "Project Camelot and the 1960s Epistemological Revolution: Rethinking the Politics-Patronage-Social Science Nexus," *Social Studies of Science* 31, no. 2 (April 2001): 171–206.

40. Roderick A. Ferguson, *The Reorder of Things: The University and Its Pedagogies of Minority Difference* (Minneapolis: University of Minnesota Press, 2012).

41. For an extensive discussion of recent debates within the discipline about this issue, see George R. Lucas, *Anthropologists in Arms: The Ethics of Military Anthropology* (Plymouth, U.K.: Altamira, 2009).

42. See Alfred McCoy, *A Question of Torture: CIA Interrogation from the Cold War to the War on Terror* (New York: Henry Holt, 2006).

43. Joe Masco, "Bad Weather: On Planetary Crisis," *Social Studies of Science* 40, no. 1 (February 2010): 16.

44. Roberto J. González, *American Counterinsurgency: Human Science and the Human Terrain* (Chicago: Prickly Paradigm, 2009).

45. González, *American Counterinsurgency*, 4.

46. Readings, *The University in Ruins*, 181.

47. See Henry Giroux, "Higher Education after September 11th: The Crises of Academic Freedom and Democracy," in *Academic Repression: Reflections from the Academic Industrial Complex*, ed. Steven Best, Anthony Nocella, and Peter McLaren (Oakland, Calif.: AK Press, 2010), 93.

48. See Ellen W. Schrecker, *No Ivory Tower: McCarthyism and the Universities* (New York: Oxford University Press, 1986), 12–23. In the 1890s, scholars such as Robert T. Ely, a prominent economist, were targeted for their critique of industrialists and what was viewed as pro-Left views. In Ely's case, a member of the University of Wisconsin Board of Regents charged him with supporting strikes and unions. Faced

with losing his job, Ely capitulated. Schrecker notes that Ely's victory was an important sacrifice in terms of the practice of "academic freedom" by "accepting the Regent's authority to censor his political views and more significantly *by accepting a restricted notion of appropriate academic behaviour*" (italics ours). See Schrecker's comprehensive and brilliant analysis of this "foundational" moment of academic "containment" (in our terms), 15–17.

49. See Schrecker, *No Ivory Tower*, 15.

50. Ibid., 18.

51. Ibid., 63.

52. Allan Bloom, *The Closing of the American Mind* (New York: Simon and Schuster, 1987); Roger Kimball, *Tenured Radicals: How Politics Has Corrupted Our Higher Education* (Chicago: Ivan R. Dee, 1990); David Hollinger, *Postethnic America: Beyond Multiculturalism* (New York: Basic Books, 1995).

53. Newfield, *Unmaking the Public University*, 268.

54. Ibid., 5–6.

55. Ibid., 3–5.

56. The bills are promoted by Students for Academic Freedom, whose webpage has the credo, "You can't get a good education if they're only telling you half the story": http://www.studentsforacademicfreedom.org.

57. See "The Student Bill of Rights," Students for Academic Freedom, http://www.studentsforacademicfreedom.org/documents/1922/sbor.html.

58. Newfield, *Unmaking the Public University*, 115–21.

59. Junaid Rana, *Terrifying Muslims: Race and Labor in the South Asian Diaspora* (Durham: Duke University Press, 2011); Roxanne Dunbar-Ortiz, "The Grid of History: Cowboys and Indians," in *Pox Americana: Exposing the American Empire*, ed. John B. Foster and Robert W. McChesney (New York: Monthly Review), 31–40.

60. Chatterjee and Maira, "An Open Letter to All Feminists."

61. Maira, "'Good' and 'Bad' Muslim Citizens."

62. Judith Butler, "Judith Butler's Remarks to Brooklyn College on BDS," *The Nation*, February 7, 2013, http://www.thenation.com/article/172752/judith-butlers-remarks-brooklyn-college-bds#.

63. For example, David Horowitz's ad in the *New York Times* in 2011 defaming 150 U.S. scholars who supported the academic and cultural boycott of Israel as anti-Semitic proponents of "blood libel" against Jews.

64. For example, the notorious public transit ads in San Francisco and other cities by Pamela Geller's Stop Islamicization of America campaign stated, "In any war between the civilized man and the savage, support the civilized man. Support Israel. Defeat jihad." See interview with Geller by Jamie Glazov, "Is Islamic Jihad Not Savagery?," *Front Page*, November 26, 2012, http://frontpagemag.com/2012/jamie-glazov-is-islamic-jihad-not-savagery/.

65. "The Top Ten Anti-Israel Groups in America," Anti-Defamation League, October 4, 2010, http://www.adl.org/main_Anti_Israel/top_ten_anti_israel_groups.htm?Multi_page_sections=sHeading_2.

66. See Steven Salaita, *Israel's Dead Soul* (Philadelphia: Temple University Press, 2011).

67. Max Ajl, "Academic Freedom Controversy Brewing at University of California," *The Electronic Intifada*, May 20, 2009, http://electronicintifada.net/content/academic-freedom-controversy-brewing-university-california/8242.

68. Jasbir Puar, *Terrorist Assemblages: Homonationalism in Queer Times* (Durham: Duke University Press, 2007), 45.

69. Nora Barrows-Friedman, "Bogus Allegations of 'Anti-Semitism' Create Real Climate of Fear for Arab, Muslim Students in US," *The Electronic Intifada*, August 8, 2012, http://electronicintifada.net/content/bogus-allegations-antisemitism-create-real-climate-fear-arab-muslim-students-us/11563; Yaman Salahi, "The Echo Chamber of Campus Anti-Semitism," *Al Jazeera*, August 29, 2012, http://www.aljazeera.com/indepth/opinion/2012/08/201282991348710688.html.

70. See Salaita, *Israel's Dead Soul*, 14.

71. Ibid., 3.

72. Joseph A. Massad, *Desiring Arabs* (Chicago: University of Chicago Press, 2007); Puar, *Terrorist Assemblages*.

73. Schrecker, *No Ivory Tower,* 18.

74. Clyde Barrow, *Universities and the Capitalist State: Corporate Liberalism and the Reconstruction of American Higher Education* (Madison, Wis.: University of Wisconsin Press, 1990), 227.

75. Ibid., 228.

76. Ibid., 14.

77. Ibid., 229.

78. Cary Nelson, *No University Is an Island: Saving Academic Freedom* (New York: New York University Press, 2010), 1.

79. Robert Post, "The Structure of Academic Freedom," in *Academic Freedom after September 11*, ed. Beshara Doumani (New York: Zone Books, 2006), 65. Lovejoy had, in fact, resigned from Stanford in protest over the dismissal of faculty in 1900 for opposing exploitation of Asian immigrant labor.

80. Ibid., 71.

81. Ibid.

82. Ibid., 75.

83. Schrecker, *No Ivory Tower*, 23.

84. Judith Butler, "Academic Norms, Contemporary Challenges," in *Academic Freedom after September 11*, ed. Beshara Doumani (New York: Zone Books, 2006), 107.

85. Ibid., 128.

86. Joan W. Scott and Harold F. Linder, "Introduction to Academic Boycotts," *Academe* 92, no. 5 (September–October 2006): 35–38.

87. Joan W. Scott, "Changing My Mind about the Boycott," *Journal of Academic Freedom* 4 (2013), http://www.aaup.org/reports-publications/journal-academic-freedom/volume-4.

88. See Lisa Taraki's essay in "[Critics] of the AAUP Report," *Academe* 92, no. 5 (September–October 2006): 56.

89. Omar Barghouti's essay in "Critics of the AAUP Report," *Academe* 92, no. 5 (September–October, 2006): 44; Judith Butler, "Israel/Palestine and the Paradoxes of Academic Freedom," *Radical Philosophy* 135 (January–February 2006): 8–17.

90. The AAUP called for divestment from corporations complicit with apartheid South Africa in 1985 and acknowledges that this was a "form of boycott," if not an academic boycott as such. Joan W. Scott et al., "On Academic Boycotts," AAUP, http://www.aaup.org/report/academic-boycotts.

91. It is interesting to note here the chilling parallels of Dominguez's surreal interview with FBI agents at UCSD with what happened in the McCarthy period: "It was not uncommon for a faculty member to be called to an administrator's office to be interrogated in the presence of an agent of the FBI or some other government operations. It was believed quite appropriate for academic administrators to initiate an investigation into the political life of faculty." See Lionel S. Lewis, *Cold War on Campus* (Piscataway, N.J.: Transaction Publishers, 1987), 251.

92. Nelson, *No University Is an Island*, 113.

93. Ibid., 110.

94. This was made ever more apparent in the controversy that erupted about the issue of AAUP's *Journal of Academic Freedom* on academic boycott that included several articles in support of the boycott and was followed by a rebuttal by Nelson and criticism by pro-Israel academics. See *Journal of Academic Freedom* 4 (2013), http://www.aaup.org/reports-publications/journal-academic-freedom/volume-4.

95. Best, Nocella, and McLaren, "The Rise of the Academic-Industrial Complex," 29.

96. Ibid.

97. Ibid., 27, 29.

98. Readings, *The University in Ruins*, 144–45, 171.

I

Imperial Cartographies

1
_____

New Empire, Same Old University?

Education in the American Tropics after 1898

Victor Bascara

> *¡LA UPR ES DE TODOS!*
>
> —*Graffiti at University of Puerto Rico, Rio Piedras, circa 2010*

> *Different racial beauties lend charm to Hawaii's wonders, and they gather from all the islands of the group at the University of Hawai'i. Truly, the march of student life has no beginning and no end.*
>
> —Ka Palapala, *University of Hawai'i student yearbook, circa 1937*

Figure 1.1. ¡LA UPR ES DE TODOS! (THE UNIVERSITY OF PUERTO RICO IS EVERYONE'S!). Graffiti seen on a dumpster at University of Puerto Rico, Rio Piedras, circa 2010. Photograph by Victor Bascara.

The Uses and Idea of the Imperial University

In *The Uses of the University* (1964), University of California president Clark Kerr outlines "two great clichés about the university" in relation to social change: "One pictures [the university] as a radical institution, when in fact it is most conservative in its institutional conduct. The other pictures it as autonomous, a cloister, when the historical fact is that it has always responded, but seldom so quickly as today, to the desires and demands of external groups. . . . The external view is that the university is radical; the internal reality is that it is conservative. The internal illusion is that it is a law unto itself; the external reality is that it is governed by history."[1] These two clichés are no less apt for approaching the uses and idea of imperial universities, particularly when considering their histories of emergence. This chapter looks to and emphasizes possible linkages among the diverse institutional histories of the University of Hawai'i (UH), the University of the Philippines (UP), and the University of Puerto Rico (UPR). All three universities were founded within a five-year span between 1903 and 1908. This chapter, through a discussion of these three richly complicated sites, is a consideration of the intersections of "the idea of a university"[2] and the idea of empire. These intersections are legible in official university discourse and the material culture of these universities themselves as these institutions emerged and developed in the post-1898 era, serving U.S. possessions in Hawaii, the Philippines, and Puerto Rico.[3]

What follows, then, is a consideration of discursive formations from these universities that grapple with the meaning of the new imperial university— and of liberal education in particular—in the early years of three vastly separated institutions with potentially resonant concerns. And those common concerns may emerge at sites where the mission of the university and the mission of the empire either converge or diverge, perhaps even imagining a university *of* an empire but not necessarily for it, as Dr. Francisco Benitez recently noted in his speech on the occasion of his being installed as president of Philippine Women's University (PWU) in February 2011: "Let us recall that PWU was a house of learning founded [in 1919] by teachers who were at the same time citizens with a social consciousness and a missionary zeal. Establishing a school under the aegis of empire, theirs was a fundamental belief that education cultivated a capacity for the participative citizenship required of a strong democratic and independent republic."[4] Founding a university under imperial conditions can demand an appreciation for the role such institutions may play in envisioning and realizing postimperial conditions worth working toward. That is to say, Benitez carefully draws out ways in which higher education established "under the aegis of empire" can ironically be an apparatus *against* the project of future imperial formations, pursuing this by inculcating and emphasizing anticolonial political ideals also evident in empire's genealogy. In doing so, he implicitly helps us appreciate how the imperial university may be at risk of aligning the demands of postconquest militarism with postcolonial neoliberalism, as legitimated notions of security and development have substituted for older narratives of pacification, domestication, and civilization.

In grasping what is at stake in how these imperial demands are both addressed and challenged, this chapter appreciates not only how the university, as an institution, is a contact zone but also how the imperial university is a contact zone within a contact zone. And as such it can both legitimate and challenge the terms and conditions of contact in the colony in the ways that it practices such contact and figures its significance. For in apprehending how the imperial university conceptualizes its role in the imperial project, we can also see how that institution provides terms for conceptualizing and realizing the transition to postimperial conditions. This chapter is an examination, if partial and not encyclopedic, of specimens of discourse from archives at UP, UH, and UPR in order to analyze objects through which we can recognize the role of the university in the erection and dismantling of empire.

A key rationale behind the establishment of colonial institutions, in general, is that aligning peripheries to the core requires formal as well as informal means of producing proper subjects of the empire, as will be explored in this chapter. During and after the Cold War especially, progressive and even radical dimensions of these institutions significantly manifested in their connections to countercultural, oppositional, and decolonizing movements. But historically these institutions were not always so readily aligned with constituencies at odds with the empire. Then and now, such selective and elite universities are both stratifying and democratizing. The dilemma of this contrapuntal vision is critically expressed in the graffiti quoted previously, where, in theory, "¡LA UPR ES DE TODOS!" (which might be translated as "The University of Puerto Rico is everyone's!"). Yet differential access to higher education and the presumed rewards of a university education in the labor market seem to indicate otherwise; that is, the university may belong to all ideally, but in practice it trains a select few who benefit from that exclusivity. That is what universities do. Universal university access is a widely held idea that stretches back historically,[5] especially to public and land-grant universities where chants of "Whose university? Our university!" resound at rallies today.

Given the plausible notion of the "two great clichés" of the radicalism and conservatism of the university articulated by Kerr, the imperial university emerges as a revealing site for both contending with and affirming imperial projects. That empires and universities are connected is neither new nor even really debatable; Kerr acknowledges how the university came of age in response to "two great new forces [in nineteenth-century Germany]: science and nationalism."[6] And that idea is not alien to the uses and idea of the imperial university, as natural and national histories are evident in legitimated knowledge production in higher education.

The considerable material and ideological resources that have been necessary for operating, and indeed founding, such institutions would likely have been unattainable without the blessings and budget allocations of the U.S. empire. From the very land occupied and sometimes environmentally devastated by universities[7] to the bodies of workers reconcentrated on that land and the bodies of knowledge putatively preserved there, universities are institutions of, and presumably for, the civilizations they teach to and about. In this respect they are a related infrastructure to fortresses or missions along literal and metaphorical frontier lines. Indeed, the founding of U.S. universities in colonized sites soon after the waging of wars of conquest and pacification can hardly be seen as a mere coincidence.

This chapter draws on the early twentieth-century discourse of the universities of Hawaii, the Philippines, and Puerto Rico—all universities founded under U.S. administration of island colonies, or colony-like possessions, between 1903 and 1908. To examine the mission of these universities, and of the educational apparatus in the colonies in general, the focus here is on the implicit and explicit institutionalization of liberal education at these institutions. That is to say, this work analyzes primary documents from the archives of each of the institutions, mainly via the genre of the general catalog and related university discourse. Whether technically compliant with American Association of Collegiate Registrars and Admissions Officers (AACRAO) guidelines or not, these materials nevertheless manifest a textual sameness across time, space, and circumstance that, despite the difference of conditions, communicates a concomitant sameness of vision. There were certainly local differences from archive to archive, but overall these general catalogs were, for the most part, exemplary of this still widely produced genre, albeit in paperless forms today. Amid this sameness, both with the imperial core as well as with coperipheral sites, this chapter isolates discursive formations that articulate negotiations between the sameness and difference that both empire and its universities are premised upon. This predicament is a condition that a headnote to the English department curriculum of a 1923–1924 University of the Philippines general catalog ambiguously referred to as "the peculiar demands of the university." What, we might reasonably ask, were those "peculiar demands of the university" under these conditions—namely, that of U.S. territorial acquisition in the era soon after the watershed events of 1898?

Considering the foundings of UPR in 1903, UH in 1907, and UP in 1908, the origins of these institutions clearly follow on turn-of-the-century imperial acquisitions. While the foundings of these universities did not really have significant administrative overlap, the coincidence of these geographically disparate foundings was likely not coincidental, given the growing and innovative globality of the United States' imperial reach.[8] Though the varying transitions to decolonizing or neocolonizing futures of the Philippines, Hawaii, and Puerto Rico were yet unknown, the emerging vision of a new empire is discernible in comparable university documents across these sites. As will be analyzed and discussed later, these universities served as both an outpost of the imperial center as well as an emerging and illuminating network of empire's contradictions.

Cartographies of Imperial and Educational Reform, circa 1898 and After

To grasp the relationship of these universities to the imperial conditions in which they were founded and developed, it helps to consider the particular conceptions of empire contemporary with their foundings at the outset of the twentieth century. U.S. extraterritorial imperialism is understood as a liminal position between the age of high imperialism and the coming world order of the neocolonial and the neoliberal.[9] Various manifestations of U.S. extraterritorial imperialism were palimpsestic in that they were built on the displacement of Spain and then replaced by direct and/or indirect U.S. control, thereby setting the terms for U.S. empire as managing to be both a break and a continuity. The perceived and perhaps actual role of the flagship university may, as I argue later, be that of both dramatizing a break with some pasts and establishing continuities with other pasts and their real and imagined futures.

Even in the immediate aftermath of the Spanish-American War in 1898, the statuses of these three island locations were different but were lumped as the insular cases in the Bureau of Insular Affairs.[10] Soon after the end of World War II, the Philippines would finally become an independent republic by virtue of a decades-long legislative effort to gradually implement independence. And it remains an independent republic, in conventional political terms at least. In 1952, Puerto Rico would become the political entity it currently is: an associated free state. And in 1959, Hawaii would become the fiftieth U.S. state. On paper and in material infrastructure, these three destinies are substantially different, despite the various commonalities of their moments of incorporation into the sphere of U.S. control, ranging from economic (inter)dependency, cultural influence, and formal plenary power. The history of each could well serve as distinct test cases in the diverse realization of U.S. world power, along the lines of what Henry Luce, in 1941, famously referred to as the "American Century," observing, "American jazz, Hollywood movies, American slang, American machines and patented products, are in fact the only things that every community in the world, from Zanzibar to Hamburg, recognizes in common. Blindly, unintentionally, accidentally and really in spite of ourselves, we are already a world power in the trivial ways—in very human ways."[11] Manifesting "world power" through the "trivial" and the "human" now seems prophetic, as neoliberal globalization has proliferated and formal administration of empires has declined over the twentieth century. Though the Luce family has long had prominent ties to academic philanthropy and institution building, especially in Asia, one item Luce interestingly does not list here is the American university,[12] implying perhaps that such direct administration is exceptional and perhaps a residual form of exercising "world power."

Well before the current political fates of Hawaii, the Philippines, and Puerto Rico were realized, U.S. imperial infrastructures at these sites emerged. And as concerns this chapter, 1903, 1907, and 1908 saw the foundings of the University of Porto [sic] Rico, the College of Hawaii (later the University of Hawai'i in 1920), and the University of the Philippines (the original Manila campus), respectively.[13] These geographically disparate locations with unique histories and political relationships with the United States would each establish what were similarly planned as, and would go on to be, the premier research universities of their respective sites. For instance, there was already a thriving infrastructure of higher education in the Philippines older than Harvard's (which was founded in 1636, a quarter century after the University of Santo Tomas). The local variations are, of course, too numerous to catalog here; revealing, however, are plausible parallels in the era of U.S. control between these sites that are just coming to terms with imperial cohesion. I argue that these terms are tellingly visible in attempts to reconcile the concept of "liberal education" with the practice of imperialism, for that echoes the attempts of U.S. imperial discourse to legitimate its emergence. In many ways, that reconciling, then as now, is not difficult, as the connection of the secular civilizing mission to the uplifting educational apparatus is fairly easy to see when ideology and state apparatuses converge conspicuously in schools, from curricula to pedagogies to disciplining. We might now more readily recognize this as neoliberalism, a way of seeming to reconcile integrated markets with localized freedoms.[14]

It may then be reasonable to ask why these universities would be founded at all, especially given the familiar traffic in students from the colonies to the metropole and back. From Mohandas Gandhi to Frantz Fanon to José Rizal, there is a clear tradition in the history of modern Western empire of having institutions located in the imperial center to educate the elite of the colonies. This is not alien to the limited imperial experience of the United States—for example, the *pensionado* program brought Filipinos from the territory to major U.S. universities.[15] The figure of the quasi-foreign student is a motif abundantly dramatized, often celebratorily and at times critically, in representations of empire. That ambivalence is dramatized in Doroteo Ines's 1938 silent film *A Filipino in America*, made at the University of Southern California (USC) while Ines was in a graduate cinematography program.[16] The film's ending presents something of a dilemma for Asian American consciousness, as the unnamed protagonist opts to return to the Philippines at the conclusion of his studies in mining engineering at USC. Ines's film was produced through his graduate program at USC (and does not actually reflect what he ended up doing himself).[17] Here we have a story that is not unfamiliar, even in the present. A foreign student comes to the United States for advanced training in a specialized field—presumably a training program not available in the sending state or other administrative unit. And at the conclusion of that training, the student—sometimes funded through explicit programs established by the sending, receiving, or both administrative units—is expected to return.

It is important to note that the protagonist in Ines's film does attempt to stay in the United States by putting his USC mining engineering degree to work. But given the labor market of the Depression years and the realities of a racially segmented labor market, his efforts to find employment commensurate with his education predictably end in failure, within the metropole at least. And so he must return to a frontier zone to participate in the process of nation building, a path on which the Philippines was put since the passage of the Tydings-McDuffie Act of 1934,[18] if not earlier. The U.S. government efforts to repatriate Filipinos from the formal United States to the territory of the Philippines were under way, though largely unsuccessful at removing Filipinos in substantial numbers.[19]

The educational cartography that this narrative resolution makes visible at once links the core and the periphery through the evidence of these intraimperial circuits. But this mapping also simultaneously demonstrates the material divisions of underdevelopment and overdevelopment that make the idea and practice of migration meaningful, especially for these students and the knowledges and skill sets they carry with them after matriculating. A question that then emerges concerns what is lacking in the university at the periphery that makes it apparently necessary for there to be an internal migration of students, not as an occasional aberration in an educational infrastructure, but as a constitutive part of it.[20] The needs that this migratory formation implies both parallels and is an integral part of the underlying logic for the establishment of colonial institutions in general— that is, producing proper subjects of the empire. This at least is the presumed theory behind the founding, or refounding, of educational systems in the colonies at the primary and secondary levels certainly.[21] But does it hold true for higher education in the periphery? Is the imperial university located in the territories the marker of empire's highest attainment—the installation of "liberal education" for indigenous subject populations, albeit frequently the elite of those populations?

Education was a central trope in turn-of-the-century U.S. imperial discourse. In the rich tradition of imperial and anti-imperial illustrations from that era, one of the more well-remembered and expressive renderings of U.S. imperialism and its educational mission in its new possessions is Louis Dalrymple's "School Begins" cartoons from an 1899 issue of *Punch*. The image depicts Uncle Sam, rod/pointer in hand, admonishing the apparently squirming children in the front row of the classroom in the following caption: "Uncle Sam (to his new class in civilization)—'Now, children, you've got to learn these lessons whether you want to or not! But just take a look at the class ahead of you, and remember that in a little while, you will be as glad to be here as they are!'" The wriggling brown children are wearing ribbons that indicate "Philippines," "Hawaii," "Porto [*sic*] Rico," and "Cuba."

Across a vast number of illustrations from cultural texts of the period, education indeed came to stand in for both the hopes and despair of the new colonial civilizing mission.[22] The empire is a classroom writ large, and the classroom is a microcosm of empire. In this particular image, Dalrymple pointedly included past attempts to manage racialized populations, with the presumably Chinese child standing at the classroom door, the American Indian child sitting just inside holding his ABC book upside down, and the African American looking on while washing the classroom window. Schooling is certainly a metaphor for the process of "civilization," but it has also clearly been an actual instrument of it. For example, philosopher Louis Althusser, in his influential work on ideology and ideological state apparatuses, calls attention to the overwhelming role of education:

> Nevertheless, in this concert [of ideological state apparatuses], one ideological State apparatus has the dominant role, although hardly anyone lends an ear to its music: it is so silent! This is the School. It takes children from every class at infant-school age, and then for years, the years in which the child is most "vulnerable", squeezed between family State apparatus and the educational State apparatus, it drums into them, whether it uses old or new methods, a certain amount of "know-how" wrapped in the ruling ideology (French, arithmetic, natural history, the sciences, literature) or simply the ruling ideology in its pure state (ethics, civic instruction, philosophy).[23]

In Althusser's analysis, the hegemonic role of education implies its perhaps more dominant understanding as liberatory, empowering, and counterhegemonic. As the saying goes, if you think education is expensive, try ignorance.[24] We might adapt this to the colonial context to say if you think education is imperial, then try decolonizing without it. And this indeed may be what U.S. educators in these new possessions in the wake of the Spanish-American War had envisioned the situation in which they found themselves. One such commentator—Adeline Knapp of Berkeley, California—both links and likens territorial conquest to pedagogical incorporation at the turn of the twentieth century. Aboard the storied USS *Thomas*,[25] sailing from July 23 to August 21, 1901, and filled with U.S. primary educators bound for the Philippines, she made the following pronouncement, which I quote at length:

The Spanish-American war has been the direct cause of three remark-able expeditions by sea, any one of which is notable among the enter-prises of great nations. Taken together the three form a significant commentary upon that faith in "the other man" which is so marked a characteristic of the American genius. Of these three expeditions the first was that which carried the vanquished Spanish army back to the Peninsula; the second, which brought the Spanish-American teachers from Cuba to the mainland to study American methods and ideas in a great summer school at Harvard University, is yet fresh in the minds of many. It was a generous and grateful act on the part of this government, and this expedition was as joyous as the other was sad. The third and most notable of these expeditions is, like the second, one for educational purposes; but has grown out of other conditions than those which prevail in Cuba, and is designed to meet another sort of problem. In the Philippine Islands there exists no already established body of native teachers; few teachers at all, in fact, trained or otherwise, are there to carry on the education that shall fit the Filipinos for their new citizenship. She bears no armed force, yet it is nonetheless an army with banners, with standards and ensigns . . . hence the gathering of this great army of instruction. . . . Soon the soldiers shall be scattered over the insular field, fighting each his battle with what might is given him.[26]

I include this extended quotation to convey and trace the epistemologi-cal challenge of figuring and almost literally mapping a new conception of empire. Knapp acknowledges the singularly "remarkable" voyages that can be appreciated on their own, while she also seeks to make connections between them recognizable. The overt conceit may be that of the sea voy-age, but the point she is making is that the crossing of space simultaneously defines distance while also describing the heroic bridging of those distances, a simultaneity that has inspired her own work. That bridge is the "Ameri-can genius" of "faith in 'the other man.'" The parallel between soldiers and educators may seem to enact the biblically inspired pacification narrative of turning swords into plowshares and unlearning the very idea of war.[27] Yet in this narrative, the activity of the presumably male soldier becomes the tem-plate for the variously gendered Thomasite, figured as a "soldier . . . scattered over the insular field, fighting each his battle with what might is given him."

Those battles are waged on behalf of, if not also perhaps against, the newly recolonized.

Knapp's vision of education in the new colony resonated not only with the biblical but also with au courant ideas about the role of education in producing properly disciplined citizen-subjects seeming to emerge from New England.[28] The educational system she envisioned would transform this population that the U.S. imperialists, from McKinley to Beveridge to Taft, described as "unfit for self-government" through an education "that shall fit the Filipinos for their new citizenship." Whether that citizenship was to be to the United States or possibly even a postcolonial nation-state, citizenship emerges as a compelling speculative concept that not only stands at the endpoint of an educational process but also serves as a crowning rationale for erecting both educational systems in general and specific educational institutions in particular.[29]

Knapp's reference to the idea of "faith in 'the other man' which is so marked a characteristic of the American genius" can be understood in the context of her era's attempts to reconcile Enlightenment ideals that the United States is presumed to stand for (e.g., liberty, equality) with what it was actually doing (e.g., conquest, subordination). The project on which she and her fellow teachers, and her fellow soldiers, embarked is expansionism but somehow benevolently undertaken.[30] And through her notion of "three remarkable expeditions by sea," an imperial network emerges, linking the Caribbean to New England to California to the Philippines. With the USS *Thomas* making a stop in Honolulu on its way to Manila, a map of U.S. education not coincidentally overlays a map of U.S. military control.

Colony as Laboratory

Such maps of empire are not only spatial but also developmental, with the core at one end of development and the periphery on the other. Knapp's, Dalrymple's, and Ines's conceptions of both education and empire emerge to situate the metropole as the core to the colonial frontiers' periphery, albeit most likely to different ends. Across these examples there is a consistent sense of the metropole being the fountain of knowledge and civilization and the colonies being on the receiving end of that flow. For Knapp's 1901 journal, the educational apparatus and its agents displace the military apparatus and its agents. For Dalrymple's 1899 cartoon, the latest set of students— this time from the new possessions of Hawaii, Puerto Rico, Cuba, and the

Philippines—file into the seats formerly occupied by the successes, and fail-
ures, of previous classes. And for Ines's 1938 film, technical training acquired
in mining engineering can then be brought back to the Philippines, in a critical reversal of the "brain drain" that will presumably contribute toward the
infrastructure of the on-its-way-to-postcolonial Philippines by extracting
resources.[31] In these familiar narratives of colonizer–colonized relations, the
developed core transplants its ideas and institutions in the colonies. In this
logic, putatively fully formed programs in "social engineering"[32] and governance more generally are applied to new contexts.

There have been needed and strategic inversions of this narrative in
examinations of such institutions as public health, policing, and schooling.
And in such cases, the colonies are therefore seen not only as "backward" but
also as visions of the future governmentalist management of analogous populations within the metropole. For example, Warwick Anderson has demonstrated how public health under the U.S. colonial administration in the
Philippines would later go on to shape public health practices in the United
States. Alfred McCoy has traced how the history of the innovative forms of
policing and surveillance of the U.S. colonial administration in the Philippines would later go on to shape law enforcement theory and practice in
the United States. And Meg Wesling provocatively proposes that the defining
and teaching of American literature had crucial formation in the real and
imagined classrooms of the Philippines under U.S. colonial administration.[33]
In each of these cases, the colony was considered a kind of laboratory for the
metropole to learn from. That is, the flow of influence was not as unidirectional empire would have it. This idea also echoes one of the main insights
of Edward W. Said's *Orientalism*—that is, that the West becomes knowable as
the West when it seeks to manage its Oriental alterity.[34]

So we observe that the imperial university can be seen not only as a lofty
site for imparting technical knowledges and imperial cultural values but also
as a laboratory for subject formation not only for the empire that founded it
but also for the coming world order being tested out in the tropics and on
new subjects being integrated into an ever-changing and expanding educational apparatus. In the field of U.S. educational reform, the idea that those
who are in an educational system transform the system by their incorporation and integration into it has been a crucial one. Perhaps no more celebrated articulation of this exists than the 1954 U.S. Supreme Court decision
of *Brown v. Board of Education*:[35]

Today, education is perhaps the most important function of state and local governments. Compulsory school attendance laws and the great expenditures for education both demonstrate our recognition of the importance of education to our democratic society. It is required in the performance of our most basic public responsibilities, even service in the armed forces. It is the very foundation of good citizenship. Today it is a principal instrument in awakening the child to cultural values, in preparing him for later professional training, and in helping him to adjust normally to his environment. In these days, it is doubtful that any child may reasonably be expected to succeed in life if he is denied the opportunity of an education.

Here we find an emerging articulation of race-conscious liberal education, identified as the making of "good citizenship." Importantly, education is understood as the unidirectional imparting of knowledge not only from teachers to pupils but also from pupil to pupil. The justices unanimously make a telling distinction between "tangible," or material, factors and "intangible," or "psychological," factors. And in doing so, the *Brown* decision articulates the educational importance of diversity in the classroom.

To separate [students] from others of similar age and qualifications solely because of their race generates a feeling of inferiority as to their status in the community that may affect their hearts and minds in a way unlikely ever to be undone. . . . A sense of inferiority affects the motivation of a child to learn. Segregation with the sanction of law, therefore, has a tendency to [retard] the educational and mental development of negro children and to deprive them of some of the benefits they would receive in a racial[ly] integrated school system. Whatever may have been the extent of psychological knowledge at the time of *Plessy v. Ferguson*, this finding is amply supported by modern authority.

The court is making an abstract argument not necessarily for interracial mixing for the sake of interracial mixing but rather, and more implicitly than explicitly, for a recognition of the fact and history of that mixing. To erect barriers to that mixing in the educational apparatus is unsustainably delusional and promotes "a sense of inferiority." These integrationist sentiments were not new in 1954, as Derrick Bell and others have rightly noted.[36] What was different was that the U.S. Supreme Court was also articulating these ideas in this way and for this new legitimating purpose. The court was, in effect, making a case for multiculturalism and recognizing the role of the educational apparatus itself—not just the curricula—in reckoning with the past, present, and future of diversity, thereby "awaking the child to cultural values." And that future was not one of "separate but equal" (or "equal but separate," as the phrase also appeared in the statutes upheld by *Plessy*) but rather in the brave new world of desegregating schools to reflect de facto interracial existence and, in theory, produce interracial harmony.

Here, the school must be appreciated as a contact zone in a society where such contact is actual if not always acknowledged; the imperial university, then, is a contact zone within an explicit contact zone. In this way, the histories of U.S. universities in Hawaii, Puerto Rico, and the Philippines provide resonant precedents for these conditions as U.S. administration proceeded. Of course, the sites have vastly different and highly specific histories in relation to such developments as diverse plantation economies, the Atlantic slave trade, missionary activity, creole settlement, and militarization. We can then better appreciate how, for these sites, the idea of the U.S. imperial university sought to align these island possessions with U.S. modernity and, in doing so, potentially made empire's contradictions both evident and resonant.

Rainbow Coalitions: Literary Study in the Early Years of UH, UPR, and UP

A late 1930s edition of *Ka Papala* celebrates the symbol of the University of Hawai'i: "The Rainbow. It has spread its harmonious colors over our 400 acre campus continuously and symbolizes a college where the varicolored customs of nationalities are blending together." Though the unanimous *Brown* decision was persuasively contended nearly two decades later, here we see the school being appreciated as an interracial contact zone to reflect and produce the extant and future diversity of the constituents served by that school, with possible implications for conceptions of a nation's citizenry and an empire's subjects. Self-conceptions of the university in the periphery anticipate this use and idea of the educational apparatus. In an era of constitutionally protected segregation, the racial mixing at the University of Hawai'i is instead held up, already in the 1930s, as a progressive site for diversity management, as articulated in the previous quotation. More than a decade before that, in a 1924 UH biennial report, a statement such as the following indicates the value of diversity going forward: "The future of Hawaii is going to be deeply affected by the contacts of the young men and women in the University where they learn to understand and respect one another's qualities, and learn that a man is to be classified primarily by what he is and can do, rather than by his ancestry."[37]

One can readily see how Rev. Dr. Martin Luther King Jr.'s justly celebrated "I Have a Dream" speech echoes these island sentiments almost four decades later. And like Dr. King's speech, this discourse points to an actual state of judging not by the "content of one's character" but rather by racial ideas. That is to say, that UH needed to declare these values indicates not only that the university has these values but also that (1) they are not the current state of things and (2) the university's role is to realize those values. In other words, ¡LA UH ES DE TODOS!, as is, we might also presume, UP.

What, then, does an elite, imperial, flagship university do to manifest this defiant future? Examination of specimens of discourse from archives at UP, UH, and UPR provides a glimpse of instances where we can recognize a testing ground for future ideas that the postimperial university was particularly well situated to imagine if not realize.

The iconography and related discourse of universities have ideas that resonate with the imperial project of bringing enlightenment to those "sitting in darkness."[38] *Fiat lux*, or "Let there be light," is the God-of-the-Old-Testament-sounding motto on the seal of the university system where I and the editors of this volume work(ed): the University of California system. *Malamalama* is on the seal of the University of Hawai'i, meaning "light of knowledge" in Hawaiian. (The actual motto of UH is *Ma luna aʻe o nā lāhui a pau ke ola o ke kanaka*, sometimes dubiously translated as "Above all nations is humanity."[39]) Darkness and light have a long history in both the educational apparatus and imperial projects, as have the "nation" and "humanity." But there is also an important history of liberatory movements strategically, if not also earnestly, invoking illumination and enlightenment, and this dilemma may emerge in the spread of American literature as a means of liberal education under conditions of explicitly formal colonization.[40]

If it is a reasonable premise that all universities emerged to serve the empire that established them, then subsequent resistance to empire can be said to take up the contradictions of the terms of imperial incorporation. A subsequent commonality that may be emerging across UP, UH, and UPR is not only their shared transplantation of the curriculum of Anglophone and American literature but also perhaps their possible ambivalence toward that curriculum and its role in meeting "the peculiar demands of the university."

And the curriculum of the early twentieth century in a peripheral site may then be seen as not necessarily so different from one a century later in the metropole. This is not to denigrate the important interventions that generations of educational reformers have made in the twentieth century, especially in the past forty years. But in the main, certain basic curricular priorities were in place in the first decade of the twentieth century, and they're not so different from curricular priorities today at, say, UCLA or UW–Madison. In the 1924–1925 UCLA catalog, the English department offers courses in public speaking, a priority that it was not alone in having.

But literature as a medium of national culture persists, thereby upholding one of the "two great new forces"—that is, nationalism and science—of the nineteenth-century university that Kerr described. And when transposed to the imperial periphery, nationalism faces new tests and impacts when deployed for taking up "the white man's burden." In the study of English literature, a plausibly defensible emphasis on British culture also persists—for instance, reinforcing Terry Eagleton's narrative in "The Rise of English."[41] Knowing English literature means knowing its history. However, such defenses may not necessarily serve arguments about relevance and practical applicability, despite some degree of persistence of fairly high numbers of English majors in the U.S. university. Arguments about either inculcating humanity (in a liberal education model) or communication skills (in an industrial education model) or even the elusive notion of "it's what I enjoy" (in a consumerist, felicific calculus model of education) are probably the more likely explanations offered to, say, parents who ask English majors why they have chosen that major in a tight job market or to administrators who ask English professors for budgetary justifications in lean times. Therefore, majoring in English may be less discussed as a field for knowing Chaucer, Milton, and Shakespeare and more discussed as a course of study for practical knowledge of language and expression, with English as the useful medium of the imperium of the English-speaking world.

Another narrative of the rise of English is also instructive here: that of Gauri's *Masks of Conquest: Literary Study and British Rule in India*, where Viswanathan reminds us, among other things, that "England was obligated to promote the 'interests and happiness' of the natives and that measures ought to be adopted [and here she quotes from the 13th Resolution of the 1813 Charter Act], 'as may tend to the introduction among them of useful knowledge, and of religious and moral improvement.'"[42] Though Viswanathan is mainly discussing British India—a highly diverse region—the insights of Viswanathan's work are particularly instructive for appreciating the histories of UPR, UH, and UP. That is, her study, in attending to the anxieties of empire that educational systems implicitly attest to, provides terms for the decline of formal empire manifested in educational systems, military presence, and direct governance in general and the rise of empire manifested in, to borrow Luce's terms, "blind," "unintentional," "accidental," "trivial," and "human" ways of exercising "world power." In other words, the subject formation that is arguably the main output of any formal educational system can be achieved more effectively by other means, such as "American jazz, Hollywood movies, American slang, American machines and patented products." Between the high, formal empire as practiced by the British and French and the informal empire as apparently practiced by no one (nation) in particular but nevertheless serving the interest of late capitalist development, a liminal condition of blended formality and informality may have taken hold across disparate and distant U.S. possessions.[43]

The university then functions as a site of commonality for imperial cohesion, sometimes literally, as well as ideologically and metaphorically, culturally as well as politically and economically. The aforementioned logo with the light of knowledge was adopted when the College of Hawaii became the University of Hawai'i in 1920. The seal would be later changed to indicate 1907, when the College of Hawaii was founded. The earlier seal mainly depicts a ship sailing toward shore. And that earlier seal also has near its top a small illustration of the Pacific side of earth with Hawaii at its center with nine vectors linked to various points through the Pacific Rim. The message of that image is clear: connection, in all its promising and perhaps sinister potential. (The later seal also has an image of the Pacific side of the earth, which comes to take up the entire field of the seal. Gone are the vectors; it has a book and torch at is center, where Hawaii is.)

Articulations in a 1937 yearbook convey both the challenges and potential of a University of Hawai'i in the early middle twentieth century, quoted earlier. The fuller quote reveals just how explicit this vision of integration was, as well as UH's role in its achievement:

> Symbolic of the assimilation of races on our campus, is the
> familiar . . . frequently too familiar emblem of the Deans . . . the
> Rainbow. It has spread its harmonious colors over our 400 acre
> campus continuously and symbolizes a college where the varicol-
> ored customs of nationalities are blending together. Though thirty

years old, the University is still in its period of growing up. The rapid increase of enrollment necessitates expansion and to this end a ten year building program has been formulated and presented to the territorial planning board for approval. . . . This growth indicates an optimistic future for an institution, devoted to the understanding and study of the peoples of the Pacific area.

A perhaps even more suggestive and bold vision of this idea of intermixing is rightly sexualized.[44] A full-page photograph of six racially diverse female UH students has the following caption: "Different racial beauties lend charm to Hawaii's wonders, and they gather from all the islands of the group at the University of Hawai'i. Truly, the march of student life has no beginning and no end."

The linkage of co-ed conditions with multiracial conditions further emphasizes the utopic, and, as, for instance, Topeka, Kansas, in the 1950s; Oxford, Mississippi, in the 1960s; Davis, California, in the 1970s; Berkeley, California, in the 1980s; and Ann Arbor, Michigan, in the early twenty-first century demonstrate,[45] the instruments and stakes of racial management

Figure 1.2. "Different racial beauties lend charm to Hawaii's wonders, and they gather from all the islands of the group at the University of Hawai'i. Truly, the march of student life has no beginning and no end." Kapalapala, 1937, University of Hawai'i Archives. Image used with permission from The University of Hawai'i Library

in education inspire passions—at times libidinal passions—as well as legal argumentation.

These images and ideas of the university—any modern university—as a "gathering place" (which is the literal translation of Oahu, the island on which UH–Manoa was erected) of celebratorily diverse people is something ahead of its time in U.S. educational history. We can see such things as the "Excellence amidst/through Diversity" ethos that would become a marketing campaign for the University of California in the late twentieth century.

Reading *As You Like It* in Manila, San Juan, and Honolulu

If we take a closer, though admittedly selective, look at the course offerings and descriptions themselves, we may find suggestive moments of compliance and resistance that capture the predicament these universities faced. Neoliberalism may, I argue, become anachronistically legible in the forms of contained resistance that may be discerned. Comparison and contrast of material from the University of Puerto Rico in the 1920s and UCLA today may hint at what shared and divergent stakes were involved in the study of English literature. The catalog offers the description for a general introductory English course: "English Literature: a study of the long poem, the drama and a form of prose fiction—the novel or short story. This course, though designed primarily for second year Normal students, will emphasize cultural rather than professional values, but the problem of effective presentation and appreciative interpretation of literary masterpieces will be frequently discussed." The description suggestively makes the distinction between "cultural rather than professional values," to distinguish between literary studies for presumptive liberal arts education rather than for a more immediately practical skill, as with, for instance, a course on public speaking or business writing. The goals of liberal education are so presumed in a contemporary description (from a recent UCLA listing) that there is no mention of "cultural values" over "professional" ones: "Introduction to literary analysis, with close reading and carefully written exposition of selections from principal modes of literature; poetry, prose fiction, and drama."

And here are two descriptions of Shakespeare courses, one from UPR in the 1920s and the other from UCLA today. First, a description for UPR, circa 1921: "A study of six plays. The aim of the course is to enable the student to read the works of the Master Dramatist with intelligent appreciation, and to accomplish this aim it will be necessary to study the Shakespearean language carefully. At the same time the qualities that made Shakespeare both a successful popular playwright and a permanent force in literature will be emphasized." Second, a description for UCLA, circa 2011: "Survey of Shakespeare's plays, including comedies, tragedies, and histories, selected to represent Shakespeare's breadth, artistic progress, and total dramatic achievement." Clearly there are subtle and significant differences between the two sets of descriptions—particularly the reference to "Normal" or teacher-training education in the first example. (Though UCLA, before it became UCLA in 1927 and UC Southern Branch in 1919, was State Normal School from 1882 to 1919.) In many respects these descriptions could be interchangeable across geography, across historical periods, and across primary spoken languages. It may perhaps be the triumph of the field—and the civilization it reproduces and reflects—that little has changed. Shakespeare, in particular, is about as enduring and translocal as Anglophone literature gets.

Yet there may be something engagingly progressive about the way that, in 1921–1922, the English department of the University of Puerto Rico—a university founded in 1903 by the U.S. territorial legislature—would present an approach to Shakespeare that is, in broad strokes, an affirmation of a New Historicist / cultural studies approach that sees Shakespeare as both part of a localized, "popular" culture for the groundlings in its early modern day as well as a "permanent force in literature" in 1920s Puerto Rico and, by implication, to this day and everywhere. There is a potentially contentious interplay among temporally, geographically, and linguistically localized conditions and those that outlive and reach beyond the local. Might that latter form of reading be called "transnational" and perhaps "imperial"? One might want to see in that formulation the seeds of critique, sown in the colonized periphery. They weren't teaching *The Tempest* that year; instead, they may have still been living it.

Postscript—Manila, February 2011: "The Thickening of Older Imperial Networks," or the Uses and Idea of the Postimperial University

In February 2011, Dr. Francisco Benitez was installed as the new president of Philippine Women's University (founded in 1919), and in his installation ceremony speech, he eloquently reflected on this situation. For universities straddling an ambiguous historical line between formal colonization/occupation and independent nation/state/estado-libre-asociado, as UP, UPR, and UH do, the legacies of their foundings and early years may be a call to reflect on not only how things have changed but also how they have stayed the same. Benitez called on those assembled (including congresswoman and PWU alumna Imelda Marcos and other dignitaries) to remember imagined futures from the educational past: "Let us recall that PWU was a house of learning founded by teachers who were at the same time citizens with a social consciousness and a missionary zeal. Establishing a school under the aegis of empire, theirs was a fundamental belief that education cultivated a capacity for the participative citizenship required of a strong democratic and independent republic." Cognizant of the inherited discourse of imperial universities and postcolonial desires, President Benitez notes that

> as the conditions of empire and the nation changed, so too did the university's response to the persistent national need for participative citizenship. Despite formal independence for colonies, today's imperial globalization carries many of the same challenges as yesterday's colonial imperialism. Large sectors of the world still wallow in poverty, a condition of unfreedom that Nobel laureate for economics Amartya Sen terms the "global injustice of capacity deprivation." At the same time, globalization has created distinct conditions for the thickening of older imperial networks, these networks have further facilitated the flow of information, knowledge, goods, labor, and capital.

Benitez is careful to characterize the role of PWU in particular and implicitly of the university as an institution in general in relation to the past and future of imperialism. The earlier one was frankly colonial, while the current one invokes the imperial more as a modifier to globalization. In doing so, he critically engages with the "two great clichés" to which Kerr referred nearly a half century earlier. President Benitez carefully avoids ultimately endorsing the tenets of neoliberalism, instead recognizing and enabling a postimperial university wary of ways in which institutional persistence has tended to mean imperial persistence.

Notes

This research has been supported by grants from the University of California Center for New Racial Studies, the University of California Pacific Rim Research Program, and the UCLA Academic Senate Committee on Research Faculty Research Grant

Program, as well as funding from the University of Wisconsin, Madison, Graduate Research Committee Grants Program and the Mellon Interdisciplinary Workshops in the Humanities Program. I also gratefully acknowledge the feedback from audiences at the University of Florida; the Los Angeles and Riverside campuses of the University of California; and panel attendees at the Modern Language Association, American Studies Association, and Association for Asian American Studies conferences.

1. Clark Kerr, *The Uses of the University* (Cambridge, Mass.: Harvard University Press, 1963), 94.

2. Here I invoke the phrase from Cardinal Newman's influential tract occasioned by the founding of the University of Dublin. John Newman, *The Idea of a University* (1846; repr., New Haven: Yale University Press, 1996).

3. Those seeking the unique and complex stories of the individuals and organizations that mobilized to establish these institutions of higher learning would be advised to look elsewhere. Universities customarily offer these stories readily. See http://www.hawaii.edu, http://www.upr.edu, and http://www.upd.edu.ph.

4. Dr. Francisco Benitez, speech delivered at his installation as president of Philippine Women's University, February 21, 2011, Philippine Convention Center, Manila, Philippines.

5. See Mike Murase, "Ethnic Studies: Higher Education for Asian Americans" *in Counterpoint: Perspectives on Asian America,* ed. Emma Gee (Los Angeles: UCLA Asian American Studies Center, 1976), 205–23.

6. Kerr, *Uses of the University,* 11.

7. On the physical plant of the educational apparatus on Oahu, see the work of Noelani Goodyear-Ka'opua, Association for Asian American Studies presentation, Honolulu, 2009.

8. See Julian Go, *American Empire and the Politics of Meaning: Elite Political Cultures in the Philippines and Puerto Rico during U.S. Colonialism* (Durham: Duke University Press, 2008).

9. For the main articulations of this argument about informal empire, see William Pomeroy, *American Neocolonialism and Its Emergence in the Philippines* (New York: International Publisher, 1970); Walter LaFeber, *The New Empire: An Interpretation of American Expansion, 1860–1898* (Ithaca: Cornell University Press, 1963); William Appleman Williams, *Empire as a Way of Life: An Essay on the Causes and Character of America's Present Predicament along with a Few Thoughts about an Alternative* (New York: Oxford University Press, 1980); Thomas McCormick, *The China Market: America's Quest for Informal Empire, 1893–1901* (Chicago: Quadrangle, 1967).

10. See Amy Kaplan, *The Anarchy of Empire in the Making of U.S. Culture* (Cambridge: Harvard University Press, 1995); Allan Isaac, *American Tropics: Articulating Filipino America* (Minneapolis: University of Minnesota Press, 2006).

11. Henry Luce, *The American Century* (1941; repr. New York: Ferris Printing, 1941), 33.

12. See Walter Guzzardi Jr., *The Henry Luce Foundation, a History:* 1936–1986 (Chapel Hill: University of North Carolina Press, 1988).

13. Other post-1898 acquisitions and related holdings did not quite establish universities in the same moment, such as the University of Guam in 1952. And centuries-old institutions of higher learning already existed in such cities as Manila (e.g., University of Santo Tomas, 1611–present), Santo Domingo (e.g., Universidad Autonoma de Santo Domingo, 1538–present), and Havana (e.g., Universidad de Habana, 1728–present).

14. See Chandan Reddy, *Freedom with Violence: Race, Sexuality, and the U.S. State* (Durham: Duke University Press, 2011); Roderick A. Ferguson, *The Reorder of Things: The University and Its Pedagogies of Minority Difference* (Minneapolis: University of Minnesota Press, 2012); Jodi Melamed, *Represent and Destroy: Rationalizing Violence in the New Racial Capitalism* (Minneapolis: University of Minnesota Press, 2011).

15. For example, see Rick Baldoz, *The Third Asiatic Invasion* (New York: New York University Press, 2011); H. Brett Melendy, "The Tydings-McDuffie Act of 1934," in *Asian Americans and Congress: A Documentary History,* ed. Hyung-Chan Kim (Westport, Conn.: Greenwood Press, 1996), 283–308; Mae Ngai, *Impossible Subjects* (Princeton: Princeton University Press, 2003); Linda España Maram, *Creating Masculinity in Los Angeles's Little Manila* (New York: Columbia University Press, 2005).

16. Information at http://www.filipinoamericanlibrary.org/ines.html (formerly Pamana Foundation).

17. As related in a personal anecdote by his distant relative Florante Ibanez (Loyola Marymount University law librarian), Ines actually remained in the United States.

18. After more than a decade and a half of intermittent Philippine delegation hearings in Congress, the Tydings-McDuffie Act of 1934 granted a twelve-year program toward "complete independence" of the Philippines. See Melendy, "The Tydings-McDuffie Act of 1934."

19. See Ngai, *Impossible Subjects.*

20. Ongoing campaigns by Pacific Islander student organizations today make the provocative case that students from locations and unincorporated territories such as American Samoa should be eligible for in-state tuition at public U.S. universities, largely due to the lack of comparable institutions in such locations.

21. See Solsiree Del Moral's excellent history *Negotiating Empire: The Cultural Politics of Schools in Puerto Rico, 1898–1952* [2013].

22. For instance, see Abe Ignacio et al., *The Forbidden Book: The Philippine-American War in Political Cartoons* (San Francisco: T'boli, 2004).

23. Louis Althusser, "Ideology and Ideological State Apparatuses (Notes Toward an Investigation)," in *Lenin and Philosophy and Other Essays,* trans. Ben Brewster

(New York: Monthly Review Press, 1971), 127–86. Althusser actually devotes most of his critical analysis to Christianity rather than education, though he conveys here that education has likely become a more potent and pervasive ideological state apparatus than Christianity, perhaps because "it is so silent!"

24. This quotation is usually attributed to Derek Bok, president of Harvard University, 1971–1991.

25. See Mary Racelis and Judy Celine Ick, eds., *Bearers of Benevolence: The Thomasites and Public Education in the Philippines* (Pasig City: Anvil, 2001).

26. Adeline Knapp, quoted in U.S. Embassy, *To Islands Far Away: The Story of the Thomasites and Their Journey to the Philippines* (Manila: Public Affairs Section, 2001).

27. Isaiah 2:3–4: "He shall judge between the nations, and shall decide disputes for many peoples; and they shall beat their swords into plowshares, and their spears into pruning hooks; nation shall not lift up sword against nation, neither shall they learn war anymore."

28. Meg Wesling, *Empire's Proxy: American Literature and U.S. Imperialism in the Philippines* (New York: New York University Press, 2011).

29. For example, see the persuasive and eloquent articulations of current Philippine Women's University president Dr. Francisco Benitez at the end of this chapter.

30. In the Puerto Rican context, Del Moral describes how the first instructors were U.S. military men, soon to be replaced by female teachers from the United States. See Del Moral, *Negotiating Empire*.

31. Given the prominence of mining interests in the Philippines, this occupation likely is not random for Ines and his protagonist. More recent environmental critiques of mining and drilling industries and economies may yield concerns about the implications of this line of work as a metaphor for postcolonial nation building. For example, see Jared Diamond, *Collapse. How Societies Choose to Fail or Succeed* (New York: Penguin, 2006).

32. See Glenn May, *Social Engineering in the Philippines: The Aims, Execution, and Impact of American Policy, 1900, 1913* (Westport: Greenwood, 1980).

33. See Warwick Anderson, *Colonial Pathologies: American Tropical Medicine, Race, and Hygiene in the Philippines* (Durham: Duke University Press, 2006); Alfred W. McCoy, *Policing America's Empire: The United States, the Philippines, and the Rise of the Surveillance State* (Madison: University of Wisconsin Press, 2009); and Meg Wesling, *Empire's Proxy: American Literature and U.S. Imperialism in the Philippines* (New York: New York University Press, 2011).

34. Edward W. Said, *Orientalism* (New York: Vintage, 1979).

35. Brown v. Board of Education, 347 U.S. 483 (1954).

36. Derrick A. Bell Jr., "*Brown v. Board of Education* and the Interest-Convergence Dilemma," *Harvard Law Review* 93 (1980): 518–33.

37. "Report of the Board of Regents to the Governor of the Legislature of 1925," *University of Hawai'i Quarterly Bulletin* 3, no. 4 (December 1924): 12.

38. This is Twain's phrase. See Susan Harris, *God's Arbiters: Americans and the Philippines, 1898–1902, the War That Sparked Mark Twain's Conflict with America* (New York: Oxford University Press, 2011).

39. Thanks to Kehaulani Kauanui for alerting me to the dubiousness of this particular translation.

40. See Wesling, *Empire's Proxy*, particularly on the subject of American literature in primary and secondary educations in the archipelago as well as the idea of American literature in these contexts.

41. Terry Eagleton, *Literary Theory: An Introduction* (Oxford: Basil Blackwell, 1983).

42. Gauri Viswanathan, *Masks of Conquest: Literary Study and British Rule in India* (London: Oxford University Press, 1989), 24.

43. On the new, informal empire, see LaFeber, *The New Empire*; McCormick, *The China Market*; Appleman Williams, *Empire as a Way of Life*. On the structures of formal governance under U.S. colonialism, see Go, *American Empire and the Politics of Meaning*; May, *Social Engineering in the Philippines*. Regarding the actual informality of that new empire, see Thu-huong Nguyen-Vo, *The Ironies of Freedom* (Seattle: University of Washington Press, 2008); Saskia Sassen, *Globalization and Its Discontents* (New York: New Press, 1998); Robyn Rodriguez, *Migrants for Export: How the Philippine State Brokers Workers for the World* (Minneapolis: University of Minnesota Press, 2010); Melamed, *Represent and Destroy*.

44. Thurgood Marshall, who argued *Brown*, well recognized the open secret that the primary concern that the segregationists had was of a sexual nature—that is, that classrooms are spaces were libidinal predilections were formed and perhaps acted upon. See Alfred H. Kelly, "The School Desegregation Case," in *Quarrels That Have Shaped the Constitution*, ed. John A. Garraty (New York: Harper Torchbook, 1975), 254.

45. James Meredith was the first African American to enroll at the University of Mississippi in 1962. *Bakke v. Regents of UC* (1978) and *Gratz v. Bollinger* (2003) involved UC Davis and University of Mississippi, respectively.

2

Militarizing Education

The Intelligence Community's Spy Camps

Roberto J. González

In July 2005, a select group of fifteen- to nineteen-year-old high school students participated in a week-long summer program called "Spy Camp" in the Washington, DC, area. The program included a field trip to the CIA's headquarters in Langley, Virginia, an "intelligence simulation" exercise, and a visit to the $35 million International Spy Museum. According to the Spy Museum's website, visiting groups have the option of choosing from three different "scavenger hunts," in which teams are pitted against one another in activities ranging "from code-breaking to deceptive maneuvers. . . . Each team will be armed with a top secret bag of tricks to help solve challenging questions" that can be found in the museum.[1]

On the surface, the program sounds like fun and games, and after reading about the program one might guess that it was organized by an imaginative social studies teacher. But for some, "Spy Camp" was more than just fun and games—it was very serious business. The high school program was carried out by Trinity University of Washington, DC—a predominantly African American university with an overwhelmingly female student population—as part of a pilot grant from the U.S. Office of the Director of National Intelligence (DNI) to create an "Intelligence Community Center of Academic Excellence" (or IC Center).

According to the Office of the DNI, the goal of the IC Center program is to increase the pool of future applicants for careers in the CIA, the FBI, the Defense Intelligence Agency (DIA), and the dozen or so other organizations that make up the U.S. "intelligence community"—in less euphemistic terms, America's spy agencies.

The idea for IC Centers came about in the wake of the September 11, 2001, attacks, when both the U.S. Senate and House of Representatives held hearings about how the country's spy agencies missed clues that might have foiled the World Trade Center and Pentagon attacks. As part of the response, Congress passed a sweeping law called the Intelligence Reform and Terrorism Prevention Act (S 2845). In the House Intelligence Committee hearings prior to the bill's passage, California representative Jane Harman (Democrat from California and chair of the House Intelligence Committee) put it bluntly: "We can no longer expect an Intelligence Community that is mostly male and mostly white to be able to monitor and infiltrate suspicious organizations or terrorist groups. *We need spies that look like their targets*, CIA officers who speak the dialects that terrorists use, and FBI agents who can speak to Muslim women that might be intimidated by men" (emphasis added).[2]

For this reason, the IC Center program wasn't aimed at students attending Harvard, Yale, Princeton, or other Ivy League schools or internationally renowned universities like Stanford or Berkeley or the University of Chicago. The program's architects consciously directed it at schools where minority students are the majority—predominantly African American and Latino universities, which are chronically underfunded. Perhaps this reflects the shape of "multiculturalism" in a militarized society: the government's spy agencies and armed forces recruit minority students from low-income regions in order to "monitor and infiltrate" people ("targets") that look and speak like them.

Since 2005, Trinity's IC Center has had its funding renewed, and "Spy Camp" has continued every summer since. In fact, beginning in 2006, the director of National Intelligence dramatically expanded the IC Center program (of which the "Spy Camp" is only one part), and today there are a total of twenty-one such centers throughout the country. These are located at California State University, San Bernardino; Carnegie-Mellon University; Clemson University; Clark Atlanta University; Florida A&M University; Florida International University; Howard University; Miles College (Alabama); Norfolk State University (Virginia); North Carolina A&T University; Pennsylvania State University; Tennessee State University; Trinity University; University of Maryland, College Park; University of Nebraska; University of New Mexico; University of North Carolina, Wilmington; University of Texas, El Paso; University of Texas, Pan American; University of Washington; Virginia Tech; and Wayne State University (Michigan). Significantly, most of these universities have large numbers of minority students, which corresponds with the original objectives of the IC Center program's architects. Tens of millions of dollars have been appropriated for the programs, with some centers receiving individual grants of up to $750,000. According to the *Washington Post*, the

DNI planned to expand the program to twenty universities by the year 2015. Apparently, it has met this goal far ahead of schedule.[3] (Since 2008, the DNI has included universities with significantly higher percentages of "white" students. It appears that the DNI quickly exhausted its supply of predominantly Hispanic and African American universities.)

This is by no means the first time that U.S. military and intelligence agencies have funneled large sums of money into universities to advance their interests. The 1958 National Defense Education Act led to the creation of dozens of language and area studies programs focused on Russia, Latin America, and Southeast Asia, but those centers generally did not limit scholars' ability to pursue a wide range of research, including critical social science research building upon anti-imperial and leftist scholarship.[4] By contrast, there are clear indications that the IC Centers and other new recruitment programs have much more focused and narrow objectives that threaten core educational values that have underpinned American universities for many years.

Judging from some students' responses, it seems that the DNI programs are making an impact. News reports from college newspapers begin to tell the story. Najam Hassan, a nineteen-year-old student at Trinity University, said, "It's a good opportunity. I have interest in the FBI." Reagan Thompson, who is seventeen, told a reporter, "I want to be a spy when I grow up. You learn different perspectives and it opens your mind." Meriam Fadli, also seventeen, said, "I was like 'Oh my God, I am so joining the FBI'. . . . She [the speaker] made it seem so interesting. It's not like a dull office job." Leah Martin, a twenty-one-year-old, decided that she wanted an intelligence career after getting involved in the program: "You get to travel, to do something different every day, you're challenged in your work and you get to serve your country. How cool is that?"[5] The picture that emerges from these and other comments is that students are drawn to the IC Centers because they offer exciting, challenging experiences that will serve the country—not unlike the reasons that many young people decide to enlist in the armed forces. Television series that glorify law enforcement agents (*CSI: Crime Scene Investigation*), intelligence operatives (*24*), and military personnel (*JAG*) have greatly romanticized these careers.

University administrators and faculty like the IC Centers for other reasons. Obviously there are the issues of funding and job placement for graduating students. But some also emphasize the importance of building an ethnically and culturally diverse pool of intelligence agents who might blend in more easily abroad. Norfolk State University geology professor David

all have "Kids' Page" websites that include games, puzzles, and, occasionally, sanitized histories of the agencies.) Nearly all universities that have received funding for IC Centers have created high school outreach programs. For example, Norfolk State's program included a simulation exercise in which faculty asked Nashville-area high schoolers to locate ten simulated "weapons of mass destruction" hidden in the city using GPS locators.[9]

The name "Spy Camp" was only used once, at Trinity University. Now the high school outreach programs are known in many places as "Summer Intelligence Seminars."

Recruiting Intelligence?

What makes the new IC Centers across the country different from other institutes or research centers? Though there are numerous differences from one school to the next, several universities appear to be involved in three kinds of activities apart from high school outreach programs like "Spy Camp."

Curriculum development—especially the creation of new classes—is a common process for IC Center schools. Many participating universities are creating new majors and minors in "intelligence studies" and developing new courses to meet the demands of spy agencies. For example, Trinity University developed a new course titled "East vs. West: Just War, Jihad and Crusade, 1050–1450." While the title itself is benign (though it conjures up images of the "clash of civilizations" popularized by historian Samuel Huntington), the syllabus reportedly states that the course "seeks to develop the critical/analytical and writing skills that are particularly important to the intelligence community."[10] (We are left to wonder what the costs of favoring some kinds of writing—perhaps intelligence briefs and PowerPoint presentations—over others might be.) In some cases new masters' programs are also being developed, which might result in new faculty hiring. New classes in languages deemed important to U.S. security are being established as well (particularly in Arabic and Mandarin), and many campuses are purchasing books and films to support these new courses.

Another group of activities includes organized events such as academic colloquia and guest lectures. Like all university special events, these can be intellectually stimulating, particularly when a thought-provoking or controversial speaker is invited to speak. But what should occur when a guest lecture or other campus event becomes a recruiting pitch for spy agencies?

Finally, nearly all the IC Centers include scholarship and travel abroad programs. The same law that brought the IC Centers into existence also created the new "Intelligence Community Scholarship Program" (ICSP). Scholarship fellows take required intelligence-related courses and are typically eligible for study abroad experiences and internships with spy agencies. According to the law, ICSP students who do not take jobs with U.S. intelligence agencies after graduating are required "to repay the costs of their education plus penalties assessed at three times the legally allowed interest rate."[11] Like PRISP (the Pat Roberts Intelligence Scholarship Program, a $25,000, one-year scholarship for undergraduate and graduate students that requires them to work for the CIA after graduation), the identities of students are not publicly announced. Congress established PRISP in 2004 as a kind of academic version of the ROTC (Reserve Officer Training Corps) program: it was designed to combine intelligence training skills with academic areas of expertise, such as anthropology or political science. Since its creation PRISP has placed hundreds of students in an unknown number of university classrooms. Although critics have referred to such programs as "debt bondage to constrain student career choices," President Barack Obama's director of National Intelligence, Dennis Blair, announced in 2009 plans to make PRISP permanent.[12]

In and of themselves, these activities sound benign, even desirable. After all, who could argue against funding for new courses, films, guest speakers, conferences, and scholarships, particularly during this period of chronic underfunding of higher education? But there is a subtle danger posed by the deluge of funds reaching universities through IC Centers—a danger similar to that posed by military funding. Anthropologist Hugh Gusterson has written eloquently about the ways in which this can twist the education process over time. A wide range of problems comes into focus:

> When research that could be funded by neutral civilian agencies is instead funded by the military, knowledge is subtly militarized and bent in the way a tree is bent by a prevailing wind. The public comes to accept that basic academic research on religion and violence "belongs" to the military; scholars who never saw themselves as doing military research now do; maybe they wonder if their access to future funding is best secured by not criticizing US foreign policy; a discipline whose independence from military and corporate funding fueled the kind of critical thinking a democracy needs is now

compromised; and the priorities of the military further define the basic terms of public and academic debate.[13]

In short, the IC Centers could further threaten the notion of the classroom as a free "marketplace of ideas"—a process that is well under way due to the powerful influence exerted on college campuses by multinational corporations and other commercial interests. The fact that the "intelligence community" includes heavy representation from Pentagon agencies (such as DIA and Marine Corps Intelligence, to name but two) and is closely linked to military contract firms further underscores the significance of Gusterson's words.

Close to Home

For me, learning about the IC Centers struck close to home—literally. I first found out about IC Centers from an anthropology professor at a participating university, the University of Texas, Pan American (UTPA), located along the U.S.–Mexico border deep in south Texas. The professor was interested in seeing an article I had written in which I criticized the "military-anthropology complex"—a web connecting U.S. social scientists to the Pentagon and military contract firms for counterinsurgency work. I learned that some of the key players at UTPA's IC Center were anthropologists (including a college dean), and to their credit, they were interested in learning more about the history of such relationships and ethical dilemmas that might arise as a result. I sent my article to the anthropology professor, along with a request to interview the dean of the College of Social Sciences—a request that was rapidly granted.

UTPA is located seven miles away from my childhood home, and my parents both graduated from the university when it was called Pan American College. My first "academic" job was at UTPA more than twenty years ago, where I tutored local high school students as part of the Texas Pre-Freshman Engineering Program. I planned a trip to the university's anthropology department that would coincide with a summer visit to my hometown.

Arriving at the university brought back many memories. As I walked toward the social science building in the sweltering tropical heat of a south Texas summer afternoon, the sprawling campus, the long arched corridors connecting its buildings, and the beautiful palm trees lining its perimeter made a renewed impression on my mind.

UTPA is not a small university—it has nearly thirty thousand students, nearly 90 percent of whom are Latinos. More than one out of three faculty members are Latino, and it has more full-time Latino faculty members than any other Texas university. I learned that like many other universities around the country, UTPA has not grown quickly enough to meet local demand. Administrators and donors have tended to give strong support to UTPA's engineering, health science, and business schools, while social science and humanities departments have sometimes struggled.

For these reasons, the IC Center grant was especially attractive to the College of Social Sciences. The applicants were able to get faculty from each of the colleges to support the grant proposal and letters of support from the university president and a local school district superintendent. Their efforts paid off handsomely: in October 2006, the DNI awarded UTPA a grant of $500,000 a year for five years for a total of $2.5 million.

Within a year, UTPA's IC Center staff organized a high school outreach program—a five-day "camp" involving twenty local students—which took place in August 2007. They called it "Got Intelligence?" (students wore black T-shirts with the phrase silk-screened across the chest), and according to the UTPA magazine *Los Arcos*, students "heard from speakers from intelligence community agencies, such as the CIA and FBI."[14] Other activities included workshops for geographic information systems training, resumé preparation, and a solar-powered vehicle competition.

Just two months earlier, a smaller group of UTPA students had an even more dramatic experience: a one-month all-expenses-paid study abroad trip to Qingdao, China. This was reportedly the first trip ever taken by a UTPA group to China. Accounts of the trip in *The Monitor* (the local daily newspaper) did not mention the word "intelligence" nor the Office of the Director of National Intelligence. Instead, the "Center for Academic Excellence" was described as "promot[ing] international research and analytical thinking skills." Later, the study abroad program was expanded to include Morocco.[15]

The dean was very optimistic about the future of the IC Center. He described ongoing efforts to create a new minor in "intelligence" and eventually a master's degree program in "global security studies and leadership." He noted that courses in Mandarin Chinese would soon be offered for the first time at UTPA, and there were plans to introduce Arabic language courses in the near future. When I asked about whether he was concerned about the possibility that students might be corralled into dangerous careers with agencies that have a record of human rights abuses, the dean emphasized that this was primarily a program for better global understanding, not an intelligence gathering program. (In fact, the IC Center eventually changed its name to the "Integrated Global Knowledge and Understanding Collaboration" or IGKNU.) Even so, he acknowledged that the IC Center offered "many opportunities for dialogue" with "agency people" for internship opportunities and career placement for college graduates.

The UTPA IC Center staff were cordial, but they seemed to have a benign view of spy agencies, even naïve, given headlines in recent years. For example, they expressed the idea that in future generations, a more ethnically diverse "intelligence community" would likely lead to better policies. Others seemed convinced that they would be able to keep the program focused on sharpening students' "critical thinking" and other skills not limited to spy work. They repeatedly emphasized the idea that in a period of scarce resources, the IC Center grant was beneficial because of the generous funds that were made available to students and faculty. There was little concern that UTPA's base of knowledge might be "bent in the way a tree is bent by a prevailing wind."

Dissenting Voices

Not everyone at UTPA approved of the IC Center. A group made up of students from the university's chapter of MEChA (a nationwide Chicano student organization) and faculty members voiced opposition to UTPA's participation in the DNI grant before it had been awarded, and I contacted several of them.

These critics brought up a wide range of concerns. Some expressed concern that the center might lead to bias in the classroom or a biased orientation of books and other materials purchased in the library. In the words of a professor opposed to the IC Center, "I don't think they're going to be buying history books that examine the CIA's crimes in Central America or the abuses of graduates of the School of the Americas." (I heard later that some university staff designated one section of the main library the "spy room" because it houses a large number of intelligence-related journals and books acquired for the IC Center.) The professor noted that IC Center personnel appeared to suffer from a lack of awareness of the dark history of the CIA, the FBI, and other agencies making up the "intelligence community."

UTPA political science professor Samuel Freeman argued that "just as intelligence agencies are penetrating our universities today with phony 'Intelligence Community Centers of Academic Excellence'—like the center recently established at UTPA unfortunately—the CIA, in the 1950s and 1960s conspired with unethical university professors and administrators."[16] Freeman's concerns linked intelligence agencies' current recruiting efforts on college campuses to a broader history of co-optation on university campuses.

Some critics were concerned about the way in which the intelligence agencies might be manipulating "diversity" to meet their own interests rather than the interests of students. A graduate student I spoke with was particularly galled by the cloak of "multiculturalism" used by the DNI and the IC Center to promote the program. Another student, Nadezhda Garza, reportedly said of the UTPA program, "At this point, you have to decide if opportunity is really opportunity. . . . The [intelligence community] isn't pushing you academically, it's pushing you to recruitment. The [intelligence community] has its own agenda."[17] A report in the *San Antonio Express-News* appeared to confirm Garza's words, noting that "CIA recruiters were on [the UTPA] campus visiting mainly with students in the program who are earning an intelligence studies certificate."[18]

Still another concern expressed by critics of the program had to do with the safety of UTPA students participating on study abroad programs. "What kind of risk are students in China going to face if that country's government knows that they are connected to the Office of the Director of National Intelligence?" asked a professor. He argued that Chinese officials might view them as spies.

Finally, both students and professors were alarmed at the possibility that academic freedom at UTPA might be threatened by the IC Center. What would happen to students or faculty who refused to go along with the current produced by waves of IC Center funding? How would university administrators (or campus police) deal with students or faculty who actively protested guest speakers from the CIA or FBI? According to the minutes of an April 2006 UTPA faculty senate meeting, a group of MEChA students expressed concerns over the proposed IC Center ranging from "possible restrictions to academic freedom" to "exploitation of UTPA students by intelligence communities."[19] When local media ran a handful of stories on the UTPA IC Center in 2007, reporters generally ignored the many criticisms that had been raised by concerned faculty and students. The CIA, FBI, and other spy agencies appeared to be scoring a "silent coup" at UTPA, a pattern that would be repeated at other universities as the IC Center program diffused throughout the country.[20]

Ignoring the Elephant in the Room

Once I began combing through dozens of documents, articles, government reports, websites, and interview transcripts, it became clear that many university administrators, congressional representatives, and educators were ignoring the elephant in the room: outrageous and illegal actions that U.S. spy agencies have been involved with over the last sixty years. I began to ask, what happened to teaching "critical thinking skills" at the IC Centers?

As Stephen Kinzer has noted in his book *Overthrow*, the CIA has been deeply involved in orchestrating coups, assassinations, and civil wars in such diverse places as Iran, Guatemala, Chile, Indonesia, and El Salvador, among many others over the past century.[21] We now know that the CIA supported social science research throughout the 1950s and 1960s to perfect psychological torture techniques that were outsourced to Vietnam, Argentina, and other countries.[22] Phillip Agee was so shocked by the CIA's covert operations in support of Latin American dictatorships that in 1968 he quit the agency and spent the rest of his life criticizing it.[23]

Over the past decade many people have exposed illegal acts carried out with impunity by the "intelligence community." For example, in December 2002, the *Washington Post* ran a front-page story describing how CIA operatives sent suspected members of al-Qaeda to third countries for brutal interrogations.[24] In November 2005, journalist Dana Priest revealed the presence of a secret CIA network of overseas prisons in Eastern Europe, Southeast Asia, and other regions. The "black sites" were located in countries whose police and intelligence agencies are infamous for their egregious human rights violations, which have been extensively documented by human rights organizations.[25] In April 2006, Former AT&T technician Mark Klein issued a public statement in which he described AT&T's cooperation in a secret National Security Agency (NSA) operation that would allow it to conduct "vacuum-cleaner surveillance of all the data crossing the internet," a form of wiretapping prohibited by the U.S. Constitution. In December 2005, the *New York Times* described the NSA and Defense Intelligence Agency's use of illegal wiretapping at the request of the Bush administration.[26] In February 2007, an Italian court indicted twenty-six U.S. intelligence agents, most of them from the CIA, for the 2003 kidnapping of an Egyptian cleric, Usama Nasr. Nasr was taken to Egypt where he was held for four years and reportedly tortured before being freed by an Egyptian court that ruled his detention to be "unfounded."[27] In January 2007, a German court issued arrest warrants for thirteen U.S. intelligence agents (mostly CIA) involved in the 2003 kidnapping of a German citizen, Khaled el Masri. Masri was taken to Afghanistan, jailed for five months, and physically and psychologically tortured before being released without charges.[28]

Although these events (and many other similar violations) were making headlines at the time the IC Centers were established, few of the news articles about the centers mentioned any dilemmas that might be posed by university collaboration with the agencies in question. Nor did they ask whether it was appropriate for institutions of higher education to be accepting money linked to such sources. It was as if the 1975–1976 Church Committee reports of the U.S. Senate—which famously and publicly exposed the legal and political abuses carried out by U.S. intelligence agencies—had never existed.

Some scholars did make these connections and raised questions that were inconvenient for proponents of the program. For example, independent scholar and writer Kamala Platt noted that in south Texas, "decades of being among the poorest and most underserved regions of the country have laid the groundwork" for the program. In many ways, student participation in IC Centers resembles participation in JROTC programs. As anthropologist Gina Pérez argues, JROTC is "deeply rooted in notions of citizenship [and service to country] . . . [and] informed by the realities of a local political economy with extremely limited employment opportunities for working-class youth." Consequently, IC Centers and JROTC might be seen as programs in which "notions of exceptional citizenship [are] anchored in a distinctive and particularly valorized military culture."[29]

But a militarized culture can lead to intellectual, moral, and ethical dilemmas. According to Kamala Platt, a range of contradictions inherently accompany such initiatives:

> Underlying ICC's interest in these [academic] fields is the identification, fear, and domination of "enemies" and the blowing up of bridges of communication. . . . The intelligence community's interest in these disciplines defiles them, and I could never in good conscience (i.e. with intellectual or moral integrity) participate in these junctures of university and IC-CAE. I could never teach a Chicana novel in a classroom where I knew some of the students were being trained to read the literature for knowledge that might endanger sister barrios.[30]

It seems likely that once critics started to raise such points, some IC Centers began to drop the words "Intelligence Community" from their names. Now many are known simply as "Centers for Academic Excellence." Similarly, the "Spy Camp" at Trinity became simply "Summer Intelligence Seminar," while UTPA's version became the "Got Intelligence?" camp.

It may be that the DNI's primary goal in creating the IC Centers is to increase the pool of minority youth seeking employment in spy agencies. But an important secondary goal appears to be a public relations goal: to give an extreme makeover to the CIA, the FBI, the NSA, and other agencies for a generation too young to know about their past abuses and too overworked and distracted to be aware of their current ones. Only by whitewashing the past can the director of National Intelligence hope to normalize spy work.

Learning from Fulbright

Is the IC Center program as benign and generous as its proponents claim? Is it really the "win-win relationship for everyone involved," to quote a sympathetic article?[31] Or somewhere down the line, does someone lose?

From one point of view, the program appears to be creating new opportunities for young people, especially African American and Latino students who are excited at the possibility of challenging, adventurous work in service of country. But on the other hand, we might ask, couldn't these young people play a more constructive role in our society if they were aggressively recruited into careers in medicine, engineering, or education?

We might also ask ourselves, what kind of a society is it whose citizens define "serving your country" in terms of employment with the military or intelligence agencies, as if other institutions didn't matter? This propaganda strategy in the DNI's effort to recruit "intelligence"—modeled after the military's techniques for recruiting soldiers—deserves much criticism, whether such methods are targeted at minorities and recent immigrants to our country or to the general populace.

It is clear that many of the IC Centers expose students to unrealistic scenarios if not outright deception. Like most recruitment processes, whether for messianic cults, the military, or other totalistic institutions, there is an element of undue influence—what psychologists call "coercive persuasion."[32] If these centers soften children up through scavenger hunts and other exciting activities, we might ask whether they are being given the chance to freely explore other options. If a charismatic CIA analyst or military intelligence officer pumps up junior high or high school kids with stories about their global travels, many are easily convinced that it "beats having an office job!" In the official IC Center literature from the DNI, the histories of the agencies are sanitized. Full disclosure is nonexistent. Nowhere are CIA assassination plots, COINTELPRO (the FBI's illegal domestic surveillance program), or secret prisons in the War on Terror mentioned. This is not much different from the military recruiter who promises high school students money for college and the chance to see the world without mentioning that they might be sent to the front lines of Afghanistan or Iraq for a year or two. Such techniques are egregious, but they are even more egregious when children are the victims.

UTPA professor Samuel Freeman observes, "The [IC] Spy Center is part of nothing less than an attempt to legitimize the illegitimate, to manipulate us into condoning the unpardonable, and to accept the crimes of US intelligence agencies as actions that are legitimate, acceptable, and even respectable. . . . Hopefully, protests raised by students and faculty will send a message to other UTPA organizations that consorting with IC-CAE/IGkNU is not worth the cost."[33]

Will students and faculty eventually mobilize themselves against the "intelligence community" on America's college campuses? It is still too early to tell. The IC Centers have largely succeeded because they have countered local resistance efforts that have tended to be isolated from each other. David Price has noted that those opposed to IC-CAE are more likely to succeed if they forge alliances nationwide for a common cause: "Something like an 'IC-CAE Watch' or 'CIA Campus Watch' website could be started by a faculty member or grad student on an IC-CAE campus, providing forums to collect documents, stories, and resistance tactics from across the country."[34] In addition, Price recommends that concerned students, faculty, and staff make use of state public records laws and the national Freedom of Information Act to request records related to IC-CAE and that tenured professors at IC-CAE funded universities take a leading role in asking tough questions about the program.

But in the meantime the IC Centers are spreading, while students are getting sucked into scholarship programs like PRISP that require mandatory service to intelligence agencies. Another initiative, the Stokes Program (sponsored by the CIA, the FBI, and the NSA), targets high school seniors with the promise of paid tuition and a government salary in exchange for mandatory employment with these agencies. In the case of most of these programs, the cloak of secrecy surrounding the scholarships is extremely troubling. Typically, students secretly receive money from the DNI and no one—neither peers, professors, nor administrators—knows that they are receiving financial support. Under these circumstances, what is to keep the intelligence agencies from demanding that PRISP or Stokes Program participants monitor political student groups, international students from the Middle East or central Asia, or professors for "subversive" activities such as participating in antiwar rallies or demonstrations opposing torture? The very possibility that these scenarios might play out is enough to have a chilling effect at a time when college campuses are already under pressure as the result of the PATRIOT Act and the proposed HR 1955 (the so-called Violent Radicalization and Homegrown Terrorism Prevention Act), passed by the U.S. House of Representatives in 2007 but not yet passed by the U.S. Senate.

Perhaps it is not surprising that in a speech delivered to the Association of American Universities on April 14, 2008, Defense Secretary Robert Gates announced the creation of the $60 million "Minerva Consortium" project, which would provide Defense Department funding for new social science research projects related to national security. (The project is named after the Roman goddess of wisdom and warfare.) Gates outlined four areas of interest: Chinese military studies, religious studies, Iraqi and terrorist perspectives, and the "New Disciplines Project," a program that would help the Pentagon develop expertise in anthropology, history, and sociology. But the very idea of a Minerva Consortium is ill-conceived. There are many urgent priorities that could be addressed instead. The $60 million spent on Minerva could pay for the annual tuition and fees of approximately 15,000 students at a public university, to hire more than one thousand new professors, or to update the library collections of many colleges.

IC Centers, PRISP, the Minerva Consortium, and their like will likely erode academic freedom and distort the education of university students. Classes that support the needs of the "intelligence community" and the Pentagon will likely have ample funding; those that expose the historical crimes of the CIA, FBI, and other spy agencies will not. Professors who accept the goals and perspectives of the DNI will likely be supported in their efforts to secure tenure, internal grants, and facilities; those who don't accept them will not. Similar situations in the past—in which universities have succumbed to the pressures of commercialization—have tended to produce these results, and as a new wave of intelligence-based commercialization hits, we need to be wary of the dangers that it poses to academic freedom and the core principles of higher education.[35] The university itself runs the risk of selling its soul for a quick financial fix that, in the end, does a disservice to the students and the entire society. That the structures of the IC Center programs, PRISP, and other initiatives threaten to constrain free and open intellectual inquiry on our campuses should concern us all.

As noted earlier, this is not the only time that military and intelligence agencies have aggressively infiltrated college and university campuses. In many ways, the stage was set as early as the 1980s, when public universities began shifting to a profit-driven corporate model. As state governments began cutting back public funding for higher education, universities came to rely more and more on external funding, especially from corporations and other private sources. The private, profit-driven model has all but replaced our country's public university system. In the process it has inflicted widespread damage to a part of American society that is still greatly admired around the world.[36]

Universities in the United States have strayed far from their core values: academic freedom, open scientific inquiry not subject to secrecy, and commitment to high-quality education for the benefit of students, not for some ulterior motive.[37] But there is still time to turn things around. In this context it is worth remembering the words of Senator William Fulbright (for whom the Fulbright Fellowship program was named). Just over forty years ago, in the midst of the Vietnam War, he said the following on the floor of the Senate:

> More and more our economy, our government, and our universities
> are adapting themselves to the requirements of continuing war. . . .
> The universities might have formed an effective counterweight to
> the military-industrial complex by strengthening their emphasis
> on the traditional values of our democracy, but many of our lead-
> ing institutions have instead joined the monolith, adding greatly to
> its power and influence. . . . Among the most baneful effects of the
> government-university contract system, the most damaging and
> corrupting are the neglect of its students, and the taking into the
> government camp of scholars, especially those in the social sciences,
> who ought to be acting as responsible and independent critics of
> their government's policies. . . . When the university turns away from
> its central purpose and makes itself an appendage to the govern-
> ment, concerning itself with techniques rather than purposes, with

expedients rather than ideals . . . it is not only failing to meet its responsibilities to its students; it is betraying a public trust.[38]

Fulbright's words are as relevant today as when he first spoke them in 1967. It is left now to students, faculty, and citizens of conscience to ensure that wisdom and good judgment will prevail over a marriage of convenience between universities and spy agencies.

Notes

1. "Special Events: Scavenger Hunts," International Spy Museum, http://www.spymuseum.org/special/hunts.php.

2. Jane Harman quoted in U.S. House Intelligence Committee, "Building Capabilities: The Intelligence Community's National Security Requirements for Diversity of Language, Skills, and Ethnic and Cultural Understanding," November 5, 2003, http://www.fas.org/irp/congress/2003_hr/110503hpsci.pdf.

3. U.S. Office of the Director of National Intelligence, "Intelligence Community Centers of Academic Excellence Program," Intelligence Community Centers of Academic Excellence, http://www.dni.gov/cae/institutions.htm. See also Walter Pincus, "Howard, Virginia Tech Join US Intelligence Program," *Washington Post*, September 7, 2009.

4. See, for example, Bruce Cumings, "Boundary Displacement: Area Studies and International Studies during and after the Cold War," *Bulletin of Concerned Asia Scholars* 29, no. 1 (1999): 6–26. See also Christopher Simpson, ed., *Universities and Empire: Money and Politics in the Social Sciences during the Cold War* (New York: New Press, 1999).

5. Joshua Garner, "University's 'Spy Camp' Lets Teens Learn about Intelligence Gathering," *Catholic News Service*, July 17, 2007, http://www.catholicnews.com/data/briefs/cns/20070717.htm; Richard Willing, "Intelligence Agencies Invest in College Education," *USA Today*, November 27, 2006.

6. Peter Galuszka, "Black Colleges Involved in Efforts to Boost Intelligence Community Talent Pool," Diverse Online, January 11, 2007, http://diverseeducation.com/article/6874/black-colleges-involved-in-efforts.html.

7. Ryan Poulous, "UTEP Camp Shows the World of Intelligence," *El Paso Inc.*, http://www.elpasoinc.com/showArticle.asp?articleId=1471.

8. U.S. Office of the Director of National Intelligence, *United States Intelligence Community Centers of Academic Excellence in National Security Studies: Program Plan for Fiscal Years 2005–2015* (Washington, DC: Office of the Director of National Intelligence, 2005), 6–7, http://www.trinitydc.edu/programs/intel_center/ICCAEApplicationApril05seal.pdf.

9. Galuszka, "Black Colleges Involved."

10. "Cloak and Gown," *Texas Observer*, April 21, 2006, http://www.texasobserver .org/archives/item/14790-2188-political-intelligence-marchers-mccain-y-mas.

11. Hugh Gusterson and David Price, "Spies in Our Midst," *Anthropology News* 46, no. 6 (September 2005): 39–40.

12. Ibid. See also David Price, "Obama's Classroom Spies," *CounterPunch*, June 23, 2009, http://www.counterpunch.org/price06232009.html.

13. Hugh Gusterson, "The US Military's Quest to Weaponize Culture," *Bulletin of the Atomic Scientists*, June 20, 2008, http://www.thebulletin.org/web-edition/ columnists/hugh-gusterson/the-us-militarys-quest-to-weaponize-culture.

14. "Center for Academic Excellence Creates New Opportunities for Valley Students," *Los Arcos: The University of Texas Pan-American* (Fall 2007): 18.

15. Daniel Perry, "The China Connection: UTPA Students Experience Chinese Culture, Academics," *The Monitor* (McAllen, Texas), July 24, 2007, http://www .themonitor.com/articles/china-4002-students-center.html.

16. Samuel Freeman, "Intelligence Agencies Are Penetrating Our Universities Today," *Rio Grande Guardian* (McAllen, Texas), April 10, 2007, http://www.riograndeguardian .com/index.asp.

17. Jesse Bogan, "Intelligence Grants in Valley Rile Some," *San Antonio Express-News*, December 2, 2006, http://www.mysanantonio.com/news/MYSA120306_04B _intelligencealert_2715c86_html8625.html.

18. Ibid.

19. "University of Texas-Pan American Faculty Senate Minutes," April 26, 2006, https://portal.utpa.edu/portal/page/portal/utpa_main/daa_home/senate_home/ senate_imagesfiles/fs_060426_lm.pdf.

20. David Price, "Silent Coup: How the CIA Is Welcoming Itself Back onto American University Campuses," *CounterPunch*, January 16–31, 2010, 1–4; David Price, "The Spook School Program," *CounterPunch*, February 1–15, 2010, 7–8.

21. Stephen Kinzer, *Overthrow: America's Century of Regime Change from Hawaii to Iraq* (New York: Times Books, 2007).

22. Alfred McCoy, *A Question of Torture: CIA Interrogation from the Cold War to the War on Terror* (New York: Metropolitan Books, 2006).

23. Phillip Agee, *Inside the Company: CIA Diary* (New York: Bantam, 1984).

24. Dana Priest and Barton Gellman, "US Decries Abuse but Defends Interrogations," *Washington Post*, December 26, 2002.

25. Dana Priest, "CIA Holds Terror Suspects in Secret Prisons," *Washington Post*, November 2, 2005.

26. James Risen and Eric Lichtblau, "Bush Lets US Spy on Callers without Courts," *New York Times*, December 16, 2005. See also "NSA Whistleblower Warns Domestic Spying Program Is Sign the US Is Decaying into a 'Police State,'" *Democracy*

Now! (syndicated by Pacifica Radio), January 3, 2006, http://www.democracynow .org/2006/1/3/exclusive_national_security_agency_whistleblower_warns.

27. Tracy Wilkinson and Maria De Cristofaro, "Italy Indicts CIA Agents in Kidnapping," *Los Angeles Times*, February 17, 2007.

28. Mathias Gebauer, "Germany Issues Arrest Warrants for 13 CIA Agents in El-Masri Case," *Spiegel Online*, January 31, 2007, http://www.spiegel.de/international/ 0,1518,463385,00.html.

29. Gina Pérez, "JROTC, Citizenship, and Puerto Rican Youth in Lorain, Ohio" (presentation, annual meetings of the American Anthropological Association, Philadelphia, Pa., December 6, 2009). See also Gina Pérez, "JROTC and Latina/o Youth in Neoliberal Cities," in *Rethinking America*, ed. Jeff Maskovsky and Ida Susser (New York: Paradigm Publishers, 2009), 31–48. For analysis of the legal and political implications of Latino noncitizens in the military (and their conversion to citizens), see Luis F. B. Plascencia, "The Military Gates of Non-Citizenship: Latino 'Aliens' and Noncitizen Nationals' Performing Military Work in the US Homeland" (presentation, annual meetings of the American Anthropological Association, Philadelphia, Pa., December 6, 2009).

30. Kamala Platt, "How Can We Sleep? The Birthing of an Intelligence Center on University Grounds," *La Voz de Esperanza* (San Antonio, Texas), May 2007, 6. See also Kamala Platt, "Latino/a Students and Covert 'Securities': The Integration of Academic and Intelligence Communities," *Latino Studies* 6: 456–65.

31. "Intelligence Studies Initiative," *Trinity Magazine*, Fall 2005, http://www.trinitydc .edu/news_events/mags/fall05/intelligence_studies_initiative.php.

32. Edward H. Schein, *Coercive Persuasion* (New York: H. H. Norton, 1971).

33. Samuel Freeman, "PACE and the 'Spy Center's' Shills," *Rio Grande Guardian*, January 30, 2009, http://www.riograndeguardian.com/index.asp.

34. Price, "Silent Coup," 4.

35. Early examples of commercial pressures that eroded academic freedom and the university system are described in Mary O. Furner, *Advocacy and Objectivity: A Crisis in the Professionalization of American Social Science, 1865–1905* (Lexington: University of Kentucky Press, 1975); and David Noble, *America by Design: Science, Technology, and the Rise of Corporate Capitalism* (New York: Oxford University Press, 1979).

36. See, for example, Henry A. Giroux, *The University in Chains: Confronting the Military-Industrial-Academic Complex* (Boulder, Colo.: Paradigm Publishers, 2007); Gaye Tuchman, *Wannabe U: Inside the Corporate University* (Chicago: University of Chicago Press, 2009); and Christopher Newfield, *Unmaking the Public University: The Forty-Year Assault on the Middle Class* (Cambridge, Mass.: Harvard University Press, 2008).

37. Derek Bok, *Universities in the Marketplace: The Commercialization of Higher*

Education (Princeton: Princeton University Press, 2004). As this book goes to press, news reports have described how a professor at Yale University plans to create a training center for U.S. Special Forces interrogators, using New Haven's immigrants as research subjects. See Amy Goodman and Juan González, "An Interrogation Center at Yale?," *Democracy Now!*, February 21, 2013, http://www.democracynow.org/2013/2/21/an_interrogation_center_at_yale_proposed.

38. J. William Fulbright, "A Point of View," *Science*, December 22, 1967, 1555.

3
_____

Challenging Complicity

The Neoliberal University and the Prison-Industrial Complex

Julia C. Oparah

This chapter suggests that our analysis of the relationship between the academy and U.S. imperialism would benefit from an examination of new regimes
of mass incarceration and their imbrication within the fabric of institutions of
higher education. I argue that a symbiotic relationship has arisen between
the academy and the "prison-industrial complex"—a conglomeration of
state surveillance and punishment machinery—and corporate profit making
that has emerged as a response to the rising numbers of "refugees" displaced
by and troubling to global economic and political elites. I argue that transnational technologies of mass incarceration are a key weapon used by contemporary imperial regimes to control marginalized populations and suggest
that effective anti-imperialist scholar activists need to pay greater attention
to the challenges and complicities posed by this hidden alliance between
higher education and the transnational prison-industrial complex. The
chapter identifies four ways that carceral dependency ties the university to
the political economy of prisons. Finally, I reflect on the challenges of decoupling these dangerous complicities and explore what it would mean to work
toward the abolition of the academic-military-prison-industrial complex.

Dangerous Complicities: Funding the Neoliberal Academy

2012: Students and faculty meet in the student union of Atkins College,[1] a
West Coast liberal arts college, to read excerpts from Arizona's "banned
books"—books removed from public school classrooms in the wake of the
passage of Arizona State Legislature 15–112, a measure designed to eradicate Mexican American studies from publicly funded schools.[2] Transcend-
ing hierarchies between paid staff and students, those gathered commit
to working in solidarity with organizers in Arizona to challenge the state's

censorship of antiracist scholarship. Two weeks later, queer and transgender antiprison activists at a gathering in the same room share a radical analysis of the interconnections among gender policing, racism, and criminalization and encourage the audience to get involved in local struggles against the racialized surveillance and punishment of bodies that transgress narrow gender norms.

2011: Atkins College receives a large donation to build a new graduate business school, which is named for the "self-made," multimillionaire philanthropist who made the new building possible. The new building, with its state of the art design; striking glass, steel, and granite structures; and living roof, is in sharp contrast to the aging, inefficient but much-loved infrastructure found elsewhere on the campus, creating a disjuncture between the "old" and new liberal arts. The donor is a leading funder of colleges, universities, and high schools and is committed to opening doors for women in higher education and business. He is also a passionate supporter of Israel and has given more than $30 million to the Technion Institute in Haifa, Israel.

2011: Cornell University, in collaboration with Technion Institute, wins a New York City contest to build an engineering campus with a land grant on Roosevelt Island and $100 million for infrastructure improvements.[3] Cornell students, faculty, and local activists protest the partnership, claiming that Technion—Israel's leading technological innovator—is complicit with the illegal occupation of Palestinian territory and war crimes against Palestinians.[4] They point to Technion's role in the development of surveillance, security, and military equipment—from remote-controlled bulldozers to weapons and armor—used by the Israeli military to perpetuate the territorialized control and incapacitation of Palestinians.[5] Despite high-profile student activism against Technion at Cornell and elsewhere, students at Atkins remain muted about their benefactor's connections to the Israeli military-industrial complex.

These three interconnected stories illustrate the contradictions always present in the lives and work of scholar-activists within the imperial university. On the one hand, institutions of higher education are sites of immense transformation, particularly for undergraduate students who will go through a process of unlearning and rethinking in preparation for life beyond the classroom. This moment of openness has immense potential for transformative educational praxis that allows students to locate their own experiences within systems of dominance; to build solidarities across racial, gender, class, and national lines; and to imagine and begin to enact forms of resistance.

On the other hand, there are dangerous complicities implicit in our attempts to carve out sites of resistance from within the neoliberal university. While schools like Atkins College provide an insurgent space for the development of scholarship that names and resists state violence and repression, globalization, militarism, and empire, they are also deeply embedded in and reliant on the very processes interrogated by these disciplines. As higher education has become increasingly corporatized, scholars have noted the consolidation of an academic-military-industrial complex, an interdependent and mutually constitutive alliance whereby corporate priorities and cultures, including the intellectual needs of the military-industrial complex, increasingly shape the face of academia. Those concerned with this trend have predominantly focused their attention on the large "research one" universities that receive the most government and corporate funding to develop intellectual commodities that advance business and strategic military imperatives.[6] But as the previous example demonstrates, even college campuses that have historically upheld the value of a liberal arts education that transcends the immediate needs of the workplace or marketplace are increasingly borrowing architecture, priorities, and language from corporate elites in order to compete in the global knowledge marketplace. This corporatization of the liberal arts brings it into alignment with global relations of ruling, enforced by the U.S. military-industrial complex and U.S.-backed occupations.

Whereas intellectual collaborations with research universities provide the corporate sector with technological capital, liberal arts colleges can provide much needed *moral* capital because of their association with progressive values. In the previous example, Technion not only won a significant donation of corporate wealth but also became part of the funding portfolio of a respected philanthropist with liberal credentials gained in part through his work with Atkins College. Thus Atkins was enlisted in the normalization of an illegal military occupation that routinely violates Palestinian human rights and transgresses international law.[7] In return, the college received its largest ever donation from a single donor and was able to expand its plant and curriculum at a time of reduced state funding for higher education. The relationship between such a donation and insurgent disciplines like ethnic or queer studies is complex. All students and departments can arguably be seen to benefit from an infusion of cash at a time of resource restriction via a trickle-down effect, and administrators solicit such donations in part to support the financial sustainability of the institution as a whole. The progressive critical engagements by Atkins College students and faculty in relation to the attack on ethnic studies and the policing of gender nonconformity are thus undergirded, if indirectly, by the financial support provided to the college's new business school. However, the lavish funding of departments that provide the most obvious returns to corporate funders—business and technology—and simultaneous shrinkage through budget cuts and furloughs of the rest also serves to delineate and exacerbate disciplinary inequalities between the "haves" and "have nots" of the new knowledge economy.

Unwarranted Influence: The Prison-Industrial Complex

2004: The Atkins College student newspaper publishes an editorial revealing that over 19 percent of the college's investments are handled by Farallon Capital Management, a hedge fund targeted by the national "Unfairallon" campaign for engaging in environmentally and socially toxic investments. Students point to the close ties between Atkins and Farallon, which was founded by a former Atkins College chairperson, and demand the college divest from the fund. The college denies that Farallon's investments are socially irresponsible. Two years later, Farallon sells its stock in Corrections Corporation of America (CCA), a leading private prison operator that has been instrumental in advancing prison privatization and tough-on-crime policies in the United States, Europe, and Australia.[8] Farallon denies that a nationwide "Dump Farallon" campaign started by Yale students influenced its decision, citing a significant profit on the sale.

While activist scholars have provided substantial analysis of the symbiotic and insidious linkages between academia and the military-industrial complex, very little has been written about the role of U.S. higher education and the prisonization of the globe. This is a particularly troubling lacuna given the central position of the United States both as the world's most avid incarcerator and as the leading proponent and exporter of mass incarceration, a mode of imprisonment that involves the large-scale racialized detention of economically and politically disenfranchised communities. As a result of four decades of tough-on-crime politics, and the biggest prison-building boom in history, the United States now imprisons more than 2.3 million people, with a further 5 million on probation or parole.[9] The cost of this social experiment in mass incapacitation is staggering: prisons, jails, juvenile halls, and detention centers drain state and federal coffers by $68 billion annually, an increase of 336 percent since 1986.[10] This prison boom has spurred the emergence of a controversial prison industry, which has turned the racialized fear of crime into a potent recipe for profit making. Mass incarceration has become a significant economic motor, providing contracts and profits for corporations that design, build, bankroll, operate, and equip prisons, including telecommunications, surveillance equipment, and architecture firms. It has also provided a reserve army of labor in the form of prisoners from racialized and low-income communities who work both for federal and state industries and for private companies such as Victoria's Secret, JC Penney, and IBM.

The interweaving of corporate motives and public correctional regimes has led activists and scholars to decry the emergence of a "prison-industrial complex." The concept is derived from the "military-industrial complex," a term coined by Dwight Eisenhower to describe the "conjunction of an immense military establishment and a large arms industry."[11] The prison-industrial complex can usefully be defined as a symbiotic and profitable relationship between politicians, corporations, the media, and state correctional institutions that generates the racialized use of incarceration as a response to social problems rooted in the globalization of capital.[12] The term "prison-industrial complex" was first used by Mike Davis to describe a multibillion-dollar prison-building boom in California that, he argued, "rivals agribusiness as the dominant force in the life of rural California and competes with land developers as the chief seducer of legislators in Sacramento."[13] Elaborated on by California-based scholars and prison intellectuals associated with Critical Resistance[14]—Ruth Wilson Gilmore, Linda Evans, Angela Y. Davis, and myself—the concept helped to explain why that state had continued a hugely expensive prison-building binge throughout the 1990s, even as crime rates were falling. If, as Davis argues, prisons not only *cost* money but actually generate large revenues for powerful corporate interests that design, build, operate, and invest in prisons and exploit prison labor as well as for local businesses and real estate owners in the towns where prisons are sited, then the apparently illogical willingness of state legislators to spend billions of dollars on a failing social policy is transformed into a rational—if immoral—economic policy.[15]

Anti-imperialist scholars have largely overlooked the close ties between militarism, globalization, and the prison-industrial complex. Where prisons have been identified as a tool of empire, the focus tends to be limited to military prisons, such as Guantanamo Bay or Abu Ghraib. This is perhaps unsurprising since the use of the prison to advance imperial military objectives—which in turn are closely allied to corporate agendas—is most clearly visible in the detention of "insurgents" and "terrorists" by the U.S. government and its allies. These prisons and the private interests that may design, build, or staff them are frequently analyzed in this context as military sites and thus a part of the military-industrial complex. What remains undertheorized in such a conceptualization are the ideological, political, and material continuities between military and civilian sites of incarceration under U.S. occupation and within U.S. borders. That is, by envisioning military prisons as part of the apparatus of war but not as part of a continuum of surveillance, punishment, and incapacitation that includes civilian prisons, these prisons are made a special case, outside of the norms of U.S. penal practices. This exceptionalization allows scholars and activists who oppose processes such as the extraordinary rendition and indefinite detention of "enemy combatants" on the grounds that those detained have been denied due process or are "innocent" to do so without critical examination of embedded assumptions about the normalcy and legitimacy of the "business as usual" of mass incarceration. It also renders invisible the linkages between the mutually constitutive nature of military and prison regimes.

Militarism and Prisons: Toward an Intersectional Analysis

Efforts to bring insurgent knowledges about the prison-industrial complex into conversation with a critical analysis of U.S. militarism have proven useful in countering this approach. Prior to the September 11, 2001, attacks, antiprison organizers paid infrequent attention to U.S. military bases and interventions abroad and tended to focus on the financial and human cost of mass incarceration in isolation from the multibillion-dollar military-industrial complex.[16] Indeed, the prison-industrial complex has often been theorized as the successor of the arms race, with the racialized fear of crime replacing the fear of "reds under the beds," domestic wars on drugs and crime replacing wars abroad, and prisons replacing the army as the primary market for technological developments and sales.[17] In the wake of the attacks of 9/11, as saber rattling reached its height and the United States prepared for war with Afghanistan, there was a marked shift as antiprison organizers witnessed a sharp (but temporary) reduction in support for abolitionist work in favor of antiwar mobilization. It was evident that the prison-industrial complex was simply not on the agenda of the mainstream antiwar movement. Contributing to this lacuna, scholars and other intellectuals who identify as being aligned with an antiwar politics had failed to produce critical analysis that unpacked the synergies between the military- and prison-industrial complexes and demonstrated the importance of challenging both simultaneously.

By 2003, as the United States bombarded Baghdad in order to "shock and awe" the Iraqi population, antiprison organizations had begun to respond to this gap. At the time, I was organizing with the Arizona Prison Moratorium Coalition (APMC) in Tucson against the construction of a new women's prison and several new federal detention centers in the Southwest. As Tucson became the site of increasingly hostile and aggressively policed confrontations between antiwar demonstrators and war supporters from families dependent on the military and local munitions industries, APMC issued a statement that sought to inform progressive activists about the intersections between the state's dependency on the military and a powerful proprison lobby.[18] Pointing to the ideological, technological, financial, and political synergies between militarism and prisons, APMC argued that "we are witnessing the consolidation of a powerful military-security-prison industrial complex that is driving an agenda of policing and aggression at home and abroad." It concluded, "If we are to undo the U.S. culture of militarism, we must also attack our politicians' profitable relationship with prisons." APMC's multifaceted critique rejects the separation of movements against state violence. In so doing, it recognizes and makes visible the multiple faces of imperial force—from prisons and immigration detention centers to army bases and military bombardments.

APMC's analysis was prescient of how the war and subsequent occupation would unfold in Iraq. The ideological, political, and economic synergies between prisons and the military have played a critical role in the invasion and reconstruction of Iraq. Long before the war was declared, the U.S. populace was prepared for a punitive and violent response to 9/11 through the saturation of news and popular media with images of crime and retributive "justice." The death penalty, in particular, plays a key role in legitimating state-sanctioned killing as a rational and ethical response to threats to (national) security. George W. Bush presided over 152 deaths during his eight years as governor of Texas, a number not achieved by any governor before or since, despite the emergence of DNA counterevidence and exposes of egregious miscarriages of justice.[19] The dehumanization of those deemed to have offended by the state, the normalization of state-sanctioned death, and the callous disregard for evidence of guilt or innocence were also essential components of the hunting down of al-Qaeda, the assassination of Bin Laden and his family, the indefinite detention without trial and torture of alleged enemy combatants, and the misinformation supplied to the public about weapons of mass destruction in Iraq.

While the ideology of retributive justice is central to the prison-industrial complex, scholars and activists have resisted an understanding of mass incarceration that is overreliant on an analysis of the ideological realm at the expense of an understanding of the material relations of commodification and exchange. While racialized ideologies of crime and retribution are essential to the U.S. War on Terror at home and abroad, it is the materiality of mass incarceration within the United States, the emergence of a powerful prison industry and proprison lobby, and technological innovations in security equipment and architecture that have resulted in the spread of high-tech superjails as a corollary of war and occupation. Colonial occupations have always been accompanied by and reliant on the prison; prisons were introduced to the Americas, Africa, and the Caribbean by European settlers, replacing or coexisting alongside indigenous systems of mediation, redress, and, in egregious cases, banishment. As Viviane Hanna-Saleh points out in the West African context, prisons have historically provided an essential service to empire by incapacitating those deemed to trouble contested relations of ruling.[20] In the contemporary context, as Gilmore elucidates, they also absorb those whose lives and labor are surplus to the new global imperial order, thus incapacitating and disappearing large, potentially insurgent populations. Prisons insulate and legitimize (neo)colonial occupations by reframing dissent as "crime" and insurgents/resistance fighters as criminals or terrorists. They also operationalize "preemptive strikes" by isolating individuals whose lived realities provide powerful motivation for involvement in anti-imperialist social movements.

This dual function of the imperial prison is visible in the invasion and occupation of Iraq and Afghanistan. Leniency toward the raiding of hospitals, museums, and libraries by looters (including the U.S. military) in the early days of the occupation of Iraq swiftly hardened when U.S. troops, allies, and infrastructure became a target. When a plethora of groups opposing the occupation, from Ba'athists to Sunni and Shia religious followers, began to take violent direct action, paternalism was replaced with a tough, punitive attitude. Blaming the violence on "criminals" released by Saddam Hussein from Iraqi prisons during the invasion, the U.S. administration sought to mask the extent to which gun violence, armed militias, and a pandemic of violence against women were a direct consequence of the vacuum created by an occupying power with little legitimacy on the streets. At the same time, the focus on "terrorists" and foreign opportunists distracted attention from the growing resistance movement.[21] The criminalization of dissent in Iraq proceeded so rapidly that Paul Bremer's $87 billion reconstruction budget announced in September 2003, just four months after the official end of the war, included $400 million for two 4,000-bed prisons. Seeking to replace the dilapidated prisons of the Hussein era with U.S.-style, multimillion-dollar, high-tech superjails, the U.S. Army Corps of Engineers invited private corporations to bid for the opportunity to design and build the new prisons. Utilizing a model tried and tested in rural America, authorities won support from local Iraqi politicians for the new prisons by promising economic development in the form of jobs to the economically devastated population.

The Khan Bani Sa'ad prison, located in the desert northeast of Baghdad, is illustrative of the symbiotic relationship between the U.S. military and a prison-industrial complex and suggests that a new conceptualization that foregrounds these synergies would be helpful. It is also indicative of the unpredictable outcome of imperial planning when it comes into conflict with local insurgencies and complex political realities. Ground was broken on the $40 million, 3,200-bed prison by Parsons, a global U.S.-headquartered firm that specializes in complex engineering and construction projects, as part of a $900 million infrastructure contract issued in 2004 by the U.S. Army Corps of Engineers.[22] Citing massive cost overruns and delays, the Coalition Provisional Authority terminated Parsons' contract two years later. The partially built prison was ultimately abandoned by the U.S. Army and handed over to the Iraqi Ministry of Justice, which was reported in an audit to have no intentions to complete the project.[23]

The failure of the military-prison-industrial complex to take root in this instance is an important example of the vulnerability of imperial power to local, uncoordinated, and unpredictable insurgencies. However, the continuing rise in the Iraqi prison population and accompanying overcrowding suggest that as the transition to neocolonial domestic rule is completed, the transnational private prison industry will find new opportunities to expand its marketplace as a legacy of U.S. occupation. An indication of future developments in Iraq and other parts of Southwest Asia and the Middle East can be seen in the extensive use of imprisonment by the Israeli state to incapacitate the Palestinian population and silence dissent from occupation.[24] Israeli prisons routinely detain fighters and leaders of the fractured Palestinian resistance movement as well as adults, youth, and children who participate in political activism and demonstrations or engage in acts of civil disobedience.[25] At the same time, if reports of the Israeli government's decision to build a 7,000-bed detention center for "infiltrators" on Israel's southern border prove accurate, it will be further evidence that the U.S. model of mass incapacitation, with its two-pronged role in suppressing dissent and incapacitating entire communities, is becoming a global solution to the problem posed by disenfranchised, volatile, and border-crossing populations.[26] Israeli detention centers can hold asylum seekers in administrative detention for up to three years and members of "enemy" states indefinitely, mirroring the targeting of migrant and racialized communities in the U.S. prison-industrial complex and neatly tying together the rhetoric and machinery of military security with the language of illegalization. The flow of incapacitation and termination technologies is not only one way. The training of senior police, FBI, and security officials from the United States by the Israeli National Police and Security Agency allows counterinsurgency knowledge and equipment designed to contain Palestinian resistance to be used by U.S. police forces to target Occupy protesters and immigrant communities in U.S. cities.[27] This multidirectional traffic of racialized surveillance, policing, and detention technologies constitutes a global network that promotes antidemocratic security "solutions" under the guise of counterterrorism and national security.

Unmasking the Academic-Prison-Industrial Complex

If anti-imperialist scholars are to heed APMC's call to develop a multifaceted analysis that simultaneously addresses militarism and prisons, then our critical interrogations of the imperial university must make visible its reliance on and contributions to the prison-industrial complex. Elsewhere, I have argued that universities and colleges educate a global knowledge elite who will become the "prison wardens"—literally and metaphorically—of the nonuniversitied majority and produce technological advances that permit the use of incarceration on a massive scale as a solution to the social ills and unrest caused by the globalization of capital and military repression worldwide.[28] While this critique remains pertinent, the widespread use of policing and repression against students involved in Occupy protests and other expressions of dissent against neoliberal attacks on students and workers is a reminder that enrollment in an elite institution of higher education is no guarantee of protection. Students who choose not to ally themselves with the priorities of ruling elites or to adhere silently to the strictures of "patriotic correctness" but instead confront the neoliberal state can quickly be removed from their positions of privilege and rendered part of the "criminal class."

Antiprison activists often posit schools and universities as the inverse of the prison-industrial complex. In many ways, this makes sense. As campaigns for "Education Not Incarceration" point out, it costs far less to send a young person to a university than it does to imprison him or her, yet young people of color in the United States are more likely to go to prison or jail than to higher education. Demanding that the funds put into policing and detaining young people be invested instead into failing public schools and underfunded institutions of higher education is one way of galvanizing educators and students and their families against prison expansion.[29] Low-income families of color see education as a pipeline for their children out of the economically disadvantaged neighborhoods that the prison-industrial complex feeds on. Similarly, advocates of educational programs inside prisons have demonstrated a correlation between access to K–12 and college education for prisoners and successful reentry after incarceration.[30] However, although the education/incarceration dichotomy is a useful strategic tool for activist projects, it also masks the ways in which schools, universities, and spaces of confinement are linked and mutually reinforcing.

In the case of public schools, this linkage is now being explored by racial justice and antiprison activists, nonprofit organizations and scholars. Public schools in low-income neighborhoods serving predominantly black and Latino young people have become training grounds for the juvenile detention centers, jails, and prisons that await many of their students, and they serve as fertile soil for army recruiters.[31] School budgets are increasingly spent on surveillance equipment and policing, including surveillance cameras in corridors and classrooms, metal detectors for entranceways, and security personnel.[32] Systemic underfunding, a reliance on highly regimented and disciplined regimes, and a culture of surveillance and control have led activists and scholars to decry the emergence of a "school-to-prison pipeline." At the same time, aggressive military recruitment in high schools alongside legislation forcing public schools to allow the military unfettered access to their pupils point to a "school-to-war pipeline."[33] This prisonization and militarization of urban public schools is a sharp contrast to the belief in education as a pipeline to social and economic mobility that is held by many low-income parents.[34]

Whereas public schools have been absorbed into the prison-industrial complex as a producer of raw material—"juvenile delinquents," "criminals," or army recruits—the relationship between the university and the prison-industrial complex is more multifaceted and has largely been overlooked by scholars. I have identified four functions that tie the university to the military-prison-industrial complex, revealing a mutually reinforcing relationship between systems of higher education and mass incarceration. First, as the Atkins College case reveals, universities invest in prisons and the military. With an eye for ways to grow their endowments, colleges and universities in the 1990s became major financiers of private prisons and the military-industrial complex through direct investments and less visible financing via endowment management companies that own sizeable stakes in prison corporations and the defense industry.[35] In tying endowment growth to the success of private prison and defense corporations, university managers have created a stake for students, faculty, and administrators in the continuation of the prison buildup. More prisoners mean more profits for shareholders; that translates into new buildings, better facilities, improved technology, and even financial aid packages.

What Henry Giroux calls the "corporatization of academia" has also embedded higher education in the political economy of prisons.[36] In 2001, student activists working with the national campaign, Not with Our Money—Students Stop Prisons-for-Profit, drew attention to the connections between the private prison industry and the privatization of services on campus. After learning that Sodexho Marriott, a leading provider of contracted food services in colleges and universities across the country, was a subsidiary of Sodexho Alliance, a Paris-based multinational corporation that at the time owned more than 10 percent of Corrections Corporation of America, students organized an effective series of local campus campaigns leading to the cancellation of contracts in a number of schools. The Sodexho campaign revealed only the tip of the iceberg. With both prisons and higher education institutions outsourcing services from food and health care to security, it is more and more difficult for schools to find suppliers that are not invested in the military-prison-industrial complex.

Second, universities produce an educated workforce for the prison-industrial complex. Global economic restructuring has produced new patterns of employment in industrialized countries, with full-time unionized jobs increasingly being replaced by seasonal, low-waged, casual, or offshore labor. At the same time, decades of dramatic penal expansion have generated a plethora of new employment opportunities, including probation and parole officers and drug enforcement, immigration enforcement, homeland security, law enforcement, and corrections personnel. Colleges and universities have responded to the demands of the prison-industrial complex for trained workers by proliferating new courses in corrections and law enforcement administration, from certificates and associate degrees for entry-level staff to masters programs targeted at those already working in the field who wish to ascend to management positions. These academic programs are premised on the continued ascendance of mass incarceration, and indeed candidates are recruited with promises of projected growth in criminal justice–related jobs. The paucity of programs focusing on restorative justice, peacemaking, or alternatives to incarceration is in sharp contrast to the innumerable programs on retributive criminal justice approaches available to potential students. As students who enroll in these programs invest in their anticipated career mobility, colleges and universities benefit from their tuition and graduate students and junior faculty find more openings for tenure-track positions specializing in criminal justice. In this sense, graduate students who are committed to antiprison scholarship as well as those whose work promotes carceral logics may well gain their first faculty position precisely as a result of the university's stake in training the foot soldiers and generals of the penal war on people of color and poor people.

Third, universities mine prisons as a source of data. For the past three decades, scholars have testified to the rise of postindustrial knowledge societies in which knowledge has become a valuable commodity.[37] These knowledge industries are peopled by the "experts," or powerbrokers, who, through professional training, are positioned as legitimate producers of knowledge and rewarded through salaried positions and professional recognition. They are also peopled by the human subjects who serve as the raw material for knowledge production, whether as experimental subjects, participants of social science research, or objects of mass media news stories. These relationships, between scientist and experimental subject, social scientist and research participant, are embedded in imperial global inequities and domestic patterns of subordination; the social relations of knowledge production position those without economic or political power, or racial, national, and gender privilege, as objects of investigation and raw materials for knowledge industries. As Senator Edward Kennedy observed during Senate hearings on human experimentation in 1973, "Those who have borne the principal brunt of research—whether it is drugs or even experimental surgery—have been the more disadvantaged people within our society; have been the institution-alized, the poor, and minority members."[38]

Histories of experimentation on prisoners demonstrate that the social death that accompanies incarceration is also a powerful determinant of an individual's role within the knowledge economy. As recently as the 1970s, prisoners in the United States and Canada have been used as subjects in experiments involving infection with life-threatening diseases and exposure to mind-altering drugs, chemical warfare, and radioactive isotopes. Entering Holmesburg Prison in Philadelphia in the 1960s, Dr. Albert Kligman, a pro-fessor at Pennsylvania Medical School, was ecstatic at the potential for scien-tific experimentation, telling a newspaper reporter, "All I saw before me were acres of skin. It was like a farmer seeing a fertile field for the first time."[39] The predominantly African American, impoverished male prisoners were paid a few dollars for their involvement in potentially life-threatening experiments by Kligman's research team; many were permanently mutilated or suffered from psychological problems. Similar experiments in the Kingston Peni-tentiary for Women (P4W) were revealed when one of the victims, an Afri-can Canadian woman who was subjected to behavior control experiments using mind-altering drugs and electroshock, sued the Correctional Service of Canada.[40] Although ethical review committees at universities aim to pre-vent research that imposes clear physical and psychological harm on indi-viduals, the social relations of research that made possible the Holmesburg and P4W experiments remain largely unchallenged. Prisoners continue to serve as objects of research rather than subjects of their own narratives. The dichotomy between researcher and researched is rarely examined critically within prison studies, and prisoners' lived experiences are either rendered invisible through the dehumanizing tendencies of quantitative research or refracted through the expert analysis of the (nonimprisoned) researcher. At the same time, economic, racial, and national privilege continue to shape the researcher–researched binary, so that the latter is both a reflection and con-stitutive element of systems of power and dominance.

The fourth prong of academic–prison symbiosis highlighted here is that universities produce knowledge that undergirds and legitimates penal tech-nologies. Radical criminologists have long noted the role of the discipline as a handmaiden of the punishing state.[41] Rather than producing forms of knowledge that enable criminalized communities to challenge state vio-lence and coercion, academic "experts" have dedicated themselves to pro-ducing new and more effective technologies for apprehending, controlling, and disciplining unruly populations. This synergy between scholarship and systems of social control is evident in the annual meeting of the American Society of Criminology. Among the hundreds of panels and presentations, the voices of prisoners, people on parole or probation, and their families, as well as those of criminalized and policed communities, are largely absent. Absent in the field of criminology is any deep interest in what criminalized communities are doing to resist state surveillance and control, evidenced by the lack of panels on movement building or local community organizing.[42] Although there are many progressive criminologists—including minority and feminist criminologists, who produce scholarly work that challenges gender and racial discrepancies in the criminal justice system or promotes decarceration—few embed themselves in community organizing or dedicate time and resources to support movements that press for these changes. In contrast, academic entrepreneurs who work closely with the mainstream media, conservative think tanks, and politicians have been highly influential in providing scholarly justification for the punitive "tough-on-crime" measures that have fueled dramatic penal expansion. For example, James Q. Wilson and George Kelling's "broken windows" thesis, which argued that minor social disorder led ultimately to violent crime, has served as scholarly justification for the introduction of quality-of-life policing across the country, resulting in crackdowns on socially excluded groups, from squeegee operators to street-involved youth.[43] Similarly, the selective incapacitation theory, which argues that crime can be reduced significantly by incapacitating the small group of "repeat offenders" who are supposedly responsible for the majority of criminalized activity, has provided scientific rationale for harsh sentencing practices—such as the "three-strikes" law—that have swelled prison populations and targeted low-income communities of color.[44]

We should not be surprised by the synergistic relationship between academic expertise and penal technologies. As Biko Agozino argues, criminology was developed "to serve imperialism as a tool for the repression of others."[45] In the "battle of ideas"[46] that characterizes criminal justice policy, academic expertise carries a weight of authority that can lend legitimacy to politically driven, costly, and violent penal technologies. But the prison-industrial complex does not just rely only on conservative criminology. When public opinion periodically turns against the high social and economic cost of ever-growing rates of incarceration and racially discrepant criminal justice policies, reforms find scholarly backing in the work of progressive scholars. In this way, the prison-industrial complex can retrench, reshape, and find new ways to continue its inexorable expansion. As Foucault warned us, liberal reform efforts, far from challenging carceral regimes, continually reconstitute and undergird the prison.[47] This pattern is visible in the contemporary shift toward "gender-responsive strategies" (GRS). Promoted by liberal feminist criminologists as a corrective to practices that ignore women's particular life experiences and pathways into the criminal justice system, the gender-responsive model has been adopted by the U.S. Department of Justice as the best practice for work with "women offenders."[48] For example, in California, a GRS commission, convened by the Department of Corrections and Rehabilitation in 2005, identified 4,500 women who it deemed low risk and proposed that they should be relocated from the huge penal warehouses currently holding women prisoners. However, rather than promoting decarcerative strategies that would return women to the community and build community-based supports to address emotional, health, educational, and housing needs, the commission advocated for the construction of "female rehabilitative community correctional centers" that would add 4,500 prison beds to the state's already bloated prison system.[49] The gender-responsive model ignores the violence of imprisonment, rearticulates prison expansion as a means of meeting women's needs, and thus undermines efforts to redirect public funds from punishment into community programs, housing, welfare, and other supports for women. By positing the possibility of a humane, woman-centered, rehabilitative prison, these liberal feminist scholars move us farther away from the possibility of ending our reliance on mass incarceration by temporarily alleviating its contradictions. In this way, scholars produce knowledge that sediments the prison and its corollary, mass racialized incarceration, as inevitable and necessary, even when they appear to critique specific penal regimes. Thus the academy is a major (re)producer of carceral logics.

The economic, ideological, and technological synergies between the university and mass imprisonment suggest that the academy is not just complicit with the prison-industrial complex; it is a constitutive, if overlooked, part of it. Indeed, we can argue that students, faculty, and administrators, regardless of our political positions for or against penal warehousing, are by virtue of our location active participants within the academic-prison-industrial complex. As the university underwrites and legitimates processes of mass incarceration, it falls to insurgent subjects within the academy to challenge and ultimately sever the symbiotic relationship between penal and educational systems. In the following section, I briefly explore the possibilities of dismantling penal dependency.

Toward a Postcarceral Academy

In my earlier work on the academic-prison-industrial complex, I suggested that activist scholars were producing and disseminating countercarceral knowledge by bringing academic research into alignment with the needs of social movements and interrogating and reorganizing relationships between prisoners and researchers in the free world.[50] Given the history of epistemic and physical violence and exploitation of research subjects by the academy, such a reorganizing of relationships and accountabilities is clearly urgently needed. Yet no matter how radical and participatory our scholarship is, we ultimately fail to dismantle the academic-military-prison-industrial complex (academic-MPIC) if we address it only through the production of more knowledge. Since knowledge is a commodity, marketed through books, articles, and conferences as well as patents and government contracts, the production of "better," more progressive or countercarceral knowledge can also be co-opted and put to work by the academic-MPIC.

An abolitionist lens provides a helpful framework here. Antiprison scholars and activists have embraced the concept of abolition in order to draw attention to the unfinished liberation legislated by the Thirteenth Amendment, which abolished slavery "except as a punishment for a crime."[51] Abolitionists do not seek primarily to reform prisons or to improve conditions for prisoners; instead they argue that only by abolishing imprisonment will we free up the resources and imagine the possibility of more effective and less violent strategies to deal with the social problems signaled by harmful acts. While early abolitionists referred to themselves as prison abolitionists, more recently there has been a shift to prison-industrial complex abolitionism to expand the analysis of the movement to incorporate other carceral spaces— from immigrant detention centers to psychiatric hospitals—and to emphasize the role of other actors, including the police and courts, politicians, corporations, the media, and the military, in sustaining mass incarceration.[52]

How does an abolitionist lens assist us in assessing responses to the academic-MPIC? First, it draws our attention to the economic basis of the academic-MPIC and pushes us to attack the materiality of the militarization and prisonization of academia rather than limiting our interventions to the realm of ideas. This means that we must challenge the corporatization of our universities and colleges and question what influences and account-abilities are being introduced by our increasing collaboration with neoliberal global capital. It also means that we must dismantle those complicities and liberate the academy from its role as handmaiden to neoliberal globaliza-tion, militarism, and empire. In practice, this means interrogating our uni-versities' and colleges' investment decisions, demanding they divest from the military, security, and prison industries; distance themselves from military occupations in Southwest Asia and the Middle East; and invest instead in community-led sustainable economic development. It means facing allega-tions of disloyalty to our employers or alma maters as we blow the whistle on unethical investments and the creeping encroachment of corporate fund-ing, practices, and priorities. It means standing up for a vision of the liberal arts that neither slavishly serves the interests of the new global order nor returns to its elitist origins but instead is deeply embedded in progressive movements and richly informed by collaborations with insurgent and activ-ist spaces. And it means facing the challenges that arise when our divest-ment from empire has real impact on the bottom line of our university and college budgets.

Andrea Smith, in her discussion of native studies, has argued that politi-cally progressive educators often adopt normative, colonial practices in the classroom, using pedagogical strategies and grading practices that rein-scribe the racialized and gendered regulation, policing, and disciplining that PIC abolitionists seek to end.[53] In this sense, there could be no "postcarceral" academy. Certainly, sanctions for undergraduate and graduate students and faculty who challenge the university's regular practices—from failing grades and expulsions to tenure denials and deportation—are systemically distrib-uted, along with rewards for those who can be usefully incorporated. Yet uni-versities and colleges also hold the seeds of a very different possible future, evoked, for example, by the universal admissions movement or by student strikes in Britain and Canada that demand higher education as a right, not a privilege of the wealthy. Rather than seeking to eradicate or replace higher educational institutions altogether, I suggest that we demand the popular and antiracist democratization of higher education.

The first step toward this radical transformation is the liberation of aca-demia from the machinery of empire: prisons, militarism, and corporations. Speaking of abolishing the white race, Noel Ignatiev argues that it is neces-sary for white people to make whiteness impossible by refusing the invisible benefits of membership in the "white club."[54] Progressive academics are also members of a privileged "club," one that confers benefits in the form of a paycheck, health care, and other fringe benefits; social status; and the freedom to pursue intellectual work that we are passionate about. But we can also put our privilege to work by unmasking and then unsettling the invisible, symbiotic, and toxic relationships that constitute the academic-MPIC.

Decoupling academia from its velvet-gloved master would begin the process of fundamental transformation. Without unfettered streams of income from corporations, wealthy philanthropists, and the military, universities and colleges would be forced to develop alternative fund-raising strategies, relationships, and accountabilities. Can we imagine a college administration aligned with local Occupy organizers to protest the state's massive spending on prisons and policing and demand more tax money for housing, education, and health care? Can we imagine a massive investment of time and resources by university personnel to solve the problem of how to decarcerate the nation's prisons or end the detention of undocumented immigrants in order to fund universal access to higher education? Can we imagine a university run by and for its constituents, including students, kitchen and garden staff, and tenure-track and adjunct faculty? These are the possibilities opened up by academic-MPIC abolition.

Notes

1. A pseudonym.
2. Arizona State Law 15–112 states that school districts may not offer classes or programs that "1. Promote the overthrow of the United States government. 2. Promote resentment toward a race or class of people. 3. Are designed primarily for pupils of a particular ethnic group. 4. Advocate ethnic solidarity instead of the treatment of pupils as individuals." As a result of the law's passage, the Tucson Unified District terminated its Mexican American studies program and removed a list of "banned" books from its classrooms. "Fiftieth Legislature—Second Regular Session," Arizona State Legislature, http://www.azleg.gov/FormatDocument.asp?inDoc=/ars/15/00112.htm&Title=15&DocType=ARS.
3. Oliver Staley and Henry Goldman, "Cornell and Technion Chosen by NYC for Engineering Campus," *Business Week*, December 20, 2011, http://www.businessweek.com/news/2011-12-20/cornell-and-technion-chosen-by-nyc-for-engineering-campus.html.
4. Occupied Palestine blog, "End Cornell University Collaboration with Technion," March 6, 2012, http://occupiedpalestine.wordpress.com/2012/03/06/end-cornell-university-collaboration-with-technion.

5. U.S. Campaign for the Academic and Cultural Boycott of Israel, "Stop Cornell-Technion Collaboration!," http://www.usacbi.org/stop-technioncornell-collaboration.

6. Henry Giroux, *The University in Chains: Confronting the Military-Industrial Academic Complex* (Boulder, Colo.: Paradigm Publishers, 2007).

7. For a discussion of the role of normalization in Israeli settler colonialism, see Alex Kane, "'A Level of Racist Violence I Have Never Seen': UCLA Professor Robin D. G. Kelley on Palestine and the BDS Movement," February 16, 2012, http://mondoweiss.net/2012/02/a-level-of-racist-violence-i-have-never-seen-ucla-professor-robin-d-g-kelley-on-palestine-and-the-bds-movement.html. For the latest in a long series of United Nations resolutions against the illegality of Israel's occupation of territories seized in 1967, see United Nations General Assembly, "Israeli Settlements in the Occupied Palestinian Territory, Including East Jerusalem, and in the Occupied Syrian Golan," April 13, 2011, http://unispal.un.org/UNISPAL.NSF/0/6104815DF58C3C1F85257877006786A7.

8. CCA was subject to numerous complaints about failure to provide medical care, failure to control violence, substandard conditions leading to violence and protests, criminality activities by guards, and poor management practices leading to prisoner escapes. The Responsible Endowment Project, "Corrections Corporation of America," http://www.responsibleendowment.com/corrections-corporation-of-america.html.

9. The Pew Center on the States, *One in 31: The Long Reach of American Corrections*, 2009, 11, http://www.pewcenteronthestates.org/uploadedFiles/PSPP_1in31_report_FINAL_WEB_3-26-09.pdf.

10. Ibid, 11.

11. Dwight Eisenhower, "Military-Industrial Complex Speech," *Public Papers of the Presidents of the United States: Dwight D. Eisenhower, 1961* (Washington, DC: Government Printing Office), 1035–40, http://www.h-net.org/~hst306/documents/indust.html.

12. For a detailed analysis, see Julia Sudbury, "A World without Prisons: Resisting Militarism, Globalized Punishment and Empire," *Social Justice* 31, nos. 1–2 (2004): 9–30.

13. Mike Davis, "Hell Factories in the Field: A Prison-Industrial Complex," *The Nation*, February 20, 1995, 260, 229–34.

14. Critical Resistance is a national organization that aims to end the prison-industrial complex by challenging the belief that prisons make us safe.

15. Angela Y. Davis, *Are Prisons Obsolete?* (New York: Seven Stories, 2003).

16. A notable exception is the pamphlet by anti-imperialist and former political prisoner Linda Evans with Eve Goldberg, which was first published in 1998, *The Prison-Industrial Complex and the Global Economy* (PM Pamphlets, 2009).

17. Angela Y. Davis, "Race and Criminalization: Black Americans and the

Punishment Industry," in *The Angela Y. Davis Reader*, ed. Joy James (Malden, Mass.: Blackwell Publishers, 1998), 69–70.

18. Arizona Prison, *Militarism and Prisons: Making the Connections, from the War on Drugs to the War on Iraq* (Tucson, Ariz.: 2003), http://www.prisontalk.com/forums/showthread.php?t=24767.

19. Andrew Gumber, "Bush's Bid for a Death Penalty Fast Track," *AlterNet*, August 22, 2007, http://www.alternet.org/rights/59880.

20. Viviane Hanna-Saleh, *Colonial Systems of Control: Criminal Justice in Nigeria* (Ottawa: Ottawa University Press, 2008).

21. Tariq Ali, "Resistance Is the First Step Toward Iraqi Independence," *London Guardian*, November 3, 2003.

22. "Empty Iraq Prison a 'Monument' to Waste," CBS News, February 11, 2009, http://www.cbsnews.com/2100-500257_162-4298624.html.

23. Special Inspector General for Iraq Reconstruction, "Kahn Bani Sa'ad Correctional Facility, Kahn Bani Sa'ad, Iraq," July 25, 2008, http://www.sigir.mil/files/assessments/PA-08-138.pdf#view=fit.

24. As of 2012, approximately 4,600 Palestinians are held in Israeli prisons in reportedly inhumane and violent conditions. United Nations Office at Geneva (UNOG) Committee on the Exercise of the Inalienable Rights of the Palestinian People (CEIRPP), "The United Nations International Meeting on the Question of Palestine Opens in Geneva," April 3, 2012, http://unispal.un.org/UNISPAL.NSF/0/9EBE118029F480BA852579D5006B0F7B.

25. For example, Fatah leader Marwan Barghouti, who advocates noncooperation with Israel, is currently serving five life sentences for his involvement in the youth wing of Fatah. Uri Avnery, "A Palestinian Mandela," AntiWar.com, April 2, 2012, http://original.antiwar.com/avnery/2012/04/01/a-palestinian-mandela.

26. Hotline for Migrant Workers, "Israeli Government Plan for the World's Largest Prison for Asylum Seekers," January 2012, http://www.hotline.org.il/english/pdf/New_Detention_Facility_Eng.pdf.

27. Max Blumenthal, "From Occupation to 'Occupy': The Israelification of American Domestic Security," *Alakhbar* English, December 2, 2011, http://english.al-akhbar.com/content/occupation-%E2%80%9Coccupy%E2%80%9D-israelification-american-domestic-security.

28. Julia Sudbury, "Challenging Penal Dependency: Activist Scholars and the Antiprison Movement," in *Activist Scholarship: Antiracism, Feminism, and Social Change*, ed. Julia Sudbury and Margo Okazawa-Rey (Boulder, Colo.: Paradigm Publishers, 2009), 17–36.

29. Education Not Incarceration, http://www.ednotinc.org; NAACP, *Misplaced Priorities: Over Incarcerate, Under Educate*, May 2011, http://naacp.3cdn.net/ecea56adeef3d84a28_azsm639wz.pdf.

30. Michelle Fine et al., "Participatory Action Research: From Within and Beyond Prison Bars," in *Working Method: Research and Social Justice*, ed. Lois Weis and Michelle Fine (New York: Routledge, 2004).

31. Garrett Albert Duncan, "Urban Pedagogies and the Celling of Adolescents of Color," *Social Justice* 27, no. 3 (2000): 29.

32. Christian Parenti, *Lockdown America: Police and Prisons in the Age of Crisis* (London: Verso, 1999).

33. Leah Wells, "No Child Left Behind by Military Recruiters," *AlterNet*, December 9, 2002, http://www.alternet.org/story/14716/.

34. NAACP Legal Defense and Educational Fund, *Dismantling the School-to-Prison Pipeline* (New York: NAACP, 2005), http://www.naacpldf.org/content/pdf/pipeline/Dismantling_the_School_to_Prison_Pipeline.pdf.

35. Sarah Haley and Bob Libal, "Prison for Profit Loses Its Appeal," *Campus Progress News*, May 25, 2006, http://www.campusprogress.org.

36. Giroux, *The University in Chains*, 2.

37. Sung Sil Lee Sohng, "Participatory Research and Community Organizing," *Journal of Sociology and Social Welfare* 23, no. 4 (1996): 77–97.

38. Ibid, 37.

39. Allen M. Hornblum, *Acres of Skin: Human Experiments at Holmesburg Prison* (New York: Routledge, 1998): xvi.

40. Kelly Hannah-Moffat, *Punishment in Disguise: Penal Governance and Federal Imprisonment of Women in Canada* (Toronto: University of Toronto Press, 2001): 103–4; Geraint Osborne, "Scientific Experimentation on Canadian Inmates, 1955–1975," *Howard Journal* 45, no. 3 (July 2006).

41. Stanley Cohen, *Against Criminology* (Edison, N.J.: Transaction, 1998); Kerrie Carrington and Russell Hogg, *Critical Criminology: Issues, Debates, Challenges* (Devon, UK: Willan, 2002).

42. At the 2005 annual conference, held in Toronto, Canada, I organized a roundtable of local antiprison activists, which was very poorly attended. The lack of interest in such a dialogue heightened the divide between international experts benefiting from the Canadian dollar for an "offshore" conference and local communities struggling with the effect of policies influenced by criminal justice experts.

43. James Q. Wilson and George L. Kelling, "Broken Windows," *Atlantic Monthly*, March 1982, http://www.theatlantic.com/doc/198203/broken-windows; Bernard Harcourt, *Illusion of Order: The False Promise of Broken Windows Policing* (Cambridge, Mass.: Harvard University Press, 2001).

44. Franklin E. Zimring and Gordon Hawkins, *Incapacitation: Penal Confinement and the Restraint of Crime* (New York: Oxford University Press, 1995).

45. Biko Agozino, *Counter-Colonial Criminology: A Critique of Imperialist Reason* (London: Pluto, 2003), 199.

46. Ibid.

47. Michel Foucault, *Discipline and Punish: The Birth of the Prison* (London: Penguin, 1979).

48. Barbara Bloom, Barbara Owen, and Stephanie Covington, *Gender-Responsive Strategies: Research, Practice, and Guiding Principles for Women Offenders* (Washington, DC: National Institute of Corrections, U.S. Department of Justice, 2003), http://www.nicic.org/pubs/2003/018017.pdf.

49. California Department of Corrections and Rehabilitation, *Inmate Population, Rehabilitation, and Housing Management Plan*, July 2006, http://www.cdcr.ca.gov/News/docs/inmatePopRehabHMP.pdf.

50. Sudbury, "Challenging Penal Dependency."

51. Julia Sudbury, "Maroon Abolitionists: Black Gender-Oppressed Activists in the Antiprison Movement in the U.S. and Canada," *Meridians: Feminism, Race, Transnationalism* 9, no. 1 (2009): 1–29, 8–14.

52. Critical Resistance, *The Abolitionist Toolkit*, 2004, http://criticalresistance.org/resources/the-abolitionist-toolkit/.

53. Andrea Smith, "Native Studies and Critical Pedagogy: Beyond the Academic-Industrial Complex," in *Activist Scholarship: Antiracism, Feminism, and Social Change*, ed. Julia Sudbury and Margo Okazawa-Rey (Boulder, Colo.: Paradigm Publishers, 2009), 46–51.

54. Noel Ignatiev, "The Point Is Not to Interpret Whiteness but to Abolish It," *Race Traitor: Journal of the New Abolitionism* 4 (1997) http://racetraitor.org/abolishthepoint.html.

II

Academic Containment

4

Neoliberalism, Militarization, and the Price of Dissent

Policing Protest at the University of California

Farah Godrej

In this chapter, I argue that the neoliberal logic of private capital at work in the privatization of the University of California is necessarily intertwined with the logic of militarization and the criminalization of dissent. I will argue that the deliberate and systematic privatization of one of the nation's greatest public education systems engenders—and in fact *requires*—a militarized enforcement strategy that relies on criminalizing those who dissent and on being able to engage in legitimized violence against such dissenters as and when necessary. The enforcement of the tuition hikes, budget cuts, and other so-called austerity measures at the heart of the privatization strategy is an irreducibly political project, not simply because it relies on a rhetorical political strategy that cleverly assigns responsibility for privatization to recalcitrant state legislators who insist on state disinvestment in public education rather than to those elites within the UC leadership who stand to benefit from such privatization. It is political and politicized in a much deeper sense in that it is able to plausibly and powerfully squash all public dissent from this plan by casting those who dissent against its neoliberal logic as criminal, ensuring that the "price" of their dissent—whether in terms of violence, jail time, or simply public stigmatization—is high enough to discourage further dissent. It uses the legal-political resources of the neoliberal state and replicates the neoliberal state's complicity with private capital in order to build political legitimacy for its repression of dissenting views.

The basic premise of my chapter—that the leadership of the University of California has since 2009 been committed to the deliberate and systematic privatization of one of the nation's premier public education systems—should not be in question. This plan involves being complicit with the state's disinvestment in public education and shifting the burden of payment for education from society to individual students. The effect of this shift hits the least privileged the hardest, so that the accessibility and affordability of this education is eroded, particularly for those who are least able to afford this burden. Access to education in this system is now meant to require one of two routes: already having the wealth and privilege to pay the exponentially multiplied fees or taking on unimaginable amounts of student debt in order to do so, which in turn provides profitable investments for banks. The outcome of this deliberate plan is to further widen the already massive inequalities of income so as to reinforce existing privileges of race, wealth, class, income, and so forth. Indeed, as Chris Newfield has so convincingly argued, the financial and political crises of public universities are the result of a conservative campaign to end public education's democratizing influence on American society.[1] One of the greatest experiments in democracy, the University of California's commitment to accessible, affordable public education, had created unprecedented levels of social and economic mobility over the past forty or so years while creating a racially integrated mass middle class. But Newfield skillfully demonstrates how the expansive vision of an equitable America that emerged from the postwar boom in college access has gradually been replaced by the emergence of the antiegalitarian "corporate university," which contributes to the ongoing erosion of the college-educated middle class.

The specifics of the University of California's strategy of systematic privatization should not require much exploration; vocal critiques by dissenting scholars within the UC system have repeatedly demonstrated that the so-called austerity measures such as tuition cuts, fee hikes, and budget cuts are *not* to be seen as the somewhat desperate response of a hapless and helpless UC leadership with no other choice in the face of a bankrupt state that insists on disinvestment.[2] The convincing choruses of "What else can we do?" constitute the first discursive political victory of the UC leadership, ensuring that the state is seen as the political problem and that the leadership's own abdication of responsibility for forcefully and publicly advocating for public education is utterly occluded. Indeed, what is occluded above all is the fact that privatization, rather than being a necessary evil, comes about as the result of deliberate complicity with—and in fact advocacy of—neoliberal disinvestment in the concept of education as a public good by the very people charged with protection and disbursement of this public good. And consequently, education is systematically reframed as a private good existing in the sacred neoliberal realm of individual choice, something therefore to be commodified and paid for by those who have the resources. But it is crucial to recall that such reframing is the result of a rhetorical strategy by precisely those who would profit from this commodification and privatization.

However, in order to be able to enforce the tuition hikes, budget cuts, and other "efficiency" and "austerity" measures at the heart of this privatization strategy, the UC leadership has relied on a concomitant strategy of plausibly and powerfully squashing all public dissent from this plan. I argue here that the enforcement strategy has two distinct but interrelated components. First, it uses a militarized police force in order to inflict injury and violence upon any protesters. Second, it engages in the deliberate and systematic criminalization of all dissent that arises in opposition to this plan. The two components are of course intertwined, for the one requires the other: all violence inflicted on a dissenting public must be legitimized and justified as a necessary measure in the public's own interest to maintain law and order against ostensible criminal threats. Together, these combined elements of militarization and criminalization are designed to ensure that the price of protest is so high that dissent against the privatization strategy becomes prohibitively expensive. The neoliberal language of "price" and "expense" here is of course intentionally multivalent. It includes the literal "price" in terms of financial cost of ensuing legal battles but also refers to the cost of being labeled as a criminal in the public imagination or of suffering injury by police forces. The higher these costs, the more those involved in dissent are incentivized into silence through a carefully constructed chilling effect on all forms of speech and action that criticize, protest, or dissent against the privatization plan.

Militarization

The UC protests against privatization predated both the Arab Spring and the Occupy Wall Street movements, beginning as early as 2009 in response to the UC leadership's commitment to the systematic privatization of the system along with its implicit support for the state's disinvestment in public education. By 2011, however, the moral outrage of dissenters within the UC system was largely aligned with that of the emerging Occupy movement, itself in turn inspired by the Arab Spring. Despite the obvious differences among these movements—with the Arab Spring focused specifically on the critique and removal of undemocratic military dictatorships and repressive neoliberal regimes—both movements share, in Anne-Marie Slaughter's words, the "same fundamental drivers: a deep sense of injustice and invisibility."[3] Dissenters within the UC system, like their counterparts in the Occupy movement and elsewhere, expressed public anger at the increasing power of private capital, the impunity with which it operated in enriching its own profit-making agents while impoverishing the vast majority of citizens, and the state's collusion with the self-enriching power of capital through increasing disinvestment in public services such as health care and education. And the tactics of expressing such dissent were remarkably similar in both the Occupy movement and the movement in support of public education, which involved the occupation of public spaces such as university campuses, parks, or other areas surrounding seats of local government, along with the traditional markers of nonviolent protest such as chanting, singing, sitting-in, raising slogans both verbal and pictorial, and generally drawing attention to the injustice of the overarching framework of racial and socioeconomic inequity that framed the lives of the protesters. In a few cases, the protesters engaged in specifically disruptive yet nonviolent action such as blockading the entrance to a bank or refusing to allow officials to leave a building. Across the board, the movements were mostly avowedly peaceful and nonviolent in both symbolic intent and actual practice, although, as we will see later, there were some exceptions to this.

It is therefore perhaps all the more worth noting that each of these movements was ultimately met with a violent, militarized force deeply disproportionate to its peaceful character, while the respective authorities engaged in dispersing these protests justified this militarized violence through the use of rhetoric that served to paint its targets as potentially dangerous and threatening. The Occupy encampments were systematically dismantled, throughout winter 2011–2012, by various city mayors employing police and other law enforcement authorities who sometimes manhandled or otherwise violently dragged, slammed, and beat protesters in the course of arresting or handcuffing them.

The response to protests at the Davis, Berkeley, and Riverside campuses of the University of California in 2011 and 2012 was rather more dramatically disproportionate. In November 2011, in a series of iconic images that would soon evoke international outrage, police in riot gear armed with assault weapons were recorded pepper spraying, beating, and shoving batons into the stomachs of nonresisting, nonviolent student and faculty protesters occupying the Davis and Berkeley campuses. Two months later, scenes of similarly disproportionate militarized response were seen at the Riverside campus where the UC regents were meeting, ostensibly to discuss another set of tuition hikes and budget cuts in the course of privatization. Protesting students and faculty surrounding the location of the regents meeting were faced with police in riot gear and eventually shot with lead paint bullets. While students and faculty chanted; peacefully blockaded a building; and repeated their intent for peaceful, nonviolent expression of dissent, the administration responded with a massive show of militarized force. Police from every UC campus were mobilized and eventually supplemented by officers from the Riverside Police Department and the Riverside County Sheriff's Department, while helicopters circled overhead and officers took sniper positions at high points on campus buildings, as described in the introduction to this book. Viral videos taken on cell phones showed police pushing fences into crowds of students, shoving batons into the bodies of protesters, slamming heads into the ground, dragging bodies across the ground, and shooting guns loaded with lead paint bullets.

Much was of course written and said about the moral illegitimacy of the administrative response in each of these cases. But what is worth emphasizing here is that the militarization of campuses seems crucially linked to the privatization of public universities. UC Santa Cruz professor and former president of the Council of UC Faculty Associations Bob Meister articulates the link between the privatization of public universities, the financial services industry, and the national and global security industry:

> Since 9/11 the US defense industry of the Cold War has morphed
> from being mainly in the military hardware business into a new
> role as global provider of security services that enables government
> and corporations throughout the world to outsource intelligence,
> policing, background checks, construction of secure sites and vari-
> ous operations that may need to be deniable—as well as the public
> relations efforts necessary to support such deniability. Most Ameri-
> cans do not know that there is a huge domestic market for services
> provided by the defense industry. . . . The fastest growing market for
> the defense and security services industry is in the area of local gov-
> ernment and public agencies that feel threatened by political protests,
> such as the Occupy movement, and that have reporting and other
> obligations under the Patriot Act.[4]

UC Davis professor and poet Joshua Clover, who was arrested as part of the civil disobedience movement against privatization, goes on to point out that while the specifics of such connections may vary, the systemic logic is clear:

"Heightened campus security is inextricably linked to heightened campus securitization in its two main forms: the decision of universities to pursue a certain line of investment strategies which move money away from educational services and into capital projects; and the corresponding decision to cover those educational costs by shifting burdens to students at a rate which can only be financed though student loans, concomitantly providing profitable investment for banks laden with otherwise fallow capital. The rise in tuition and indebtedness within the context of economic crisis simply is the militarization of campus; *they are one and the same*."[5]

In other words, to paraphrase UC Davis faculty member and activist Nathan Brown, police brutality is an administrative tool to enforce tuition increases[6] precisely because of the link between privatization and militarization. In short, it is no accident that we see the repeated deployment of armored, armed, militarized police forces on campuses where large crowds of students and faculty and staff gather to protest the erosion of the accessibility and affordability of public education. Nor should it have been surprising that in July 2012, the UC Berkeley police department briefly considered the purchase of an armored military tank with grant funds from the U.S. Department of Homeland Security. The UC administration is willing to, able to, and indeed does deploy militarized force in order to make the cost of dissent high. Note that its deployment of both campus police and external police forces makes the neoliberal state complicit in the militarization of these campus spaces. So this is one sense in which it is in the administration's interest to make sure that the cost of protest and dissent is high. The message is clear that if dissent occurs publicly and collectively, those involved are likely to be pepper sprayed, beaten with batons, shoved to the ground, shot with lead paint bullets, and so forth. It is better, in short, to stay home and silent rather than to participate in such events.

The extent to which the UC leadership wants to underscore its encouragement of such silence can be seen in the text of a travel advisory ostensibly issued by the UC Office of the President (UCOP) before May Day protests of 2012. The memo apparently warned UC students, faculty, and staff to avoid all rallies and demonstrations as a precaution and offered "tips for reducing vulnerability," which include "avoid[ing] all large gatherings," because "even seemingly peaceful rallies can spur violent activity or be met with resistance by security forces."[7] Furthermore, one is advised to avoid "cities with a large immigrant population and strong labour groups." If this advice is not followed, the memo offered a glimpse of the violent and militarized response that likely awaits: "Bystanders may be arrested or harmed by security forces using water cannons, tear gas or other measures to control crowds." Members of the UC community that must travel near protests should "dress conservatively . . . maintain a low profile by avoiding demonstration areas . . . [and] discussions of the issues at hand."[8] As Mark Levine notes, such advice might well have been offered to a black person in a white neighborhood forty years ago: "Dress well, stay low, don't talk to strangers, stay clear of the police, and most of all, don't do anything to draw suspicion to yourself. And for God's sake, don't mess with the one per cent."[9] When those tasked with advocating for public education issue such public messages, the thinly veiled warning to dissidents within the UC system is clear: stay away from places with lots of poor immigrants and/or wage-working people, especially those with the nerve to fight for their rights; keep your head down; keep your voice down; don't cause trouble; and don't get involved with troublemakers. Or else.

Criminalization Part I: Rhetoric

I turn now to the second component of the enforcement strategy. The second thing that the UC system needs in order to enforce privatization is the ability to make the cost of dissent high by systematically criminalizing those who protest, speak out, and dissent against privatization. This criminalization takes two forms. The first is a kind of rhetorical criminalization, which we actually saw used most effectively in the nationwide dismantling of Occupy encampments, where city and local officials justified the often violent expulsion of the occupiers with the vague and unsubstantiated threat that such people posed to law and order. The city authorities responsible for authorizing the often violent expulsion of Occupy encampments engaged in forms of rhetoric designed to justify the need for such violent response by casting the protests as potentially threatening and even perhaps criminal, with the idea that the extended occupation of public spaces by citizens (some of whom were unemployed) posed a threat to law and order. While the precise nature of the threat was rarely specified, such justifications often used the rhetorical strategy of linking the presence of protestors to unemployment, bad personal hygiene, the recreational use of alcohol and narcotics, and sometimes sexual predation. The general image evoked was that of dirty people who have no jobs and nothing better to do than to shout loudly about their anger, get drunk, and perhaps prey on innocent women. In the public imagination, it was suggested, such people should be seen as somehow threatening, and their loud, angry, and disruptive behavior—along with their somewhat questionable status on the margins of society, as evidenced by the dodginess of their personal bearing and activities and their concentration in large numbers in tents in public places—should be seen as a source of concern. And it is precisely this concern that should rightfully cause city officials to bring in the forces of law and order.

The UC leadership's rhetorical strategy in defense of its own militarized response to various protests was uncanny in its similarity. Perhaps the best example comes from Nathan Brown's excellent analysis of the Reynoso report, in which UC Davis chancellor Linda Katehi, a month after the pepper spray incident at Davis, offered her explanation of why she had to authorize police presence in order to remove protesters from the Quad: "We were worried at the time about that because the issues from Oakland were in the news and the use of drugs and sex and other things, and you know here we have very young students . . . we worried especially about having very young girls and other students with older people who come from the outside without any knowledge of their record."[10] To quote Brown, "The best rationale our Chancellor can come up with (after a month's reflection) for a major police operation against non-violent student protesters is 'the use of drugs and sex and other things' in the midst of 'very young girls'. . . . In brief, all [she] has to offer in its defense is the danger of sex and drugs, of 'older people,' and the terribly frightening specter of 'Oakland' [presumably referring to the Occupy Oakland debacle]."[11] Indeed, this rationale echoed almost exactly the somewhat absurd logic repeatedly employed by city authorities that the combination of public anger and many bodies in tents and the possible presence of sex and drugs automatically equals a potential threat that must be squashed through a militarized police response.

But other rhetorical moves made by UC leadership were rather less laughable and must be taken more seriously in their deliberate intent to criminalize dissent. Perhaps the most infamous was the attempt by UC Berkeley chancellor Robert Birgenau to rationalize the police beating of unarmed and unthreatening students and faculty by claiming that linking arms and forming a human chain in order to prevent police from gaining access to an encampment, as the Berkeley protesters did, was "not non-violent civil disobedience."[12] Indeed, such a discursive strategy, while widely reviled and thus hopefully repudiated (Chancellor Birgenau subsequently resigned, citing personal reasons), was notably never contradicted by anyone in the UC leadership. Meanwhile, its logic rested on the ability to argue that the actions of the protesters were loud enough, aggressive enough, confrontational enough, and disruptive enough—even if they were not directly violent—to warrant the violent response. In other words, protesters had provoked or invited police violence simply through the disruptiveness and provocation, and thus the subjectively perceived aggressiveness, of their tactics.[13]

But what precisely had the protesters done that could be perceived as aggressive, confrontational, disruptive, and thus deserving of violence? Or, in other words, what about their behavior could have plausibly, albeit subjectively, been interpreted as "not nonviolent"? Indeed, a wonderful analysis of these rhetorical strategies in the blog Reclaim UC reminds us that it is precisely the fact that the protesters refused to submit to the commands of the police that placed their actions outside the category of "nonviolence" according to the rationality of the police. The only thing remaining in the realm of the nonviolent, according to this logic, "is the absolute, uncritical obedience to their authority . . . in short, 'non-violence' according to the police means the uncritical compliance with the growing arbitrary power of the sovereign."[14]

Similar logic was used in the case of the UC Riverside (UCR) response to the crowd of student and faculty protesters at the regents' meeting on Riverside's campus, also mentioned in the opening vignette of this book's introduction. The administrative response to the hundreds-strong unarmed crowd—chanting peacefully, often using humorous slogans, music, drumbeats, and dance—was to declare the nonviolent assembly unlawful and to issue the command that everyone disperse or otherwise be subject to forcible removal. Through this declarative act, conducted anonymously and without any public justification (the precise responsibility for the declaration of unlawful assembly remains as yet unaccounted for by the UCR administration, despite repeated requests), every single student and faculty member doing nothing other than standing in a public space at a public university was thereby criminalized. When protesters refused to disperse and instead more actively surrounded the location of the meeting, police in riot gear escalated the situation by shoving batons and fences into the bodies of protesters and eventually shooting lead paint bullets at an entirely unarmed crowd. While the UCR leadership subsequently expressed the usual regret for the injury to protesters, at no point did their rhetoric do anything except defend such violence as regrettably necessary by pointing to the threats posed by the angry and active opposition of the protesters.

In both a public communiqué to the campus as well as a town hall meeting, then UCR chancellor Tim White repeatedly relied on the argument that the protestors were somehow potentially threatening and that they were endangering the safety and security of all present. Despite the existence of multiple videos demonstrating that it was clearly the police in riot gear rather than the unarmed protesters who had escalated the violence, the UCR administration continued to use vague, questionable, and nebulous imagery in order to argue otherwise. At a town hall meeting on March 6, 2012,[15] White projected photos of protesters carrying signs, claiming that such signs were potentially injurious. According to White, other photos ostensibly showed students menacing or threatening members of the administration, yet not a single one of these images showed anything other than protesters in various confrontational poses, sometimes expressing anger. No actual violence or threat of violence is seen in any of the photographic or video evidence. Yet the administration continued to rely on vague and unsubstantiated threats to public safety in order to justify bringing in a highly militarized police force and the subsequent escalation of violence.

A system-wide review of the various campus responses to protests was then conducted by the UC general counsel and the Berkeley Law School dean at the request of UC president Mark Yudof. Despite the lip service it paid to the importance of "free expression, robust discourse and vigorous debate," the resulting Robinson-Edley report was even more striking in the discursive gymnastics it produced in order to further widen the scope of the university's ability to respond to protest with a variety of militarized strategies. It begins by stating that civil disobedience "by definition involves violating laws or regulations, and that civil disobedience will generally have consequences for those engaging in it because of the impact it can have on the rest of the campus community."[16] Thus the report preemptively suggests that offering any resistance whatsoever to any "regulations" (without examining what can fall under the scope of such "regulations") can be construed as threatening, provocative, confrontational, and potentially violent and thus worthy of whatever "consequences" the campus authorities deem fit. In an echo of the discursive strategies that preceded it, the very presence of militarized forces on campuses is deemed to be beyond question, and at no point do these reports and strategies address the responsibility to curb the largely disproportionate responses that such militarized forces present to unarmed resisting dissenters.[17] But if unarmed protesters express any confrontation or active opposition in response to such militarization, then they have perhaps automatically declared themselves suspect and even worthy of a violent response.

In one fell swoop, the administrative response to campus protest has managed to completely subvert the logic of nonviolent protest, effectively criminalizing all forms of it by focusing on the potentially threatening nature of such protest. If the very refusal to submit to authority, and indeed the moral obligation to actively and confrontationally oppose such authority is at the very core of nonviolent resistance, then reserving the right to construe any such form of active opposition or resistance as threatening (and thus worthy of "consequences") potentially criminalizes all nonviolent protesters for undertaking the very act that defines nonviolence resistance. And in continuing to insist that civil disobedience can "have consequences" because of its "impact" on a community, these strategies serve to hint darkly that disruptive and confrontational actions that express public anger can be equated with dangerous and potentially threatening behavior, thus justifying a potentially violent response. In invoking this logic, the Robinson-Edley report seems to reserve the right to criminalize protesters for nonviolent behavior if it can be deemed sufficiently oppositional or disruptive.

Moreover, leading with the assumption that civil disobedience can have an "impact on a campus" is similar in rhetorical function to the "ticking time bomb" scenario in debates on U.S.-sponsored torture. That is, the question encourages the interlocutor to imagine a hypothetical situation that would justify the use of force and suggests that we use such hypothetical situations as the basis of policy.[18] It allows administrators to equate disruptive and potentially embarrassing student behavior with "dangerous" behavior, which requires a police presence—ostensibly for safety. At the same time, it functions to shift critical attention away from the *actual* use of repressive force, which generally has little or nothing to do with these hypothesized rationales.[19] Leading by assuming that civil disobedience requires punishment because of its "impact" seems to leave the door open for a militarized response with no justification other than the vague and unsubstantiated threat of a so-called impact on campus.

It should of course be noted that in many of these instances of protest, the behavior of protesters was often disruptive, confrontational, oppositional, and laden with anger. At Berkeley, this meant simply locking arms and the refusal to disperse. But in other cases, protesters refused to allow officials to leave and blockaded exits. Angry and perhaps offensive language was thrown at police officers. The regents' meeting was occupied by students and eventually shut down. Authorities could have responded by recognizing the underlying causes of such expressions of public anger or choosing to recognize their moral underpinnings, even while disavowing those actions that were offensive or perhaps rude. They could even have acknowledged the slipperiness of terms like "violent" or "nonviolent," recognizing that nonviolent resistance spans a wide variety of different kinds of actions, some of which can be more disruptive, aggressive, and confrontational than others, while clarifying which forms of aggression are worthy of a violent response and which are not. Any of these statements would have fallen within the realm of reasonable moral responses to such situations. Instead, the UC leadership has chosen to adhere to an uncritical, monolithic, and unrepresentative caricature of *all* confrontational and disruptive methods of resistance as always potentially threatening.

Thus the UC leadership's ability to justifiably criminalize nonviolent dissenters appears to depend on making a convincing argument that anger, disruption, confrontation, and provocation equal danger to public safety. It rests on the ability to argue that dissenting loudly and collectively about the erosion of one's access to affordable public education makes one a threat to public safety, dangerous enough to warrant a heavily weaponized response in the name of the so-called public. What remains unexamined, of course, is who in particular represents this "public" whose safety is ostensibly at risk in such situations: in a mass e-mail to the UCR community following the regents' meeting protest, Chancellor White bemoaned the fact that nine of the officers involved in the militarized response—"our coworkers who are police"—received minor injuries. The bloodied knuckles sustained by police officers in the course of shoving batons into the bodies of protesters becomes the justification for the use of force: these very injuries, the e-mail suggests, demonstrate why the police "did need to use force at times . . . to protect themselves and ensure safety for others." Such appeals to "public" safety rest on the absurd assumption that if a confrontation between unarmed nonviolent protesters and those ostensibly charged with protecting public safety results in violence, then such violence must somehow be traceable to the party that is disruptive and confrontational yet unarmed rather than to the party that adheres to the most militarized, weaponized, and militant techniques of preemptive repression ever known to humankind. The "public" whose safety requires protection is easily conflated with those who already have legitimately sanctioned weapons at their disposal (thus ostensibly representing and supposedly protecting this public), while disruptive, loud, angry, and confrontational yet unarmed protesters are cast as potential criminals.

The logic at work in such argumentation is, of course, precisely the post-9/11 logic of the neoliberal state in response to the War on Terror and the PATRIOT Act. This logic rests on convincing us that a nebulous group of potentially dangerous and threatening "others" are "out there," coming to get us. Accordingly, those charged with protecting our safety and security—who, as it turns out, are the most weaponized, militarized, and militaristic elements of society—need to use force and sometimes suspend civil liberties in order to achieve this. As the bloggers at Reclaim UC have rightly noted, "This takes us to the somewhat self-evident point that the state has successfully instrumentalized and redefined the slippery term 'violence' to repress and criminalize various forms of dissent against austerity measures, and to shrink and eliminate established spaces and practices of constitutionally protected forms of political expression."[20] These authors also remind us that such logic follows "the classical expansion of the executive authority of the state, such as, for instance, the 2012 National Defense Authorization Act, passed with a provision that allows for the indefinite detention of terrorism suspects on US land, including citizens, without trial. Much more insidiously, the police operate within the juridical regime of the liberal state, while using interpretive tactics to bend definitions of crime and expand their own power to incriminate dissenting subjects."[21] As David Theo Goldberg notes, "crisis creation, chaos fabrication and management of state terror to fight the projection of terrorism"[22] allow states to conduct legitimate violence in the name of so-called civilized citizenry. "That the figure of the 'violent protester' has become a trope in the liberal media and a target of condemnation in popular liberal discourse is a direct effect and continuation of the logic of the violent state, masquerading behind the language of peace, order, and safety."[23] It is this same logic that governs the UC leadership's criminalization of dissent, following the neoliberal state's "promot[ion] of a new ahistorical stereotype of the 'violent protester,' structured around a logic of prejudice, stigma, and exclusion—where violence against protestors appears *a priori* reasonable and justified."[24]

Criminalization Part II: Laws

The second form of criminalization evident in the squashing of dissent uses the legal power of the neoliberal state and its complicity with the forces of capital to criminalize nonviolent protestors through legal channels. In March 2012, twelve UC Davis students and faculty—including Joshua Clover—were arrested and faced twenty-one misdemeanor charges and up to eleven years in jail for nonviolently blockading the campus branch of U.S. Bank. In early 2012, Clover and the eleven students—now dubbed the "Banker's Dozen"—had conducted a nonviolent sit-in at the bank office to protest its role in, and profiteering from, the ongoing privatization of public education at UC. The sit-in was designed to draw attention to the problematic nature of the relationship between the banks and the privatizing university. University contracts with banks encourage tuition hikes because banks stand to profit directly from rising tuition while the administration comes to rely on funding from bank contracts. Thus UC Davis's contract with U.S. Bank was explicitly predicated on the continued shift of funding for education from public to private sources. When the bank was finally forced to close its campus branch office in breach of its contract with UC Davis, it held the university responsible for all costs, claiming they were "constructively evicted" because the university had not responded by arresting the "illegal gathering." Shortly thereafter, at the behest of the UC Davis administration, the Davis district attorney charged the so-called Banker's Dozen with twenty counts each of obstructing movement in a public place and one count of conspiracy. If convicted, the protesters would face up to eleven years each in prison and $1 million in damages payable to U.S. Bank.

Another case of legal criminalization was in response to a March 29, 2012, meeting of the regents at UCLA, when three students were arrested and manhandled by police, even though they were not disobeying any police orders or resisting in any way. The students were charged with criminal offences, strip-searched, and, even more onerously, forced to post bail in excess of $10,000 each, which necessitated their raising $6,000 to pay the fees for their bonds. All three students had previous records of having engaged in civil disobedience at other times and were thought to have been targeted for this reason. UC president Mark Yudof is on record as having thanked the officers who conducted their arrest. Despite the subsequent dismissal of all charges by the San Francisco district attorney, the bond money posted by the students was not recoverable.

At the regents' meeting protest at UCR in January 2012, Ken Ehrlich, a lecturer from the UCR art department, also known to have been involved in previous instances of public protest against privatization, was assaulted by several police officers, subsequently charged with felony assault, and held on

$25,000 bail. Witnesses say that at the time of his arrest, Ehrlich was doing nothing other than holding a protest sign in the shape of a book. A video of the protest shows Ehrlich being pushed into the police line and then being slammed to the ground and dragged across the pavement by police. Although all charges were subsequently dropped, Ehrlich was forced to raise funds for his legal defense in the interim, money that is yet again not refundable or recoverable.

These and other instances of legal criminalization demonstrate clearly the collusion between university and state authorities in defense of private capital. In instances where the university does not directly criminalize its own faculty and students, it appears to encourage and even assist the state's legal authorities to act against those who threaten the systemic logic of privatization and neoliberalism. Even when charges are subsequently dropped and protestors pay no price in terms of their criminal records, they are left with the literal cost of financing their own bail or legal defense to the tune of thousands if not millions of dollars. Dissent is literally made to be prohibitively expensive. In contrast to the public rhetoric and discursive strategies addressed in the previous section, we see here that the university uses a strategy that calls upon the legal resources and mechanisms of the state to replicate the state's hostility to dissent against privatization and neoliberal disinvestment in public services. What is particularly clever about such a strategy is its delivery of threats without the use of speech or discourse. The discursive message is indeed that those who do not keep their heads low and their mouths shut will be made to pay a high price, quite literally. But this threatening message is never actually spoken. Rather, it is conveyed through the use of legal prosecution in which the university itself never seems to be directly involved but is always lurking in the shadows, always willing to comply with and support—if not encourage—such prosecution against dissenters.

Conclusion

I have offered here a particular window into the ways in which the interests, mechanisms, and operations of both the university system and the neoliberal state are aligned with those of private capital. Of course, that the academy is made to strategically ally with capital as a key piece of neoliberal consolidation should not surprise us. Rather, what is worth noting, I have argued here, is the *necessity* of the linkages between disinvestment in public education, militarization, and the criminalization of dissent. These necessary link-ages demonstrate this volume's premise that the university is an institution embedded in the hierarchies and inequalities of U.S. racial, gender, and class politics and shed light on the confluence of military and industrial interests as they appear within the U.S. university. I have sought also to emphasize the systematicity and multilayered complexity of this phenomenon. That is, the various pieces of this picture necessarily go together, as rhetoric, law, bureaucracy, and the force of arms all combine effectively to produce the desired end.

The neoliberal logic entailed in the privatization of the University of California is, I have argued, necessarily interlinked with the logic of militarization and the criminalization of dissent, because it employs a militarized enforcement strategy, coupled with a political rhetoric that criminalizes the specific behaviors involved in protest and dissent against these strategies. The militarization of the university campus is thus not simply a reflection of the increasing militarization of American law enforcement based on the logic of ongoing threats to public safety encoded in years of the War on Drugs and the War on Terror.[25] Rather, such militarization is one prong of a necessary enforcement strategy designed to convey that dissent against privatization is meant to be costly in inflicting various forms of legitimized violence upon those who dissent. The second prong of the enforcement strategy also conveys that dissenters will pay a high price by being criminalized, either through rhetoric that paints them as violent and therefore marginal, unworthy, and undesirable in the public imagination or through legal machinations that force them to expend tremendous financial resources on extricating themselves from prosecution.

The language of cost and price here, of course, reminds us of the ongoing hegemony—and perhaps victory—of the conceptual frameworks of neoliberalism and its theoretical accompaniments, such as rational choice theory, predominantly featured in neoclassical economics. These strategies of criminalization and militarization rest on sending signals to adversaries, encoded precisely in these languages, wherein value and worth are measured in terms of indicators such as price or cost, and rational actors are assumed to be guided by a universally comprehensible incentive structure. Thus the strategies of criminalization and militarization rest on de-incentivizing dissent, so to speak, assuming that dissenters will measure the costs inherent in their actions and choose rationally to cease from engaging in such dissent. The continued insistence on dissent is therefore resistance to the logic of

NEOLIBERALISM, MILITARIZATION, AND THE PRICE OF DISSENT · **141**

neoliberal privatization on multiple levels: it not only calls out the complicity of the university with the neoliberal state and the forces of private capital but also continues to dissent despite the "incentives" offered in exchange for desisting from dissent. And in so doing, it should be signaling its rejection not simply of privatization but of the entire conceptual baggage of neoliberalism, including its logics of rational choice, cost, price, and incentive, as well as its logic of structural violence. In other words, the ongoing struggle against the logic of neoliberal privatization requires that dissent continue, despite its high "price."

Notes

1. Christopher Newfield, *Unmaking the Public University: The Forty-Year Assault on the Middle Class* (Cambridge, Mass.: Harvard University Press, 2008).

2. See, for instance, Nathan Brown, "Five Theses on Privatization and the UC Struggle," Distribution of the Insensible, November 15, 2011, http://distributioninsensible .tumblr.com/post/12867650744/five-theses-on-privatization-and-the-uc-struggle; Stan A. Glantz, "The Problem Is Privatization, and It Can Be Reversed," Remaking the University, September 29, 2011, http://utotherescue.blogspot.com/2011/09/ problem-is-privatization-and-it-can-be.html; Bob Samuels, "UC Might Increase Tuition 81% over the Next Four Years," Changing Universities, September 12, 2011, http:// changinguniversities.blogspot.com/2011/09/uc-might-increase-tuition-81-over-next .html; Chris Newfield, "Just Trying to Say That We Don't Care," Remaking the University, December 29, 2010, http://utotherescue.blogspot.com/2010/12/just-trying-to -say-that-we-dont-care.html.

3. Anne-Marie Slaughter, "Occupy Wall Street and the Arab Spring," *Atlantic*, October 7, 2011, http://www.theatlantic.com/international/archive/2011/10/occupy -wall-street-and-the-arab-spring/246364. See also Mitchell Hartman, "Did the Arab Spring Spark the 'Occupy' Movement?," *Marketplace*, January 24, 2012, http://www .marketplace.org/topics/wealth-poverty/did-arab-spring-spark-occupy-movement; Rebecca Solnit, "How the Arab Spring and Occupy Wall Street Started with One Tunisian Man," *Mother Jones*, October 18, 2011, http://www.motherjones.com/politics/ 2011/10/arab-spring-occupy-wall-street-protests.

4. Bob Meister, "Debt, Democracy, and the Public University," Remaking the University, December 16, 2011, http://utotherescue.blogspot.com/2011/12/debt-democracy -andpublic-university.html.

5. Joshua Clover, "Reflections from UC Davis: On Academic Freedom and Campus Militarization," *College Literature* 39, no. 2 (2012): 5. Emphasis added.

6. Brown, "Five Theses on Privatization and the UC Struggle."

7. The full text of the travel advisory e-mail no longer appears anywhere online,

perhaps because of the controversy it generated. For most of the text of the advisory, see Maryam Monalis Gharavi, "Avoid All Demonstrations as a Precaution," *New Inquiry*, April 28, 2012, http://thenewinquiry.com/blogs/southsouth/avoid-all-demonstrations-as-a-precaution.

8. For more reports on the text of the travel advisory, see Jon Weiner, "May Day Warning from the University of California President: 'Avoid All Protests,'" *Nation*, April 30, 2012, http://www.thenation.com/blog/167642/may-day-warning-u-cal-president-avoid-all-protests#. Meanwhile, there is now some controversy over whether the travel alert came from UCOP or from Connexxus, the UC travel website. See Christopher Yee, "UCOP Says That Yudof Warning Travelers to Avoid May Day Protests Was False," *Daily Californian*, May 1, 2012, http://www.dailycal.org/2012/05/01/yudof-warns-travelers-to-avoid-may-day-protests.

9. Mark Levine, "How Ego and Ideology Are Destroying the World's Greatest Public University," *Al Jazeera*, May 11, 2012, http://www.aljazeera.com/indepth/opinion/2012/05/201251195339240940.html.

10. Nathan Brown, "The Reynoso Report: A Portrait of Administrative Malice, Stupidity, Incompetence and Immaturity," Remaking the University, April 11, 2012, http://reclaimuc.blogspot.com/2012/04/reynoso-report-portrait-of.html.

11. Brown, "The Reynoso Report."

12. "Message to the Campus Community about 'Occupy Cal,'" UC Berkeley News Center, UC Berkeley Office of Public Affairs, November 10, 2011, http://newscenter.berkeley.edu/2011/11/10/message-to-the-campus-community-about-occupy-cal/.

13. Rei Terada, "Not Non-Violent Civil Disobedience," Work without Dread, November 11, 2011, http://workwithoutdread.blogspot.com/2011/11/not-nonviolent-civil-disobedience.html.

14. "On Violence and Non-Violence, Once Again: Lessons from Recent Political Developments on the Berkeley Campus (Part 1)," Reclaim UC, March 21, 2012, http://reclaimuc.blogspot.com/2012/03/on-violence-and-nonviolence-once-again.html.

15. Footage available at http://chancellor.ucr.edu/webcast_archive.html, click on Town Hall Meeting Webcast of March 6, 2012, scroll to 68:00.

16. Christopher F. Edley Jr. and Charles F. Robinson, "Response to Protests on UC Campuses: A Report to University of California President Mark G. Yudof," September 13, 2012, 2, http://campusprotestreport.universityofcalifornia.edu/documents/protest-report-091312.pdf.

17. Bob Ostertag, "Militarization of Campus Police," *Huffington Post*, November 19, 2011, http://www.huffingtonpost.com/bob-ostertag/uc-davis-protest_b_1103039.html.

18. See Bob Brecher, *Torture and the Ticking Bomb* (Malden: Blackwell, 2007); Alfred W. McCoy, "The Myth of the Ticking Time Bomb," *The Progressive*, October 2006, http://www.progressive.org/mag_mccoy1006; Conor Friedersdorf, "Torture

Opponents Were Right," *Atlantic*, May 5, 2011, http://www.theatlantic.com/politics/archive/2011/05/torture-opponents-were-right/238387.

19. I owe this point to my colleague Bronwyn Leebaw.

20. "On Violence and Non-Violence."

21. Ibid.

22. David Theo Goldberg, "Killing Me Softly: Civility/Race/Violence," *Review of Education, Pedagogy and Cultural Studies* 27 (2005): 345.

23. "On Violence and Non-Violence."

24. Ibid.

25. Norm Stamper, "Paramilitary Policing from Seattle to Occupy Wall Street," *The Nation*, November 28, 2011, http://www.thenation.com/article/164501/paramilitary-policing-seattle-occupy-wall-street.

5

Faculty Governance at the University of Southern California

Laura Pulido

If USC ever wants to be taken seriously amongst the Big Boys of higher ed, it MUST institute a faculty controlled promotion and tenure system to provide legitimacy. This is something administrators will have a hard time comprehending, because they think prestige is all about grabbing big-name profs with big money, or building big centers for this and that sexy topic, or pleasing the big donors. Those things help, and USC has done a lot of it, but in the end a university's academic prestige is a subtle thing that rests on the quality of faculty and their reputations among large networks of scholars. That is, the faculty ARE the university. Students come and go, and so do administrators. Faculty need to stay and feel respected, inside and out, for the university to succeed.

—Richard Walker, emeritus professor of geography, UC Berkeley[1]

I write as a faculty member of a wealthy, private institution, the University of Southern California (USC). While there is a rapidly growing literature that explores the current economic crisis and how it is restructuring public universities—and higher education more generally—USC is enjoying unprecedented wealth in addition to new opportunities and privileges. While in some ways, these two situations could not be more distinct, in fact, they are deeply connected. Christopher Newfield has argued that the latest round of attacks on public institutions is restructuring all higher education so that soon only private schools will make up the top-tier universities.[2] While many public school faculty are fighting privatization and the erosion of academic quality, there is no escaping the fact that the public–private chasm is growing. Already a small set of elite, private institutions are considered the pinnacle of higher education in the United States and set the standards in many areas of the academy. One sphere that is of grave concern in this moment of transition is faculty governance. While long considered a hallmark of higher education, its strength and vitality is being challenged by privatization. USC offers one example of how faculty governance works—or perhaps more accurately, does not work—in a culture steeped in privatization.

USC has spent the last twenty years working very hard to join the ranks of top-tier private institutions. While its academic profile has improved tremendously and the school continues to advance academically, far less attention has been paid to faculty governance. Yet the issue of faculty governance in a private university should be of concern to everyone in the academy, as the policies, practices, and philosophies of private elite schools are disseminated through the larger culture of higher education. However, it is equally true that care must be taken not to draw too stark a distinction between public and private universities. While there are significant differences, USC *is* a nonprofit institution that is tax exempt and supposed to serve the public good. While USC routinely uses its private status as a shield to deflect any demands for openness, I wish to problematize the supposed sanctity of its private status in light of the massive public subsidies it receives. In reality, this latest round of "privatization" in higher education is the latest struggle over "who learns, who teaches, what, and to what end."[3] It is my intent in writing this chapter to encourage all members of the academy to reflect on the importance of faculty governance and the price it exacts—either by ignoring it or by fighting for it. A second purpose is to encourage USC faculty in particular to reflect on the current state of faculty governance on our campus and whether this serves us, students, and the larger community.

The focus of this chapter is a struggle over USC's tenure process. Because many people have and are participating in this effort, this chapter should in no way be seen as a definitive or comprehensive account. For one, the story is too vast to be told in the allotted pages. In addition, I am writing from my personal vantage point and experience, with particular attention to issues of faculty governance. It is my hope that others will write their own experiences so a more robust and accurate narrative will emerge. There is much to be learned, analyzed, and shared.

I write this chapter as someone involved in critical ethnic studies (CES). My disciplinary affiliation and identity is important because from my perspective, CES, and Chicana/o studies in particular—my intellectual roots— have always been committed to *both* the production of scholarly knowledge as well as opening up institutions of higher education to people who have historically been excluded from its reach. As a working-class Chicana and high school dropout, I was saved from a life of working at Kmart only by the goodness of California taxpayers and the community college system.[4] Accordingly, I have always felt that keeping institutions open, accountable, and transparent is part of my mission. And despite the fact that I have worked in a private institution for almost twenty years, I carry that experience with me: a commitment that has brought me into conflict with USC's administration.

The first part of this chapter sets the stage by focusing on USC's unprecedented efforts to improve its academic standing. The second part details how such dynamics have played out in the tenure process and how USC responded to faculty efforts to challenge its practices. In the conclusion I bring the story up to date and consider where USC might go from here.

Keeping Up with the Harvards

USC was established in Los Angeles in 1880 as part of a major wave of U.S. higher education institutions. From the beginning it played a key role in training professionals for the Los Angeles region, including social workers, dentists, lawyers, doctors, architects, and many others. Such a mission was in keeping with the culture of higher education at the time insofar as it provided the knowledge-power to extend the United States' international reach as well as provide domestic training and skills.[5] Partly because of its historic focus on the professions, it only recently developed a serious liberal arts program. For many years the well-known UCLA–USC rivalry was centered primarily on sports, as there was no real competition when it came to academics. Indeed, I recall when I first joined the faculty in 1993 being somewhat shocked at the dramatic range of student abilities—including some who were barely literate. I remember thinking, "Oh, so this is what affirmative action for the wealthy, white, and connected looks like."[6]

But unbeknownst to me, big changes were afoot under President Steven Sample, who served from 1991 to 2010. A decision had been made that USC was going to become a serious academic institution. Over the next two decades, through a combination of long-range planning, public relations, fund-raising, and highly centralized control, USC began changing. Major initiatives were undertaken to improve both graduate and undergraduate programs and to recruit top faculty. Billions were invested in new buildings (especially in the sciences) and well-conceived public relations campaigns. Over time I saw a difference in my classroom. My classes were soon peppered with students who could have gone to any university in the country. Indeed, in the 1997–1998 academic year, USC accepted fewer than half of its freshman applicants—a bellwether indicator for the university.[7] It was also in the 1990s that it began its "Building on Excellence" campaign, which netted USC $2.85 billion. Since then, it seems that there is always some fundraising campaign under way, and USC has certainly proven its capacity to raise funds.[8] Currently, it is seeking to raise $6 billion through its "Campaign for the University of Southern California."

This fund-raising is seen as key to improving the academic reputation of the university. Perhaps because it was long considered an academic backwater, USC has had an inferiority complex that it is in the process of overcoming. The mantra of the new president, Max Nikias, is for USC to enter the ranks of "undisputed elite institutions," which are defined as the Harvards, Princetons, Caltechs, and Stanfords of the world. Indeed, in a recent annual address to the faculty, President Nikias boasted, "The freshman class houses almost three times as many Caltech-caliber students as Caltech itself." He went on to explain that Caltech has about 200 students with almost perfect GPAs and SAT scores, while USC has 550 such students.[9] While recruiting Caltech-caliber students is certainly one indicator of academic quality, and I respect the desire to improve academically, I am equally concerned with the *culture* of the institution. What is it like to be a worker there? Especially for tenure-track faculty? What is the culture of a private university aspiring to elite status?[10]

It is often heard on the USC campus that the school has undergone the most dramatic improvement in U.S. academic history over the shortest period of time. I don't know if this is true or not, but I would not doubt it. One of the factors that allowed this phenomenal shift is the fact that USC is an extremely hierarchical institution with very limited faculty governance. At the highest level, USC is governed by a board of trustees. This includes fifty voting members as well as a slew of honorary and emeriti trustees. While most are drawn from corporate leadership, there are also a number of lawyers, top USC administrators, and a community leader or two. Examples include Rick Caruso, a major developer; Yang Ho Cho, the CEO of Korean Air; and Ray Irani of Occidental Petroleum.[11] While there are many assets that such individuals undoubtedly bring to the job, I am unsure how important building an accountable, transparent system of faculty governance is to them, given that most come from private corporations—not necessarily known for transparency.

Second-in-command at USC is the senior administration. This includes the president, the provost, and the people who oversee USC's hospitals, business operations, and fund-raising efforts.[12] Historically, both the board and senior administration have operated somewhat as an old boys' network, but this is beginning to change. Board appointments are carefully and strategically made to enhance the university's wealth and profile. For instance, there has been a concerted effort to cultivate Asian trustees to parallel USC's growing Asian presence. Moreover, the current provost, Elizabeth Garrett, is a female—something the university takes pride in.

The third tier consists of a group of elected bodies, including the academic senate. USC describes its governance as follows: "USC is governed by a Board of Trustees and led by President C. L. Max Nikias in conjunction with a senior administrative team responsible for managing institutional operations through administrative units and schools. Additionally, the academic senate, Undergraduate Student Government, and Graduate and Professional Student Senate have power to make studies, reports and recommendations to the president in matters pertaining to their constituencies."[13] This arrangement is known as "shared governance." Although governance is supposedly shared, note that the academic senate is presented on the same level as student government and is relegated to making reports and recommendations. Few faculty see it as an independent entity. One reason is that the vice-provost for faculty affairs regularly attends academic senate meetings. Crucially, the individual serving in this post is *appointed* by the administration, which I see as a tremendous conflict of interest. The presence of the vice-provost for faculty affairs at academic senate meetings can preclude free-flowing debate among faculty, as a representative of the administration is always present. The university website describes the vice-provost's duties as follows: "As Vice Provost, he serves as the senior executive officer responsible to the Provost for USC's 4300 faculty."[14] Note who the vice-provost is responsible to: the provost. Although the members of the academic senate are elected, as we have seen, the body itself does not have any real power—they can only make recommendations. There is no directly elected individual or body with real power that is accountable to the faculty.[15]

I spend this time reviewing USC's administrative structure because it has been instrumental in allowing the institution to achieve such academic heights in a short period of time. There was scant need for faculty input, and major academic reforms were certainly not faculty led. Of course, the administration would often convene committees to rubber-stamp plans or otherwise provide a front of legitimacy—but make no mistake, this was all from the top. In my own experience, I have sat on university committees that were pointless. Circa 2005 I sat on the Vice-Provost Task Force on Graduate Education. We met twice. I recall the chair of the committee being frustrated that we, the faculty, did not seem to be coming up with the kind of ideas and suggestions she wanted. As far as I know, nothing ever came of the committee: no report, no recommendation. It was simply an exercise in creating the illusion that faculty had meaningful input. While a small event in itself, it illuminates a larger culture characterized by backroom deals, a lack of transparency, no real faculty governance, a commitment to avoiding a paper trail, and a merciless drive to become a top-ranked institution. I now turn to how these dynamics have played out in the tenure process.

Tenure at USC: The Black Hole

Not surprisingly, as USC underwent this dramatic transformation, there were profound changes for faculty. Some of these were most welcome, like being able to hire colleagues without a national search through the "Senior Hiring Initiative." This was an effort to bring academic stars to USC to bolster its rankings or otherwise "transform" certain fields and departments. Others changes were simply bothersome. I recall that one year when I was undergraduate advisor, I was charged with getting my colleagues to call potential incoming students that had indicated an interest in my department and encourage them to come to USC.[16] Still, other changes were extremely damaging, including the tenure process. Because for so long USC was not academically rigorous, there are some older faculty who would not, by the new standards, be considered academically competitive. Indeed, I know faculty who never published after the dissertation. But this was the new USC. In order to advance in the academic rankings, tenure standards were going to have to change. Thus there was a new and unprecedented set of pressures and expectations placed on junior faculty.

To clarify, I agree that tenure standards needed to change. I don't think anyone benefits from faculty who don't publish past the dissertation. Having said that, however, I believe that the standards need to be reasonable, fair, transparent, and adhere to a consistent set of procedures. This has been unattainable to date at USC. The new expectations coupled with a culture of secrecy and a lack of accountability have led to serious problems. As a result, there were many who saw tenure as an ever-moving target. Indeed, at a recent tenure workshop for junior faculty (a new innovation at USC), a colleague reported that the workshop leader explained that even if a candidate did all that was expected, he or she may be denied tenure simply because he or she did not fit with the dean's vision for the unit. The fact that nobody at the workshop questioned this statement and what it meant for the procedure just outlined is a powerful testament to the kind of political culture that USC is intent on cultivating among its faculty. Moreover, such a practice would partially explain the seemingly capricious nature of some tenure decisions. Exacerbating the problem was the fact that substantive reasons are not regularly given for tenure denials. As a senior member of the department, I felt the tenure process for my junior colleagues was a black hole that not only depressed faculty morale but often led to major problems in terms of staffing, program building, and emotional devastation.[17]

Tenure became a growing problem as the 2000s wore on. My department regularly put faculty up for tenure—with positive votes—and they would be rejected in a variety of ways. The *ways* that tenure decisions were rendered, or not, is illuminating, as it shows how private universities can operate. For instance, it was stated in the faculty handbook that tenure decisions were to be made by commencement (around May 15). In the case of one colleague, commencement had come and gone and there was no decision. He then received a phone call from an administrator who told him that they wanted permission to delay his decision until June 30. He was told there was a "snafu." Not feeling he had any real options, he agreed. Certainly, most people would not read this as a good sign. As it turned out, this person had also applied for a job elsewhere (as is common for USC tenure candidates), and he had received an offer with tenure. Unfortunately, this new university was not willing to wait until June 30 for USC's decision. He informed USC of his other offer and there was a resounding silence. Not surprisingly, my colleague took the new job. This happened to at least two people in my department—both men of color. In these cases, delaying tactics were used to deny someone tenure without having to actually say it. This is a clever strategy on the part of USC as no tenure denial is ever recorded. Thus the record never shows that two men of color were denied tenure. While this tactic may help USC's racial diversity data, it is disastrous to faculty and student morale.[18]

Another strategy was simply to ignore the deadline altogether. In one case a woman of color had received a retention offer that included the promise of coming up early for tenure. Unfortunately, this was never put in writing (a pervasive tactic), and she came up at the originally planned time (in 2006). Although her department voted unanimously in support of her tenure, near commencement in 2007 the dean called to inform her that the decision was being postponed. No explanation was given. Indeed, the dean himself said he did not understand the delay. Finally, in 2008 this faculty member received tenure, after two years of tremendous anxiety and frustration.

In yet another instance, a woman of color was told in her job offer letter that she would be given a tenure decision by commencement 2009. In May of that year, she was informed by the senior associate dean of her school that the decision had been "deferred." Despite the candidate's best efforts, no explanation was forthcoming. She was then told that her decision would be rendered by the end of the summer, then by the end of fall, and then sometime in February. In March 2010 she was asked to submit additional materials on multiple occasions. She was finally granted tenure in May 2010. No explanation for the delays was ever provided.

Other cases have impacted candidates more materially. In one instance, a woman of color was offered a position as an associate professor with tenure. Delighted, she resigned from her home institution and passed on the tenure process there. Three months later, she received a call from the departmental chair (acting on orders from above) informing her that the terms had been changed: she was now being offered a job without tenure. Unfortunately, by the time she received word of the revised job offer, it was too late to apply for tenure at her home institution. It was only through the hard work and commitment of her colleagues at her current university that she was eventually able to come up for tenure, but not after significant cost to herself and her family in terms of anxiety, money, and damaged careers for both her and her partner.

Finally, in the most recent case, a woman of color was denied tenure after receiving the full support of her department. This time, however, she hired a lawyer and filed a grievance claiming discrimination, among other things. During the course of the proceedings, it was revealed that the dean had made cold calls inquiring with outside scholars about the candidate—dossier unseen. When she charged that this practice represented a violation of USC's tenure procedures, we collectively learned that was not the case. Not only does the provost have the right to engage in all manner of outside communication, but she "may authorize exceptions or waivers to this manual or other policies." Such a policy essentially renders the entire established process moot.[19]

You will note that in none of these instances do I discuss the merit of individual tenure cases. While important, it is an entirely different matter. People

Figure 5.1. Flyer from Tenure Forum, 2010. Courtesy of Sarita See.

of goodwill can and do disagree on tenure requirements. My concern is the question of *process*. How should faculty be treated in the tenure process? What rights might one reasonably expect to have? Whether we conceive of faculty as workers or colleagues, I believe that they should be treated with honesty, respect, and in a dignified manner. These are values that are elusive to the USC tenure process. USC can function with limited accountability like the private corporation that it is because the administration knows there are few avenues for faculty recourse. It was against this backdrop of tenure problems that a small group of faculty began to mobilize in 2010.

Challenging the Tenure Process at the Corporate University

The precipitating event for this faculty mobilization was yet another tenure denial. While many felt that "Lisa" certainly warranted tenure, her denial could not readily be separated from this larger history and context. For me personally, it felt like it was the last straw in a long line of deeply disappointing decisions that were never fully explained nor embodied a logical and transparent procedure. A group of Lisa's colleagues convened and discussed various options. Calling ourselves the Committee for Tenure Justice (CTJ), we drew from the experience of faculty at the University of Michigan in 2008, when several women of color were simultaneously denied tenure.[20] We began by writing a letter to the administration stating our concerns in regards to both Lisa's case as well as the larger issue of tenure denials, particularly among women of color. We then circulated an online petition that was delivered to the administration and began a national letter-writing campaign among those in Lisa's fields in support of her tenure. In addition, we convened a forum on the USC tenure process that included several scholars who had previously been denied tenure at USC (see Figure 5.1).

It is important to note how the administration responded to these efforts. First, if it is not already evident, this is *not* the kind the activity that the administration had come to expect or deem appropriate. This was entirely counter to USC's culture: on the part of both faculty *and* the administration. While I am very critical of the administration, it must be underscored that USC faculty have been complicit in creating this culture. Over the decades we have allowed this system to flourish by *not* regularly challenging the administration in any substantive or collective fashion. USC is an ideal place for those who simply wish to do their research and teach or, alternatively, for those who want to garner a modicum of power by becoming one of the handful of professors who regularly interface between the administration and the faculty. It is precisely because of this culture that outspoken criticism was considered aberrant behavior. The fact that the members of CTJ were already located on the fringe—as primarily women of color and queer faculty—facilitated the university's efforts to dismiss our concerns by ignoring us and disciplining us.

The college dean, along with Lisa's departmental chair and the vice-dean for college diversity, responded by writing letters to all outside faculty who had written letters of support. In it, they stressed the validity of the USC tenure process and the need for privacy and championed USC's diversity record (you will hear this last point repeatedly). They closed their letter stating, "To make baseless suggestions about improper conduct or disturbing patterns is ill-informed and irresponsible."[21] Specifically, they were responding to the letter writers' charges of discrimination in the tenure process, but they did so in a way that speaks volumes about the culture of USC as a whole. Not only is the mere suggestion of discrimination or a problematic tenure process dismissed, but they imply that no one has the *right* to question USC's decisions. To do so is supposedly a violation of the institution's rights.[22] Despite the administrators' claims to the contrary, it turns out that such charges of discriminatory or unjust tenure review processes were hardly baseless.

Another avenue pursued by the CTJ was to request a meeting with the dean's office. The dean himself did not meet with us, but his right-hand man did as well as two administrators, the vice-dean of college diversity and a special advisor to the provost, both of whom are men of color. The fact that two senior men of color were involved is hardly incidental but part of USC's practice of "racial management." The bodies of these two men of color performed important ideological "work." Their positionality enhanced USC's ability to dismiss any charges of racism. Collectively, strategically located colored bodies, the diversity statistics, the existence of the Office of Equity and Diversity (more on that later), and the adamant dismissal of all criticism constituted USC's shield in these early battles.

At the meeting, we in CTJ stated clearly our concerns as well as a list of demands. One of the demands that merits elaboration was for an independent investigation into a perceived pattern of racial and gender bias in the tenure process against women of color. The administration responded in two ways. First, in a follow-up memo, the administrators said that these concerns were best referred to the president of the University Committee on Academic Promotion and Tenure (UCAPT). In some institutions this might actually mean something substantive, but at USC it meant nothing would happen and, not surprisingly, nothing did. Indeed, the follow-up memo stated that they also thought our call for an independent investigation was "jumping the gun."[23]

The other response, based on our allegations of possible discrimination, was to refer "the case" to the Office of Equity and Diversity (OED) for an investigation. This last move posed a definite challenge to the CTJ and its allies. On the one hand, this was entirely in keeping with USC's—and perhaps most institutions'—normal procedures. Any charge of discrimination must be investigated. On the surface, this seems like a good thing. In reality, there were several factors complicating such an investigation. First, transforming Lisa's tenure denial into a "case" served to legalize the problem and response. Legal cases often parallel the act of an arrest: they serve to isolate and individualize collective problems.[24] This meant that Lisa's tenure decision would be investigated, but the larger pattern may be ignored. While we certainly supported any move that might provide Lisa with grounds to appeal her case, we knew that this course of action would not address the larger problem. The second problem with the OED's investigation is that many of us had heard of or been involved in previous investigations—and they all resulted in the same conclusion: no evidence of discrimination. Thus we knew that this was simply a legal exercise that USC had to undertake in order to exonerate itself.[25] The third problem with this strategy was that it put us on legal terrain—and there was no way we could win against USC lawyers. The institution has very deep pockets, both in-house lawyers as well as outside ones on retainer, and a history of paying off employees in exchange for silence. And finally, an investigation is very much in keeping with the institution's overall strategy of racial management.

I should clarify that I do not think USC is unique in this regard. But as a litigious society that is structured to reproduce the power and rights of corporate capital and that has commodified the entire process of dealing with social transgressions, we have created a system that at this particular juncture is largely incapable of addressing structural racism or sexism. Not only is the methodology of the investigation limited to revealing overt forms of discrimination, but it requires either self-confession, a witness, or other forms of tangible evidence to legitimize the claims. While certainly none of this is conducive to dealing with structural inequality, the process is especially pernicious because it masquerades as a form of relief. In other words, nothing else needs to be done. The affirmative action investigation is one of the most powerful tools of racial management and social control that universities have at their disposal. Consequently, it is utterly useless to USC employees but extremely useful to the administration.

Because of all the problems surrounding the investigation, people had varied feelings about participating in it. One compelling reason to participate was that should Lisa ever decide to take her case to court, she would not have a legal leg to stand on if she did not exhaust the university's internal process. A minority believed that the OED offered a path to dealing with real problems.[26] Still others, myself included, did not want to participate in what we saw as a sham in the first place. Thus there were a range of responses that no doubt contributed to the "investigation's" conclusion—big surprise— that there had been no problem with Lisa's tenure process and certainly no discrimination.[27] In a letter from the provost that accompanied the findings of the OED's report, it stated, "As we do whenever a charge of discrimination is raised, I referred your letter of last September for investigation by the Office of Equity and Diversity. I am enclosing the investigative report sent to me. I trust you will be pleased as I am that the investigation does not support a finding of discrimination."[28]

The investigative report itself is worthy of its own study. Here I will limit myself to a few observations. For the most part, it simply compares concerns voiced by interviewees with written policy or, in some cases, concludes that the faculty who raised the initial charges were confused. There is no mention of actual interviews with administrators or others who played key roles in Lisa's denial of tenure.[29] For instance, a commonly heard complaint across the college was the lack of transparency with the tenure process.[30] The report noted this as a faculty concern, but instead of seriously engaging with it, the OED's report simply states, "It appears (as set forth in a-6 of the UCAPT manual) that USC places great value on respecting the confidentiality of tenure evaluations, so as to promote honest and unbiased evaluations, free of lobbying or pressure."

This response merits a bit of elaboration. First, to a certain extent, it is a sleight of hand, as the response continues a pattern of suggesting that we wished to know the identities of the evaluators. At no time did we ever ask to know the identity of tenure evaluators. Rather, we simply wanted to know the *content* of the letters, even in summary form. But the university consistently glossed over this crucial distinction by responding as if we wanted to know individual identities—something that few people at USC (and elsewhere) would support. By not dealing with the specificity of our demands, the university sought to portray our demands as unreasonable.

In addition, the OED's response is particularly frustrating because it consists of a reference to a value stated in a manual, which does not tell us anything except what USC says about itself. As far as we can tell, the OED pursued no real investigation beyond the faculty handbook. Questions that might have been explored include the following: What constitutes transparency? Is there are a relationship between transparency and discrimination? Lastly, the OED's response also reveals who it sees as the actual subject that constitutes USC. In this rendering, USC is not the faculty or other workers who, for the most part, do not benefit from secrecy. Rather, it is the administration. This is a central issue that we need to be discussing: Who benefits from secrecy? Who benefits from transparency? While beyond the scope of this chapter, some academics are beginning to discuss this sacred cow.[31]

The issues of "privacy" and "transparency" are central to this entire story precisely because USC claims them as values but they actually are tools of domination. Privacy/transparency can be seen as objects of class struggle between faculty and administrators. Knowing other faculty do not always labor under conditions such as ours, I researched other schools' tenure procedures and developed a "Tenure Bill of Rights" as practices that USC should consider adopting in order to promote greater transparency.

A Proposed Tenure Bill of Rights

1. The right to know why one was denied tenure—a detailed explanation in writing
2. The right to see redacted outside letters
3. The right to know the content of the chair's letter(s)
4. The right to know which outside scholars one is compared to in the evaluation process
5. The right to know the results/methods of any quantitative analysis (e.g., cohort analysis, citation count, etc.)
6. The right to know the vote/deliberations at the departmental level
7. The right to know the vote/deliberations at the college level
8. The right to a clear decision by commencement
9. The right to a clear appeal process
10. Institutional respect for departmental decisions. Any decision counter to the department's should be accompanied by a full written explanation to the department.
11. The right to know who sits on the UCAPT (university tenure committee)
12. The academic senate should appoint the UCAPT—not the administration
13. The right to see statistics on tenure outcomes, including methodology and data sources (provided confidentiality is ensured)

I culled these practices from various institutions, primarily public, as few private schools make their tenure practices public. When we shared these practices with the administration, a common response was, "But those are *public* schools. What do the *private* schools do?" Here, once again, we see how USC is consciously producing itself in relation to the private elite schools it aspires to. It wishes to emulate Harvard, not merely the University of California. This, in turn, begs the question, what is the connection between privacy and elitism? Privacy allows USC to operate with minimal challenge, but it is also a practice that contributes to the cultivation of a particular image. In turn, this image is thought to enhance the status of the institution. Thus privacy actually produces value in the economy of higher education. Privacy functions as an asset in the accumulation of prestige. The practice and rhetoric of privacy goes far beyond the tenure process and is key to positioning oneself in the academic hierarchy.

Another privacy issue is the composition of the UCAPT itself. At USC, the membership of the UCAPT is largely unknown. Over the years various colleagues have shared when they were on UCAPT, but never was the full membership disclosed. When we brought this issue up at our meeting with representatives of the administration, we were told by the special advisor to the provost that, in fact, the membership of the UCAPT was not a secret. I quickly followed up in an e-mail asking for the list of members. I was then informed that it turns out that this information is *not* for university-wide consumption. This seemingly small point illustrates at least two things. First, the fact that there was confusion on the part of the administration regarding whether this information is public or not is a microcosm of the larger tenure process. If there is not agreement within the administration itself whether the composition of the UCAPT is a secret, one can imagine how much room there is for confusion along the full spectrum of the tenure process. Second, in subsequent e-mails and discussions with representatives of the administration, I was consistently told that the identities of the UCAPT had to be kept private in order to prevent lobbying and pressure. This speaks volumes about how USC views its faculty. It is a form of infantilization to believe that we could not handle such information in a responsible manner. At most universities such information is known and lobbying does not seem to be an issue.[32]

The administration also rejected our demand for an independent investigation into the larger pattern of tenure denials.[33] Following the suggestion of one of the dean's representatives, we tried to work through the college's faculty council, asking it to undertake or commission an independent study or, at the very least, request the data from the college. Since the university administration would not give us the data on tenure outcomes by race and gender, we thought perhaps the college administration would share its data with the college's elected representative body. It was denied.

Instead, the OED's report included a statement on tenure outcomes: "An analysis of University-wide data shows no statistically significant difference in tenure success rates between male and female candidates, or between minority and non-minority candidates, during the period 2006 through 2009. Thus it appears that there is neither intentional discrimination against minorities, women, or minority women."[34] There are several problems with this analysis, starting with the fact that we have no idea who conducted it.

Presumably it was someone in the administration or commissioned by the administration. Apparently we are supposed to believe what the administration tells us, despite its history and the lack of faculty governance. Precisely because a university self-study has little credibility, we called for an independent investigation in the first place. Second, we have no knowledge of the data used or methodologies employed. I find it deeply ironic that a university would conduct a study employing a set of practices that it would never accept as legitimate scholarship from its faculty. One example of why there is a need for a clear methodological statement is the issue of who counts as a minority. With the best of intentions, people may disagree on how to categorize various populations. For example, do Asian immigrants in the sciences count as a minority? How about 1.5 generation immigrants? There are obviously important political implications to the process of racial counting—a crucial part of racial management.[35] In my time at USC, there have been several lively discussions about who counts as a minority and much speculation about how exactly the university has achieved its much-vaunted status as being a leader in faculty diversity. As ever, the provost noted in her letter accompanying the report, "As you may know, Government statistics show that USC is #1 for faculty diversity among AAU private universities."[36]

In the face of such intransigence, one faculty member decided to conduct her own analysis of tenure outcomes based on the university catalog. She tracked the faculty in each department and counted who was promoted to associate professor and who was not. While not a perfect dataset, it is the best available to faculty. Based on her analysis of the social sciences and humanities faculty in the college from 1998 to 2012, it was determined that 91.9 percent of white men received tenure, but only 55.1 percent of women and minorities received tenure. While we suspected a pattern of discrimination, we had no idea how severe the discrepancies were. While the data itself is clearly incriminating, equally significant is its juxtaposition with the administration's claim that minorities were awarded tenure at a higher rate than nonminorities.[37] Although their claims were based on university-wide data from 2006 to 2009, it strains credulity to imagine that both findings are correct. Is the administration lying? Should the administration's findings simply be dismissed since they will not reveal their data and methods? While the administration has not denied the findings to date, it did secure the testimony of a professor at a grievance hearing who sought to discredit the analysis. He suggested, for example, that the skewed tenure rates may be due to top female and minority candidates being recruited by more prestigious institutions than USC prior to tenure. Alternatively, he offered that perhaps white men who are poor scholars are more likely to be advised to leave prior to tenure, and thus the resulting pool of white male tenure candidates is simply stronger.[38] Such logic illuminates the degree to which the USC is willing to go to avoid the truth.

The Aftermath and the Future

In January 2011 the administration sent out a memo to all faculty introducing some positive changes to the UCAPT manual. While such revisions are welcome, in no way do they go far enough or address the central issues embodied in the tenure bill of rights.[39]

In December 2010, my department was charged with selecting a new chair. Two candidates were advanced—both of whom, including myself, had been active in CTJ. The dean rejected both candidates, which threw the department into a tailspin. Particularly illuminating is how the dean treated us. While it is the dean's prerogative to accept/reject chair nominations, and there may have been valid reasons for rejecting us, the *way* he did it was noteworthy: He never bothered to inform us personally, whether in person, over the phone, or in writing. He never bothered to explain why we were unacceptable candidates. When a departmental delegation went to argue for our candidacy, he would not reconsider. In short, the dean treated us disrespectfully because he could. I am a woman of color and my colleague is queer. Already marginal to the university, he did not have to bother explaining his actions to us, as we were not worthy of his time and effort. Moreover, his actions were clearly intended to discipline us for being outspoken as well as the larger department for challenging his authority. In this sense, he was very purposeful in his disregard of us.

This larger culture of disrespecting faculty of color has left the department a shell of its former self. According to my count, between 2007 and 2012 eight faculty who were affiliated with my department left for tenure reasons, and another eight senior faculty chose to leave, primarily because of the administration and culture of USC. A recent external review of the program described the situation as follows: "It is unfortunate that many of the negative tenure decisions and most of the faculty who departed were scholars of color. Rightly or wrongly, there is a perception that the administration did not value the scholarship of these junior faculty, or appreciate the accomplishments and intellectual stature and high regard in which the senior faculty who departed were held in their fields."[40]

It is a telling yet sad commentary that a university that desires both diversity and top-ranked status cannot manage them both. As I have stressed, USC has actively sought and continues to seek racial/ethnic and gender diversity—as long as its politics can be contained. Challenges to the tenure process, on the other hand, were seen as uncontainable.[41]

In response to the most recent tenure denial and grievances, the Equal Employment Opportunity Commission has agreed to conduct an investigation of USC. Specifically, USC has been charged with violating Title VII of the 1964 Civil Rights Act. This process has just begun, and it is uncertain how it will end. I can only hope that USC will take this opportunity to come clean, share its data, move toward a more transparent tenure process, and follow the lead of such institutions as MIT. My desire for USC to model itself after MIT is not because of its national ranking but because it seriously grappled with gender discrimination in the sciences when confronted with the evidence.[42] Instead of USC emulating the "undisputed elite institutions of the world," it is my hope such institutions will one day emulate USC for its openness, diversity, and commitment to justice.

Notes

I thank the editors of this volume, Piya Chatterjee and Sunaina Maira; David Lloyd; and Ruth Wilson Gilmore for their generous comments, as well as all the people who allowed me to share their stories. I alone am responsible for any shortcomings. A version of this was presented at the Critical Ethnic Studies Conference at UC Riverside in 2011. Epigraph quoted from e-mail to author, November 9, 2010.

1. Richard Walker, e-mail to the author, November 9, 2010.
2. Christopher Newfield, *Unmaking the Public University: The Forty-Year Assault on the Middle Class* (Cambridge, Mass.: Harvard University Press, 2008).
3. Ruth Wilson Gilmore, "Decorative Beasts: Dogging the Academy in the Late Twentieth Century," *California Sociologist* 14 (1991): 129.
4. In many ways, I am a poster child for how California's higher education plan was supposed to work: I enrolled in the community college system, transferred to California State University, and ultimately received my PhD from UCLA. Although I did benefit from affirmative action at various points, I believe the significance of my story is the democratizing power of public education for everyone. I currently have a number of younger cousins in the same position I was thirty years ago—but

there is no space for them at the community college. Manuel Pastor, among others, has argued that some of the most effective policies to improve the well-being of the poor and people of color are inclusive policies that embrace everyone: the community college is one such example. See, for example, Manuel Pastor, Juan de Lara, and Justin Scoggins, "All Together Now: African Americans, Immigrants and the Future of California" (Los Angeles, Calif.: Center for the Study of Immigrant Integration, University of Southern California, 2011).

5. I am grateful to Ruth Wilson Gilmore for this insight.

6. The USC application has a box to check for "Scions," or legacy students. These are students with preexisting family ties to USC. In 2011, 20 percent of the incoming freshman class were scions. USC Freshman Profile, 2011, http://www.usc.edu/admission/undergraduate/apply/fresh_profiles.html.

7. For USC's version of its history, see http://about.usc.edu/history/.

8. As an example, in a recent letter to all USC "ambassadors" (of which I am apparently one), President Nikias identified the following gifts: $110 million from Julie and John Mork for undergraduate scholarships; $10 million from the Harmon Family Foundation for an Academy of Polymathic Study; $10 million from William and Sharon Schoen for scholarships for military veterans; and $3.8 million from the Stamps Family Charitable Foundation for undergraduate scholarships. I believe that all these gifts were given in 2011 and 2012. Letter from C. L. Nikias to Laura Pulido, March 30, 2012, author's personal files.

9. C. L. Max Nikias, "Annual Address to the Faculty," University of Southern California, February 2012, 3.

10. On the struggles of low-wage USC workers, see Donna Houston and Laura Pulido, "The Work of Performativity: Staging Social Justice at the University of Southern California," *Environment and Planning D: Society and Space* 20 (2002): 401–24. One aspect of USC's culture that has been scrutinized is its athletic program. Mike Garrett, a former Trojan himself, was USC's athletic director from 1993 to 2010. Under his leadership the Trojans broke many NCAA rules, eventually resulting in the school returning Reggie Bush's Heisman Trophy. The scandal became a huge embarrassment to USC, and President Nikias responded promptly and firmly by replacing Garrett with Pat Hayden, who was thought to have an impeccable reputation. Though corruption seems endemic to university athletics—witness the recent Penn State scandal—we tend to treat athletic corruption as completely removed from an institution's academic culture. I believe that this question merits further investigation.

11. For a complete list of trustees, see http://about.usc.edu/administration/board-of-trustees.

12. For a complete list of the senior administration, see http://about.usc.edu/administration/.

13. http://about.usc.edu/administration.

14. http://www.usc.edu/academe/faculty/vice_provost_faculty_affairs/.

15. I am grateful to David Lloyd for clarifying this relationship. An additional example of such a conflict of interest is in my own department, where a faculty member in the dean's office also participated in departmental meetings. When I raised this as a possible conflict of interest, some, unfortunately, interpreted this as a case of personal conflict. The fact that it was interpreted as such and not seen as a conflict of interest testifies to how entrenched such practices are at USC. It must be acknowledged, however, that some departments have banned this practice.

16. All undergraduate advisors in the college were charged with this task by the dean's office. My colleagues actually did place the phone calls, but most reported that the students did not understand why they were calling and were somewhat baffled by the whole thing.

17. I received tenure in 1997. The changes at USC had definitely started, but they were not yet fully manifest in the tenure process. I was told I needed to produce a specific amount of scholarly work and I did. However, I do not think that the amount of work I was told is/was necessarily reasonable: one book and approximately twelve journal articles/book chapters. I assume that such a high bar was set to ensure my record was beyond reproach. It worked. But the important questions we need to be asking are the following: Is it reasonable and desirable to require someone doing qualitative social science to produce so much? Am I really a better scholar because I hit that magic number? Was the emphasis on research worth the trade-off of less-than-stellar teaching (something I am still working on)?

18. As it happens, both men were outstanding teachers with sizeable student followings.

19. Tania Modeleski, "The Death of Shared Governance at the U. of Southern California," *The Chronicle of Higher Education*, January 11, 2013, http://chronicle.com/blogs/conversation/2013/01/11/; Memo from Steve Kay and Heidi Rummel to Members of the Grievance Hearing Panel, "Hearing Brief," December 7, 2012, 4, author's personal files.

20. Michigan students mobilized and launched a national letter-writing campaign, convened a conference, and pursued many other activities; see, for example, Robin Wilson, "Protest Heat Up at Michigan over Tenure Case of Expert in Native American Studies," *Chronicle of Higher Education*, February 28, 2008; "Campus Lockdown-Tenure for Andrea Smith!," Greater Detroit website, February 29, 2008, http://www.greaterdetroit.wordpress.com/2008/02/29/campus-lockdown-tenure-for-andrea--Smith. See also Sarita E. See, "Talking about Tenure: Don't Be Safe, Because There Is No Safety Anyway," in *Written/Unwritten: Tenure and Race in the Humanities*, ed. Patricia Matthew (unpublished manuscript, Rutgers University); Andrea Smith, "Life after Tenure Denial," in *Mentoring Faculty of Color: Achieving Tenure and Promotion*

at Predominantly White Colleges and Universities, ed. Dwayne Mack, Elwood Watson, and Michelle Madsen Camacho (Jefferson, N.C.: McFarland, 2013), 195–204.

21. Letter from Howard Gilman, George Sanchez, and Donald Miller to Paul Spickard, July 26, 2010, author's personal files.

22. I cannot help but see the parallels between USC's attitude and the Citizens United case; Citizens United v. Federal Election Commission (2010).

23. Memo from Michael Preston, Michael Quick, and George Sanchez to David Lloyd, October 27, 2010, author's personal files.

24. Allen Feldman, *Formations of Violence: The Narrative of the Body and Political Terror in Northern Ireland* (Chicago: University of Chicago Press, 1991).

25. I personally was invited by a colleague to accompany her to meetings with the affirmative action officer to discuss the results of an investigation. My friend, a woman of color, filed a charge of discrimination in 2008 after she was denied tenure. The process was a rude awakening to us both and served as a shocking reminder of how utterly meaningless the entire "investigation" was. The essence of the meeting was the affirmative action officer telling my friend that she had interviewed the individuals who handled the case and no discrimination was found. No names were shared, no evidence was cited, no methodology was made explicit: we were simply supposed to trust the word of the officer.

26. Several faculty who agreed to speak with the affirmative action officer noted that she seemed genuine and caring and even cried. She cried so often that we would joke about carrying around a box of tissues for her.

27. An additional problem with the internal investigation was that the affirmative action officer informed us that we could not talk about the case. Indeed, throughout the process, people contacted me asking what I thought about participating in the process, and I was told by Jody Shipper that I could not talk about it with anyone. E-mail from Jody Shipper to Laura Pulido, November 18, 2010, author's personal files.

28. Letter from Elizabeth Garrett to Laura Pulido, August 9, 2011, author's personal files.

29. In previous encounters with Shipper, she has pointed out that all her research/interviews are confidential, which is in keeping with the best practices of her field. While I can appreciate this as a scholar, it is completely unacceptable in terms of workers' rights. The lack of transparency demands an alternative procedure and methodology. It is NOT acceptable to simply be told to trust the word of an administrator, who ultimately is accountable to and paid by the administration.

30. Whether one thinks USC's tenure process is legitimate or not, there is a valid case to be made for greater transparency. Consider the outside letters. In many universities, faculty are allowed to see redacted letters written by outside colleagues. Why is this important? First, reading other people's evaluations of your work is of value in trying to ascertain why one did or did not get tenure. Second, after having

reviewed the letters and disagreeing with some element of them, one can potentially respond to specific points and provide counterevidence. This can obviously help one's case. Third, I have been told by numerous colleagues that reading these letters is quite helpful in terms of one's scholarly development.

31. While there is an argument to be made for confidentiality, this position is problematic in that it assumes (1) we cannot truly be honest with our colleagues because it would be difficult and uncomfortable, and (2) the converse: it sanctions a lack of honesty in order to maintain the illusion of harmonious relations. Such an arrangement clearly does not benefit the candidate and presumably has the comfort of the tenured faculty in mind. But we must question the value of any system that does not require, or at least encourage, full honesty with ourselves and others. I find it deeply ironic that an entire institution, higher education, which supposedly is committed to the pursuit of truth, is ultimately predicated on a lack of honesty. Personally, I believe that if faculty have the power to fire, then they should have the courage to tell that person to their face. Is this difficult? Yes. But not only might this encourage a more thorough review (i.e., more professors might actually read the full dossier), but the candidate would understand how/why the decision was made, and we would all grow as human beings by being forced to publicly be honest. See "Talking about Tenure"; Andrea Smith, "Confidentiality," *Religious Studies News*, May 2012, http://www.rsnoonline.org/index.

32. At the University of California, Berkeley, the membership of the committee is actually online: http://academic-senate.berkeley.edu/committees/bir. As this chapter was going to press, USC issued a new policy on the UCAPT: "At the end of each academic year, the University makes public the names of UCAPT members from the past two years." This passes for transparency at USC. UCAPT Manual, March 2013, 3.

33. E-mail from Michael Preston, Michael Quick, and George Sanchez to David Lloyd (cc'd to Laura Pulido), October 27, 2010. Independent investigations are not without precedent. For example, the Illinois American Association of University Professors (AAUP) conducted an investigation of DePaul University's tenure process after protests over a perceived discriminatory pattern. See http://www.insidehighered.com/news/2011/01/04/minority_faculty_contest_depaul_tenure_denials.

34. Letter from Jody Shipper to Elizabeth Garrett, July 27, 2011, author's personal files.

35. Since we don't actually know how racial counting occurs and have never seen the actual numbers, rumors abound. One colleague, a Latina with South American origins, once speculated that perhaps she is counted as white when it is convenient to do so and as minority when that is advantageous to the university.

36. Letter from Elizabeth Garrett to Laura Pulido, August 9, 2011, author's personal files. It is my understanding that such reports are actually based on data submitted by the university itself—thus, there is plenty of room for interpretation on the part

of the institution. Moreover, USC's status as number one is not necessarily impressive as it simply reflects how deplorable things are at other institutions (public *and* private). For example, in the college itself, according to my calculations, there are five Mexican American or Chicana/o full-time tenure-track faculty. This is out of approximately 400 tenure-track faculty in a city that was once part of Mexico and has the largest Mexican American population in the United States. To me, these are not impressive statistics. It is not my wish to disparage USC's efforts at faculty diversity—which have indeed been real—but rather to put such claims in context, especially when such rankings are used by the administration in a self-serving way to dismiss charges of discrimination.

37. This was stated by both the affirmative action officer and the previous dean. The latter wrote, "I looked over the time period for which I have data at hand, the year since 1996, and see that the percentage of under-represented faculty succeeding in their promotion to tenure in the College happens to be higher than for white faculty. Thus the statement in your letter that there is a 'longstanding pattern of inexplicable tenure decisions that have disproportionately affected faculty of color' is contrary to the data." Letter from Howard Gilman to Laura Pulido, September 13, 2010, author's personal files. More recently, the revised *UCAPT Manual*, which is authorized by the provost, states, "From academic year 2006–2007 through academic year 2011–2012, 86 percent of the 164 tenure-track faculty who completed the UCAPT process were granted tenure . . . The proportion of women receiving tenure was nearly identical to the rate for men (1.2 percent higher for women). The tenure rates for faculty who identified themselves as non-Hispanic whites and those who identified themselves as ethnic minorities also were essentially the same (1.2 percent lower for ethnic minorities). These inter-group differences are not statistically significant." UCAPT Manual, USC, March 2013, 9. As always, we have no idea how the administration derived these figures. The actual report is a memo from Jane Junn to Phil Ethington, October 10, 2012, author's personal files. See also Audrey Williams June, "Tenure Decisions at Southern Cal Strongly Favor White Men, Data in a Rejected Candidate's Complaint Suggest," *Chronicle of Higher Education*, http://chronicle.com/article/Tenure-Decisions -atSouthern/135754/?cid=at&utm_source=at&utm_medium=en.

38. Memo from Mark Weinstein to Heidi Rummel, November 30, 2012, "Jane Junn, Analysis of Data on Tenure at USC Dornsife," author's personal files.

39. Memo from Elizabeth Garrett, Peter Conti, and Leo Braudy to the Faculty, January 28, 2011, "Tenure, Promotion and Appointments." Highlighted changes include the following: the creation of a FAQ; recommendations on how best to evaluate collaborative scholarship; expanded advice to candidates, departments, and school committees; and expanded sections on promotion to full professor and designation as clinical scholar.

40. Melvin Oliver, Ruben Rumbaut, Priscilla Wald, Kenneth Warren, and William

Vega, "External Review of USC's Department of American Studies and Ethnicity (ASE)," May 20, 2012, author's personal files.

41. Andrea Smith, "Native Studies and Critical Pedagogy: Beyond the Academic-Industrial Complex," in *Activist Scholarship: Antiracism, Feminism, and Social Change*, ed. Julia Sudbury and Margo Okazawa-Rey (Boulder, Colo.: Paradigm Publishers, 2009), see esp. 40–46.

42. On women in the sciences at MIT, see http://web.mit.edu/fnl/women/women.html.

6

The Boycott, Divestment, and Sanctions Movement and Violations of Academic Freedom at Wayne State University

Thomas Abowd

The movement for Boycott, Divestment, and Sanctions (BDS), orga-nized in the United States and globally as a response to several decades of Israeli human rights abuses against the Palestinian people, has spread at a rate unimaginable ten years ago. Responding to a call from activ-ists in Palestine in 2005, BDS has been a nonviolent campaign comprising actions meant to end Israel's illegal occupation of Palestinian land.[1] These varied and proliferating campaigns have in some cases emanated from the grounds of the fortressed "imperial university" in the United States, where increasingly students and professors are opening up and broadening discussion on Palestine/Israel in ways never seen before. The gains of this nascent movement are not, to date, mammoth if measured against the formal successes of BDS activists and campus campaigns against apartheid South Africa in the 1970s and 1980s. However, measured by the growth of public awareness in the United States and elsewhere concerning Israel's ongoing, sixty-five-year theft of Palestinian land, the victories have not been meager.

Dynamic broad-based organizing of this kind has increasingly arisen within Palestine rights circles in the United States since 2002. And perhaps it is evidence of the potential of a dedicated, effective, nonviolent movement that BDS efforts have caused such fear and fury among those who wish to sustain Israel's violent military rule over the Palestinians. Those familiar with activism of this sort are also well aware that Israeli officials and consulates have deemed these activist projects to be among the greatest "threats" to the Jewish state. These proliferating popular campaigns have compelled Israeli officials and pro-Israel activists to intensify their own responses, seeking to garner support in the United States through at times quite racist rhetoric about the threats "the Arabs," "fundamentalist Islam," or anti-Zionist activ-ists pose to *their* security. But despite the Israeli government's endless ire against an Iranian nuclear weapons program that does not exist or forms of Palestinian militancy that pose no capacity to win back one inch of Palestinian land, the project that generates some of the most intense trepidation among Zionists in Israel and elsewhere has been these emerging nonviolent BDS initiatives.

These campaigns have been diverse and waged nationally and locally in a range of places: from those targeting food cooperatives selling Israeli products to those directed at universities that invest in companies that benefit from the Israeli occupation of Palestinian land. For example, the U.S. Campaign for the Academic and Cultural Boycott of Israel (USACBI) has sought to forge academic and cultural boycotts of Israeli academic and cultural institutions. Efforts of this sort now list among their supporters internationally known figures as diverse as Jimmy Carter, Pete Seeger, Bishop Desmond Tutu, Alice Walker, and Roger Waters. Endorsers of the USACBI campaign have included such prominent U.S. academics as Angela Davis, Judith Butler, Robin Kelley, Richard Falk, Alan Wald, and hundreds of others. Even some of Israel's most prominent Jewish academics and writers, such as Ilan Pappe, Moshe Behar, and Tanya Reinhart, have affirmed the need to support BDS efforts of various kinds.

The Rise, Fall, and Rise of Palestine Solidarity Work: The Campus as Ideological Battlefield

My involvement in Palestine solidarity work as an Arab American student-activist at the University of Michigan and Columbia University was, like that of so many others, born of the experiences and struggles of the first Palestinian Intifada (1987–1993). This popular revolutionary uprising against Israeli military occupation had innumerable positive outcomes. For one, it punctured old axiomatic ways of regarding Palestinians and the state of Israel in the United States and elsewhere. The Intifada completely transformed the international solidarity movement on behalf of the Palestinians, broadening support in the late 1980s for one of the world's remaining colonized communities. In fact, I argue that it made that solidarity movement possible.

The impact of Palestinian struggles under Israeli occupation was multi-layered. For one, it thrust the issue of the several decades-old Israeli colonization of their land onto the agendas of progressives the world over. Until the Intifada began to be widely covered in major media outlets, progressives and leftists had known very little about Israeli human rights abuses. It also undermined the prevailing myth in the United States and elsewhere that a benign and democratic Israel was beleaguered and threatened by "Palestinian terrorism," a racist stereotype that Zionist organizations like the so-called Anti-Defamation League (ADL) have incessantly sought to promote for decades. Many have forgotten about the 1989 ADL fund-raising letter signed by B'nai B'rith president Seymour Reich, who alleged that the "Arab presence on the college campuses is poisoning the minds of our young people." Reich's racist screed, directed against Palestinians and other Arabs by a major Zionist figure, was reminiscent of classic anti-Semitism. And this was not lost on American Jews, several of whom on the University of Michigan campus alone condemned this letter and its source.

The brilliant organizing of Palestinians revolting with stones and direct action against the region's most powerful army were potent images. This fundamental power dynamic began to be laid bare and understood. "David," as U.S. church groups were beginning to see, was contesting a well-armed "Goliath." Those gravitating toward Palestine rights work at the time were frequently left asking who the real terrorists were and why the U.S. government was arming and providing moral sanction for the Israeli regime and thousands of violent Jewish settlers. The moral force of these struggles even made it impossible for thousands of erstwhile supporters of Israel to continue defending polices such as destroying Palestinian homes and breaking the bones of Palestinian children who resisted Israeli military occupation, as then Israeli defense minister Yitzhak Rabin instructed his troops to do.

Those of us involved in what were then referred to as "Arab-Jewish dialogue groups" in the late 1980s and early 1990s witnessed many if not most of the so-called liberal Zionists in these groups eventually abandon Zionism within a few months or years of coming to terms with the magnitude of Israeli human rights abuses. One fellow student activist, now a prominent anti-Zionist intellectual, was keen to tell the story of how in the early 1990s, during her first year at the University of Michigan, she became president of the "Progressive Zionist" organization and by her senior year, she was president of the "Palestine Solidarity Committee." Seeing how those socialized into a particular kind of politics around Israel could challenge these hegemonic and prevailing perspectives in the United States, once presented with other views, was an enormous lesson in the importance of meeting people where they are at politically.

However, the signing of the Oslo Accords in 1993 between the Palestine Liberation Organization (PLO) and the Israelis brought the First Intifada to an end. During the quiescent years of political disillusionment produced in the cauldron of "Oslo" (1993–2000), a good deal of activism in the United States opposed to Israel's military occupation dissipated nearly as quickly as it arose. It was not until the outbreak of the Second Intifada and the return of Israeli gunships, death squads, and attack helicopters over Palestinian refugee camps and cities that a new energy in the solidarity movement reemerged. Since fall 2000, the intensity of organizing within traditional Palestinian rights communities has not only returned to the levels of the early 1990s but also far exceeded it in crucial ways. By 2002 or 2003, the movement had become deeper, broader, and far more inclusive and forged alliances with other struggles in much more meaningful ways. Calls for an end to Israeli policies and practices of colonial domination, torture, and settlement building have even entered the mainstream of American public opinion like never before. Imagine, for instance, a major mainstream figure such as former U.S. president Jimmy Carter using the term "apartheid," as he did in his 2006 book, to refer to Israeli actions in 1986 or 1996.

As a professor (for the most part in the anthropology department at Detroit's Wayne State University from 2003 to 2009), my work with the Palestinian people and the Israeli progressives who support the end to their government's military occupation has coincided with the relatively recent rise of BDS globally. In the last five to ten years, broader, more enhanced solidarity has come from a myriad of political and cultural corners: from gay rights activists and the "Occupy" movement to African American churches and ever broader elements within U.S. Jewish communities. Commitment to Zionism among American Jews has been gradually fraying for at least the last decade and with this has come ever greater criticism of Israeli human rights abuses by Jewish individuals and organizations.[2]

But in my case and that of innumerable other academics, it has been possible to witness the responses to this political shift on college campuses and beyond. I am thinking primarily about those actions and statements exemplified by the words of Larry Summers, the former president of Harvard, who referred to BDS campaigns as "anti-Semitic in their effect if not their intent."[3] These are attacks that seek to denigrate faculty and students who dare to criticize Israeli human rights abuses or implicate the United States and "imperial universities" in violations of international law. There are also schemes that, in effect, straddle the university and local and national Zionist organizations, such as the Jewish Federation, Hillel, and the ADL, pressuring universities to silence voices critical of Israeli human rights abuses.

Increasingly, Jewish students who support BDS and wish to be part of campus Hillel chapters are being told in various ways that they are not welcome at Hillel. The recent 2013 firestorm that erupted when American Jewish scholar Judith Butler was invited to speak at Brooklyn College in support of BDS campaigns against Israel underscores the hostility against BDS that links the university and the communities in which it is embedded. In this case, the New York City Council issued a call to defund Brooklyn College if this event went forward, underscoring the attack against civil liberties in which Zionist organizations continue to be involved. I will return to the specific instances of discrimination and harassment that I experienced at Wayne State University in the following pages. First, however, I would like to flesh out a bit the political context in which the BDS movement has arisen in the United States.

Since about 2000, progressive activist projects focused on Palestine/Israel have been nearly as interested in securing the rights of at least 4.5 million Palestinian refugees as in ending Israel's illegal military occupation. This remobilization of mass energy grew in response, first, to the rise of the Second Intifada in the fall of 2000. It was then further amplified by Israel's violent reoccupation of Palestinian cities of the West Bank in early 2002, an onslaught condemned the world over. It involved the Israeli Defense Forces targeting Palestinian civilians with F-16s, torturing and writing numbers on the bodies of Palestinian prisoners, and other documented war crimes. These invasions were grim portents for Israel's attack on Lebanon in 2006 and on Gaza in 2008–2009, in which Israeli forces killed and maimed thousands of civilians and created hundreds of millions of dollars of destruction to homes and infrastructure. That this violence was made possible through the backing of the U.S. government increasingly began to be understood by American progressives and radicals but also others more in the mainstream. With Israel's escalation of violence and illegal settlement construction, however, came the intensification of global criticism and the growth of BDS.

BDS-U.S. grew out of the campus and community activism of groups such as *al-Awda*, the U.S. Campaign to End the Occupation, Jewish Voice for Peace, Jews against the Occupation, Sabeel, and others. One of the earliest BDS initiatives with a genuine, international component arose in 2002 when Nobel laureate Bishop Desmond Tutu and other South African activists and progressives endorsed a campaign to divest from Israel. The call of Tutu lent the legitimacy and moral sanction of one of the world's most respected human rights activists to a budding movement smeared so often then—as now—as an "anti-Semitic" campaign to "destroy Israel." Tutu's involvement eventuated in a statement he authored in 2002 in which he condemned continued abuses against the civilian population of Palestine. He noted the similarities between Israel colonial authority and that of South African apartheid, as well as the historic—but little known—cooperation between these two states between 1948 and 1994. Calling for the need to divest, he wrote, "We [anti-Apartheid forces in South Africa] would not have succeeded without the help of international pressure—in particular the divestment movement of the 1980s. Over the past eight months a similar movement has taken shape, this time aiming at an end to the Israeli occupation of Palestinian territories captured during the 1967 military campaign."[4] In the wake of this early intervention there arose a wave of initiatives formulated and organized on U.S. campuses and in other cultural spheres, from important labor unions to the Presbyterian and Methodist churches. Sustained and serious campaigns calling for divestment, such as those at Columbia University, Hampshire College, and UC Berkeley, made national and international headlines. They drew students and faculty into these politics, most for the first time. But these battles did not overwhelmingly impel college administrations to support these efforts. Instead, their response (again, often under pressure by outside Zionist groups) was typically to engage in denials of, or silence about, Israeli violations of international law and the involvement of their university in those abuses.

In 2003–2004, at my alma mater, Columbia University, President Lee Bollinger discredited himself among wide swathes of liberal and left opinion on campus and beyond when he issued a statement condemning that school's faculty-led BDS initiative. Bollinger's statement was coarse and unrefined. I and others in support of this BDS campaign saw similarities between it and what a right-wing, pro-Israel organization, such as the ADL or the American-Israel Political Action Committee (AIPAC), might have written. Bollinger dismissed the very moderate call from dozens of faculty members for the end of university investment in defense firms that do business in the occupied territories and that provide support for Israeli human rights abuses. It was, in other words, a campaign directed primarily at U.S. corporations, not Israel.

The once well-regarded civil libertarian became a veritable laughing stock among progressive organizations in New York and elsewhere when he, among other things, referred to Israeli human rights abuses—including torture—as "alleged." In fact, Israeli human rights and civil liberties organizations had issued similar (even far harsher) critiques of their own government than did the faculty behind the Columbia BDS initiative. When this was brought to light, Bollinger appeared as ignorant as he was insensitive to the suffering of civilians maimed and killed by the Israeli state.

Wayne State University: The Paradoxes of Institutional Racism

Whereas Columbia's 2003–2004 BDS initiative was primarily the work of faculty members, a 2003 effort at Wayne State University (WSU) was largely the work of students. WSU, a school I taught at for five years before resigning in 2009, has not been known in recent decades for much in the way of student activism. Like other urban universities comprised overwhelmingly of undergraduates who do not reside on or in the vicinity of the campus, this "commuter school" has, for that reason, lacked the critical mass of consistent political energy that other schools with significant resident populations possess. Without the vigorous involvement of students in the movements of the day, universities, as faculty well know, can be very sedate places. It was ever thus.

But despite such realities and limitations, activists at WSU should count among their achievements the fact that the student council was one of the very first in the United States to vote in favor of its administration divesting from Israel. The text of this resolution (passed in spring 2003) was forthright and principled. It condemned Israeli torture and other human rights abuses and correctly pointed to their university's and the U.S. government's financial links to this regime. Further, the resolution, following the critiques of Bishop Tutu, Nelson Mandela, and other South African progressives, drew parallels and connections between the Israeli and South African apartheid regimes. Faculty and students on campus at the time generally felt that the initiative was supported by a substantial number (if not, in fact, a majority) of the campus community.

But if the BDS initiative enjoyed majority support among students and faculty in the wake of this successful student initiative, it received hostile opposition by a minority within the WSU administration and among some on the board of trustees, including one or two committed Zionists who openly supported elements in Israel who had committed war crimes. The reactions of a small number of anti-Palestinian and anti-Arab individuals in the administration ranged from confused and ignorant to hostile and racist. And on this campus with one of the largest Arab and Muslim student communities in the nation (upwards of 20–22 percent of the student body), what I witnessed was a small number within the administration, among the faculty, and in the local Jewish community continually vilifying the divestment initiative and those supportive of it. Efforts to oppose the student campaign were considerable. The knives came out in the predictable ways: smears of anti-Semitism and "Israel-bashing" were the first responses, and they were usually articulated without any rational argument about why the critiques of Israeli human rights abuses were supposedly unfounded.

In a range of cases of reprisal for criticism of Israeli policy, including mine, those regarded as "anti-Israel" or "anti-Semitic" were targeted in vicious campaigns. Among WSU's first acts, I believe, was to fire an extremely talented and popular administrator, who had a PhD in Arabic linguistics and was a Middle East specialist. As a high-level administrative official, he had begun to build a nationally known language study program in collaboration with the Middle East and other parts of the world. He had also served as an advisor to then president of WSU Irvin Reid on how to foster productive relationships between WSU and universities in the Arab world. That he was also as knowledgeable about the Palestine/Israel conflict as he was critical of Israeli human rights abuse, not to mention supportive of the student divestment campaign, was not, informed observers believe, a small element in his ouster.

The paradox of this political firestorm at WSU was that this had been a campus where very little, if any, Zionist activism had taken place among students or faculty in the last two or three decades. It is a school embedded in a city with a comparatively tiny and insipid Zionist and pro-Israel community. And it was and continues to be, for this and other reasons, a curious cultural context for witnessing just how influential a small and shrill group of anti-Arab racists and right-wing Zionists can be, particularly when there is not sufficient endurance, stamina, and growth in Palestine solidarity work in the local community.

In the Detroit area, much of the real activist energy since 2000 around Palestine/Israel politics has been the product of well-organized and progressive Jewish groups like Jewish Voice for Peace; American Jews for a Just Peace; and a range of interfaith, joint Christian, Muslim, and Jewish political clusters. Jewish American groups articulating more chauvinist or mechanical "support for Israel," such as the so-called Jewish Federation or the moribund WSU chapter of Hillel, produced little in the way of programming or solidarity demonstrations during the period that I was on campus. During

Israel's invasion of Gaza in 2008–2009, innumerable pro-Palestinian demonstrations and events across southeastern Michigan dwarfed, by a factor of ten, those organized by right-wing elements in the Zionist community. Some of these pro-Israel groups actually defended the mass killing of Palestinian civilians in the name of "Israel's security."

During my five years at WSU, it was possible, literally, to count on one hand the number of events held on campus that sought to support Israel's expansionist and discriminatory policies. With the fingers on the other hand, it was possible to compute the number of pro-Israel activists at WSU among students and faculty. When Hillel-sponsored events did happen, they rarely drew more than a few people. However, though there have been a scant few Zionist activists on campus for at least a couple of decades, I had been warned upon arriving at WSU by longtime activists in the Detroit area that, unlike other schools, the "pro-Israel" community in and around WSU, though relatively small, had a much fiercer, more narrowly right-wing character than in other places. Historically, there had even been supporters of the most racist Zionist elements, such as Kahane Chai and others who explicitly supported the ethnic cleansing of the Palestinians and worse.

What then can explain the degree of hostility to nonviolent opposition to Israeli human rights abuses among university administrators? I argue that unlike in decades past when Zionist activists on U.S. campuses were growing and the voices in support of rights for Palestinians were very small, today the way power is mobilized against movements trying to end the Israeli occupation of Palestine tends to be through more secretive, behind-the-scenes campaigns, including those that arise from noncampus elements. The point that must be remembered is that these universities are embedded within broader relations, constraints, and pressures—corporate and community.

During my five-year stay at WSU, I taught roughly nineteen classes and several hundred students. My sense was that among the Jewish students on campus who were interested in what happens in Palestine/Israel, there was a sizable percentage—perhaps most—who were actually critical of Israeli policies toward the Palestinians. Two young Jewish women, whom I came to know as students in three of my classes, were involved in the 2003 BDS campaign on campus. They and the majority of the other Jewish students and faculty I came to know wanted nothing to do with what they perceived to be the chauvinism and even anti-Arab racism that pervaded WSU's Hillel and Cohn-Haddow Center for Jewish Studies.

The political effort among WSU students and faculty to call attention to

Israeli human rights abuses and its demand that Wayne State divest "the university from its investments in Israel" coincided with initiatives generated by the university president at the time to create small but meaningful institutional relationships between WSU and universities in the Middle East. At least, that is how the first few years of his administration, in the late 1990s and early 2000s, began. President Reid sought advice from regional specialists on how to make connections of this sort. One of his chief advisors was the administrator mentioned earlier who was fired soon after the student council vote.

Zionist members of the WSU board and in the administration, one of whom is widely understood to be a supporter of some of the Jewish state's worst war criminals, then sought to presumptuously and undemocratically "recast" the ideological posture and orientation of the school. In the wake of the student council divestment vote, some of these pressured WSU's administration to send out "assurances" to the area's Jewish and Zionist communities affirming that Reid was "a strong supporter of Israel." WSU's administration also sent out, on at least one or two occasions, officials to various synagogues to issue similar messages on behalf of the university.

It was, incidentally, during the months leading up to the student council vote to divest from Israel and the subsequent affirmations of WSU's "friendliness to Israel" that the Israeli army had used F-16s against a defenseless civilian population in Palestine, killing hundreds, including the massacre in Jenin refugee camp. Respected human rights organizations—some in Israel—had branded these Israeli attacks "war crimes" and called for an end to them. It was violations of human rights like these that made being an Israeli general or politician traveling to certain European democracies, such as the United Kingdom, an increasingly tricky business, lest they be picked up on a warrant for war crimes under the principle of universal jurisdiction.

A Professor Bumps Up against the Limits of Liberalism

My involvement in educational and activist events on campus began my first semester at WSU in 2003. Unlike the range of controversies and complaints that arose on other campuses against many dozens of professors who criticized Israel, in the course of teaching about Palestine/Israel and the Middle East, not one complaint was made to me, my chair, or others in the administration concerning any alleged "bias" in my classroom. Only about one-third of my courses related principally to the Middle East. In those classes in which Palestine and Israel were discussed, I had overwhelmingly positive experiences with students. They generally were among the most open-minded young scholars a professor could hope for.

However, as one of several faculty who had helped organize roughly ten events related to Palestine on campus between 2003 and 2008, I and others did, in fact, experience hostility and protest in response to activities that were open to the broader academic community. There was occasionally outright hostility at the criticism of Israeli torture and demolition of Palestinian homes, with some right-wing Zionist students even seeking to disrupt one or two fora. But usually opposition was expressed behind the scenes. There were instances in which the administration simply refused to fund our events or programming initiatives for more expansive offerings on the Middle East. There was even a case, in 2007, in which the university cancelled a talk they had asked me to give (gratis) to WSU alumni once I chose as my topic the newly released book by Jimmy Carter, *Israel: Peace not Apartheid*. When I demanded to know why my talk had been cancelled, the university would provide no answer, nor would they propose another date. My sense then and now was that someone in the Alumni Office had been instructed to cancel this invitation from "higher-ups."

At an event on campus in fall 2005 featuring Israeli activist, scholar, and Nobel Prize nominee Jeff Halper, a small group of right-wing Zionist students passed out defaming fliers meant to smear the speaker. It was becoming increasingly evident to me, then, that, despite the tiny Zionist presence on campus, there were at least a half-dozen students and professors whose views meshed with the most racist and extremist Israeli political parties, some advocating the ethnic cleansing of Palestinians. The fliers accused Halper, known for his brilliant nonviolent, direct action campaigns and his courageous efforts to block the destruction of Palestinian homes by Israeli forces, of defending the "killing of Jewish children," "support of terrorism," and "bus bombings."

A few of these aggressively pro-Israel activists followed up this protest with complaints against me, a third-year, untenured faculty member at the time and the principle organizer of Halper's talk. One of the protestors, who I had seen passing out the defamatory fliers, sent a letter to the president, the dean, the chair of the department, and others claiming that I had threatened him and other Jewish students at the event and made them feel "uncomfortable." Though the charges against me were baseless, this began to put me and other faculty on the radar of an administration containing a few prominent individuals quite unsympathetic to Palestine rights activism and ready to believe that Israel's critics on campus were, indeed, anti-Semitic.

But what would also become clear is that, though the administration did not respond to this Zionist student's grievance, neither did they reach out to me to assure me that these unfounded assertions would not harm me. When I asked repeatedly for a meeting to respond to what were serious charges, I was ignored. As other equally baseless complaints were made against me and others in the wake of this incident by similar students and "pro-Israel" racists in the Detroit community, they began, I believe, to leave traces among elements of the administration—precisely the situation I feared. "Where there's smoke, there's fire" is a dangerous assumption, particularly when, as I was told off the record by one very supportive administrator, those hostile to my politics may have been trying to find ways to undermine me within the university.

The student who initiated the first complaint against me would later be involved in hosting at WSU the well-known anti-Arab and anti-Muslim xenophobe, Daniel Pipes. Pipes, a failed academic and one of the founders of the notorious "Campus Watch," was making the rounds of U.S. colleges in fall 2007. After I spoke at a campus protest against Pipes the day of the event, two young Pipes supporters approached me and demanded to know why I had supposedly said "slaughter the Jews" during my speech. I told them to get away from me and that if they repeated this allegation, I would take legal action against them.

"Are you threatening me?" one of them then asked as I walked away.

About a week later, I received a letter from WSU's Office of Equal Opportunity, stating that I would be questioned for alleged acts of anti-Semitism. When I looked carefully at the complaint, I could see that the two young men who had approached me after the Pipes demonstration had filed it. It also became evident that neither complainant was even a student at WSU. They had issued two corroborating narratives that claimed that I had "harassed" them at the event and made them "feel uncomfortable as Jews." With alacrity, the university pursued an investigation based on this complaint and demanded that I submit to questions about this alleged harassment.

Further, in violation of a 1975 Supreme Court ruling (*NLRB v. J. Weingarten, Inc.*), the university's rather pathetic general consul staff refused to allow me to bring a faculty union representative to witness this encounter and inquiry. The university also stated that I could not cross-examine those who made these specious charges.[5] After the legal intervention of the union's lawyer, WSU's general consul's office was forced to let a union representa-tive attend the more than two hours of questioning that I was subjected to. The line of questioning included several queries of my ideological positions, my views on Zionism, and whether I had engaged in threatening behav-ior toward the two complainants who were not even members of the WSU community.

But the lawyer from the Office of Equal Opportunity who engaged in this interrogation, Amy Stirling, who earlier in the year had sought to investi-gate whether I had engaged in "antiwhite" racism, also did something that she and WSU are surely quite sorry they ever tried to do. Namely, in the course of investigating this alleged instance of "anti-Jewish" discrimina-tion, Stirling demanded *three* times of me, "Are you Muslim?" This she did in the presence of the third party, the union representative, and once in a hostile tone. When I refused to answer this question the first time, she asked me twice more a few minutes later. When the union representative and I both demanded to know what could possibly be the relevance of this line of questioning, Stirling dismissively asserted that the question *did* have rel-evance and that she expected an answer from me. She might have expected a lawsuit or complaint because that is precisely what I was prepared to do in the wake of this discriminatory and totally offensive line of questioning. And it was evident at that point, too, why WSU did not want any third-party wit-ness in the room, for had I been alone, it would have been very much more difficult to convince others that she had actually engaged in such actions.

My family members and I would, in the months to come, be the victims of threatening and harassing anonymous e-mails and posts on our respective websites.[6] But as it became clear that I was being targeted by the university, I was also the subject of a fairly intense campaign of solidarity from across the United States and beyond. University officials—including Stirling—received hundreds of calls, e-mails, and letters from fellow activists, scholars, and community members from as far away as the United Kingdom, Egypt, Palestine, and even Israel. This occurred in spring and summer 2008 and coincided with the university having to conclude, after interviewing me and several others on campus, that the charges of anti-Semitism and "anti-white" racism were baseless and unfounded. When WSU could not prove that I had expressed any anti-Jewish sentiments, they dug in and defended their employee's own racist language toward me. In the months after this instance, the WSU general consul's office even *promoted* this person as they continued to attack me.

My conflict with the administration at WSU came to a head around a series of clumsy violations of my union contract by the dean of the college at the time. It eventuated in him and my chair trying to get rid of me two months later, in May 2008, by not renewing my contract and refusing to give a reason for what is nearly always a pro forma renewal of a faculty contract. In fact, I had been renewed on this tenure-track contract without question three years previously. And that, combined with the fact that the year before WSU had awarded me the university's highest teaching award and had also given me the largest merit-based salary increase of any other junior faculty member in my department, seemed to indicate that their actions were driven by and in response to a campaign of political exclusion.

About one week before the university tried to not renew my contract, the department chair at the time and at least one other senior faculty member in the department (against whom students and faculty of color had long-running complaints) deliberately falsified my end-of-the-year evaluation. After senior faculty had written me a string of positive evaluations since I arrived on campus, they mysteriously left out some of the strongest elements of my record this time. They then sought to send this evaluation to the dean's office for review before I had a chance to see it. When I obtained a copy of the evaluation by a sympathetic senior faculty member and quickly pointed out the errors to the chair, she ignored my requests to formally correct the record.

My strong belief, and those of many other faculty members familiar with my case, is that my criticisms of Israeli human rights abuses had infuriated a small but influential number of Detroit-area Zionists at a moment when the university sought to prove that they were "strong supporters" of racist elements in Israel and among Zionists in the Detroit area. Their opposition toward me, I believe, filtered down to the department level. It was taken up by those who already saw me as "trouble" for encouraging two female graduate students—who came to me with complaints of sexual harassment against the former chair of the department—to take action against the former chair and others who tried to cover up similar instances of abuse against students. That the department chair at the time did not support me *even privately* during the time university officials were violating my contractual rights or demanding to know what my religion was underscored, I believe, the fear they felt from the administration—not simply their lack of political principle.

Conclusion

One lesson about the functioning of universities illustrated by my conflict with WSU is that even when a Zionist presence on campus among students and faculty is not particularly strong, campus administrations that raise money from Zionist community members and alumni can create the most top-down sort of realities. WSU continues to promote and hire individuals sympathetic with racist policies and acts of discrimination against the Palestinians while inventing claims of anti-Semitism to try to smear critics of Israeli human rights abuses. This is happening while, among faculty and students, such chauvinist views enjoy little support and those who hold them are unable to successfully defend them when freedom of expression and open debate reign.

But my experiences at Wayne State indicate just how far university administrations might go in trying to attack, marginalize, or even remove critics of Israel in their employ, including those that they, themselves, have honored for their teaching and mentoring record over several years. This is done not simply through sheer apologia for and ideological commitment to Israeli state terrorism. Nor is it usually in response to a wellspring of narrow nationalist solidarity among students or faculty with an increasingly apartheid-like Israel. It has arisen at WSU and at other places because university administrators, otherwise ignorant of Middle East politics, have been made keenly aware of the dangers that these political views present in scaring away wealthy donors and alumni.

My case and countless others also underscore the rank hypocrisy that many schools—in their claims to racial equality and academic freedom—display when racism toward Muslims and Arabs comes to the fore. When accusations of anti-Semitism are leveled (real or baseless), schools like WSU are capable of mobilizing rapidly with investigatory interviews, intimidation, and condemnation. But they have too often been sluggish to address a myriad other expressions of racism and harassment—institutional and noninstitutional—committed against Arabs, Muslims, African Americans, or other targeted groups.

The irony is, of course, that WSU would love to aspire to be an "imperial university," one with a global reputation that can successfully chase sizable funds from the Department of Defense and pull in huge grants from the National Endowment for the Humanities and National Endowment for the Arts. In fact, recent efforts to build a "security studies" program at

WSU, one used potentially to recruit Arabic speakers and others into U.S. intelligence branches, was about the only significant interest higher-level administrators on campus have shown in Detroit's Arab and Muslim American communities. Further, these actions engaged in by this institution as it seeks to chase money (and chase talented faculty away) can filter down to departments seeking to prove their obedience to, and curry favor with, the administration in an age of economic scarcity.

It should be noted that the anthropology department, under two different chairs, not only refused to support my educational work in the Arab American community but largely squandered the legacy of Dr. Barbara Aswad, one of the founders of Arab American studies, who had taught at WSU for more than thirty years. Her several decades–long research and political involvement with Arab Detroiters and with progressive communities in the area is legendary. After she retired, I was hired to fill the slot of "Middle East anthropologist," a position that she had held since the late 1960s. We both received very little in the way of support for our work with area Muslim and Arab populations.

That I have been one of the very few Arab American scholars ever hired in a full-time position in this and several other departments at WSU, a campus with one of the highest percentage of Arab American students in the country, is quite telling. Since my resignation from the department of anthropology in 2008, they have not been able to hire and retain for more than a year another Middle East anthropologist. Nor have they appeared to care very much about doing so. With my departure, substantial efforts to work with and in solidarity with the three-hundred-thousand-strong Arab American community of Greater Detroit is all but dead. And as dozens of faculty and students of color at WSU have expressed, this mirrors the broader contempt the school has exhibited toward this and the other Detroit-area communities of color within which it is so spatially embedded but from which it is so ideologically and intellectually removed.

What BDS campaigns across the country have helped begin to create is the end of the default position of support for human rights abuses in the name of "support for Israel." In realms unimaginable two decades ago, the vilification of the Palestinians as congenitally driven killers and anti-Semites has been confronted and contested with ever greater energy. What is seen on campuses is a growing resentment toward those that fling the charge of "anti-Semitism" in efforts to quell debate around Israel's military rule and quiet its critics. BDS efforts should, therefore, count among its achievements the insertion of a vital anti-racism into the political cultures in and around college campuses—a politics that Arabs, Jews, and others have increasingly claimed and promoted.

Notes

1. Recent campaigns across American and European campuses, alone, have grown each year. For more information and insight about various BDS campaigns, see http://www.bdsmovement.net.

2. In 2010, Peter Beinart wrote a highly perceptive, intelligent piece titled "The Failure of the Jewish Establishment." Its potency, to my mind, lies largely in the fact that he is a thinker sympathetic in many ways to Zionism and the state of Israel. Observing college campuses over the last two decades, he is quite right to point out the drift away not simply from xenophobic Zionisms among U.S. Jewish youth but also from an interest in Israel altogether. What he downplayed was the extent to which substantial numbers of American Jewish youth are not just moving away from Zionist politics but actually forming the backbone of *anti*-Zionist activism on innumerable U.S. college campuses, including the most elite ones. At Tufts and Harvard University, for instance, lively and growing Palestine solidarity work has been organized in the last ten years. In both cases, more than one-third of the membership of these campus-based groups has been Jewish.

3. These and other comments by former president Summers were reported in the *Boston Globe*, September 20, 2002.

4. *The Nation,* June 2002.

5. NLRB v. J. Weingarten, INC 420 U.S. 251 (1975) ruled that employees in unionized workplaces have the right, under the National Labor Relations Act, to the presence of a union steward during any management investigatory interview that the employee reasonably believes may result in discipline. These rights have become known as the "Weingarten rights."

6. My younger brother, a journalist and a recipient of two or three of these unwanted attacks, actually—through some fine sleuthing—traced the e-mails back to a WSU law student who had sent at least one of them from the Detroit-area law firm where he was clerking at the time. The student in question was a well-known supporter of the most racist elements in Israel. When he was caught, the harasser's plea not to alert his boss at the firm where he had been engaging in the threatening and harassing e-mails was a curious and pathetic display. He begged the very same Arab American he had threatened to turn over to the FBI for "terrorism" to not tell his boss, lest he be punished. Other harassers by phone and Internet went undiscovered.

7

Decolonizing Chicano Studies in the Shadows of the University's "Heteropatriracial" Order

Ana Clarissa Rojas Durazo

> *Chicana Feminism is the refusal to participate in colonial activity.*
>
> —Teresa Córdova, "Power and Knowledge, Colonialism in the Academy"

I came to Chican@ studies as a young student at UC Santa Cruz in the early 1990s. The school and university system had kept me from accessing the histories of people who shared roots with me, the poetry of people that spoke like me. There was a profound resonance indicative of something you've been unknowingly thirsting for, the foreshadowing of something that will be with you for a long time. Most importantly, I developed a language and analytics through which I could imagine a resistance to the structures of oppression that had produced the multitude of violences that crossed my path as a young Chicana/Mexicana border migrant.

The university was among the hostile institutional structures that, like the experience of many that came before me and after me, persistently reminded me of my exteriority.[1] I drank from the spirit of survival that glistened off the pages of tell-all testimonios and resistance literatures. The one constant among teachers and mentors at UC Santa Cruz and San Francisco State University, where I later pursued graduate study, was their passion—the deep love and conviction they shared for their communities and for what they taught. That love was contagious and inspires me to this day. I write this as a kind of love letter to Chican@ studies, to honor my teachers (inclusive of students) and to honor the spirit of resistance, struggle, and social transformation that their dreams imagine. I write knowing that imbricated within the revelatory practice of naming and assessing the institutional violence we experience in academic institutions as queer/trans/mujeres femenistas lies the possibility for deep transformation.

I write at the moment that marks my temporary exile from Chicano studies.[2] Weathered from the battles of colonization begun long before me, I seek other grounds from which to continue the struggle. The battle waged is a battle forged at the institutional site where colonial politics emerge through the invention of nation projects that order difference within the site of the university. As these politics play out in the twenty-first century, the battle aims to control, subdue, and exteriorize—if not exterminate—recalcitrant queer, trans, and feminist Chican@ politics and subjectivities. For some of us, our queer and feminist decolonial politics render us dangerous subjects to Chicano studies because these politics threaten to unhinge the imperial university's tethering toward a colonial heteropatriarchal Chicano studies. This chapter concerns itself with the ways the imperial university's "heteropatriracial" ordering engenders a heteropatriarchal Chicano studies that "exiles" Chicana feminist and queer subjectivities by attacking, subordinating, and externalizing us.

This story is less about me and the institutional actors it involves than it is about the history and trajectory of imperial projects to inscribe and rearrange imperial subjects through the university. This story is about all of us at the university because we are all implicated as imperial subjects in imperial projects, and our survival depends on our ability to recognize, disentangle, and dislodge the complicated terms of our engagement. Chicano studies is not separate, nor is it immune to these politics; rather, it operates as a location from where the colonial and neocolonial battle against us ensues in the twenty-first century. In the neoliberal imperial age, attacks on ethnic studies and Chican@ studies not only are engineered from outside these academic units but emerge from within its very ranks when Chicano studies colludes with a heteropatriracial colonial project.

In 2008, I accepted a tenure-track position at California State University, Long Beach, in Chicano/Latino studies. Within days of beginning my post, I found myself fending off a series of attempts to demean, intimidate, silence, and recruit me into the politics of a heteromasculinist Chicano studies. I was not alone in my experience; there was a revolving door of arrivals and departures by Chicanas and queer Chican@s that preceded and followed me; one senior scholar shared with me the soul wounds of a decade of surviving Chicano studies. In the years that followed, a few of us built and nurtured a community of Chicana feminist insurgencies to continue the decolonial work begun long ago at CSU–Long Beach. From 2008 to 2012, we rose up to transform Chicano studies into a queerer, more feminist, more radical version of what it had become. Intensifying the structural and daily ways Chicano studies already deployed violence against us, we faced an additional barrage of retaliatory attacks aimed at inhibiting our insurgencies. This chapter considers the structural and historic roots of the imperial university's engagement with Chican@ studies to better understand what shapes and creates this mode of academic colonial violence.

Epistemologies of Empire

A day before his passing, Cuban revolutionary and writer José Martí railed against the U.S. empire's persistent pursuit to dominate and demean "Our America." He wrote, "I have lived inside the beast and know its entrails."[3] Those of us at the university have lived—and some of us have survived—the institutional entrails of U.S. empire. In the university, conquest is digested, and indigenous peoples and people of color's lives, beliefs, cultures, languages, and remains are masticated: collected, acquired, accumulated, cataloged, and subjugated. We are morphed and manipulated and ultimately expelled into the byproduct excrement of neocolonial institutions vying to keep us all in our place. Violence courses through the halls, the site, and the birth and rebirth of the European imaginary of rationality, history, and thought.[4] The university classroom is riddled with violence. Among its primary tasks are the colonizing tactics of indoctrinating Western "civility."

Edward Said reminds us, "The most readily accepted designation for orientalism is an academic one."[5] "Higher education" becomes the producer of epistemic violence that deploys narratives of domination enacted through the erasure of the other, the persistent subjugation of the other driven by the classificatory objectification, the commodification and fetishization of the other, and the structural institutional legitimation of this order.[6]

The university's violent past excluded once, and still, the voices of indigenous and communities of color. The exclusion was necessary so as to effectively constitute the "objective" narratives of domination it is tasked to produce in its role as producer of meanings that animate the existing (colonial) social order. While exclusion remains its practice (and a feature of colonialism), in the neoliberal state formation, the state also acts through incorporation, coaxing racial- and ethnic-based social movements toward a professionalized amalgamation that is dislocated from community and the politics of decolonization.[7] The university's historic and continuous colonial epistemological and ontological underpinnings and structural configuration make Chican@ studies, like ethnic studies, perennially precarious and complexly implicated formations.[8] As Rusty Barceló reminded us last summer in her plenary talk on institutional violence at the MALCS Institute at UC Santa Barbara, "These are not 'our' universities."[9]

The inclusion of people of color into the university in the latter half of the twentieth century emerged when the cultural lexicon of empire invoked a heightened logic of imperial benevolence seen through the Western-driven global development of human rights organizations, the United Nations, global notions of "universal rights," and the U.S. development of civil rights. In the late twentieth and increasingly in the twenty-first century, the university's stated commitments to the liberal multiculturalist pedagogy of diversity (which ethnic studies plays a role in producing) evinces usurpation of radical anticolonial and antiracist movements and politics. Concerns and calls for diversity in the university are dangerous imperialist strategies insofar as they obscure a colonial agenda.[10] Deeply implicated in the university project is a colonial agenda's ghost ontologies of feminicide and genocide through permanent/unending wars, of carceral institutions of confinement, and of the criminality of migration.[11]

From the many shadows of the university, prisoners make classroom desks; the A/V equipment is made in Juarez, Mexico; and the pillaged historical documents of Baghdad become an archive at Stanford. Henry Giroux assesses the role of the imperial university as he considers what Eisenhower once called the *academic*-military-industrial complex, later developed by William Fulbright as a term intended to signal grave concern for the overdetermining influence that the conjoined war industry and the state were increasingly wielding over the production of knowledge and universities in the United States.[12] Angela Davis considers the relationship between the prison-industrial complex and the military-industrial complex as a symbiotic one with mutual support, promotion, and shared structural organization and technologies.[13]

Julia Oparah suggests that countercarceral politics also reveal a "symbiotic" relationship between universities and prisons through university investment in prisons, the use of prisons for research, and the university's production of knowledges that legitimate the prison-industrial complex and train its staff.[14] In *Are Prisons Obsolete?*, Angela Davis addresses the use of prisoners for medical experimentation, which gave rise to the pharmaceutical industry.[15] In her book *Medical Apartheid: The Dark History of Medical Experimentation on Black Americans from Colonial Times to the Present*, Harriet Washington also references Albert Kligman's career exploitation of prisoners in the development of dermatological practice and research at the University of Pennsylvania.[16]

The convergence of an academic-military-prison-industrial complex produces the shadows of the university, the places where people of color are rendered exploitable and expendable. We are reminded that the university operates as a space for the ongoing recruitment, management, and production of imperial violence against us and our communities as it imagines, articulates, and arranges the spaces of symbolic and material necropolitics within and beyond the university.[17] My earlier commentary suggests that the university project in the United States has historically been tied to colonial interests in service to, practice of, and design of imperial and Eurocentric knowledge formations.[18]

When assessing the liberatory projects of Chican@ studies and ethnic studies, it becomes necessary to consider the compositional role that the university has as a site for the production of knowledge emerging from and toward the ends of imperialism. The particular shifts in the organization of the twenty-first-century university show an intensification and reconstitution of U.S. campuses toward militarism and the policing of dissent that marks a deepening of its imperial efforts and has particular implications for both the communities under attack and the making of imperial subjects.[19]

In the post-9/11, increasingly militarized university campus, intensified surveillance of communities of color has led to heightened abuses of police power and police violence. Latina students at San Francisco State University (SFSU) reported to me what they experienced as an increase in sexual harassment by campus cops with the increase in campus policing after 9/11.[20] Women of color and men of color are always suspect in the university—surveilled, regulated, and disciplined. In 2005, also at SFSU, Africana studies professor Antwi Akom was arrested and jailed as he entered his own office in the College of Ethnic Studies building; he didn't have his ID card. On the night before my dissertation defense in 2007, I too was accosted by security at the University of California, San Francisco's (UCSF's) Genentech Hall, who insisted I show them my ID card, which I purposefully did not carry in solidarity with the millions of migrants across the country who don't have IDs. And when security called backup, I decided it was time to flee, and as I headed for the door to walk out of the building, the security guard pointed his gun at me, threatening to shoot. I was unsure if I would make it through the door, but I walked out, knowing my stint with the academic-industrial complex at UCSF was coming to a close—the graduate school experience that began with me being racially profiled as a daycare job interviewee (university administrators revealing their apparent inability to imagine a Chicana graduate student at UCSF) ended with another kind of gun pointed at my back.

As the militarization of university campuses intensified through increased police presence, a surge in racial and heteropatriarchal violence closely followed. In 2010, UC San Diego's "Compton Cookout" escalated to symbolic references of lynching found all over campus; the "Vatos Locos Party" at the University of Washington was one of similar themed parties across many university campuses. Antiqueer and antitrans violence also emerged quite publicly at many universities across the United States, including CSU–Long Beach where hate violence was deployed as an intimidation tactic against Chicana Feminisms Conference organizers and speakers. Violence in the university is no aberration; it is as constant as the university's refusal to return sacred belongings to indigenous communities. The techniques of a neoliberalist mix of exclusion and/through incorporation emerge through violence. Violence codes, surrounds, and carves the moment of inclusion/exclusion in the university project.

"Ghost ontologies" emerge alongside imaginaries and structures of citizenship, of belonging, of the American Dream, and of civil and human rights—a cultural lexicon imagined in the university. The War on Terror, the War on Drugs, the war on migrants, and relevant repressive feminicidal and genocidal maneuvers all invoke an appeal to security and freedom—ideologies that travel from and through the university. Through the diversity project at the university, the brutal violence of war is deployed alongside the refrain of feigned rescue that metaphorically conceals the attempt at takeover.[21] Empire emerges, as Michael Hardt and Antonio Negri posit, through the frame and form of democracy, brandishing perilous convergent practices and logics of inclusivity.[22] The acquisition of imperial subjects is an epistemological project of force. Ontologies of violence turn on the inclusion of citizenry through education into the cultural lexicon of empire.[23]

Empire's persistent drive toward the expansion of geopolitical territorial/economic acquisition extends to, even hinges on, the acquisition of minds/bodies, on the production of imperial subjectivities to buttress and assume the labor of maintaining and upholding the walls of empire. Empire rests, especially in twenty-first-century iterations, as a seemingly inconsistent, even contradictory, yet codependent, co-constitutive set of simultaneous maneuvers that posit the violence of exteriorizing through material, symbolic, representational, and social deaths alongside inclusive, at times even inviting gestures that seem to loosen the bounds demarcating the imperial subjects' access to citizenship, "recognition," and some (albeit often slight) protections from the scythe of premature (legal, representational, social, or material) deaths.[24]

Ethnic Studies: In the Shadows of the University

In 1968, Third World Liberation Front Strike leaders at SFSU carried off the longest student strike in U.S. history; the struggle birthed the independent College of Ethnic Studies.[25] As Chicano studies academic units emerged over the decades that followed, a unique combination of counterhegemonic visions, local sociopolitical histories, and institutional policies and practices combined to manifest a variety of formations that can in no way be homogenized.[26] The ontological, epistemological, and administrative particulars of each unit emerged from multidirectional processes with Chicano movement forms outside and inside of the university.

At CSU–Long Beach, Chicana student leader Anna Nieto-Gomez, who participated in the development of Chicano studies, shared her observations about the university's hunger for new federal funds from the Civil Rights Act of 1964 and the Higher Education Act of 1965.[27] California legislators seemed uninterested in accessing these funds, so CSU–Long Beach president Carl McIntosh extended admissions to students of color through a special program that flexed the admission requirements for athletes. With increased numbers of students of color, colleges successfully lobbied California legislators to allow the CSU to receive federal funds.[28] As Maylei Blackwell historicizes, a mostly Chicana-driven recruitment effort led to five hundred Chicanas and Chicanos enrolling at CSU–Long Beach in fall 1969, a significant increase from the sixty students of color admitted in spring 1967.[29] In conversation with Chicano student organizers at CSU–Long Beach, an advisory board made up of faculty and administrators guided students who, in conversation with the U.S. Department of Higher Education, developed a proposal for Chicano studies and other ethnic studies units. While Chicano studies formations in California emerged out of Chicano student protests and movements, they also emerged out of the university structures and under federal mandates (and in particular with the university's aim to secure funds through these federal mandates).

Roderick Ferguson's assessment of ethnic studies in *The Reorder of*

Things: The University and Its Pedagogices of Minority Difference speaks to the incredible negotiations that take place at the time of absorption into the university. His approach considers the university as an institutional form centrally organized by the state and reflective (and derivative) of state and private interests that work to produce an "adaptive hegemony" that compromises oppositional movements through incorporation.[30] He argues that while social movements imagine they can shape institutions like the university to reflect their politics, the university's "recognition" of difference aids in legitimating the state and private sphere as it appears to resolve its tendency toward social exclusion.[31] Ferguson recognizes the entrapment social movements face at the university: "The will to institutionality is itself a mode of subjection," he says. "The subject's agency depends on the very administrative forms of power that manage and discipline forms of difference."[32]

According to Anna Ochoa O'Leary, from very early on, Chicano/a scholars/activists expressed regular consternation about the prospects of housing Chicano studies in a hostile university environment and its ability to effectively challenge the dominant academic paradigms that might be oppositional to its goals or vision.[33] Several articles and discussion circulated that expressed concern with the rise of university administrative control and the effects of having to organize into structures that were coherent to the university.[34] As the field emerged, criticism over the impact of "academic colonialism" on Chicano movements and Chicano studies followed.[35] Chicano studies has always existed in a complicated relationship with the university, suggests Michael Soldatenko in *Chicano Studies: Genesis of a Discipline*, because the administrative legitimation it needs also pressures it away from radical thought and praxis.[36] The public university, as a state institution, is modeled by state politics to maintain heteropatriarchal racialized asymmetries within and beyond the university. All of us who traverse it, and especially academic units, are pressured toward such an arrangement. In fact, Anna Nieto-Gomez argues that an organized patriarchal structure within the Chicano student movement at CSU–Long Beach became entrenched at the moment United Mexican American Students (UMAS) was formalized and received "office space" within the university structure, a shift that required a hierarchical organizational order that reproduced the university's patriarchal model and eschewed Chicanas out of leadership positions.[37] Additionally, Chicana leadership at CSU–Long Beach was forestalled through early hires in Chicano studies that mirrored the university's predominant male faculty population at the time. Chicanas would be denied leadership roles in Chicano studies at CSU–Long Beach for decades to come.

Heteropatriarchal Violence in Chicano Studies

Soon after I arrived at CSU–Long Beach in 2008, I witnessed and directly experienced a version of Chicano studies that was insidiously hostile to Chicanas and queer Chican@s through the deployment of routine violence, inclusive of normatized structural inequities. The structural inequities were critical because they ensured the abuse of the chair's power to intimidate through discipline, to unequally distribute resources, to assign and take away courses, to organize scheduling, to determine department priorities, and so on. Chicanas served as mentors, offering independent studies courses for which male faculty were formally credited; they were unequally granted course releases and frequently taught four-day-a-week schedules, leaving little to no time for research and writing. Chicanas were kept out of teaching core courses, thereby facing an increased risk of not meeting enrollments and having classes cancelled, sometimes leading to semesters teaching five courses to make up for a cancelled course.

Within two to three weeks of having arrived at CSU–Long Beach, the courses I had agreed to teach the upcoming spring semester were taken away from me. It was made clear to me that I had no say in the matter regardless of whether those courses were in my job description. In fact, as of this date, my requests to teach an available class that was in my job description were never met—in violation of the union faculty contract. The structural inequities ensured male leadership in designing and facilitating the faculty meeting agenda, and I found the meetings to be a space where Chicanas were verbally harassed. At my first faculty meeting, I witnessed the use of meetings as a space to attack, demean, and humiliate a senior female faculty colleague. She was undermined, yelled at, and belittled. This happened constantly. I found that faculty meetings repeatedly expressed two ideological frames (through many examples and presentations): One was marked by the expression of consternation over the hostile and racist university structure that demeans and threatens Chicano studies. The second was marked by the expression of consternation over Chicana power. The first usually led toward defeatist, accommodationist, and/or oppositional sentiments and strategies. The second led to a display of demeaning and intimidating attacks on Chicanas and queer Chicano/as.

What was it about the convergence of Chicano movement and Chicano studies politics with university politics at this location and at this historical conjuncture that elicited this form of violence? The perceived (and very real, material) positioning of Chicano studies in the shadows of the university conjured a Chicano studies mired in the politics and practices that engendered a kind of racialized heteropatriarchal violence. To help understand the production of this form of violence, we can further consider how colonial projects (like the university) structure and perform heteropatriracial ordering that produces and enlists subordinated racialized Chicano heteronormative misogynous violence against feminist/queer Chican@s. The term *heteropatriracial* reminds us of the synchronic and indivisible racial/sexual politics of colonialism that stymie and redirect the potential of resistance and decolonization into violence directed at the community from within the community, thereby maintaining and reproducing the colonial social order. Living in the shadows of the university, we learn to cast the persistence of shadows.

CSU–Long Beach opened in the post–World War II era of increased regulation and surveillance that ushered in the Cold War. That tendency combined with the fact that Long Beach hosts the central office for the CSU chancellor and has strong ties to Orange County resources (students, staff, funding, and faculty) created a more conservative centralized culture under heightened administrative control.[38] I had previously taught at UC Davis where Chicano/a studies, like San Francisco State, had comparatively and significantly more autonomy than at CSU–Long Beach, a feature that also contributed to the repressive culture within the department. Additionally, while the student demographics reflect a majority student of color population with approximately ten thousand Latin@ students, the faculty and administrative structures maintain a clear hierarchy of white male authority while people of color are kept out of most powerful posts. Whereas Latin@ students make up roughly one-third of the student population, Latina tenured and tenure-track faculty at CSU–Long Beach are slightly higher than a mere 1 percent of the total faculty population. Latino faculty demographics are closer to 2 percent. These numbers help ensure the precarious positioning of Chicano studies, not just by the obvious demographic minoritization of Latin@s, but also by the patriarchal structural inequities that contribute to heteropatriarchal violence within Chicano studies. The statistical data as it appears on the university's website does not stipulate the count for tenure-track versus tenured faculty, which reflects one of the structural inequities in

Chicano studies during these years. Whereas most of the men were tenured (four tenured, one untenured—although he successfully went up for tenure in 2011), most of the women were not (one tenured, two untenured).

The convergence of these heteropatriarchal logics and structures was also made evident through curricular design and redesign. Chicana faculty had struggled for over two decades to get a core course that focused on Chicanas and Chicana feminisms. Every semester at least one of the only two courses focusing on Chicanas was cut due to low enrollments. The male leadership expressed clear opposition to what was framed as an exclusionary and irrelevant course that would prioritize content that only affected half of the population and would be hostile to Chicano students. In her analysis of Mario García's state of the field analysis, Sandy Soto argues that Chicana feminists are construed as "outside threats to the field . . . positioning their scholarship as completely irrelevant to the needs of Chicanos . . . radically irreconcilable with . . . Chicano scholarship."[39]

This dismal situation got worse when we began organizing, building a community of support, and countering the sexism in Chicano/a studies. A senior Chicana colleague approached me soon after I arrived. She asked me to organize a way to counter the ways Chicanas were treated in the department. Four Chicana tenure-track, tenured, and lecturer faculty began to meet to strategize. Heightened attacks followed. The verbal assaults escalated in department meetings. My office door was vandalized twice, my office was taken away from me more than once, and it was made nearly impossible for me to take needed medical leave to help my mother through surgical treatment for advanced cancer. When former San Francisco State University colleagues invited me to represent CSU–Long Beach at a meeting convened to discuss the future of ethnic studies in the state of California, I was blocked from representing the department.

The psychological abuse was constant. For example, what a trusted colleague called a "witch hunt" was started when female faculty and students whom I worked with were called in to meet with male leadership where they were interrogated and exhorted to divulge information about me. I was setup to be investigated by the dean of personnel. Rumors were started that in this era of attacks on ethnic studies and budget cuts, I would be responsible for the downfall of Chicano studies because I had aired the dirty laundry when I reached out to the campus's Office of Equity for support.

While the rumors were clear isolationist tactics, the attacks intensified when an adjunct who began to counter the misogyny in the department was fired for speaking up. Some of the female faculty who were organizing were enticed to support the male leadership through structural incentives as well as through the display of intimidating threats that frightened them into acquiescence. Worried about my well-being, trusted colleagues pleaded with me to "not put myself in the line of fire," but the bullets were already coming and would continue to slowly take each one of us (Chicanas and queer Chican@s) down and kill our spirit—resisting was the only way.

Women of Color Feminisms: Deciphering Harm, the Malinchista Refrain

I came of college age with a fountain of words written by women of color to craft and tell of a politic born out of their material realities. Since then, the "theories of the flesh" scribing Chicana and women of color feminisms have guided me, showing me the way through to the other side of harm.[40] Their words, along with my mother's and grandmother's, made it possible for me to resist, and now I invoke some of their voices in an effort to further understand the makings of the situation, of a heteromasculinist Chicano politics at CSU–Long Beach.

I begin with the vital lesson that Emma Perez's "decolonial imaginary" imparts: the reminder to be heedful of misogynous tendencies in Chicano emancipatory projects.[41] The invocation of Chicanismo's "patria" deploys a highly gendered nation-building imaginary mobilized in response to a misrepresentation of the university's and the state's white supremacy as primarily, if not exclusively, targeting the figurative (narrativized as heterosexual) Chicano male subject.[42] Chicana faculty and students are endangered, in this analytic frame, to the extent that they are "Chicano"; in this synecdoche, Chicanas are subsumed under another subject, a role framed by this heteropatriarchal Chicano nationalist imaginary. As Armando Rendón argues, "macho" is a reference to the nation.[43] In this frame the assertion of gender/racial/sexual subjectivities other than heteronormatized Chicano are perceived as threatening to the Chicano heteropatriarchal nation's imaginary. When queer and trans Chican@s and Chican@ feminists reject our submission, we are "exiled," framed as a threat to the nation's project through the colonial gendered racial sexual political imaginary of malinchismo: we are cast as traitors, untrustworthy, and outsiders.[44] We must be taken down for the survival of the Chicano. Chicanos expel and attack us because they recognize we have the power to deeply transform/decolonize their "Chingón politics," their version of Chicano studies that perceives itself as a microcosm of the nation; we have the power to reveal the limits of an implausible hetero-masculinist anticolonial resistance.[45]

Chicana Feminists have thoroughly critiqued Mexican and Chicano nationalisms that imagine the historical Nahua figure, Malintzín Tenepal, as Malinche, the indigenous woman eager to be delivered to the colonizer, complicitous in conquest, and on whom colonization is blamed.[46] The term *malinche* becomes a feminized noun and figure of speech in Mexican Spanish that comes to mean betrayal. Mexican-Chicano colonial misogyny utilizes the Malinche myth to deepen coloniality by organizing violence within the community through the persecution and repression of Mexicanas/Chicanas. In "Chicano Manifesto," Armando Rendón argues, "Malinches attack their own brothers, betray our dignity and manhood."[47] Here, the subject who derides the violence she endures, she who speaks, becomes a threat that must be contained; she must be muted. Violence is deployed to silence the subject. As Chicana feminists note, Malinche's force was her (multilingual) tongue.[48] "That's enough out of you, woman," yells the chair of Chicano studies, with his finger pointed at me as I express my concern at a meeting about the sex inequities in the department. That would be the first of several times I would be verbally silenced and attacked for speaking up at a faculty meeting and for calling out sexism. Speaking of the violence committed against us is deemed the betrayal that divides the community while the violence delivered against our voices, bodies, and minds is routinized instead of recognized as the violent betrayal of the community that it is.

Once during a faculty meeting where we discussed the possibility of a core course on Chicanas and Chicana Feminisms, "the guys" tag-teamed their opposition. I countered their machista moves again and again and then noticed that the conversation shut me out. They addressed each other as if I were no longer in the room, but they had shifted the subject of discussion to an interrogation of my loyalty to the department and my wicked feminist intentions. Unable to successfully counter, or unsteady the logic I put forth, they resorted to the tactic I call a "malinchista refrain"—the ways the political imaginary of malinchismo are deployed when a litany of other heteropatriarchal technologies of subjection prove ineffective.

The malinchista refrain would be repeated over and over again with me and other Chicana faculty and students—as it was with Chicana feminists in the Chicano movement—in order to discredit the character that does not conform and defer to the politics of male authority.[49] That meeting was called to a close on that note, and I approached the male faculty with a senior

Chicana colleague for support (always recommended!). I expressed concern for how the discussion echoed a malinchista refrain. They expressed a total lack of awareness for how that was playing out, I explained, citing movement references, and they responded, "We're not part of *that* Chicano movement that does that." Yet they taught the books that taught *that* Chicano movement history. Denial was a constant and pervasive feature of the psychological abuse we endured. Everything the female faculty expressed concern for or opposition to with regard to sexism in the department was denied. That can really get to you and you find yourself asking, did that really happen or am I making this up? Working collectively in groups can interrupt the ways we might internalize attempts at gaslighting, which can otherwise throw us off our footing; colegas can help affirm the series of events.

I remember at the last department meeting I attended that my internalized self-doubt had grown to the point where I had to confirm with another colleague if a display of homophobic hate speech was really that or if I was making it up. I realized how much my own intuition had grown cloudy, how far I had strayed from trusting my own sense of what qualifies as abuse. I saw the toll of being disciplined into tolerating abuse, the result of a nearly everyday assault on my integrity and dignity.

Maylei Blackwell's assessment and oral histories of both the gender/sexual politics of Chicano nationalism and the way these politics played out in student organizing at CSU–Long Beach illustrate how the university in particular produced what Anna Nieto-Gomez identifies as hyperbolized campus hypermasculinities.[50] Comparing her experience on campus to working in the community, she said, "Back on campus, it seemed guys were role-playing the exaggerated stereotypical macho and forced women to play out their passive role. . . . [I]f these guys deviated from this hyper macho role, they were criticized for being wimps or Anglicized because Anglo men were stereotyped as weak."[51] Betita Martinez's theory of "Chingón politics" helps interpret the way Chicanos inhered colonial sex/gender dominance tactics that led to practices of effeminizing the enemy and playing out a gendering politics of dominance within the Chican@ community.[52]

Yvette Flores-Ortiz's theory of "culture freezing" considers how deepened gendered asymmetries of power produce violence against women in heterosexual Latino relationships.[53] In her application of "culture freezing," she argues that when Latino immigrants are immersed in gringo cultural contexts that are antagonistic and hostile to Latinos and Latino cultural forms, one of the responses can be to exaggerate idealized and exacerbated rigid sex/gender roles that entrench a hypermasculine, authoritarian protectorate perceived as better equipped to negotiate the public space. This response in turn domesticates, isolates, and demeans the role of Latinas who become servant nurturers of the combatant, masculinized Latino leader and family. This analysis can elucidate what Anna Nieto-Gomez calls the "hyper macho role" on campus that expected Chicana student leaders, as part of their movement duties, to clean the notoriously unkempt "Brown House" where Chicano (male) students lived.[54] When Chicanas were elected to leadership positions within UMAS, it was this "hyper macho role" that prompted Chicano students to ask Chicana leaders to step aside and fake an organizational structure with male leadership to appear more respectable in public.[55] We can consider the interaction between the university's hostile institutional form, which has privileged Eurocentric knowledges and white heteropatriarchal authoritarian structures, and heteropatriarchal Chicano movement tendencies and how these have combined to create an exaggerated heteropatriarchal Chicano student movement politic that births and shapes, through the university's heteropatriracial ordering, Chicano studies at CSU–Long Beach.

Further, colonialism orders genders and sexualities through racial projects. In *Sexual Conquest,* Andrea Smith argues that colonialism works by marking indigenous women's bodies as "inherently violable" but also by marking indigenous men as inherently violent. She cautions of the ways indigenous communities internalize colonial sexual politics.[56] These colonial mappings gender indigeneity in ways that produce misogynous violence within indigenous communities. In "Heterosexualism and the Colonial/Modern Gender System," María Lugones argues that colonialism imposed a new hegemonic asymmetrical gender system that destroyed peoples, cultures, and communities as it built the West in part through the deployment of violence against indigenous women.[57] Oyeronke Oyewumi argues that the educational institutional form served as a key site through which women in Yorubaland were "invented" as subordinated subjects in a colonial process that eroded women's agency while it mobilized men's dominance.[58] This analytic strain offers a historical context to help understand how the university emerges as a site for the continuous engendering of racial sexual politics through heteropatriracial ordering that organizes/subordinates communities of color through the deployment of racial projects that hinge on asymmetrical dimorphous sex/gender ordering, which then produces violence against Chicanas, Chicana feminisms, and queer and sex/gender nonconforming bodies. The legacies and contemporary structuring of universities through imperial forms and interests, as addressed earlier, situates the university as a key institution through which colonial heteropatriracialities are produced epistemologically and ontologically. Heteropatriracial ordering acts to reinforce the subordination and precariousness of Chicano studies in the university system by producing heteropatriarchal structures that erode Chicana and queer Chican@ agency, divide Chican@/Latin@ communities, and inhibit decolonial praxis.

Las Rebeldes and ConFem: Decolonizing Chicano Studies

I called us "Las Rebeldes," invoking a needed spirit of zapatista *rebeldía hacia un nuevo amanecer* (a spirit of rebellion on the way toward a new beginning). When we started meeting and planning, we strategically met a few times for dinner or drinks after faculty meetings so we could deconstruct the *mala onda* (bad vibe) and redirect it. We prioritized addressing issues of sexual harassment. I had witnessed a student being sexually harassed by one of the male faculty right in front of me in the middle of the day. I could only imagine what went on in private.[59] We strategized how to back each other up at meetings and interrupt the abuse and also set the goal of getting a core course that focused on Chicana feminisms, which we succeeded in having unanimously approved in 2011.[60] I met with the university's Office of Equity with a former civil rights organizer who became an ally and agreed to attend our faculty meetings to encourage less aggressive behavior. Her presence was effective and reminded me of the dangers of isolation and the ways we were isolated into the department structure and of the power of breaking isolation as a step in transforming violence.

The faculty agreed to have a departmental retreat sponsored by the Office of Equity. In one of many moves to deny the problem, the retreat name and focus was changed by male leadership in the department from addressing sexism in the department to addressing "the culture of the department," but Las Rebeldes knew what we were there to do. One of the items we discussed was the use of department meetings as spaces for abuse. A female colleague at the retreat broke down in tears addressing one of the male faculty; she expressed feeling so belittled when she was yelled at, being made to feel so small and humiliated in front of the rest of the faculty. She was sitting just a few inches away from him. He smirked and responded with no other response, physical or verbal, except to say, "I guess I don't know what the difference is between speaking in an academic tone and a hostile one."

The response pointed to this Chicano studies scholar's troubling conflation of academic work practice with violence against women.

In early fall 2009, two of us met with the newly formed Conciencia Femenil, a recently formed Chican@ student collective, and we began planning the first Chicana Feminisms Conference. I knew reaching out to Chicana feminist scholars, activists, and communities was necessary for our survival, but I also knew that the problems we faced extended far past CSU–Long Beach, and building community and movement was key. We organized across the hierarchical divisions the university imposed on Chicanas and queer Chican@s. Doing so disrupted the institutional power assigned differentially to faculty and student roles, and it proved to be vital in building community and movement and in rupturing the isolation that compounds the risk of violence.

Soon we would experience firsthand a particular kind of violence deployed vehemently against *las que no se dejan* (the ones who will not submit). Early Chicana feminist Anna Nieto-Gomez and CSU–Long Beach Chicana feminist student group Hijas de Cuauhtemoc learned early on at CSU–Long Beach that although violence against Chicanas is constant, when Chicanas resisted the submissive role, greater violence was unleashed. Although Chicanas experienced sexual harassment and violation as routine in organizing work for the *movimiento* (movement) at CSU–Long Beach, escalated rituals of violence and systematically organized attacks on Chicanas were deployed against Anna, Hijas de Cuauhtemoc, and Chicana leaders—when Anna vied for (and won) a leadership position, and when they contested the heteropatriarchal sexual politics of UMAS/MEChA.[61]

In 2010, we gathered with members of Hijas de Cuauhtemoc at the Chicana Feminisms Conference at CSU–fLong Beach to honor and remember their legacy. They spoke of the historic event that symbolically killed Anna Nieto-Gomez and Chicana feminist leadership at CSU–Long Beach. Chicano students used antiwar props, turning them into caskets with the names of Chicana feminist leaders. These were carried in a mock funeral procession leading to the site of their lynched effigies. This violence against Anna and Hijas de Cuauhtemoc was made possible at the site of the university; however, whereas the caskets had previously represented the carrying of beloved young bodies of Chicanos killed during the Vietnam War, they now were made to mock the mourning of Chicanas. The caskets enacted an exiling of Chicanas symbolically killed for their presumed feminist betrayal of Chicano heteropatriarchy.

Organizers did not recognize the inconsistency between the use of the same props from a Chicano antiwar movement action that symbolically mourned the loss of Chicanos in the Vietnam War on the one hand and using the caskets to symbolize a war against Chicanas, Chicana feminisms, and Chicana leadership on the other. In the first case, the perceived enemy responsible for the atrocities is imagined as the war machine, racist Uncle Sam, and U.S. imperialism, while in the second case the perceived enemy is Chicana feminists who, it is imagined, tried to take down Chicanos when they called for attention to Chicana concerns, when they contested the move-ment's patriarchal organization, and when they vied for leadership within its organizational structure. This shows an interesting sleight of hand where the subject perceived as a threat to Chicanos—the subject the movement mobi-lizes to fight and take down—shifts from U.S. racism to Chicana feminists.

This shift was also visible in faculty meetings, as discussed earlier, and reminds us of the ways we are made colonial subjects, marked by and mark-ing difference with violation, driven misguidedly into the pursuit of the specter of dominance. This marks the coconstitutivity of heteropatriracial violence that deploys violence against colonized sexed and queered others by ordering, and producing through colonial violence, racially subordinated hypermasculinist violent subjectivities. We won't get very far in our efforts to counter racism as long as that fight is derailed into attacking the queered/feminized or otherwise marginalized in our very own communities.

In spring 2010, at the same time that we were honoring the legacy of Hijas's historic contributions to Chicana feminism and the Chicano move-ment, we experienced a similar escalation of the attacks in addition to the already everyday heteropatriarchal violence we faced in Chicano stud-ies. Again, the initial attackers were antiwar activists, some of whom were CSU–Long Beach Chicano studies graduates. They attacked the organizers and keynote speakers at the Chicana Feminisms Conference. "Hociconas," we were called, a term rarely gendered in the masculine; it emerges exclu-sively as a tactic to silence speaking women, deriding us with its meaning, "the mouth of an animal," as in "she speaks when she should not (have the capacity)."[62] Chicanos posted comments on the campus newspaper's website, the *Daily 49er* (if that's not a reference to the university's heteropatriracial order, I don't know what is), calling for the death of conference organizers, whom they named "lesbians" disguised as "feminists" and "jotos" disguised as allied Chicanos. In a Chicano heteropatriarchal order, the brandishing of lesbian or joto is imposed as a kind of social death that renders the subject exiled from their ability to participate in the movement by reducing their character (in clear reference to the malinchista refrain) to a sexually framed inherent tendency toward betrayal. In the early days of student organizing at CSU–Long Beach, Chicanas were called lesbians when they resisted the sexual advances of Chicanos (because their prescribed movement role presumed their sexual availability to Chicanos).[63] The comments also inferred death to those who talked back: "el infierno eterno te espera" ("eternal hell awaits you"), they claimed.

The comments were published while the conference was under way. The comments posited the university as a threat to "decent Latino families" insofar as it "promotes sexual deviance" (by hosting queer speakers). Reminiscent of Yvette Flores Ortiz's notion of "culture freezing" addressed earlier, the Chicano movement nationalist imaginary hinges on the unit of the heteropatriarchal family as the birthplace of culture ("la familia es la cuna de la cultura") as it exiles queer Latinidades into the (conflated as) queer non-Chicano "university." The commentary does not seem concerned with the kind of sexual deviance (or can we really call it "deviant"?) that produces staggering rates of sexual violence against Chicanas on college campuses like CSU–Long Beach.

The commentary included anonymous posts by Latinos and Latinas inside the university as well as community members outside the university. It cited an opposition to the "wasting of time and university resources" on matters of sexuality and the "recruiting (of) effeminate (Chicano) types as students" while the "real Chicano victim subject," "youth exhibiting normal heterosexual behavior," is incarcerated. Ironically, the heteropatriarchal Chicano is animated as the primary victim of the movement while matters of sexuality are deemed irrelevant; additionally, whereas social scientific knowledges of sexuality are used in the earlier (deviance) commentary to critique the university as a space for knowledge production about sexuality, the spending of university resources to produce knowledges about sexuality are deemed wasteful. Not only does the logic of this commentary deny histories of colonial violence and contemporary law enforcement harassment and violence against criminalized queer and gender nonconforming people of color, but it also obscures the university's heteropatriarchal order.[64] Consistent with heteropatriracial colonial politics and histories, sexuality and the bodies of Chican@s—queer and straight—become the site where the battle is played out between Chicano studies and the imperial university.

Chicano studies is even imagined as having been "taken over" by lesbians and "jotos." Further, La Voz de Aztlán writes that it is "the enemies of Chi-canos" that promote "the homosexual lifestyle . . . in order to destroy our culture." Enemies that "have infiltrated our organizations and groups within our culture . . . their purpose is to weaken the social fiber of 'La Cultura Mex-icana.'" "One movement that was invented by our enemies was the so called 'feminist movement.' The enemy empowers lesbians to lead this one partic-ular movement." Here the slip emerges yet again between construing "the enemy" as the hostile university institution or a perceived racial threat to "the culture" and language that frames the victimization of "the culture," the movement, and even Chicano studies as spearheaded by Chicana feminists, lesbians, and "the homosexual culture." The rightful, if not sole, Chicano vic-tim is again framed as a heterosexual male. I am left to wonder what was it about Chicano antiwar (and even antiprison) organizing that allowed its ranks to so easily shift the target of protest into a display of violence against Chican@ feminists and queer Chican@s?

After we began investigating who some of the attacks were coming from, I found that I had stood side by side with one of the groups responsible for the hate violence at an antiwar and Palestinian solidarity protest they co-sponsored. It is compelling that the very groups that challenged the vio-lence of war and empire, first protesting the Vietnam War and then the War on Terror, are the groups who have turned the protest of empire into the deployment of violence against Chicana feminists and queer Chican@s. This raises important questions about the limits of the historic hypermas-culinist cultural form of Chicano antiwar protest politics that, in reference again to Betita Martinez's "Chingón politics," internalize the misogynist ordering of colonial war projects while displaying hypermasculinist mili-tancy. This militancy and its concomitant sexual politics are engendered in a resistance that emerges while it engages the state's heteropatriracial police/militarized repression. This signals the dangers of a political strategy that potentially colludes with the colonial project of heteropatriracial ordering through the deployment of colonial sexual violence against Chicanas and women of color.[65]

How is it that the anti-imperialist protest calling out the "take over" of lands and peoples inhered the modalities it critiqued by "taking over" orga-nizations and engaging in the symbolic killing of one's own community? What is it about Chicano students getting a little piece of land in the uni-versity—a trailer assigned to UMAS, the predecessor to MEChA and Raza, by CSU Long Beach—that created the first entrenched heteropatriarchal hierarchical "official" order? Andrea Smith argues that land is commodified through colonialism, a presumption that fuels the heteronormative nation, which must then rely on boundaries to include and exclude.[66] What is it about the heightened militarization of culture and campus alike during an intensified moment of war—such as the Vietnam War and the current War on Terror—that produces escalations in the violence deployed against Chicanas on campus? And how is the marked increase of sexual harassment of Latinas by an expanded number of security officers on campus (in the incidents cited at San Francisco State University) after 9/11 related to the other forms of violence against Chicanas this piece addresses? This marks a key moment of convergence, how the university's heteropatriracial project turns on Chicano studies to exclude at the moment of inclusion. Because the subject must be made recognizable to the hegemonic frame, social movements that vie for recognition are in the process being remade through incorporation. What ensues in this particular example of Ferguson's "adaptive hegemony" is a heteropatriarchal Chicano studies.

Exclusion ensues at the moment of inclusion because the form of ethnic studies that is legible to the state is heteropatriarchal. Chicana and trans and queer Chican@ feminisms and bodies are illegible to the "heteropatriracial" project and are therefore exteriorized for violence to expunge the recalcitrant sexed, queered other while enlivening a set of practices that conjure a heteropatriarchal reordering of the racially minoritized subject. It is through the colonial violation of racialized ordering that Chican@s/Latin@s become legible subjects in that our violation affirms white supremacy. The racialized ordering of colonial violence is deployed through sexual and gendering means that forge the heteropatriracial project within Chicano/Latino communities. Chicanas and queer Chican@s become legible subjects to the heteropatriracial project through our violation. When Chicanos and Chicano studies recast us as violable, they are affirming the colonial hegemonic order. Insurgent feminisms have been a constant at CSU–Long Beach, as has been the exiling of queer/Chicana feminists because, when attempts to mute/mutate us into a heteropatriarchal artifact fail, we are exiled. Decolonial projects are ingested and become legible in the university insofar as they maintain the hegemonic order.

Si Hay Otro Modo de Vivir (There Is Another Way to Live)

As Chicanas and queer and trans Chican@s, we face great dangers to our well-being in Chicano/Latino studies formations in the imperial university. As Renato Rosaldo has stated, institutions of higher learning tell the previously excluded to come in, sit down, and shut up. You are welcome here as long as you conform to our norms.[67] Managed and regulated in the disciplinarity of empire: the proper quiet junior faculty *mujer* will shut up until tenure. The heteropatriracial ordering of the university imposes silence upon us, a silence we learn how to keep by the time tenure rolls around, a silence heteropatriarchy in Chicano studies builds on, feeds from, and is dependent on. Empire and Chicano studies converge upon the muzzled gendered/racialized subject. As an institution entrenched in the practices of a colonial state, the university is more interested in having us acquiesce to some sort of muted formation of a professional token representative, expected to sever our affiliations to the poor, queer, feminist, indigenous, and decolonial commitments in order to cash in on the careers of the few selected Hispanics fortunate enough to have been allowed in.

But having seen so many women of color suffer endlessly through the process of tenure—often denied tenure—I entered a tenure-track position with the conviction that tenure was not worth sacrificing my dignity or my politics. I couldn't let that yoke me so I did the only thing I could do when honoring and embracing my own dignity and my sisters' (fellow faculty and students): I resisted.[68] I prioritized my dignity and spoke out whenever I was being undermined or other Chicanas were, because I don't think that sitting in a room listening to the constant derision of women's labor and work is not or won't eventually become violence more explicitly targeting me; it will and is already. I walked into the university disinvested from it because my prior experiences organizing in universities against the War on Terror and the occupation of Palestine revealed its colonial investments. As Cynthia Enloe cautions of the brutality of being "married to the military": institutions domesticate us into propping up and maintaining the colonial heteropatriarchal order by deploying violence against women.[69] That is how I am able to write and publish this article before I go up for tenure. Invoking the courage these actions demand when swimming in postgrad school debt ensures that I am protected; it does not guarantee tenure, but it builds a path that is even better, a path shaped by a commitment to honoring myself, my sisters, and my community.

How do the politics of conquest arrive in your day-to-day life at the university? If the organization of heteropatriracial projects at the university coconstitute violent heteropatriarchal Chicano studies, then how can we transform these projects that simultaneously render death worlds in Iraq, on the U.S.–Mexico border, or in prisons, while Chicana feminisms and queer or trans Chican@s face becoming the living dead through exile and the "chronic erasure" of our being, our voice, and our resistance?

Still, I posit that Chicano studies is also marked with a complex and contradictory legacy of resistance in search of decolonization, determined to assert the silenced narratives of our communities, intent on carving liberatory and transformative spaces amid the colonial project of higher learning in the academic-industrial complex. Ethnic studies was born and in many formations continues to be a project to transform the (epistemic and exclusionary) violence of the university. But transforming the colonial violence of the university hinges on our ability to account for and transform intracommunity violence.

What does the project of Chicano studies—the curriculum, the structures, the everyday—look like if our lives as queer and trans Chican@s and Chicana feminists become audible to Chicano studies? What must change profoundly, at the very roots and in the imagination of Chicano studies, for our lives and resistant knowledges to be central to its project—not peripheral, irrelevant, illegible? How has Chicano studies assumed the logic and practice of colonialism, and how has it been tainted by Enlightenment-based projects of knowledge production and structuration that perform heteropatriracialities? How do we assert a decolonial Chican@/Latino@ studies in light of heteropatriracial logics that arm the project of the colonial university? How can the practice of naming and assessing the deployment of imperial violence against and *through* our communities conjure up an opening for healing and transformation for greater justice and liberatory possibilities?

These questions are consistent with the liberatory projects and visions that birthed ethnic studies and Chicano studies; our task is to expand our capacity to listen to the voices muted by the university's heteropatriracial ordering and continue our work of building greater justice and liberation for all our communities.

Notes

1. Theresa Cordova, "Power and Knowledge, Colonialism in the Academy," in *Living Chicana Theory*, ed. C. Trujillo (Berkeley, Calif.: Third Woman Press, 1998); Maria Cotera, "Women of Color, Tenure and the Neoliberal University," in *Academic Repression: Reflections from the Academic Industrial Complex*, ed. Steven Best, Anthony Nocella, and Peter McLaren (Oakland, Calif.: AK Press, 2010).

2. I want to signal the distinction between *Chicano studies* and *Chican@ studies*. I use *Chicano studies* to signal a heteropatriarchal Chicano studies. *Chican@ studies* invokes a shift in the conceptualization and framing of the field of study to one that centers a critical approach to bifurcating gender structures and the racialized heterosexism emergent through said structures. Instead *Chican@ studies* (as the term *Chican@* also) offers a decolonial approach that opens up gender and sexual possibilities beyond a bifurcated heterosexist imaginary.

3. José Martí, "Carta a Manuel Mercado," in *José Martí: Letras Fieras* (Havana, Cuba: Editorial Letras Cubanas, 1981), 137.

4. Cordova, "Power and Knowledge, Colonialism in the Academy"; Jodi Byrd, *The Transit of Empire: Indigenous Critiques of Colonialism* (Minneapolis: University of Minnesota Press, 2012); Gayatri Spivak, "Can the Subaltern Speak?," in *Marxism and the Interpretation of Culture*, ed. Lawrence Grossberg and Cary Nelson (London: Macmillan, 1988).

5. Edward Said, *Orientalism* (London: Pantheon Books, 1978).

6. Grace Hong, "The Future of Our Worlds: Black Feminism and the Politics of Knowledge under Globalization," *Meridians: Feminism, Race, Transnationalism* 8, no. 2 (2008): 95–115; Roderick Ferguson, *The Reorder of Things: The University and Its Pedagogies of Minority Difference* (Minneapolis: University of [Minnesota] Press, 2012).

7. Roderick Ferguson, *The Reorder of Things*; Byrd, *The Transit of Empire*; Clarissa Rojas, "Fighting the 4th World War and Violence against Women," in *The Revolution Will Not Be Funded: The Nonprofit Industrial Complex,* ed. INCITE (Boston: South End, 2007); Amina Mama, "Gender Studies for Africa's Transformation," in *Gender Studies for Africa's Transformation*, ed. Thandika Mkandawire (London: Zed Books, 2006).

8. Ferguson, *The Reorder of Things*; Fabio Rojas, *From Black Power to Black Studies: How a Radical Social Movement Became an Academic Discipline* (Boston: Johns Hopkins University Press, 2010).

9. Rusty Barcelo in a speech delivered at Mujeres Activas En Letras Y Cambio Social (MALCS) Institute, California State University, Los Angeles, 2011.

10. Cordova, "Power and Knowledge, Colonialism in the Academy"; Ferguson, *The Reorder of Things*; Dylan Rodriguez, *Suspended Apocalypse: White Supremacy,*

Genocide and the Filipino Condition (Minneapolis: University of Minnesota Press, 2009).

11. See Michelle Alexander, *The New Jim Crow* (New York: New Press, 2012); Ruth Wilson Gilmore, *Golden Gulag: Prisons, Surplus, Crisis, and Opposition in Globalizing California* (Berkeley: University of California Press, 2007); Andrea Ritchie, Joey Mogul, and Kay Whitlock, *Queer (In)Justice: The Criminalization of LGBT People in the United States* (Boston: Beacon, 2012).

12. Henry A. Giroux, *The University in Chains: Confronting the Military-Industrial-Academic Complex* (Boulder, Colo.: Paradigm Publishers, 2007).

13. Angela Davis, *Are Prisons Obsolete?* (New York: Seven Stories, 2003).

14. Julia Oparah, "Activist Scholars and the Antiprison Movement" (paper delivered at *Catalyzing Knowledge in Dangerous Times,* Center for Race and Gender, University of California, Berkeley, 2011).

15. Davis, *Are Prisons Obsolete?*

16. Harriett Washington, *Medical Apartheid: The Dark History of Medical Experimentation on Black Americans from Colonial Times to the Present* (New York: Doubleday, 2006); Davis, *Are Prisons Obsolete?*

17. See Giorgio Agamben, *Homo Sacer: Sovereign Power and Bare Life* (Palo Alto, Calif.: Stanford University Press, 1998); Gilmore, *Golden Gulag*; Ferguson, *The Reorder of Things.*

18. See Joy James, "Teaching Theory, Talking Community," in *Academic Repression: Reflections from the Academic Industrial Complex,* ed. Steven Best, Anthony Nocella, and Peter McLaren (Oakland, Calif.: AK Press, 2010); Ramon Grosfoguel, Nelson Maldonado-Torres, and Jose David Saldivar, *Latino/as in the World-System: Decolonization Struggles in the 21st Century U.S. Empire* (Boulder, Colo.: Paradigm Publishers, 2006); Emma Perez, "Decolonial Critics for Academic Freedom," in *Academic Repression: Reflections from the Academic Industrial Complex,* ed. Steven Best, Anthony Nocella, and Peter McLaren (Oakland, Calif.: AK Press, 2010).

19. See Henry A. Giroux, "Higher Education after September 11th: The Crisis of Academic Freedom and Democracy," in *Academic Repression: Reflections from the Academic Industrial Complex,* ed. Steven Best, Anthony Nocella, and Peter McLaren (Oakland, Calif.: AK Press, 2010); Steven Best, Anthony Nocella, and Peter McLaren, "The Rise of the Academic-Industrial Complex and the Crisis in Free Speech," in *Academic Repression: Reflections from the Academic-Industrial Complex,* ed. Steven Best, Anthony Nocella, and Peter McLaren (Oakland, Calif.: AK Press, 2010).

20. While many universities throughout the United States have increased law enforcement presence on campus, some have added local, federal, and even private police forces. Giroux, *The University in Chains.*

21. Juan González, *Harvest of Empire* (New York: Penguin Books, 2001).

22. Michael Hardt and Antonio Negri, *Empire* (Boston, Mass.: Harvard University Press, 2000).

23. Partha Chatterjee, "Empire after Globalisation," in *The New Imperial Histories Reader*, ed. Stephen Howe (New York: Routledge, 2010).

24. Gilmore, *Golden Gulag.*

25. Raye Richardson, *40th Anniversary Third World Liberation Front Strike* (San Francisco: San Francisco State University, 2009).

26. Michel Soldatenko, *Chicano Studies: The Genesis of a Discipline* (Tucson, Ariz.: University of Arizona Press, 2009).

27. Anna Nieto-Gomez, personal conversation, May 15, 2012.

28. Anna Nieto-Gomez, personal e-mail communication, March 13, 2013.

29. Blackwell, *Chicana Power.* (Austin: University of Texas Press, 2012).

30. Ferguson also comments that the tension is multidirectional in that through the university site, capital and state forms are also influenced by the lexicon of difference. Ferguson, *The Reorder of Things.*

31. Ibid.

32. Ibid., 214, 224.

33. Anna Ochoa Leary, *Chicano Studies: The Discipline and the Journey* (Dubuque, Iowa: Kendall Hunt, 2007).

34. Soldatenko, *Chicano Studies.*

35. Charles Ornelas, Charles Ramirez, and Fernando Padilla, *Decolonizing the Interpretation of the Chicano Political Experience* (Los Angeles: UCLA Chicano Studies Center, 1975).

36. See Soldatenko, *Chicano Studies*; Mario Garcia, "The Chicano University," in *Ghosts in the Barrio: Issues with Bilingual-Bicultural Education*, ed. Ralph Poblano (San Rafael, Calif.: Leswing, 1973).

37. Anna Nieto-Gomez, presentation of Maylei Blackwell's *Chicana Power,* Long Beach Historical Society, 2011.

38. CSU–Long Beach was initially named Orange County State College.

39. Sandra K. Soto, *Reading Chican@ Like a Queer: The De-Mastery of Desire* (Austin: University of Texas Press, 2010), 12.

40. Gloria Anzaldúa and Cherríe Moraga, eds., *This Bridge Called My Back* (New York: Kitchen Table, 1983).

41. Perez, "Decolonial Critics for Academic Freedom."

42. Cynthia Orozco cautions of the Plan de Santa Bárbara's dangerous omission of Chicana subjectivities in Cynthia Orozco, "Sexism in Chicano Studies and the Community," in *Chicana Voices: Intersections of Class, Race, and Gender,* ed. Teresa Cordova (Austin: Center for Mexican American Studies, University of Texas, 1986).

43. Armando Rendón, *Chicano Manifesto* (New York: Macmillan, 1971).

44. Rolando Romero and Amanda Nolacea Harris, eds., *Feminism, Nation and*

Myth: La Malinche (Houston, Tex.: Arte Público, 2005); Norma Alarcón, "Chicana Feminism: In the Tracks of 'the' Native Woman," *Cultural Studies* 4, no. 3 (1990): 248–56.

45. Elizabeth Betita Martinez, "Chingon Politics Die Hard," in *Living Chicana Theory*, ed. Carla Trujillo (Berkeley: Third Women, 1998).

46. Sandra Messinger Cypress, "'Mother' Malinche and Allegories of Gender, Ethnicity and National Identity in Mexico," in *Feminism, Nation and Myth: La Malinche*, ed. Rolando Romero and Amanda Nolacea Harris (Durham and London: Arte Público, 2005), 14–27. Please see text above in its entirety in addition to Adelaida del Castillo's "Malintzín Tenepal: A Preliminary Look into a New Perspective," in *Chicana Feminist Thought: The Basic Historical Writings*, ed. Alma García (New York: Routledge, 2007), 122–26; and Norma Alarcón's "Chicana Feminism," 248–56.

47. Rendón, *Chicano Manifesto.*

48. Alarcón, "Chicana Feminism," 248–56.

49. Marisol Moreno, personal e-mail communication, March 15, 2013.

50. Blackwell, *Chicana Power.*

51. Ibid.

52. Martinez, "Chingon Politics Die Hard."

53. Yvette Flores-Ortiz, "La Mujer Y La Violencia: A Culturally Based Model for the Understanding and Treatment of Domestic Violence in Chicana/Latina Communities," in *Chicana Critical Issues*, ed. Mujeres Activas en Letras y Cambio Social (Berkeley: Third Woman, 1993).

54. Anna Nieto-Gomez, personal conversation, May 15, 2012. Also see Blackwell, *Chicana Power.*

55. Blackwell, *Chicana Power.*

56. Andrea Smith, *Conquest: Sexual Violence and American Indian Genocide* (Boston: South End, 2005).

57. Maria Lugones, "Heterosexualism and the Colonial/Modern Gender System," *Hypatia* 22, no. 1 (2007).

58. Oyeronke Oyewumi, *The Invention of Women: Making an African Sense of Western Gender Discourses* (Minneapolis: University of Minnesota Press, 1997).

59. In *Chicana Power,* Maylei Blackwell addresses how at CSU–Long Beach, Chicano movement politics narrowed the possibilities for Chicana political commitment in terms measurable by their sexual availability to Chicano students. Sexual harassment and assault, including initiation into UMAS through sexual assault, were common, and, regretfully, some of the offenders became faculty in Chicano studies at CSU–Long Beach. Blackwell, *Chicana Power.*

60. We had other goals that included developing a separate track for the arts. Since all the guys were in the social sciences, we figured creating autonomy (they weren't in the least bit interested in the arts) would be one way to get them off our backs. We

also wanted to change the name of the department from Chicano/Latino Studies to one that reflected our presence and analytic.

61. Blackwell, *Chicana Power.*

62. Gloria Anzaldua, *Borderlands, La Frontera* (San Francisco: Aunt Lute Books, 1987).

63. Blackwell, *Chicana Power.*

64. Ritchie, Mogul, and Whitlock, *Queer (In)Justice.*

65. Antonia Castañeda, "History and the Politics of Violence against Women," in *Living Chicana Theory,* ed. Carla Trujillo (Berkeley: Third Woman, 1998).

66. Andrea Smith, "Queer Theory and Native Studies: The Heteronormativity of Settler Colonialism," *GLQ: Journal of Lesbian and Gay Studies* 16, nos. 1–2 (2010): 42–68.

67. Renato Rosaldo, *Culture and Truth: The Remaking of Social Analysis* (Boston: Beacon, 1993).

68. In the neoliberal era of outrageous student fees and student loan indebtedness, working-class women of color have the added strain of fearing job loss and inability to pay back student loans/credit card debt acquired while in graduate school.

69. Cynthia Enloe, *Maneuvers: The International Politics of Militarizing Women's Lives* (Berkeley: University of California Press, 2000).

III

Manifest Knowledges

Normatizing State Power

Uncritical Ethical Praxis and Zionism

Steven Salaita

In spring 2009, I was near the end of my yearlong tenure and promotion review at Virginia Tech. Tech is a research university that requires a decent amount of publication from its humanists, though its expectations are not what most would consider rigid or excessive. My tenure and promotion case had the added complication of being a year ahead of schedule (potentially four years, depending on the viewpoint). Counting my three years on faculty at the University of Wisconsin, Whitewater, I applied for tenure and promotion in my sixth year out of graduate school rather than during my seventh, as is customary at Tech. My strong record of publication and teaching provided me a good reason to go forward a year early. It was also a practical decision: because my research and writing deal with controversial material, I did not want to give fanatical groups and individuals any more time than they needed to derail my career (though tenure is no foolproof protection against politically inspired termination). This concern was not merely quaint paranoia, unfortunately: various right-wing groups, aided both tacitly and directly by more liberal colleagues, have successfully damaged the academic careers of scholars such as Norman Finkelstein, Joel Kovel, Margo Ramlal-Nankoe, Thomas Abowd, and Tariq Ramadan. Given the volatile nature of academe, it didn't seem prudent for me to bide any time.

Although I have published widely and have spoken at every available opportunity in support of Palestinian freedom and indigenous rights more broadly, I toil away more or less undetected, happy to belong to a small but devoted group of scholars and activists whose work assesses comparable themes with the same type of committed methodological approach. I enjoy a productive and comfortable professional life, one that puts me in a better economic and existential position than the vast majority of the world's population. This lucky reality often causes me to chuckle at professorial claims of

218 of STEVEN SALAITA

untenable busyness or inordinate stress: our lives for the most part are those of comfort and privilege, and we are remarkably fortunate to be paid to write and then talk about what we write. I place a high value on my job, then, and I am eager to protect it. Navigating promotion in higher education is tricky, as anybody who has done it knows, for me mostly because I find it difficult to balance my antiauthoritarian viewpoints with the pressures of conformity that tacitly dominate professorial advancement. As tenure is so profoundly intertwined with institutional loyalty, notions of scholarly responsibility, and other implicit expectations, tenure is useful for university administrators because it socializes faculty into particular modes of thinking that virtually eliminate meaningful contestation.

I bring up these points because it's important to think about what it means to act ethically and responsibly in academe, in terms of both institutional presuppositions and communal commitments—two phenomena that do not usually correspond. While most scholars and university administrators talk glowingly of engaging broad audiences and working to improve the world, such talk is invariably in the abstract, denoting a reproduction of ideals and not actual change—at least not the type that would threaten the socioeconomic privileges most administrators and professors ardently protect. It is sometimes from within this gap between discursive showmanship and substantive praxis that controversies over faculty activism and scholarship arise. Without judging the quality or veracity of their efforts, I would suggest that scholars who commit themselves to any sort of advocacy that contravenes institutional sensibilities or interests earn a reputation (or notoriety) as consciously "political," rather than equally active scholars whose advocacy happens to reinforce or complement institutional sensibilities. This observation seems obvious, but it is one that warrants further exploration. At stake are people's livelihoods, professional futures, and conceptions of responsibility. The issue of the political in academe therefore deserves a closer reading than its general treatment to this point. It is an issue that exists most conspicuously and contentiously in the interrelated frameworks of Zionism and the Israel/Palestine conflict. To be more specific, charges of unjustifiably politically motivated research and of unwarranted politicization of scholarship work overwhelmingly—sometimes implicitly but often explicitly—to maintain Zionism's normative status and to protect Israel from any serious criticism, no matter how demonstrable and legitimate.

I am deliberating these matters frequently nowadays, inspired by the hostile atmosphere in academe toward junior scholars devoted to justice for

Palestinians and my own experience with tacit articulations of such hostility. I became interested in the uses of the word "political" after having received a favorable letter from my department's personnel committee—which decides tenure and promotion cases on behalf of the entire department—in response to my request that the committee assess the viability of my early candidacy. I excitedly read the letter stating support for my decision to seek early promotion and tenure. Among the nice things the committee had to say is, "It is clear to the Committee that you are a devoted and passionate teacher. We are very impressed."

However, nestled within the glowing prose were some nettlesome suggestions in the form of inexact adjectives. I found myself rereading the following two sentences, somehow annoyed, and increasingly agitated: "In the area of research, the Committee understands your significant contributions in two areas—political literary analysis and the polemical political essay—both of which strive to put the situations of Palestinians and Arab-Americans at the center of public and intellectual debates in the United States." The assessment continues to note that I "have produced a formidable amount of searing, impassioned, and seemingly groundbreaking work." These observations struck me as adjective-happy, but not merely as a result of poor writing.

The word "polemical" stands out as a judgment of my politics rather than an evaluation of my work's scholarly quality. The word "political," seemingly innocuous, is even more disturbing. First of all, there are problems of connotation in the letter's prose: essays are by their nature political and often polemical in their style (though it is not an adjective I would use to describe these particular essays). Moreover, the committee appears to have created an entirely new category of writing especially for me: "political literary analysis." As flattered as I was to defy categorization so lustrously, I suspected that the new category wasn't meant to inspire admiration. I tried my best not to be insulted by the backhanded compliment the committee offers: "We look forward to the future development of your research and scholarship." Taken together, these curious uses of adjectives signaled the presence of a story I feared would remain hermetic. Something dubious was afoot. The word "political" was all it took to trigger my suspicion.

It turns out my suspicion was valid. Although my tenure and promotion case successfully made it out of the department—and subsequently the college and university—it apparently invoked some intense controversy, particularly around my writing focused on critical analysis of colonial discourses, including various Zionist narratives. Especially vexing to certain members of the committee was the commitment, expressed in different ways in some areas of my scholarship, to communally oriented and proactive methodologies—a commitment that I would love to claim I invented but that in reality exists in the mainstream of indigenous studies as well as in a cross-section of critical and postcolonial approaches. This commitment relegated my scholarship to various delegitimizing taxonomies intimating a lack of professional seriousness or objective scholarly gravitas. Ultimately, it was the unusual quantity of my research that ensured my success; had I not produced a large body of research, I am certain I would have faced a much more hostile judgment. My politics were protected by my profuseness. I've been aware of this possibility since graduate school, which is one of the reasons why I have been such an ambitious writer: I knew that if I planned not to shy away from my ethical commitments (particularly to Palestinian liberation) then I'd better be able to conjure a dossier whose productivity was unimpeachable. Though I am a highly biased observer, I feel that my scholarship is of a solid theoretical and rhetorical quality, so I do not wish to imply that prolificacy is or should be an effective means of concealing substandard research. I merely want to point out that it is a necessary protective mechanism for those who challenge power structures, whether or not they are adroit scholars.

The entire process, which reinforced my informed cynicism about the ability or willingness of most academics to actually practice instead of merely theorizing justice, has taught me much about the uses of rhetorical connotation and coded discourse in all manner of promotion in academic communities. In the following sections I will contextualize my admittedly tame experience within a broader analysis of tacit modes of ethical and methodological conformity in academe. I will examine in particular how academics committed to some form of Zionism deploy the term "political" as a destabilizing and denunciatory mechanism, one that is effective because it has become self-explanatory. I use the term "normatization" rather than the more familiar "normalization" to denote a discursive process of rendering Israel normative in narratives of multiculturalism and modernity. Whereas "normalize" generally (but not always) refers to a geopolitical relationship between nation-states, including economic and cultural exchange, "normatize" highlights the ways that a particular discourse becomes accepted as natural or commonsensical. Focusing on Israel's normatization, then, draws attention to its position as a standard of responsible morality and acceptable intellectual citizenship.

Political Action; "Political" Acting

Let's look at what the following term means and what it connotes: "political," adjectivally, as in "political literary analysis" and "political essay." When we assess the phrase "political literary analysis," the term "political" does not supplement or elucidate the act of analysis; instead, it devalues and delimits it. The adjective is both a signal—something of a sophisticated wink-wink— and a denunciation. At its most basic it tacitly signals denunciation without technically denouncing anything. It is a passive-aggressive commentary that relies on a number of malformed assumptions. The term, when used to describe another person's scholarship, functions as polite denunciation because of its ability to signal a disapproval that need not be articulated. These days, after decades of culture wars, its connotations are clear and largely specific, but the term retains its self-invented pretense of disinterest, rendering it safely hostile—that is, hostile without displaying explicit hostility. The adjective "political," an imputation disguised as a descriptor, is both accusatory and exclusionary.

The malformed assumptions underlying the use of that adjective are worth analysis. The most noteworthy assumption inherent in its use is that people can make judgments from a genuinely nonpolitical place. Other noteworthy assumptions include the notion that political scholarship can be identified based on immanent or enunciated positions that are unsavory, not on the mere fact of stating a position itself; the belief that ostensibly disengaged scholarship is not attached somehow to sociopolitical phenomena; and the idea that acceptable scholarship is timeless and amaranthine in such a way that it transcends history altogether. There is a clear demarcation for designating scholarship as "political": academic work that systematically challenges state power and other forms of entrenched institutional authority. Those who offer the designation are inevitably in the thrall of state power or in some way embody institutional authority. There is no demonstrable exception to this formula. The deification of objectivity and the bastardization of the political reinforce a status quo that renders academe remarkably conservative intellectually and institutionally conformist (i.e., conformity to dominant ethical and intellectual paradigms becomes a prerequisite for advancement).

I am certainly not the first person to critique the power-serving functions of academe, nor have the uses of the word "political" to that end gone unnoted.[1] Edward Said's *Orientalism* explores the matter. Said writes, "What

I am interested in doing now is suggesting how the general liberal consensus that 'true' knowledge is fundamentally nonpolitical (and conversely, that overtly political knowledge is not 'true' knowledge) obscures the highly if obscurely organized political circumstances obtaining when knowledge is produced. No one is helped in understanding this today when the adjective 'political' is used as a label to discredit any work for daring to violate the protocol of pretended suprapolitical objectivity."[2] Said was aware in his later years that the problem he described grew progressively worse; by the time of his death in 2003 the problem had become nearly intractable. Now a description of an academic's scholarship as political can be debilitating if it is raised as part of an organized movement to threaten his or her career.[3]

By now, theorizing politicization in particular areas of scholarship has become something of an industry. A new organization recently came into existence based explicitly on the mythology of nonpolitical scholarship (itself an unacknowledged but unmistakably politicized secession). This new organization, Association for the Study of the Middle East and Africa (ASMEA), was cofounded by the well-known Orientalist (and Said antagonist) Bernard Lewis and neoconservative commentator Fouad Ajami as an antidote to the supposedly radical Middle East Studies Association (MESA). When ASMEA was first incorporated, Lewis offered the empirically and theoretically indemonstrable complaint that "the study of the Middle East and of Africa has been politicized to a degree without precedent."[4] The irony of ASMEA's move to disaffiliate from a space it conceptualizes as unjustifiably political is that its most prominent members, Lewis, Ajami, and Kanan Makiya, have been high-level advisors for George W. Bush, Dick Cheney, and other powerful leaders. All three scholars advocated for the 2003 invasion of Iraq, a war that Makiya was especially adamant about. ASMEA's notion of political thus refers not to activities or to methodologies but to ideology—more specifically to whether one's ideology supplements or challenges state power. By uniting their ideologies with the exercise of foreign policy, ASMEA's leaders delimit the range of scholarly inquiry and produce a highly injunctive culture of methodological evaluation.

Contentious topics in academic communities, then, often arise from the nexus of ideological contestations that find expression through tendentious diction, the term "political" being the most frequently used and heterogeneously connotative. The "political" in academe, however, is invariably associated with the actual exercise of power, which is why there is more at stake than mere semantic quibbling. Our ability as intellectuals to cultivate ethical purpose in our work as proactive scholars depends on the anatomization of the same terms that normatively discredit the idea of scholarship as a form of humane engagement. Few scholars have analyzed the important role Zionism has played in these phenomena, an analysis I shall now undertake.

Apolitical Zionism; "Political" Palestinians

To discuss Zionism in an analysis of scholarly culture and state power presents myriad difficulties. Before I enter into this analysis, though, it would be useful to contextualize my usage of the terms "Zionism" and "Zionist." As I indicate earlier, the terms are heterogeneous, but there is one common element to all versions of Zionism that render it cohesive: the notion, in whatever form, that Israel should exist as a Jewish nation-state culturally and demographically, an entity to which Jews anywhere in the world have access (a privilege withheld from the native Palestinians). I would identify Zionist as any belief that proclaims or assumes that Israel has a normative claim to Jewish majoritarianism or any narrative that treats Israel as timeless and exceptional. There are ways in which such narratives can be delivered crudely and ways that they are imparted subtly. Their articulation in any fashion is a reasonable criterion for identifying a Zionist orientation. The term "Zionist," in any case, is not usually eschewed by Israel's supporters or by liberal multiculturalists. It is the sort of term that can be deployed as an insult or accusation, but more generally it articulates an unthreatening commitment to Israel as a nation or an idea. Although I try to avoid employing the descriptor "Zionist" as either insult or accusation, I do conceptualize it as connotative of unjust and unethical viewpoints.

First, to criticize Zionism as a political movement or a philosophical commitment is practically verboten. (Indeed, it is sure to earn one's work the label of "political.") Second, Zionism is highly disaggregated politically, temporally, and morally. Third, most Zionist academics vociferously deny playing any role in the marginalization of pro-Palestine scholars[5] and in fact portray themselves as devoted civil libertarians. And finally, numerous allegiances among academics also play a role in the circumscription of acceptable (read: state/corporate sanctioned) politics. Profoundly colonialist structures pervade North American academic institutions based on a history of ethnic cleansing and the subsequent unwillingness to allow indigenous peoples academic or political self-determination. The majority of these allegiances to power among corporatist and colonialist university officials are affiliated with or complementary of Zionism.

In addition to these problems, other phenomena play crucial roles in the contentiousness of university culture wars: interpersonal conflicts, budgetary squabbling, inveterate conformity, rhetorical ineptitude, hegemonic ideals, and simple political cowardice. I want to limit my analysis to the predominance of Zionist narratives and their austere expectations because of their particular institutional function: one that can be detected and interrogated and one that has gone largely uncommented. Zionist academics and organizations focused on the academy, both liberal and conservative, are without question the largest impediment to the development of justice-oriented intellectual communities in American universities.

An entire right-wing industry has arisen in opposition to "political" scholarship in the past two decades. This industry includes David Horowitz's many enterprises, Daniel Pipes's CampusWatch, and the National Association of Scholars, in addition to frequent editorializing in venerable publications such as *The New Republic, Weekly Standard, National Review,* and *Commentary*; mainstream periodicals frequently join the chorus. This industry has been discussed ad infinitum, and I don't want to rehearse that discussion here.[6] I bring it up to identify the policy leanings of ostensibly nonpolitical actors, which are inevitably located within whatever at the time is considered by the state to be the national interest. Such actors make no secret of their political underpinnings or intentions. A more interesting site of analysis involves a class of generally progressive scholars who work in areas such as feminist studies, labor studies, or American studies and uphold the ideals of liberal discourse through emphasis on free exchange, empiricism, and theoretical inquiry. These scholars predicate a substantial portion of their scholarly production on concocting a form of critical exceptionalism for Israel, one in which both Zionism and the idea of a Jewish state are spared the type of hard inquiry we direct at other issues and geographical regions.

Zionism, however, is customary to the point that self-identified progressive scholars can endorse or even promote it without any real sense of contradiction. In fact, articulating support for Israel is actually necessitous of proper multicultural consciousness; it is how one indicates that he or she has entered into the spaces of modernity rather than wallowing in the barbarities of an uncultured Third Worldism. The viewpoints outwardly critical of Zionism get burdened with labels like irresponsible, anti-Semitic, and the ubiquitous "radical." Examples of this phenomenon are numerous. I shall provide a few so that we can explore the discursive features that render Zionism a form of apolitical politicizing. The phrase "apolitical politicizing" is both descriptive and oxymoronic, one that juxtaposes my own viewpoint with a more general observation about the tendentiousness of deduction in most academic discourses. My own viewpoint, one informed by evidence I will present later, is that Zionism's supporters are political in the same way that many culture warriors use the term to describe supporters of Palestinian liberation—that is to say, it is a type of commitment that aspires to a particular material outcome. Zionism, however, has achieved a normative status as a discourse and a commitment that allows its advocates to conceptualize their work as apolitical. In this sense, the terms "normative" and "apolitical" are coterminous, sometimes interchangeable. Because Zionism has achieved (or created for itself) a normative status, its purveyors have appropriated the stubborn ideal that scholarship can and should be disinterested to assume a policing function on the supposed politicization of scholars and campuses. Zionism, then, has become a force of apolitical power, compelling a class of scholars to identify and condemn politics in academe not because the political itself is objectionable but because the wrong kinds of politics are objectionable.

Columbia University journalism professor Todd Gitlin, for example, writes of "political intellectuals" having lost their way. In *Intellectuals and the Flag*, an appeal for more devout liberal patriotism, Gitlin assesses today's irresponsible scholars in the context of the New Left foibles of Gitlin's gilded youth in the 1960s and 1970s: "The New Left revolt against power was also a revolt against authority—sometimes, that is, against *legitimate* power [his emphasis]. It wasn't only economic, political, and military power that the student movement resisted: it was the claim to knowledge, the bedrock of professionalism itself."[7] Subsequently, the "New Left's graduates and successors pursued their quarrel with universities in manifold ways," one of the primary ones being an inveterate suspicion of patriotism.[8] By making a distinction between legitimate power and challengeable power, Gitlin sets up an arbitrary valuation that replaces the authority he attributes to irresponsible scholars with his own based on the level-headed critique of power he claims to offer.

It is worth emphasizing that Gitlin is not against the political itself; he is against the wrong type of political, that which challenges what he conceptualizes as legitimate authority. He argues in favor of a "politics of limits," noting that "there must be limits to what human beings can be permitted to do with their power."[9] The primary limit is in relation to criticism of Israel, something Gitlin is keen on suppressing (in its more radical forms) or restricting to a type of dutiful scolding, like responsible critiques of the United States: the point is not to assail it but to urge it to do a better job of upholding its unassailable ideals. Israel is the besieged canary in Gitlin's vigilant mine: "Israeli policies bring the ranters out of the woodwork, but their delusional rants and rank forgeries simmer beneath the surface, waiting for opportunity."[10] Gitlin's version of the political is profoundly injunctive; it demands a patriotic subtext in order for scholarship to assume proper responsibility.

Eric Lott has analyzed this form of coercion, suggesting that "9/11, a profoundly global event, was *hypernationalized* in its immediate aftermath [his emphasis]."[11] He later explains, "No advocate of patriotism in this era can afford not to acknowledge the way love of country is inextricably, often mortally, bound up with the power that country wields in the world."[12] Lott's identification of national power is crucial to our understanding of apolitical politicization, particularly insofar as hypernationalism is bound up with allegiance to Israel's interests. Gitlin and others suggest, without actually saying, that support of state power constitutes an assumed apolitical perspective, whereas (some?) structural critiques are indecently political, a function of what Lott calls "neoliberal culturalism." Take this passage from the eminent liberal philosopher Michael Walzer, in an article titled "Can There Be a Decent Left?": "The radical failure of the [academic] left's response to the events of last fall [9/11] raises a disturbing question: can there be a decent left in a superpower? Or more accurately, in the only superpower? Maybe the guilt produced by living in such a country and enjoying its privileges makes it impossible to sustain a decent (intelligent, responsible, morally nuanced) politics."[13] Walzer goes on to conflate anti-Israel activism and scholarship with Islamic fundamentalism, a decidedly indecent union, he argues.[14] Walzer's arguments, like Gitlin's, constitute an entrenched instance of methodological hypernationalization because they attempt to conjoin—and demand that others conjoin—an intellectual apparatus with a corporeal notion of decency, one trained on the respectability supposedly inherent in liberal nationalism. America and Israel are ideas to be sustained and exported.

Every academic who has raised this type of argument is, in fact, a self-identified Zionist, which doesn't so much point to a conspiracy as it does a discernible pattern worth discussion. It's not necessarily the Zionist outlook that produces the disturbing methodological philosophy, but there's unquestionably a correlation between support for U.S. state power and support for

Israel. This is so because Zionism is a profoundly chauvinistic ideology, one that is essentially ethnonationalist and accepted as responsible at the governmental level in the United States. As Jonathan Schanzer, writing in the neoconservative *Middle East Forum*, puts it, too many professional spaces are providing "a soap box for Palestinian apologists and Israeli detractors," which compels professors "to bully their students, apologize for jihadists, and teach fringe ideas in the classroom."[15] This sort of political commitment is apt to get one labeled, perhaps even by the eminent Henry Louis Gates Jr., a "demagogue" or a "pseudoscholar."[16] It is for this reason that the preeminent U.S.-born historian Michael Oren can serve in the Israeli military during a time of brutal attacks on Palestinian civilians—as he did during the Israeli invasion of the Gaza Strip in 2008–2009—without it being condemned as an unjustifiably political act. (So even though critiques of militarism are common among liberal academics, there is an exception in the case of Israeli militarism—writing this just after Stand with Us brought an IOF soldier to Davis and the admin attacked [falsely, it turns out] students for disrupting the talk!) The reification of state violence is itself profusely violent, but it is morally permissible because it is the covetousness of state action that most informs the ethos of academic marketplaces. This phenomenon often plays out unevenly to the extent that certain state actions are permissible to critique and less covetous in the academy than others (the invasion of Iraq is permissible to critique, for example). Yet there are very few cases in which Zionist orientations are not marketable and in which pro-Palestinian orientations are.

The interrelation of state power and academic ethos is central to the conservative disposition inherent in most contemporary scholarship. (I use the term "conservative" here not to identify a political orientation like Democrat or Republican but to denote a conventionality in methodological approaches to issues contextualized by serious moral consequences.) Outspoken or tacit support for Israel, which can include judicious scolding but not structural denunciation, is coterminous with a proper display of intellectual patriotism. The conflation of American patriotism with Zionist devotion supplements a dialectic in which notions of responsibility underline policy formation on both local and international levels. This dialectic exists in all sorts of political commitments in American universities, but most insidiously among classically liberal scholars like Gitlin, Gates, and Walzer, whose injunctive entreaties for moderation circumscribe what it means to investigate critical issues responsibly and so exert influence in fields beyond Middle East studies. The

moderation they seek is moderate only in the sense that forces more powerful than the scholars have deemed them acceptable. There is nothing inherent to any idea that can be evaluated outside of its relationship with various
historical and political forces. Proper moderation, then, merely reflects a set
of interests that are dutifully recycled by self-identified moderates, who are
not so much purveyors of their own ethical commitments as they are inven-
tions of moderation's beneficiaries.

These factors point to a reality that cannot be overlooked if we are to adequately understand the function of the political in academic promotion and
scholarly evaluation: there are economies inscribed in the production, publication, dissemination, and reception of scholarship. The circulation of academic research and its attendant value systems are indivisible from financial
inducement, career advancement, and reputational credibility. As such, academic research is necessarily tendentious insofar as it can never be produced
completely beyond pecuniary factors. This marketplace of scholarly publication affects the development of tacit judgments of the permissible and the
frequency with which certain issues are covered. That most forms of Zionist thought are not only permissible but requisite to one's rapid ascension
illuminates an engagement of state power with the structures of scholarly
production. (The forms of Zionist thought that are explicitly fascistic are dis-
couraged but certainly not absent from American universities.) By conflating
responsible scholarship with at least absence of critique of implicit devotion
to Zionism, most professors and administrators wield the term "political" in
order to disesteem potential subversives while remaining smugly oblivious
to the rudimentary intimations of their diction.

While it might be unpopular to point to Zionism as a culprit in restricting
our range of scholarly inquiry (a conspicuous factor that far too many people
tiptoe around), it is worth noting that nearly every recent instance of egregious academic harassment, those in which somebody's academic job was
threatened, was performed by self-identified and ardently committed Zionists. Universities have been subject to intense demands (often organized by
nonacademics) to fire professors or have taken such an initiative themselves,
in numerous cases: Nadia Abu El Haj at Barnard College; Norman Finkelstein at DePaul University; Joseph Massad at Columbia University; William Robinson at the University of California, Santa Barbara; Joel Kovel at
Bard College; Terri Ginsburg at North Carolina State University; and Margo
Ramlal-Nankoe at Ithaca College. There are also dozens of unreported cases

of which I am aware anecdotally in which emerging scholars were passed over for jobs or promotions because of the "political" nature of their work.

Creating an unassailable quantity of publication is not the solution to this problem, however. With four books on my CV, I still barely made it through the departmental level of promotion. The point, in any case, is that it should not be incumbent on scholars whose work might be dubbed "political" to do ungodly amounts of research in order to ensure job protection; the tenets of academic freedom are supposed to perform that task. Anyway, most of the scholars who have been pressured or dismissed produced ample and ground-breaking research, which likely drew attention to them in the first place. Researchers who focus on controversial issues or who choose to participate in the public domain need the protections, however abstractly articulated, that are so paramount to the mythos of American higher education. Rather than demanding an enforcement of academic freedom, it might be useful for us to appraise the insidious descriptive commonplaces that, like "political," undermine whatever protections academic freedom has the power to offer. The language and spirit of academic freedom cannot account for the delegiti-mization inherent in terms like "political," which can be passed off as objec-tive or normative when in reality its purveyors raise it deliberately to target scholarship or activism that threatens the preponderance of state power.

How does one challenge a phenomenon that is both abstruse and extra-legal? There is no singularly effective way, but we can work to change the archaic ethics of scholarship, which were created during an era of coloni-zation in the twentieth-century United States and in an atmosphere of near-total Eurocentrism, the perspective they in turn support and sustain. Although today's world is much more complicated than any disinterested methodology can explain, it is the myth of untainted knowledge that con-tinues to predominate in academe. No piece of scholarship has ever been nonaligned. It is a matter of whether a piece of scholarship is aligned with the right set of politics that determines whether or not it achieves the exalted status of objective and nonpolitical. The default position of state power as a coded synecdoche of responsible scholarship is constantly reinvented as normative by those who seek to uphold what they conceptualize as time-less standards of objective inquiry. There are all kinds of problems with this default position beyond merely its methodological foolishness.

Most important, by reifying the political as an unserious, unsavory pres-ence in scholarship, Zionists and other traditionalists reinforce their own power by retaining ownership over the term "political." (Regarding the term "traditionalist": Zionists may evoke all kinds of different political identities, most of them decidedly untraditional, but when it comes to their complaints about "political"—i.e., anti-Zionist—scholarship, they are the most traditional of all culture warriors.) Moreover, this strident use of the term "political" creates exclusive spaces in academe; those spaces preclude the articulation of serious, in some cases groundbreaking, research. They tacitly limit the pursuit of knowledge. They actively limit the pursuit of justice. They make American universities stupider than they need to be. No matter what the guardians of proper scholarly ethos proclaim about the need for researchers to remain disengaged, it is perplexing to me that one could produce work that has nothing to do with improving the terrible conditions of the world and in the communities we are supposed to serve. I should emphasize that it is not naïveté or romanticized distortion that leads to this perplexing injunction; it is the knowledge, at least tacitly understood, that most scholars are part of the same power structure they so intently maintain.

The Ethics of Antistate Inquiry

In calling for an ethics of antistate inquiry, I would like to offer a few comments in closing on the potential of academic research to be both responsibly meticulous and ardently unaffiliated. I would be remiss not to acknowledge the tremendous debt of gratitude I owe to the work being done in the field of native and indigenous studies. Indigenous critics such as Andrea Smith, Dale Turner, Robert Warrior, Linda Tuhiwai Smith, and Taiaiake Alfred, along with various writers working in ethnic and postcolonial studies, have explored ways that nonobjective scholarship (an inevitable and good thing) can engage communities and projustice movements.[17] In the spirit of this scholarship, I would argue that being ardently unaffiliated to institutional power is a particularly crucial aspect of reorganizing the academic ethos. Although the myth of objectivity dictates no affiliation with political parties, paid sponsors, or special interest groups, objectivity in practice implicitly demands allegiance to state power (often in the form of a commitment to Zionist ideals). It is this implicit demand that I would like to see scholars challenge and ultimately reject. It should not be the goal of research and teaching to recapitulate modes of authority or reinvent the ethos of colonialist pursuits. We should focus on searching out the truths that serious inquiry will uncover if it is unaffected by a need to overcompensate for its inherent biases by retreating to the default position of apolitical advocacy. Worldly narratives show over and again that the exercise of state power affects academic research and impedes the quest for useful knowledge; it rarely supplements or inspires such a quest. As intellectuals and researchers, we have an opportunity to productively examine the substantial gaps between unidirectional corporate ideals and the multivalent needs of diverse human communities. This opportunity will never come to fruition if we feign objectivity and avoid the political.

We can start by reclaiming the "political" from apolitical politicos. It is a term that needs to be deterritorialized from its normative position, where it is intertwined with gender, race, class, and sexuality in both tacit and obvious ways. More specifically, the term "political" needs to be taken out of the lexicon of Zionist and right-wing activists, scholarly and otherwise, who employ the word as a form of passive-aggressive attack, a coded way to betray the liberal ideals of academic freedom without technically contravening them. "Political" is an encoded signification whose connotative meaning illustrates fascistic tendencies that actually displace it from the humanistic context it claims to inhabit. It then reasserts its own form of apolitical power—that is, a power that pretends to be rational, affiliated with a politics that purports to be nonpolitical. This pattern represents the same commonsensical rationalism concealing elite authority that Antonio Gramsci highlighted nearly a century ago.

I would also suggest that humanistic scholars continue to think about what it means to produce controversial and thus "political" work. Although the connotations of political research are still overwhelmingly negative, new generations of scholars, following the lead of their courageous forebears, are undermining the venerable colonialist structures of academic work. It is a project worth joining. Doing "political" research is not merely a byproduct of its connotations. It means that somebody is upset and names work as political, which indicates that the work is challenging some type of convention, something every worthwhile piece of scholarship does. It isn't necessarily desirable or requisite that research in the humanities and social sciences is controversial, but it shouldn't be seen automatically as negative if it is. Controversy and discomfort aid the pursuit of knowledge; they do not hinder it. The pursuit of well-researched knowledge directly contravenes the propaganda apparatus on which Israeli colonization relies, a major factor in the juxtaposition of normative scholarship with fealty to Zionism as conflated with U.S. patriotism. If we do not learn to engage the "political" in useful and creative ways, American universities will have succumbed indelibly to the preponderance of state power in epistemological systems by having deferred inquiry in favor of the prestige that attends responsible complaisance.

I do not believe that a methodological norm should exist for research in which moral issues are central to both exposition and analysis. Beyond authorial integrity, there are too many variables in humanistic research to employ injunctive expectations, especially if those expectations tacitly supplement the interests of worthy subjects of critique (such as Zionism or American militarism). Scholars should, where possible, create relationships with social, cultural, and political communities, for there is nothing morally or methodologically wrong with intertwining scholarship with organic movements for justice; there is only something normatively wrong with such a move based on the antiquated ethos of the colonialist academy.

In reflecting on my own experience with being labeled "political," I realize that the word is powerful enough to displace people from their livelihoods or stall their upward mobility. This power alone is enough for principled scholars to be profoundly suspicious of the term and its connotations. By continually reinventing the myth of disinterest and objectivity, we give weight to a set of archaic values that energetically perform a tendentious neutrality. It would be more useful to assess how disinterest and objectivity are aligned with various apparatuses of power and authority and to interrogate how a commitment to Zionism is central to that alignment. Zionism is akin to the patriotic demand American society places on esteemed celebrities: it is the implicit criterion by which one's commitment to responsible pedagogy and research is determined, and so it is able to heavily influence one's market value as both an intellectual and public figure. The outspoken political orientation of those who attack "political" scholars makes this point eminently clear. Devoted and silent Zionists never face negative tenure decisions because of their use of overly "political" methodologies. Devoted and silent Zionists, however, routinely engender negative tenure decisions for others.

It is for this reason that I prefer the terms "principled" or "communal" rather than "responsible" to describe justice-oriented scholarship. Although any adjective will have unintended connotations or be wrapped up in competing paradigms, the term "responsible" has too often been used to underline the charge of "political" as a mode of disaccreditation. If it is responsible to be at least tacitly patriotic—that is, devoted to articulations of state power—then exercising responsibility in contemporary academe is contrary to humane ethics and useful theorization. The point is to make sure that describing what we do coheres with the outcomes we desire. If we desire justice-oriented outcomes, then we need to dislodge current notions of responsibility from their entanglement with Zionist and American chauvinism. The late Iris Marion Young explores these possibilities in her splendid book *Global Challenges*:

> A dictatorship is a ruling power that imposes its own political desire and interests on others even in the face of their objections or protest. I conjure the idea of global dictatorship in order to invoke the ideal of its opposite, global democracy. The institutions of stronger global cooperation and regulation that we should envision and work for have to be thought of as democratic. Among other things, this means that they do not replace institutions through which peoples exercise a right of self-determination, but provide means through which self-determining peoples can be represented in transnational decision-making on terms that insulate smaller or less powerful groups from domination and exploitation.[18]

The idea of scholarship working in conjunction with, or even in the service of, global movements for self-determination is not a new one, but it is one that remains sufficiently marginalized. I would like to suggest that we consider the possibilities of engaged scholarship not merely as affirmational but also as oppositional. I don't speak of oppositional scholarship as an entrée into contentiousness but suggest a principled, nonobjective, interested stance against the global dictatorship enforced by the interchangeable axes of American imperialism, Zionist colonization, neoliberal economies, and corporate warfare.

A productive place to locate this intellectual labor is in indigenous communities, where the juxtaposition of research with communal development is fluid and uncontroversial. There is a remarkable energy in the world beyond the academy for ground-level change, a site of action where theorization is often more germane and sophisticated than in formal academic institutions, as we saw in the early stages of the Egyptian and Tunisian revolutions. By confining ourselves to the spaces inhabited by the supposedly unimpressionable elite, we ensure a recirculation of intellectual and material resources into limited and specialized institutions. I do not believe that the production of research should be democratic, but its dissemination should not be so patently undemocratic. We need to think more about how the work we do as scholars coheres with the struggles of projustice advocates in all social and economic strata. I don't have all the answers to these propositions, but I do know that on the cusp of promotion to associate professor, I've learned a few things about scholarship: if it claims to be objective, then it's lying to you. And if it's not political, then it doesn't exist.

Notes

1. See Devon Abbott Mihesuah and Angela Cavender Wilson, eds., *Indigenizing the Academy* (Lincoln, Neb.: Bison Books, 2004). Even the journalist Chris Hedges has scathingly denounced the role of universities in an article on *AlterNet*, "The Best and the Brightest Have Led America off a Cliff," http://www.alternet.org/story/111376/?page=entire.

2. Edward Said, *Orientalism* (New York: Vintage, 1979), 10.

3. For example, see the cases of Joseph Massad and Nadia Abu El Haj.

4. See http://www.nysun.com/new-york/group-formed-to-improve-middle-east -scholarship/66110/.

5. I use the term "pro-Palestine" with some hesitation because it doesn't adequately capture the moral and historical reasoning for one's support of Palestinians. It instead implies a tendentious political orientation to which one adheres stridently or even unthinkingly. In reality, anybody with basic knowledge of Palestine's history would easily come to identify as "pro-Palestine" based on the undeniable justice of the cause of Palestinian liberation and decolonization. I use "pro-Palestine" in this sense, then, as a way to denote those in favor of justice and to identify a particular attitude that Zionists find unacceptable.

6. See Zachary Lockman, *Contending Visions of the Middle East* (Cambridge, Mass.: Cambridge University Press, 2004).

7. Todd Gitlin, *The Intellectuals and the Flag* (New York: Columbia University Press, 2007), 5.

8. Ibid.

9. Ibid., 84.

10. Todd Gitlin, *Letters to a Young Activist* (New York: Basic Books, 2003), 137.

11. Eric Lott, *The Disappearing Liberal Intellectual* (New York: Basic Books, 2006).

12. Ibid., 185.

13. Michael Walzer, "Can There Be a Decent Left?," *Dissent*, http://www .dissentmagazine.org/article/?article=598.

14. In the same article he writes, "But ideologically primed leftists were likely to think that they already understood whatever needed to be understood. Any group that attacks the imperial power must be a representative of the oppressed, and its agenda must be the agenda of the left. It isn't necessary to listen to its spokesmen. What else can they want except . . . the redistribution of resources across the globe,

the withdrawal of American soldiers from wherever they are, the closing down of aid programs for repressive governments, the end of the blockade of Iraq, and the establishment of a Palestinian state alongside Israel? I don't doubt that there is some overlap between this program and the dreams of al-Qaeda leaders—though al-Qaeda is not an egalitarian movement, and the idea that it supports a two-state solution to the Israeli-Palestinian conflict is crazy. The overlap is circumstantial and convenient, nothing more. A holy war against infidels is not, even unintentionally, unconsciously, or 'objectively,' a left politics. But how many leftists can even imagine a holy war against infidels?"

15. Jonathan Schanzer, "Middle East Studies on the Mend?," Middle East Forum, January 4, 2009, http://www.meforum.org/2041/middle-east-studies-on-the-mend.

16. These terms are taken from Gates's controversial 1992 *New York Times* op-ed "Black Demagogues and Pseudo-Scholars," which can be found at http://www.nytimes.com/1992/07/20/opinion/black-demagogues-and-pseudoscholars.html. Gates was specifically concerned with a book sponsored by the Nation of Islam about Jewish complicity in the slave trade, which he conceptualized as anti-Semitic. However, the article was widely seen by Afrocentric and pro-Palestinian writers as an unjustifiable concession to a set of Zionist political demands on black anti-Zionist scholars.

17. See Andrea Smith, *Conquest: Sexual Violence and American Indian Genocide* (Boston: South End, 2005); Dale Turner, *This Is Not a Peace Pipe* (Toronto: University of Toronto Press, 2006); Robert Warrior, *Tribal Secrets* (Minneapolis: University of Minnesota Press, 1994); Linda Tuhiwai Smith, *Decolonizing Methodologies* (London: Zed, 1999); Taiaiake Alfred, *Peace, Power, Righteousness* (Oxford: Oxford University Press, 1999); Edward Said, *Representations of the Intellectual* (New York: Vintage, 1996).

18. Iris Marion Young, *Global Challenges* (Cambridge, Mass.: Polity, 2007), 5–6.

—

9

Nobody Mean More

Black Feminist Pedagogy and Solidarity

Alexis Pauline Gumbs

> *Nobody mean more to me than you.*
>
> —Monica Dennis, student in June Jordan's 1984 class on Black English

> *I was born a Black woman*
> *and now*
> *I am become a Palestinian.*
>
> —June Jordan, "Moving towards Home"

Introduction: Becoming Nobody

Nobody black taught English at John Jay College of Police Science before Audre Lorde. Nobody dare teach "black English" in the State University of New York (SUNY) system before June Jordan. Nobody knows the trouble I've seen. Nobody knows my sorrow. Nobody Palestinian can claim home in Palestine. Nobody mean more to me than you.

This chapter is a meditation on what it means to be nobody in a university economy designed to produce somebody individuated, assimilated, and consenting to empire. Is it possible instead to become nobody in the academic space? Is it is possible to align with the illegible oppressed/contemporary subaltern, the falling apart abject nonsubject, inside a university English class?

Here I seek to reframe and refract these questions through the archive of June Jordan and Audre Lorde's teaching in the public university system from the late 1960s through the 1980s and their writing during that period. This chapter looks at the complexity of the administrative function of teaching writing in an early black studies/women's studies context through two pieces of creative poetic and nonfiction writing by Audre Lorde and June Jordan on their own teaching.

Concrete: Discipline, Discipline, Relation, and Becoming

Struggling not to reproduce nationalistic exclusion in one of the first black studies classes in New York City, Audre Lorde writes "Power," a poem about the legal sanction of police brutality, while she herself is an employee of the College of Police Science in the City University of New York (CUNY) in the early 1970s.[1] A decade later she will be using her view as a diasporic daughter of parents from Grenada to *relate* to the U.S. military invasion of the first black socialist republic, analyzing it as the imperialist exportation of U.S. racism. By the early 1990s, at the end of her life, Audre Lorde will be one of the founding mothers of Sisters Supporting Sisters in South Africa (SISA) and will be challenging the German chancellor Helmut Kohl in an open letter published in several German newspapers on behalf of people of color and immigrants in Germany suffering from neo-Nazi racist violence.[2]

Struggling to explain the relevance and urgency of black English in her SUNY Stonybrook classroom, June Jordan creates a multilayered pedagogical narrative on the intergenerational dispersal of love between her own generation and the generation of her students in a police state. Eventually, Jordan will be standing with MADRE and the women of Nicaragua against the policing of the hemisphere by U.S. neoliberal economic interests. She will also poetically explain that the fact that she was born a black woman is not a barrier to the fact that she must become Palestinian in solidarity against U.S.-supported Israeli imperialism: "*I am become a Palestinian.*"

Palimpsest: A Process of Becoming

This chapter is inspired by June Jordan's declaration on becoming Palestinian, which exclusively uses primary texts and secondary sources by black theorists writing in the Americas. It distinguishes poetics and relation in "Power" and "Grenada: An Interim Report" by Lorde and mediates on the possibility of becoming nobody in Jordan's "Nobody Mean More to Me Than You and the Future Life of Willie Jordan" and "Moving towards Home."[3] Using published texts and their unpublished contexts as primary palimpsests in a critical discourse on relating and becoming as modes of solidarity, this chapter draws on theories of poetics, relation, and becoming in Sylvia

Wynter's "Ethno or Socio Poetics," Edouard Glissant's *Poetics of Relation,* and Michelle Wright's *Becoming Black.*

In *Disciplinary Matters,* intellectual historian Nick Mitchell distinguishes between the intellectual and administrative functions of black studies as a disciplinary form.[4] Disciplines do indeed discipline, administrating norms and validating forms of knowledge, forms of life, and some embodied realities over others. Hired to manage the post–civil rights transformation of the public university population, Jordan and Lorde refused to become the "master's tools" and sought to use the classroom as a space to interrogate the violent police management of the postindustrial underclass. I argue that these pedagogical possibilities also participated in an archive of relationship and intersubjectivity that informs Lorde's and Jordan's actions as teachers in solidarity with insurgent student survivors of internalized imperialism in New York and their statements of solidarity with people threatened by the externalized imperial violence of the United States and its partners.

The palimpsestic approach that I am taking in this chapter is influenced by M. Jacqui Alexander's use of palimpsestic time in *Pedagogies of Crossing.*[5] Alexander explains that she uses palimpsestic time to move out of the dominant imperialist mode of constructing a modern, relevant, and validated "here and now" against an archaic, dehumanized, and unmournable "then and there."[6] The palimpsest, based on the metaphor of writing surfaces used multiple times, allows her to "make visible the ways that ideologies and practices traffic within multiple spheres."[7] This chapter uses a palimpsestic practice to chart the traffic of big ideas (becoming, poetics, relation) in small spaces. I am interested in histories of violence from the perspective of poets responding to imperialism inside university classrooms and on pages of text that offer insight into their university teaching and their anti-imperialist vision.

Become Poetic

At the Ethnopoetics Symposium held in 1975 at the University of Wisconsin at Milwaukee, participants investigated the possibility of poetry as a mode of preservation of indigenous cultures threatened or eradicated through genocide.[8] Sylvia Wynter and Edouard Glissant, two Afro-Caribbean scholars, advanced ideas that challenged the basic premise of ethnopoetics and defined the function of the poetic in a way that will be useful in theorizing the poetic possibility of solidarity. Wynter and Glissant hail from Jamaica and

Martinique respectively, two islands in the Caribbean where European colonizers wiped out nearly the entire indigenous community and imported and enslaved Africans. The descendants of these enslaved Africans now participate in imperialism as national leaders, despite their devastating economic entrapment through neoliberal policies. Just as black U.S. citizens must navigate a secondary relationship to settler colonialism through forced migration, those of us who theorize Afro-Caribbean nationalism must also deal with the displacement and genocide of the indigenous groups of the Caribbean. As we attempt to arrive at a poetics that can help us understand June Jordan's statement that she must "become Palestinian," the theories of these scholars from sites of genocide are sources for such a new poetics. There are more questions about why of the seven speakers invited to the symposium, the organizers asked two Afro-Caribbean scholars to speak, but it is apparent that the specificity of the critique that Wynter and Glissant offer of the use of the poetic, with questions of indigeneity in mind, is about solidarity and diaspora. Jordan and Lorde as diasporic Afro-Caribbean poets born in the United States participate in this conversation from within a different relationship to power but with a related attention to transnational poetic concerns.

It is at this 1975 conference that Glissant offers his now famous distinction between free/natural poetics and forced poetics, arguing that ethnopoetics is of the future.[9] According to Glissant, oppressive conditions, including slavery, preclude "natural" poetics—a poetics through which a people can actually speak for themselves—by cutting off the material conditions for any self-expression that does not reproduce oppression. At the same event, Wynter argues for what she calls sociopoetics, an understanding of the poetic that takes capitalism into account. For Wynter, the poetic is a name for the creative act through which human beings create their relationships to their environment. Capitalism, she points out, only allows for things to relate to things, for objectified people to relate to objects that mean power (like machines and guns and other technologies). The capacity of relation is stolen in the context of capitalism, creating the exemplary condition: a prison, a reservation, perpetual entrapment. Wynter offers a direct challenge to the conference participants, pointing out that appropriating tribal poetry out of context only perpetuates this relationship of dominance inherent in the use of the poetry of so-called others to reify the humanism of some, which is not a genuine humanism. Instead, she offers here (as she continues to offer in her body of work to this day) the idea of a larger "we," created by the truly poetic practice of developing a relationship with others that is not about negating the other to produce a human self but rather about the human poetry of creating and describing possible collective relationships to the environment. This concept of the poetic as a category distinguished by Wynter's and Glissant's analyses of racism and other oppressions is in the writing against imperialism, which we will write right over, creating our own palimpsest on which to read the words of two poets teaching writing in a context of dehumanization and oppression.

Become Police: Discipline and Discipline?

In New York City by the end of the 1960s, the City University infrastructure included drastically more people of color than ever before. Shortly after, U.S. prisons, starting in New York and spreading across the country, grew by 400 percent. Both of these institutional expansions were funded, designed, and enforced by Governor Rockefeller's administration through the Rockefeller drug laws and the strategic university plan put into place by the state government during his tenure. We can also understand the growth of disciplinary imprisonment of people of color and the growth of educational access by and to people of color in this period as two sides of the coin of population control—that is, as part of a larger project to institutionally manage a post–civil rights diasporic population. In the 1950s, seven hundred thousand white residents left New York City and a comparable number of new residents from the Caribbean (especially Puerto Rico) and the southeastern United States (especially black migrants) moved to New York.[10] During the years that followed, Lorde and Jordan were hired to teach first in the Search for Education, Elevation and Knowledge (SEEK) program (a special program designed to give "minority" students, chosen by lottery, access to the public university) and then on CUNY and SUNY campuses that were demographically transformed by open admissions and opportunity programs. Jordan and Lorde's employment as public university teachers was part of a larger management of the dispersal of white residents and the consolidation of racialized migrants in New York City at the same time that demands for unskilled labor were decreasing in the United States.

At the moment that City University decided to address economic and social disruption by expanding its apparatus to teach remedial English and math to black and Latino high school graduates, the New York Police Department addressed the same situation with a different kind of teaching:

police brutality against black and Latino youth. As the Congress of Racial Equality (CORE), the New York Civil Liberties Union (NYCLU), and a number of organizations lobbied for the creation of a civilian review board to monitor police behavior, the tensions between a largely Irish, Catholic police force and student protesters and black and Puerto Rican youth grew. This led to a grassroots propolice campaign on the part of the Irish Catholic power base, which at its most benign circulated ads warning that police autonomy was needed to protect white women from certain racialized lurking men and at its most blatant converged into a mob and attacked five members of the Black Panther Party *in a courthouse*.[11] If the expansion of the public university was one form of increased pedagogy that sought to manage the problem of migration into New York City, increasingly organized police violence was another brutal form of teaching a new population how to learn its place.

Jordan's and Lorde's support of student-led protests and occupations of CUNY campuses in the 1960s and their queer[12] interruption of the socializing function of the university, through their teaching in the 1970s, was directly linked to their respective anti-imperialist stances against the Israeli occupation of Palestine and the U.S. invasion of Grenada in the 1980s. Their teaching was queer in the ways that it interrupted the reproduction of existing norms for a new population of students perceived as deviant to the city and to higher education. They practiced what Glissant would call a "counterpoetic" approach, using spaces designed in service of the colonial project to protest that same project, with varying levels of success. Their interventions into what it would mean for their students to become somebody also extend to their challenges of the U.S. enforcement of capitalism in the Americas and U.S. support of Israeli imperialism.

Lorde and Jordan intervened against the violent political and ideological management of racialized populations in an emergent neoliberal political order. If we engage a critical history of the convergent practices of the educational and punitive arms of the New York City and New York State government in the post–civil rights era—aided by a close reading of the pedagogical and poetic responses evident in the teaching and writing of Jordan and Lorde—we find resources to address the contemporary collaboration between the university system and the Department of Homeland Security in the racialized War on Terror, including the domestic drone war. The poetics that Jordan and Lorde used during the era when neoliberalism was justifying itself through narratives about survival, pathology, and free markets (in the academic "marketplace of ideas" and elsewhere) offer us forms and precedents to refer to in the imperative we are faced with in the face of an increased security state in the United States and a narrative of terror around the world.

The Antidiasporic Desire: The Classroom Falling Apart

The teaching that Lorde and Jordan were paid to do is also legible in the terms of the institutions that conscripted their labor. They were hired *to teach composition.* In the most cynical sense, the teaching for which Lorde and Jordan were first hired was the mammy labor of the university, the reproductive labor of training students who would be workers in the norms that the English language imposes. They were not only hired to teach students to compose coherent essays (later, memos and reports), but they were also hired to teach the student population how *to be composed,* contained, and conformist in a society in transition. The enormity of this task in New York City—with a postindustrial racialized population that was not at all *composed* and in fact was relating to the state educational apparatus through protest, school takeovers, and civil rights movement–inspired protests of police brutality—required programs designed to discipline a segment of the racialized population through inclusion.

A study of the 1970 "Open Admissions Experiment" at CUNY notes that the university's plans in 1964 and 1968 expressed anxiety about the influx of migrants and the shrinking of the unskilled labor market and described the public university as an institution that could mitigate the disruption this combination of factors would cause. A new chancellor, Albert Bowker, called the expansion of CUNY "a social necessity" and lobbied the state and federal government for the money to make that happen.[13] His campaign was assisted by the concern of elite city officials that the black and Puerto Rican populations were receiving a disproportionate amount of welfare aid. There was pressure from black, Puerto Rican, and radical white students, including the takeover of City College of New York (which Lorde and Jordan assisted and supported) and a series of sit-ins at Queens College, as well as the vocal opposition of white ethnics and the Jewish majority at CUNY to programs that seemed to favor "minorities." Eventually, the protests on both ends, while they seemed to be in opposition, were collectively disruptive enough to convince city officials that the only way to order the disorder of the 1969 City University campus (which was literally set on fire at one point) was to create an open admissions policy that appeased all the groups by admitting scores of new, working-class white ethnics and also changing the demographics to include a higher percentage of black and Puerto Rican students.[14]

At the same time, the New York Police Department deployed a set of tools to teach the peers of these black and Latino students and sometimes the students themselves their proper place in the new public ecology. In the 1960s, the visibility of police violence against civil rights workers in the south resulted in the salience and renewed resonance of responses to police violence in black and Puerto Rican communities in New York City led by organizations such as the Committee on Racial Equality (CORE).[15] Of course, not all the responses were particularly organized. A number of riots erupted in New York City in response to police violence against black and Puerto Rican youth, police violence ranging from baton use and violence during interrogations to several murders of unarmed young people. The limits of disciplined behavior on the part of the police were revealed as well, as outbursts by police, too well trained in the expendability of youth of color, provoked black and Puerto Rican communities to forget to discipline themselves into submission to the police or to remember that they had nothing left to lose in riots, especially in Harlem and Brooklyn.

Campus unrest and police violence were not separate phenomena in New York City. In January 1969, when members of the SEEK program for minority students at Queens College demanded student decision-making power over SEEK administrative positions, they were in a large part protesting the actions of SEEK director and former parole officer Joseph P. Mulholland, whom they saw as privileging "law and order" over the academic value of the black and Puerto Rican studies courses they were demanding.[16] In April 1969, when City College students took over a significant portion of their campus and renamed it "Harlem University," police were called in to manage the violence that broke out after classes resumed. These are the same Manhattan police that participated in the bloody end to the student occupation of buildings in the Columbia University rebellion in 1968, during which police officers lashed out violently against fleeing students, medical personnel, and even the counterprotesters who supported their presence. If the expansion of the public university was one form of increased teaching that sought to manage the problem of migration into New York City, increasingly organized police violence was another brutal form of teaching a transformed population how (not) to participate in the political landscape.

This increasing semblance of organization in law enforcement, designed to reclaim the disciplinary legitimacy of a police rank and file gone wild, included the founding in 1964 of the College of Police Science—later named John Jay College of Criminal Justice—at the height of the controversy over the prospect of a civilian review board in New York City. Lorde was the very first black professor in the English department of John Jay College of Criminal Justice; she cotaught the first women's studies course at the College of Police Science (acronym COPS), populated by mostly male students. But first and foremost, Lorde was hired to teach *composition* to the newly *opened* student population, a course in which the administration advised literature should not be taught but rather only the mechanics of writing. The "composition" that Lorde was hired to teach became at once more crucial and more contradictory in a context in which police officers were becoming more and more notorious for losing their cool and brutalizing the protesting sons and daughters of the middle class, not to mention young people of color. It may have been believed that professionalizing the police force with a college of "police science" would restore the police force as a symbol of order. Lorde was hired to teach in this environment six years after the founding of John Jay College, when the campus had been moved to two converted factory buildings and the makeup of the students replicated the racial tensions of the police force generally (which by this point had organizations of black and Puerto Rican officers protesting racist police action from *within* the force). Between 1969 and 1974, the population of students at John Jay shifted from 86 percent white and 14 percent black, Puerto Rican, and "other" to 56 percent white and 44 percent black, Puerto Rican, and "other." The percentage of black students more than doubled and the percentage of Puerto Rican students was six times as large as it had been. Due to the open admissions policy, students from the lowest performing high schools in the city, which also were most impacted by police violence, were now training in police science alongside members of the longstanding working-class white recruits into the force.

The contradictions resound. And this police violence hit very close to home and work for Audre Lorde, who sought to teach the mechanics of composing a sentence to young working-class police officers who would not be sentenced to anything if they killed black elementary school children in 1973. Indeed, when John Jay student and police officer Thomas Shea shot an unarmed ten-year-old black child named Clifford Glover in the back and killed him, saying into his police radio, "Die you little motherfucker," a jury decided it was justifiable self-defense. Lorde was clear about the colonizing role of the police in New York City and the legacy of colonialism undergirding the possibility of the American city in general. Thus the irony of the all capital letters across Lorde's syllabus for her course on "Race and the Urban Situation": "CIVILIZATION OR DEATH TO ALL AMERICAN SAVAGES."[17] Lorde's teaching was witness and collaborator with the internal colonizing force of the New York Police Department.

While Lorde was producing the complicated and emerging publics of her classrooms, preparing middle-class (pre–open admissions) teachers-in-training at Lehman College to teach underclass New York City public school students and then teaching composition to uniformed police officers and underrepresented prelaw hopefuls, she wrote one of her most memorable poems: "Power."[18] Writing about her teaching practices, Lorde explicitly says that the exercises she chooses to teach the same group are "different the day after the police slaughter of a Black child."[19] Lorde wrote the first draft of "Power" the day that Shea was acquitted by a jury of eleven white men and one black woman, starting the poem with the lines, "The difference between poetry and rhetoric / is being ready to kill / yourself / instead of your children." What is composition in the face of genocide?

Distinguishing the Poetic: The Difference

"Power" is Audre Lorde's poetic navigation of the nightmare contradictions born of her disciplining relationship to composition in the academy and her clear understanding of the genocidal stakes of the systematic police murders of children. Lorde addressed institutionalized racism and sexism in her elective courses, but of course, as it goes, for each course she taught on institutionalized racism and sexism, she was teaching many more composition courses. What can we find in the poem "Power" that can address the multiple levels of power we confront when we look at the disciplining functions of the university and the police state converging not only in Lorde's work but also in a shared project of domestication and imperialism?

Audre Lorde kept dream journals as a primary resource for her poetry. She describes writing "Power" as a moment when keeping track of her dreams directly served her poetry, though she did not see "Power" as a poem until years later, after living through this complicated year in her life and in her teaching. According to Lorde, when she heard the Shea verdict on the radio, she pulled over her car and wrote almost verbatim the poem now published as "Power." The first stanza of the poem makes visible the intergenerational imperative that Lorde brings to this question of power.

Lorde presences her own subjectivity as a mother and identifies Glover as part of a collective of black children toward which she feels accountability and kinship. Reading this imperative in Lorde's daily teaching relationship to Shea's classmates at John Jay, we might also think of them here. Because it was actually *rhetoric*—the practice of composing a sentence and making a coherent argument—that Lorde was paid to teach. And one such student had just convincingly argued that since (as Lorde quotes in the poem) he "didn't notice the size or nothing else / only the color," the shooting of an unarmed ten-year-old was justifiable. The argument made enough sense for a jury to agree that, yes, shooting a person who you at least knew to be black in the back is a justifiable way to save your life. The centuries of rhetoric produced and circulated about the danger of black people and the specific heightened discourse about the criminality of black people in post–civil rights New York City are also at play here. So Audre Lorde needs poetry. Poetry enables her to create a speaker that can move from subject to subject or, as she will later write in her dream journal, to understand that she is every person in her own nightmare and is also accountable to everyone in her nightmare.

In the second stanza of the poem, she describes the scene of the recurring nightmares she had been having of Glover "dragging his shattered Black / face off the edge of my sleep." "Trapped on a desert of raw gunshot wounds," she actually wants to drink the blood of the murdered boy who she later refers to as "her dying son," changing places with Glover's mother, who was the first person to describe what happened on the local news as "murder," and also shifting her own son Jonathan into Glover's place. The desert she describes makes loyalty impossible; she is in the situation of "trying to make power out of hatred and destruction." Isn't this also the situation of her students? Shea specifically uses discourses of racism to justify his action. Have not his thirteen years on the police force been a practice of purporting to use power in a context overdetermined by hatred and destruction? And do not the eleven white men in the jury affirm their own terrible power by condoning Shea's choice to kill an unarmed child who was running in the other direction?

Shea, along with bullets, deployed an imperative sentence (which was picked up on his radio, the recording from which was used as evidence in the trial)—a death sentence for Glover but not for Shea. He said, "Die you little motherfucker," and the jury heard it. Where did he learn to compose such a true statement? How did its elegance seem not to contradict his statement that he didn't notice the size of the person he called a "little motherfucker"?

The genealogy of motherfucker is specific, passed down from Oedipus to enslaved Africans in the Americas forced to breed for the market and not based on their own concepts of affinity. "Motherfuckin'" is a literal term, interchangeable with the more acceptable "cotton-pickin'" label used to describe the other labor that the same people were forced to do. How do centuries of trauma, forced sexual labor, and narratives of black social death through reproductive enslavement reemerge as common sense in the courtroom Lorde imagined while she watched the news and recounts in the poem?

Later, Jordan will work out the first rule of black English with her students as the following statement: "Black English is a whole lot more than motherfuckin'." But for now, Shea, trained at John Jay College of Criminal Justice, speaks police English, in which a small black fleeing figure still translates as not human, as socially dead, dangerously disconnected, and deviant—a rhetorical distinction imperative to the colonizing function of the police in New York City in the decade that it becomes a majority people of color space.

An Imperative Sentence Is a Dangerous Thing inside the Discipline of Police Composition

Lorde, as teacher, expresses the possibility of identification not only with the seemingly bloodthirsty police force (in the dream, she admits to "thirsting for the wetness" of the murdered child's blood) but also with the one black woman on the jury that acquitted Shea. According to the poem, this 4'10" black woman juror said, "They convinced me," seemingly translating assimilation into a narrative that defines black life as a dangerous form of power within an economy of what Lorde calls "white male approval." Lorde points out that this act of being "convinced" by the composed and recomposed arguments in the courtroom and the jury room actually means "giving up the first real power she ever had." Does Lorde herself have "real power" as she navigates a classroom in a police science college, training students who are white men or who will conduct their work in a context that privileges "white male approval"? Is Lorde the juror as well, making small and large curricular and pedagogical decisions daily as the first and at the time only black faculty member in the English department at John Jay with "white male approval" looming large? What will her students do with what she has taught them? Whom will they interrogate and not interrogate with their interrogative sentences? What will they declare with their declarative sentences? And whom will they (not) impair with their imperatives?

Finally, the last stanza of "Power" allows the narrator to reveal the almost inevitability of her own brutality: "Unless I learn to use / the difference between poetry and rhetoric," Lorde writes, she warns that she will exercise power corruptly through violence against a defenseless person (in this case not a small child but an elderly woman)—through rape, assault, and arson—triggering again the dehumanizing narrative, a declarative disguised in the interrogative: "What beasts they are." The question of brutality now faces the underlying declaration of who is and who is not human, which Lorde excavates from the language of the courtroom proceedings and the contextual sense made of the shooting of a ten-year-old in the back by a thirty-seven-year-old man. But Lorde's intervention here is key to an understanding of solidarity that includes even the brutal police-students Lorde taught rhetoric and prefigures Lorde's next move to teach poetry at Hunter College. Lorde is saying that any one of us, even the speaker of the poem—continuing along the trajectory of the rhetoric through which the state defends its sensibility and its ignorance ("I didn't notice," Shea says in his own defense)—will ultimately end up in a place of brutality or violence against the defenseless.

Distinguishing the Relation

According to Edouard Glissant, "in Relation every object is a subject and every subject an object."[20] The poetics of relation as theorized by Glissant and practiced by Audre Lorde are queer in their disruption of the composed sentence. That queerness, however, is complicated. It refracts. For example, when Shea says, "Die you little motherfucker," the queerness of the black body allows the listener to interpret the object as a "little motherfucker" and never as human. It also forces the black body to become the *subject* of the sentence, the perpetrator of perceived violence even as he is shot to death in the back at the utterance of the sentence. "What beasts they are," the sentence Lorde ends "Power" with, allows for the deferred subject "they" to come after the prejudicial "beasts" in a posture of routine objectification.

Lorde theorizes relation in her own terms as a diasporic anti-imperialist daughter ten years after Glover's murder during the imperialist U.S. invasion of Grenada, the first black socialist republic and the home country of Lorde's immigrant parents. Multiple times within this essay, Lorde refers to the subject position "relative" to distinguish her relationship as a diasporic Grenadian and a U.S.-born citizen and her responsibility to the self-determination of

Grenada. She uses scare quotes to refer to the "home" that she was seeking on her first visit to Grenada in 1978, acknowledging the fact that the "home" of her mother's stories and the place she would encounter could never be the same for a diasporic daughter who was visiting. When she returned again, in mourning, after the U.S. military invasion of Grenada against the socialist New Jewel movement's socialist revolution—and especially its collaboration with Cuba—she paused the publication of her now classic book of essays *Sister Outsider* in order to include a report on what she saw.

Lorde's "Grenada Revisited: An Interim Report" is a powerful resource for contemporary understandings of solidarity not only because of Lorde's identification with the freedom impulse of the black people who live in Grenada but also because of the way she identifies her own relationship to U.S. power and the call she makes for other black U.S. citizens to act. She breaks down the media hype, government rhetoric, and coverage in the *Washington Post* and *New York Times* of the invasion and points out their inconsistencies and fallacies, almost like a professor commenting on a disjointed essay. She also offers definitions: "Revolution. A nation decides for itself what it needs. How best to get it."[21] In other words, in relation to revolution, those who have been the object of an ongoing imperialist attack should have self-determinations—subject status in the narrative. And black Americans, whom Lorde calls out specifically and whom have been the direct objects of U.S. racism for generations, must now act as subjects in relation to an imperialist U.S. government that exports racism to the rest of the world. The context of racism is what makes the relation between the black U.S. soldiers who shot black Grenadian revolutionaries and civilians a crucial one, because in racism, which is a specific relation, Glissant's insight applies. The object and the subject are not stable and must, according to Lorde, be intentional because what they sentence the other to, they sentence themselves to as well.

Lorde is teaching us what it means and what it does not mean to be relative, asking us to amplify and politicize kinship in the service of the world we deserve. Exemplifying what Lorde's mentees, M. Jacqui Alexander and Chandra Mohanty, describe as transnational feminism, Lorde explains, "Grenada is their country. I am only a relative. I must listen long and hard and ponder the implications of what I have heard, or be guilty of the same quick arrogance of the US government."[22] Being a relative, in solidarity, does not mean disindentifying with the bad guy because of a relationship to the most drastically oppressed. It does not mean declaiming our responsibility when our privilege is also complicated by oppression. It does mean remaining

clear about the definitions of revolutions we support. It does mean resisting the external manifestations of the oppressions that impact us internally.
It does mean recognizing when we are nobody and when we are somebody
in relationship to imperialism. It does mean recognizing and strategically
accounting for our privileges and proximity of power as self-interested acts
not to garner more privilege but to enable the becoming of the world we
want to share.

Meaning More: June Jordan and Black English in the Face of Police Brutality

An elementary school student and participant in Jordan's "Voices of the
Children" workshop, Michael Goode taught Jordan about the slippery links
between the educational system and the prison system, describing his school
as "not one of the best schools in New York city and it's not a jailhouse
either."[23] Jordan's student speaks here of the connection between the school-
house and the jailhouse as the landscape of discipline for black children in
1970s New York. Goode's statement not only implies that the schools in New
York City are on a continuum between educational success and incarceration but also suggests the disciplinary function of the supposedly oppositional relationship between the educational and policing arms of the state.
Goode's statement is prescient in that policing violence and incarceration are
designed to teach something and that schools are designed to discipline and
keep people in line as well, creating a totalizing framework of discipline.

By disrupting this opposition and emphasizing the connection between
police violence and the problematics of her own classrooms, Jordan, like
Lorde, seeks to create a space for and with black youth that exceeds this
paradigm. In 1983, almost ten years after Shea was acquitted for the murder of Glover, Jordan would struggle to create an intergenerational basis for
black English in a college classroom at SUNY Stonybrook. Jordan struggled
to be accountable to the public university students in her classroom, many
of whom told her they had relatives brutalized by the police and subject to
incarceration, with a response to discipline as it emerges in language use. The
first rule in Jordan's SUNY classroom was "Black English is about whole lot
more than motherfuckin.'"[24]

In "Nobody Mean More to Me than You and the Future Life of Willie Jordan," June Jordan describes the process of creating a shared language between
herself and her SUNY Stonybrook students that can try to intervene in
yet another police murder in Brooklyn. In notes for a presentation that she

would do in 1988 in Berkeley, Jordan would recall that the situation of that class at SUNY made her understand "language as an act resulting in suicide or providing for survival." Choosing to teach black English in a university classroom was therefore a serious choice, between life and death. *A whole lot more than motherfuckin'*. June Jordan was interested in articulating the politics of presence that black English allowed.

The creation of black English as a mode through which to engage in her classroom came up directly against a repressive pedagogy in the home (ironically the exact opposite of teaching that black mothers were demonized for). Jordan explains, "For most of the students, learning Black English required a fallback to patterns and rhythms of speech that their parents had beaten out of them." And Jordan herself survived severe abusive beatings in her home. "I mean *beaten,*"[25] she emphasizes.

So here we have it. These parents apply preemptive discipline in the homes to beat the beat of oppositional black speech out of their students, hoping that this will save their children from future violence. And June Jordan wants the beat back. Or is it that Jordan wants an alternative intergenerational rhythm? Jordan's practice seems to replace the temporality of trauma in which parents seek to scare their children away from the brutality that the state wages against people with black parents, with an intentional queer intergenerationality through which a teacher and her students can codevelop a language that responds to the violence that they continue to survive. "Black English is about a whole lot more than motherfuckin'," rule number one, develops out of an encounter between Jordan and a student who critiques the black English she proposes as "too clean."[26] Jordan describes the "brawl" that ensued as the generative moment for the rule. This classroom moment restages, in advance, the scene of familial violence in which parents and children struggle over appropriate language use. This time however the struggle moves in both directions. Whereas in one instance the parents beat the children, in the other both the student and the teacher "brawl." The conclusion is that black English is not simply youthful rebellion but also a matter of terms. In fact, "motherfuckin'" itself is the code word for the silent rule of maternally bequeathed worthlessness that silences black expression to begin with. Everybody and Clifford Glover's mother knows that.

At the end of her essay "Nobody Mean More to Me than You," Jordan reveals that the language practice that she calls black English is embattled at every turn, and its necessity exceeds its present. Its victory is not in expression but rather in the creation of an alternative relationality in which kinship can emerge on terms that challenge the status quo instead of reproducing it. Jordan's black English is tested when the indescribable happens: Reggie Jordan, a twenty-five-year-old black man, brother to June Jordan's student Willie Jordan, is murdered by police officers—and nobody cares. Jordan only finds out about Reggie Jordan's death when she tracks down Willie, her dedicated student who has suddenly gone missing. The class ponders the differential defeats they face as they try to respond to the tragedy in the languages available to them. To write in American Standard English, they decide, would be to align themselves with the murderers, with the logic of the system that decided Reggie Jordan was expendable. To make it all more complicated, one student brings a friend who is actually a black New York City police officer to Jordan's class on the day that they are supposed to make their decision, once again reinforcing the fact that the university is not only an ideologically policing institution but also a space inhabited by police as students and workers. The students ultimately choose not to police themselves toward privilege. To write in the black English that they have created together is the only choice, they decide, but they suspect, correctly, that none of the publications they approach will publish their statement in black English. The victory is not in the legibility of their statement; the victory is in the rival kinship that these students, who Jordan tells us have all experienced police brutality themselves or through a loved one, have created through their shared engagement in a critical language practice. "At least we don't give up nothing else," they reasoned, "And stay all the way with Reggie."

Black English becomes a language practice that validates ignored kinship across death and on the front lines. Likewise, the relevance of Jordan's work is not (only) its prescience, not (only) its beauty, not (only) its unlikely survival, but (also) in its failed perfection. An act, called poetry, produces "the people." A practice called "black English" means black people can brawl across generations and maybe live to tell a different story about it later. Maybe it also means that oppressed people can communicate across space. Willie Jordan ultimately writes his final paper for his independent study with June Jordan about apartheid in South Africa, connecting it to the police violence that his brother experienced. Jordan includes Willie's essay at the end of her own essay, underlining the importance that she gives to these transnational connections as grounds for solidarity. If Audre Lorde explains that racism is the primary export of the United States, June Jordan is interested in pointing out that the United States also funds regimes, in both South

Africa and Israel, that reflect and violently enforce a logic of dehumanization based on race.

The public space of the classroom and the production of poetry for the multiple generations create a temporal intervention into what "public" means. What can be spoken? What can be heard? What can remain visible? The poetics of survival, a queer relationality, is key to the practice of black feminist production. Nobody mean more to me than you. Accountability to the person defined as nobody is what June Jordan ended up teaching, an undisciplining impulse in the classroom, a counterproductive mode of speech demonstrating not composition but solidarity, the unjustified mourning for nobody, who mean more than the mechanics of a standard English sentence can communicate.

Become Palestinian

Michelle Wright's *Becoming Black* is a key work on the dialogic reproduction of race in the black diaspora.[27] Taking on generations of dialectic constructions of race by thinkers such as W. E. B. Dubois, Leopold Senghor, and Franz Fanon, Wright draws on Audre Lorde and Carolyn Rodgers to reveal the dialogics of race. She argues that race is reproduced in conversation and that the ideas of the mask, the veil, and the other metaphors used to describe blackness and whiteness as antithetical avoid an analysis of reproduction and displace the figure of the mother in diasporic discourse. Lorde and Rodgers, on the other hand, center the figure of the mother, and in particular poetic dialogues with their own mothers about becoming themselves. Wright offers the idea that across time, race is reproduced in discursive terms and that scholars and activists who have argued from a stance of racial purity ignore the fact that blackness keeps being remade of many things, many diverse genes, but more important through many discursive moves and social narratives. Imperialism itself is a discourse through which blackness is reproduced. Wright's analysis is crucial to the anti-imperialism of critical black diaspora studies because it recognizes blackness as a dialogue that can happen across space, without conforming to the structure of racism that places it in continually opposition to constructed whiteness. Being black (as Franz Fanon writes about it) contains an absolute; it is pure in its abjection.[28] It is not whiteness and it is also everything that whiteness is not. Wright points out the Hegelian fallacy in Fanon's distinction of "being black," most famously articulated in relationship to whiteness in the figure of the mask. Blackness and whiteness are antithetical in this conceptual world, and when Fanon arrives at synthesis through the engagement with the masks, or when DuBois arrives at synthesis in the figure of the veil, there is actually nothing new created; black difference and the antithetical relationship are simply reproduced. So where "being black" is so stable and definite that it even traps our logic, *becoming* black is a conversation, a possibility, a process. *Becoming* black is queer in that it is not based on purity, and it is not reproducing a narrative about what blackness itself is. Instead, *becoming* black works the transformative power of the shifting definition of blackness on everything: on our relation to each other, on the possibility of solidarity, on the practice of language on the invention of politics. *Becoming* black is a poetic process in the sense that Wynter distinguishes it. It is not something that can be described. It is the process of creating a relationship to an environment or a situation that displaces the dominant objectifying relationship.

The idea of becoming that is central to Wright's intervention on what it is to become black across space and time in diaspora is relevant to the anti-imperialist poetics of becoming Palestinian that June Jordan arrives at in her poem "Moving towards Home." If *becoming* black deploys diaspora as a queer intervention into the reproduction of blackness as abjection in opposition to whiteness, *becoming* Palestinian faces the erasure of Palestinian in relationship to occupation. Becoming Palestinian is an intervention against the construction of "Arab" as a landless, colonized category performed ideologically through the denial of the "Palestinian" category and physically through the displacement of Palestinians and the penetration of Lebanon. If the poetics of becoming black requires a recognition of discourse as a productive force, the poetics of becoming Palestinian requires the recognition of discourse as an obliterating force. Jordan's intervention is the inhabitation of a position designed to prevent inhabitation itself. Becoming Palestinian is an acknowledgement of the fact that the discourse through which racially different groups of people become expendable is a discourse with a shared precondition. Becoming itself is a problem because it points to a discourse that needs the presence of the construct (black, Palestinian) as a threat in order to outlaw the actual presence of the people (black, Palestinian, indigenous). Becoming is an intervention against the interchangeability in the narrative. Becoming Palestinian is becoming nobody where nobody mean more.

Jordan prefaces the poem with an epigraph from the September 20, 1982, article in the *New York Times*, using the voice of a bereaved Palestinian woman saying, "Where is Abu Fadi? Who will bring me my loved one?" After a poem struggling with not wanting to have to speak about the atrocities of Israeli imperialism, Jordan explains,

> I was born a Black woman
> and now
> I am become a Palestinian
> against the relentless laughter of evil
> there is less and less living room
> and where are my loved ones?
> It is time to make our way home.[29]

What Jordan is looking for in this poem is a relationship to the unmournable dead and the perpetually displaced that is not overdetermined by the imperialist collaboration between the United States and the state of Israel. She is looking for something that is not what Wynter would call a relationship between objects mediated by objects. She wants to find a way to respond to what she "do(es) not want to" talk about, just as at first her students do not want to speak black English but ultimately decide that they must *become* black and illegible to the norms they resist in order to have the dialogue they need to have in the face of Reggie Jordan's murder.

Like her students, Jordan must become nobody legible in order to arrive at subjectivity. *I am become a Palestinian.* The subject and the object have a bridge to walk across or a living room where they can meet. With the Israeli invasion of Lebanon in 1982, one of a series of Israeli invasions of Arab lands that has continued into the twenty-first century, the aggressive imperialist character of Israel's occupation of Palestine was blatant. The massacres against civilians that occurred, including the massacres of Palestinians at Shatila and Sabra refugee camps, were consistently reframed as strategic and necessary acts against so-called terrorist leaders in the Palestinian Liberation Organization. Kathy Engel, Jordan's close friend, was co-organizer of "Moving towards Home" in New York in 1982, a poetry reading by Palestinian and U.S. artists in solidarity with those suffering from the Israeli invasion of Lebanon, which was in full swing at the time, though the U.S. media was consistently presenting misinformation. The event was the inspiration for Jordan's poem with the same title, and Engels explained that at the time, "living room" meant more than one thing to Jordan.[30] The living room was a vision for a more livable world, and at the same time it was the place where

Jordan watched U.S. media coverage in outrage as the deaths of Palestinian and Lebanese civilians were justified, based on biased and false information. Jordan was so angry about U.S. complicity in the displacement and death of Lebanese and Palestinian people that she not only wrote a series of angry and ironic poems (including "Apologies to All the People in Lebanon"[31]) but also participated in public solidarity events and alienated herself from some editors and publishers because of her uncompromising commitment to critiquing Israel, as she also expressed her rage at the situation in her everyday life. For example, in offering a blurb for her colleague Cheryl Clarke's book of poems, "Narratives: In the Tradition of Black Women," she uplifts the truth telling of Clarke's poetry and contrasts it to the blatant and harmful lies in the media about Israeli imperialism. All things may be interconnected, but what ultimately connects truth telling about the experiences of black women to an ethics of accountability to Lebanon and Palestine for Jordan is that she takes them both personally and finds them both to be crucial. Her written outburst in the midst of this book blurb reveals that the silence and misinformation about U.S. involvement in Israel's violence was constantly on her mind during this period.[32]

and now I am: be(come a conclusion)

You may have noticed that this chapter repeats itself, looks back at itself, seems unsatisfied to not be a poem, has scenes and starts, and does not quite stay composed—unbecoming to an academic essay or chapter in a book but also predictable in the poetic tradition it relates to here. Audre Lorde asks for the poetic, for the interim report, for the listening of a relative, and for the rejection of rhetoric in the navigation of the process of being everyone in the dream while not colonizing the subjectivity of the object. June Jordan must stay poetic to become Palestinian. "And now / I am become a Palestinian," she says, offering a tense archaic in English. Is this a stronger than mandative situational subjunctive? There is movement in the statement; is there a state or more than one or none here (am, be, come)? There is a diasporic home here that imperialism would deny or destroy, a living room that the imperialist state would criminalize and that academia would marginalize now and co-opt later. In what languages do we mourn the unmournable today? With what pedagogical forms? A pedagogy of solidarity within the imperial university, a short poem written over and over itself, at a particular time and place connected to other times and places: am, be, come, nobody, mean more.

Notes

Second epigraph "Moving towards Home" by June Jordan from *Directed by Desire: The Collected Poems of June Jordan*. Reprinted with the permission from the June M. Jordan Literary Estate Trust and Copper Canyon, http://www.junejordan.com.

1. This is according to when a draft of "Power" first appeared in Lorde's personal journal. Lorde's journals are archived at Spelman College in Atlanta, Georgia.

2. More information on SISA and a copy of Lorde's letter to the chancellor (which she included in a piece of correspondence to Adrienne Rich) can be found in the Spelman College Archives. Dagmar Schultz also mentions the impact of Lorde's letter in *Entfernte Verbindungen: Rassismus, Antisemitismus, Klassenunterdrückung*, ed. Ika Hügel et al. (Berlin: Orlanda Frauenverlag, 1993), 172.

3. Sylvia Wynter, "Ethno or Socio Poetics," *Alcheringa* 2, no. 2 (1976): 81–87; Edouard Glissant, "Natural Poetics, Forced Poetics," in *Caribbean Discourse*, ed. Edouard Glissant (Charlottesville: University Press of Virginia, 1989), 120; Michelle Wright, *Becoming Black: Creating Identity in the African Diaspora* (Durham: Duke University, 2004); Audre Lorde, "Power," in *Between Ourselves*, ed. Audre Lorde (New York: Eidolon, 1976); Audre Lorde, "Grenada: An Interim Report," in *Sister Outsider* (Berkeley: Crossing, 1984), 176; June Jordan, "Nobody Mean More to Me Than You and the Future Life of Willie Jordan," in *On Call* (Boston: South End, 1985), 123–40; June Jordan, "Moving towards Home," in *Living Room* (New York: Thunder's Mouth, 1985), 132–34. Reprinted with the permission from the June M. Jordan Literary Estate Trust and Copper Canyon, http://www. junejordan.com.

4. Nicholas Mitchell, *Disciplinary Matters: Black Studies and the Politics of Institutionalization* (University of California: Santa Cruz, 2011).

5. M. Jacqui Alexander, *Pedagogies of Crossing* (Durham: Duke University Press, 2005), 194.

6. Ibid., 190.

7. Ibid., 246.

8. See *Alcheringa* 2, no. 2 (1976).

9. Edouard Glissant, "Natural Poetics, Forced Poetics," 120.

10. David Lavin, Richard Alba, and Richard Silberstien, *Right vs. Privilege: The Open Admissions Experiment at the City University of New York* (New York: Free Press, 1981), 5.

11. See Paul Chevigny, *Police Power: Police Abuses in New York* (New York: Pantheon Books, 1969).

12. Here "queer" refers to the interruption of social norms.

13. "To Help the Disadvantaged," *New York Times*, August 4, 1968, E11.

14. Ibid., 13.

15. Marilynn Johnson, *Street Justice: A History of Police Violence in New York City* (Boston: Beacon, 2003).

16. Fred M. Hechinger, "In the Colleges 'Separate' Could Mean 'Inferior' for Blacks," *New York Times,* January 12, 1969.

17. Audre Lorde, "Race and the Urban Situation Syllabus" (Audre Lorde Papers, Spelman College Archives, Box 17, Folder 60).

18. Lorde, "Power."

19. Audre Lorde, "Poet as Teacher as Human," in *I Am Your Sister: Collected and Unpublished Essays by Audre Lorde*, ed. Beverly Guy-Sheftall et al. (New York: Oxford University Press, 2011), 182; Jordan, "Nobody Mean More to Me Than You," 129.

20. Edouard Glissant, *Poetic of Relation*, trans. Betsy Wing (Ann Arbor: University of Michigan Press, 1997).

21. Lorde, *Sister Outsider,* 179.

22. Ibid., 189.

23. Student cited in "Children and the Hungering For" unpublished essays in the June Jordan Manuscript Archive at the Schlessinger Library of Women's History at Harvard University. See more in June Jordan, *The Voice of the Children* (New York: Washington Square, 1974).

24. Jordan, *On Call,* 128.

25. Ibid.

26. Ibid.

27. Wright, *Becoming Black*.

28. Frantz Fanon, *Peau Noire, Masques Blancs* (Paris: Seuil, 1952), 87; Charles Lam Markmann, trans., *Black Skin, White Masks* (New York: Grove, 1967).

29. Jordan, "Moving towards Home."

30. Personal conversation between the author and Kathy Engel, February 14, 2013.

31. June Jordan, "Apologies to all the People in Lebanon," in *Directed by Desire: The Collected Poems of June Jordan* (Port Townsend, Wash.: Copper Canyon, 2005).

32. Cheryl Clarke Papers, Black Gay and Lesbian Archive, Schomburg Library, New York Public Library.

10

Teaching outside Liberal-Imperial Discourse

A Critical Dialogue about Antiracist Feminisms

Sylvanna Falcón, Sharmila Lodhia, Molly Talcott, and Dana Collins

This chapter reflects the multiple conversations we have had since 2007 about academia and is written in a manner that retains the spirit of our feminist collaboration. Our group embodies diverse social positions as women of color and as white women, as immigrants and as children of immigrants, as queer and as heterosexual, as mothers, and as middle class. Our diverse locations, coupled with our shared commitment to antiracist/transnational feminism, produce a strength that resonates with Audre Lorde's argument about women redefining and celebrating differences.[1] Accordingly, we reproduce here our ongoing conversations, which synthesize our collective commitments with the strength of our experiential differences.

The four of us came together to form a writing group in fall 2007 when all of us were in different stages of our academic careers, from completing a dissertation, to conducting postdoctoral research, to transitioning to junior faculty positions. Though our research and fields of study vary, we each embrace the idea of teacher-scholar activism. We came together initially to share our writing with one another in a space that was safe, humane, and supportive of our political goals. Though the formation of such a group may not seem exceptional, we came to experience our exchanges as deeply transformative; in fact, we had all borne witness to the competitive individualism, territoriality, and institutional pressures that so often drive academics to isolation. Our dedication to working together to counter the hyperindividualistic and masculine culture of the academy has made our collective into a distinctive space that is both holistic and compassionate.

We initially referred to ourselves as the Feminist Writing Group or FWG, though more recently, we adopted the name CASA—Collective of Antiracist-Feminist Scholar Activists. We were searching for a new name because we had moved beyond just offering one another writing support and had entered into broader discussions about critical pedagogies, the challenges of navigating academic life while remaining engaged in diverse social justice movements, and finding sustainable ways to remain present with our loved ones while pursuing our work. We had formed, in our view, an ideal collective for us that merged our feminist politics with our activist scholarship and acknowledged the joys and hardships of our everyday lives. In Spanish, *casa* means "home," and we had indeed found an academic home with one another that countered the individualist demands of the university. This new home transformed our vision of the work we aspire to do in our teaching, research, writing, activism, and collaborations beyond the academy; it also revealed a desire to work on joint writing projects even though we had received subtle and not-so-subtle messages that doing so would not help advance our tenure cases.

Our first collaborative writing endeavor took place in 2010. We successfully coedited a special issue of the *International Feminist Journal of Politics (IFjP)* and coauthored the introduction.[2] Our topic, *New Directions in Feminism and Human Rights*, sought to explore the contradictions that emanate from, on the one hand, the institutionalization of human rights among imperial nation-states and global governmental bodies and, on the other, the growing embrace of human rights logics and languages by activists. The special issue drew on questions at the intersections of our research and filled a critical gap in the existing human rights literature.

The common practice of most peer-reviewed academic journals is to have two coeditors, yet we wanted to approach the project as a collective, meaning that all four of us would serve as coeditors. Fortunately, the managing editors of *IFjP*, a journal that emerged out of a similarly counterhegemonic academic trajectory, supported our vision to work collaboratively and in the process practiced a feminist mentoring model, which we have sought to replicate with one another and with other junior faculty. We followed the release of the *IFjP* special issue by organizing a conference at the University of California, Santa Cruz, in April 2011, during which we discussed the evolution of CASA and the collective process by which we completed the journal—a discussion that inspired others, both contributors and attendees, to fashion similar collective projects at the intersections of their own work. By the end of 2011, Routledge had published our work as a coedited book.[3]

The conversational chapter that follows contains questions we composed and addressed through a series of conference calls and e-mail exchanges. The questions grapple with the contradictory space of academia, negotiating classroom dynamics during discussions about politically charged issues, fostering an empowering pedagogy that encourages intellectual curiosities, and reflecting on CASA's collective process of knowledge production. We consolidated our responses in this chapter into a dialogue format that maintains our distinct writing style, captures our shared and differential standpoints, and reveals a range of struggles within the imperial university.

What Are Your Thoughts about the Contradictory Space of Academia as an Imperial Space, yet One That Also Offers the Academic Freedom to Teach and Learn?

Sylvanna: The contradictory space of academia means that combined with the opportunity to teach critical classes about race, class, gender, and sexuality, we also work in an institution that is racist, classist, and patriarchal. As a feminist sociologist, I understand this contradiction intellectually, but trying to navigate it can be challenging and exhausting. I remember in one of my first teaching experiences following my return from the 2001 United Nations World Conference against Racism (WCAR) in South Africa, I decided to enter the complicated terrain of the Palestinian-Israeli conflict in a course on globalization. During the WCAR, I learned so much about this issue that I felt it would be a disservice to my political awakening to not figure out ways to integrate these debates into my classroom. That said, I had never been so scared to broach a subject matter before because I had seen firsthand the heavy price other academics had paid for being critical of U.S.-supported Israeli policy. I felt like a somewhat inexperienced teacher at the time also, but I knew I needed to confront my own fears directly in the same way I expected my students to become uncomfortable when talking about issues new to many of them. And herein lies the contradiction: if I truly felt "academic freedom" in the institution, then I would not have been overwhelmed by fear in talking about an issue that I felt I had a right to discuss in my classroom and one that I believe whose resolution is truly central to anti-imperialist projects. In the end, the conversations have been surprisingly well received by the vast majority of my students, with many saying they view U.S. news media coverage more critically than before as a result of our discussions. Yet I'm mindful of the fact that it can just take one student to raise an objection with those who "occupy" positions of institutional power and my position as an untenured faculty person would be easily jeopardized.

At a time when public education is literally being dismantled before our eyes as a result of the "budget crisis," we cannot afford to be complacent because the theoretical contributions, narratives, and analyses of, for example, communities of color, queers, and feminists have shifted education away from white heteropatriarchy and have directly challenged fallacious notions of objectivity. In other words, this contradictory space of academia is *going to* become even more apparent when we see which departments, programs, and student services are being rapidly defunded, are forced to merge, or become extinct in the public education system.

Molly: I completely agree with you. I think one of the greatest challenges we face as antiracist feminist scholars is to continually remain mindful of the fact that we inhabit a deeply complex institutional position. University classrooms are among the few public spaces and places where we can have extended conversations about racism and antiracism, sexism, homophobia, and capitalism—and how to challenge all this. To move outside liberal discourse, we have to connect an analysis of gender, race and racism, and culture and identity, I think, with U.S. imperialism and with expanding forms of militarization and privatization. This space is contradictory because our very institutions, the people who write the checks, are tied to militarization projects and the privatization of the academy and many other arenas of life. So we cannot be seduced by some of the liberatory parts of the work we do. We have to maintain that oppositional consciousness that Chela Sandoval has written about and make strategic decisions at various moments.[4]

For example, I encountered some difficulty in a recent class I taught on race, class, and gender where I wanted to move the discussion beyond a liberal discourse that looks only toward dismantling discrimination but keeps deeply unequal systems of oppression, occupation, and accumulation intact globally. In my view, analyzing U.S. militarization and foreign policy is a vital part to this pedagogical goal of challenging students to move beyond an individualized and U.S.-based discrimination lens. In this particular class, I had shown a video clip about the 2012 anti-NATO (North Atlantic Treaty Organization) protests in Chicago, where U.S. veterans threw away their medals and explained their many—often anti-imperialist—reasons for doing so, which visibly gripped one of my students, a young man of color and former U.S. Marine. He disagreed with the protesters and insisted that he had fought for "our" freedom in Iraq. Other students—one whose cousin had returned from Iraq and committed suicide and another whose friends had returned from Iraq with the revised understanding that the mission had "not been what the U.S. said it was about"—challenged the former marine, producing the most heated set of conversations to date in my several years of teaching this course.

At my university in East Los Angeles—where a majority of students are working-class people of color with few avenues to higher education—the U.S. military is not typically viewed as an instrument of systematic racial, gender, and class oppression but rather one that promotes "uplift" and freedom. I knew I was treading on imperial ice by screening the protest footage, but I had to do so if I wanted to take a course on race, class, and gender beyond individualized conversations about discrimination. Conversations like these with my students remind me that we must "occupy" the imperial university and create anti-imperialist spaces of exploration within it.

Sylvanna: Your story reminds me of precisely why we need to problematize the notion of academic freedom, which I conceptualize as far beyond the debates about censorship. Academic freedom is tenuous for academics who do critical work that challenges systematic racism, sexism, heterosexism, and classism, among other subjects, as you did, Molly, by showing the anti-NATO protest clip. For me, true academic freedom includes respecting the choices we make as teacher-scholars as long as we are not intentionally belittling students in the process, including a student like your former marine. We also want to help create a classroom community where students are not disrespectful of one another.

Even though we can have the good fortune to work with amazing students and some provocative and radical colleagues, the structural expectations of personnel reviews are stark reminders that quite a bit of rigidity and sharp limits on our jobs exist. Where is this so-called academic freedom then? Since our work is heavily scrutinized, and in some cases I'd argue more heavily scrutinized than some of our colleagues, a complicated disconnect can exist between academic freedom and the realities of the profession. In other words, we can have our personnel files reviewed by colleagues who do not always understand the intense emotional labor involved in conducting social justice–oriented research and practicing an antiracist feminist pedagogy. Such work can result in mixed teaching evaluations from students, less quantifiable productivity in terms of publications, and higher numbers of coauthored works. None of this is equally valued by comparison to single-authored publications in a tenure case.

Molly: For me, being an antiracist feminist scholar in the contemporary academy is about continuously trying to work on answering the question that Kathleen Cleaver has raised in the context of her work in the Black Panther

Party, and that is, "How do you empower an oppressed and impoverished people who are struggling against racism, militarism, terrorism, and sexism too? I mean, how do you do that? That's the real question."[5] As an antiracist feminist, that is essentially my enduring research question and the broader scholarly question from which all the work I do springs. To the extent that I can work in community with others on this question, I feel that the public university is a space we need to fight to save—and to transform. Yet along with being a space where academic freedom is at least ostensibly valued, it is a space of domination and social control, where power is simultaneously wielded—increasingly by managerially minded university administrators—and evaded through opaque, top-down practices. If antiracist feminists are to survive, heal, and become whole and stay focused on addressing Cleaver's central question, we need one other, and that means we must build anti-imperial spaces, circles, and oases within the imperial university.

Sylvanna: In relation to Cleaver's question, I try to practice a politics of transparency in academia. For example, when I was on the job market, I often found myself interviewing for the same faculty positions as some of my friends. Rather than being secretive about the interview and my job application, I was very transparent about it—I shared my job materials with anyone who asked for them and I even told colleagues I knew interviewing for the same job about my interview experience. By lifting the veil of secrecy about being on the job market, I knew that I was not succumbing to the logics of the imperial university that mandate I prioritize my own self-interest. I know my openness threw off many of my colleagues at first, but I realized that if I was going to have any chance of surviving in the academy, then I had to do it according to my own political and ethical terms and not on those of the hypercompetitive culture of an institution that was never meant to include women of color faculty in the first place.

I also believe it is imperative to acknowledge the limitations of the academy and that the activism we do beyond teaching is not going to be recognized as legitimate for academic purposes. And I think we need to accept this structural fact because academia, like nongovernmental organizations, is not going to be at the forefront of any revolution.[6] As INCITE!, a grassroots women of color organization against violence, so aptly reminds us, "The revolution will not be funded"; academia is intertwined with this same funding regime that is largely invested in promulgating a liberal discourse that our teaching and research seeks to unsettle.

Molly: I also believe that, as activist scholars, we must move beyond the academy and really participate in social movements—not just study them from a distance. It's not enough to analyze and deconstruct them; we need to do our part to help build them. Noël Sturgeon has quite insightfully pointed out that in the United States especially, academic feminism has rewarded deconstruction.[7] You advance your career by pointing out flaws and omissions in other peoples' work. Now I'm not arguing against critique; we do need social critique. But sometimes when the structures of advancement (tenure, publishing, etc.) and the culture of competitive individualism in the university intersect with our practices of social critique, we're not really being that effective at building a new society or at motivating students to build new worlds that are antiracist, anti-imperialist, and feminist. As my colleagues within *Sociologists without Borders* have reminded me, this academic structure is specific to the United States. In other academic cultures (e.g., in parts of Latin America), scholarship is less focused on deconstruction and more focused on the work of building new values, cultures, and institutions that center equity, cooperation, and justice over individual success, competition, and oppression. Grace Lee Boggs, one of the most important intellectuals alive today, calls this work "visionary organizing" because it combines philosophical and intellectual work with concrete actions—urban farming and freedom schooling, for instance—that make beneficial changes to the lives of oppressed peoples. In Latin America, academics are active in political parties and grassroots movements. In the Philippines, it is unremarkable for feminist academics to be active members of GABRIELA, a radical grassroots and transnational feminist political movement. We in the U.S. academy desperately need to observe, learn from, and incorporate the practices of those working outside of it, be it Boggs (an intellectual activist Asian American woman whose PhD in philosophy in 1940 did nothing to advance her career in the apartheid United States) or others working in academies located in the global South.

In the United States, the return to public intellectualism is a really important one. But this also becomes a source of difficulty for feminists, because we've become caught to some extent in *superserviceable feminism*,[8] where ethnic, women's, and gender studies faculty end up being scholars, programmers, and being called upon to fulfill a range of university service capacities all the while trying to keep our embattled programs afloat in the face of the neoliberal-managerial assault. This is another case where I think we need to think strategically about our service work in the university. Sometimes it is strategic to be involved in certain types of service. On the other hand, these decisions need to be conscious (we need not be "yes women") and in the context of knowing we work for institutions that systemically produce inequality and suffering alongside their liberatory potential.

In What Ways Are Our Complex Subjectivities, and Those of Our Students, *Hypervisible* within the Context of Classroom Engagements with Politically Charged Issues?

Sharmila: Our presence and position within the academy, as "Othered" women, coupled with the antiracist feminist politics that inform our teaching, can at times inspire certain degrees of resistance on the part of faculty and students. I've encountered this firsthand in my efforts to elevate subjugated knowledge in response to a curricular revision at my institution that involved a shift away from the requirement of a traditionally Euro-American-centered Western culture sequence—which celebrated modernity, Christianity, and American exceptionalism—to one that was more global and interdisciplinary in scope.

As I sought to align my assignments with the learning objectives of the newly developed "Cultures and Ideas" courses, I sensed a distinct shift toward a more transnational and interdisciplinary framework of analysis. At the same time I learned of a profound sense of crisis that had emerged among some faculty members and students in response to this change, which in their view had resulted in a problematic decentering of the West. American studies scholar John Mythyala has suggested, "Eurocentrism can aspire to universalism and exclusivity *at the same time* only insofar as the presence of what makes it different and therefore exclusive and superior is marginalized, and left unaddressed."[9] In order to do so, he argues, one must adopt a "perverse kind of historical blindness" with respect to non-European cultures and peoples. In putting together the texts, the assignments, and the overarching critical framework of my "Cultures and Ideas" course sequence, dedicated to examining women's lives in a transnational perspective, I thought a lot about how my history inflects—or perhaps *infects*, depending on your point of view—my place and space in the classroom. What did it signify that I, a postcolonial, racialized, and gendered subject, was being asked to teach a course that had fought for and secured its independence from a Eurocentric framework—one that was in a sense cured of the "historical blindness" of which Mythyala speaks? What opportunities might I create for students, specifically students of color, women students, immigrant students, and first-generation college students who, like me, may have felt somewhat detached from, or at least disengaged in, compulsory courses in Western civilization? In teaching these transnational courses, I've come to find that many students can readily relate to the narratives of colonization, migration, identity, and homeland that emerge out of the literature they are reading and that they come to view their lives and experiences represented in ways they are not elsewhere in the curriculum.

Dana: There is also a certain precariousness and risk, not only for us as faculty members, but also for our students when we openly engage in such gendered critiques of globalization and Eurocentrism, which include outspoken critiques of U.S. imperialism. Teaching at California State University, Fullerton, a university that serves not only a metropolitan region but also one of the core global regions of Southern California, has challenged me to rethink vulnerability within the classroom. Students have pushed me to explore and work with the vulnerable standpoints of those at which education is directed in the imperial university. I want to share my experience with a student who spoke at length with me about his experience of vulnerability in education, in general, and, specifically, within classrooms where the subject matter centers on antiracist and anti-imperialist politics and critiques of U.S. foreign and domestic policy. This student never self-identified ethnically and racially, yet he shared with me his experiences of racial profiling when he was a high school student in Orange County. He had ongoing conflicts with a teacher who deemed him a "threat" and who eventually had him removed from the classroom by the police.

This student shared his story with me after a class where students directed our collective discussion of readings. He wanted to explain to me why he was not talking in our classes and shared his sense of vulnerability vis-à-vis the students and myself. He identified at that moment as a radical and an anarchist who has an understanding and set of critiques and politics that are critical of U.S. imperialism. Now as a university student who is taking courses that engage with politically radical ideas, the trauma he experienced in high school has become more acute. He explained how he felt "on stage" in classrooms and vulnerable to being retraumatized because he is always already read (by both students and professors) as a suspect (Arab/Muslim/Other) and a visible "threat" if he were to verbalize his critiques of the United States and anti-imperialist politics as a brown man. He was expressing his fears about speaking truth to his political standpoint, and this was particularly the case in politically left classrooms. There is a contradiction here in his experience, which parallels the experience of others in ostensibly "left" circles who find themselves simultaneously hypervisible and invisible, or at least silenced in the left's discourse on imperialism. He was silenced precisely because of his hypervisibility as a person of color who, in post-9/11 public discourse, is not allowed to hold critiques of U.S. imperialism, and this is the case for critiques of U.S. imperialism within educational institutions as well, even though such institutions are supposed to be spaces "ripe" for critical intellectual and political engagements, as Molly, Sylvanna, and Sharmila have already discussed. It is a lesson on how classes that are framed to be productive of such discourses can silence students who have been most victimized by the imperial university.

Sharmila: Yes, and then there are other students, however, who have taken issue with my gendered critiques of globalization or my deconstruction of the media's Orientalist gaze upon "Third World women" subjects. In response to the narrative evaluation question—"What concerns do you have about the course?"—I have received comments like, "She shows a tendency to be biased against white culture," "An ideological position is taught instead of healthy debate," and one that I have received repeatedly, "Instructor focuses too much on race." In reflecting on such comments, I cannot help but wonder if this resistance to who is teaching and what is being taught, in fact, mirrors more widely held anxieties around race, immigration, and gender circulating within dominant discourses.

Further, given the weight of student and faculty evaluations within the context of decisions regarding tenure and promotion, the issue of heightened intellectual risks and consequences for certain faculty members cannot be overlooked. As one senior faculty member told me quite emphatically, along the lines of Peggy McIntosh's arguments about whiteness as a privilege, "Teaching critiques of globalization are just easier for white people." The issue of the positionality one occupies within the classroom then (whether claimed or imputed) merits greater scrutiny, particularly given the assumption of bias on the basis of one's race, class, gender, sexuality, or national origin that is reflected in the evaluative comments previously described. Certainly, white, male classics or history professors are not being told in their evaluations that they spend too much time focusing on "privileged, white men." The raced and gendered identities of "postcolonial" and "transnational" teachers are marked but often in ways that resist simple translation within the U.S. racial hierarchy.

Dana: I agree, and if our commitments to antiracist feminism have encouraged our ongoing exploration of the intersections between our, and our students', vulnerabilities in such imperialist spaces, then, how do we as critical teachers continue to develop and foster an anti-imperialist pedagogy in classrooms where students and faculty face these core vulnerabilities that are part of the imperial university? My student's experience that I discussed earlier is pertinent for many other students who face vulnerability in classrooms that grapple with transnational feminist issues; here, I am thinking of undocumented students, students who have faced violence and sexual violence, students who have lost their homes in the recent economic crisis, and students who have experienced racial profiling, to name a few.

My student's experience challenged me on multiple levels, given that my whiteness had allowed me to be a vocal critic of globalization without consequence from students. I had, at that time, focused on my own vulnerabilities in the imperial university, as an out, left, lesbian, and untenured professor who teaches politically radical subject matter in a deeply conservative part of Orange County. I had made the decision to not "cower" until tenure, which meant that, daily, I navigated questions about the most strategic stances and actions I could take in my service, teaching, and research to build an anti-racist and feminist sociology. Now reflecting on this exchange, I remember how my consciousness about my positionality and teaching shifted; this student drew my attention outward, encouraging me to reflect more critically on my pedagogy to account for the invisible vulnerabilities in the classroom for students, even as I centered a critique that is the foundation of transnational feminism. I became aware of the classroom as a delicate space where radically transformative ideas and strategies, which I had always hoped would arise out of collective discussion and "open" classrooms, are created with a classroom community's engagement with students' vulnerability. So despite my attempts to practice Chandra Talpade Mohanty's "feminist solidarity or comparative feminist studies model,"[10] these vulnerable standpoints pushed me to question for whom this course was politically open and how such openness perhaps created unanticipated vulnerabilities. This experience encouraged me to rethink my assumptions about "liberatory" spaces in education, which were spaces that I assumed were critically transformative yet which were experienced as oppressive by students who are cast as "threats" by the imperial university.

Sharmila: This concept of "threat" can absolutely apply to students and even to the subject matter we teach, as demonstrated in the example Molly shared earlier. Last year, I taught a unit on gendered violence in the context of war. I began my lecture by speaking about how the rape of women and girls by soldiers has occurred during wartime for centuries, speaking specifically about the early colonization of the United States and the systematic way in which native women were targets of sexual violence during that period. To introduce a more contemporary U.S. example, I cited the lawsuit filed in February 2011 on behalf of fourteen current and former soldiers who accused the Pentagon of failing to prevent rape within the U.S. military. I shared with them a powerful digital story[11] I had come across that integrated words and phrases from the plaintiffs' complaint, alleging that the failure to act from Defense Secretary Robert Gates and his predecessor, Donald Rumsfeld, had created a culture that they suggested enabled and protected their rapists. I then cited the events in Bosnia and Rwanda as other examples of this phenomenon. During class discussion, I asked students to consider the factors that might explain the rise in gendered and sexual violence during wartime, using the works of Nira Yuval Davis, Cynthia Enloe, and Catharine Mackinnon as a point of departure.

At the close of the lecture, a white male student raised his hand and said, "While I can see how rape has been used as a weapon of war in underdeveloped nations like Rwanda and Sierra Leone, I don't think that you can say that rape has been used in the same calculated and strategic way by the U.S. The U.S. does not have this same *culture* of violence." I was a bit taken aback by his comment as my hope in starting with the United States' historical and contemporary acts of militarized sexual violence was to preempt such a foreseeable assertion of American exceptionalism. I responded that perhaps the women filing the claim against the Pentagon might disagree with his claim that the U.S. military is free of such misogynist militarized violence. Though he ultimately rejected this reasoning, it reminded me that certain types of antiracist and feminist analyses are palatable but that others inspire fierce resistance in the climate of neoliberalism and military conflict. Students seem more willing to accept historical critiques of slavery and colonialism because they don't feel as implicated in, or at least feel more detached from, this history. Yet when we enter into the terrain of evaluating U.S. military interventions in Afghanistan or explore the racialized implications of "national security," then the classroom environment is profoundly altered by a perceived threat to Western hegemony. What's also interesting to consider here is that while each of us work in radically different institutional environments, and I at a private, Jesuit, liberal arts college with particular student demographics, this particular anxiety often traverses the lines of race and class.

Given These Institutional Realities, How Can We Create an Empowering Pedagogy That Nourishes Oppositional Curiosities and Students' Voices?

Dana: I thought I'd propose some ideas that both nourish oppositional curiosities and address the issue of vulnerability in classrooms more directly. I tend to begin my courses by introducing my pedagogical approach and strategies (including readings by bell hooks[12] and Mohanty,[13] who have influenced my approach) and have the first exercise center on a class discussion of the merits and limitations to this pedagogical approach to teaching and learning. A central part to this discussion could be students' exploration of their vulnerabilities with the course's subject matter, including the ways in which vulnerabilities can inhibit social justice. Additionally, the class could strategize on how to employ methods of teaching and learning that address these vulnerabilities, having the class visualize what a classroom community could ideally look like when vulnerability is more directly engaged with. It would also be important to encourage students to offer at least one core strategy of teaching and learning that the class could employ throughout the semester to develop *community*. I have also found that case method teaching is an excellent way for *all* students to assume different social positionalities and hence to step outside of their own vulnerable positions and into someone else's, particularly when case methods require students to take on a character and to argue from that character's standpoint. During the case's debriefing, we could add a discussion of the vulnerabilities that students experience by having to take on other social positionalities and how they see their character grappling with these vulnerabilities. Finally, I have incorporated weekly exercises that facilitate a class's exploration of each week's social issue and explore ways to create *solidarity* across positionalities. Thus as a classroom community, we visualize strategies for working together despite our different positionalities, our disagreements, and our potential sentiments of anger and fear. Students have expressed gratitude for having the space to articulate why they felt "frightened or uncertain" when they played a character in a case method teaching exercise. Students have also expressed their agency over their learning when presented with the opportunity to build unforeseen solidarities with one another and in relationship to social justice issues. In short, my students have been thirsty for these more transformative and solidarity-building moments in their education.

Sharmila: The purposeful strategies you've outlined remind me of a powerful talk given by Nigerian author Chimamanda Adichie, who spoke with profound insight about the dangers of a single story about a place or a region. She said, "Power is the ability not just to tell the story of another person, but to make it the definitive story of that person."[14] Like you, I've endeavored to create opportunities in the classroom for allowing different stories to be told, especially since students have a wealth of knowledge to share with one another. One strategy I use is adopting digital storytelling assignments as an additional method of evaluating student learning in a course. In one such assignment, students are asked to draft and record a narration and put together images of a place, a person, an accomplishment, or a memory and to tell that story through the critical lens of our class. What emerges are powerful stories of migration, education, and family as well as stories of cultural constraint, intimate violence, and the lived experiences of racism or sexism that have not otherwise surfaced within class discussions. I've found that the student's work in crafting and then sharing these projects at the end of the quarter is a very powerful learning and community-building experience, both for them and for me.

Molly: Most students at my public institution are attending university against all odds; many went to high schools that resemble prisons, and getting a bachelor's degree is a way "up and out." The kind of teaching I am able to do is very promising, because we don't have to spend a lot of time convincing students that "privilege" exists as a structure of oppression and unearned advantage, as is often the case in majority-white institutions. My students know intimately what it is to be followed in stores, surveilled and abused by police, and barely able to make ends meet. And yet, as working-class and poor folks trying to move into the middle class, they nevertheless retain a capacity to "Other" their peers as a way to explain why they were able to get to university against multiple obstacles and why others have ended up in prisons.

Because incarcerated peoples are the ultimate Others, I make it a point to discuss the rise of this new caste system in connection with the War on Drugs. When we discuss the fact that the very desks we sit in are made by prison laborers and purchased through the California Prison Industry Authority, we are able to see that a mere drug conviction or two lies between their position as a student sitting in the desk and a prisoner making the desk. It's a very thin line, especially when you live in a heavily policed community where the police increasingly operate like an occupying force. These are vital conversations at my particular institution because CSU–Los Angeles students are the future police officers, prison guards, and parole officers in

California's enormous prison-industrial complex. Their ability to understand the emergence of this caste system is crucial to the building of anti-imperialist consciousness among a group of people who are so oppressed by U.S. empire and yet are being offered the chance to eke out a living if they are willing to preside over the oppression of their own communities.

Sylvanna: The teaching environments you have all described remind me of how creating a "safe space" in the classroom can be silencing and stifling. It is impossible to make a space safe when you are talking about colonialism, racism, patriarchy, and injustice, as well as the complicated and intertwined nature of our lives and the blurry lines of oppressor and oppressed. In addition, you do not grow politically and intellectually from being safe—you grow from discomfort, dissent, and being challenged. I am not just talking about white students here, either; all our students need to grow. Creating a space of respect is more what I attempt to do in the classroom now; being respectful does not mean having consensus and it should mean having heated discussions.

The students I have are similar to Molly's and Dana's—many are the first to go to college, predominately Latina/o, some undocumented, and they can lack cultural and social capital. Yet their social location does not automatically make them critical thinkers. So I try to develop interactive exercises—through the use of case studies and student-led presentations on social movement organizing—and even bring in pop culture references that permit them to come into their own as budding scholars. And I don't think the results are immediate either. I've received e-mails from many students well after the term has concluded about the impact of my classes. I try to put into practice what bell hooks so powerfully states about pedagogy: "I celebrate teaching that enables transgressions—a movement against and beyond boundaries. It is that movement which makes education the practice of freedom."[15] And these transgressions may not be immediate for students. They may occur well after our classes have concluded.

In What Ways Has Your Academic Creativity, Curiosity, and Critical Pedagogy Grown from the Collective Process of Knowledge Production That CASA Has Fostered?

Sharmila: CASA has enabled us to foster a meaningful community of sharing, support, and encouragement in both our research and teaching. I am profoundly grateful for our collective and I can say with great sincerity that I would not be in my tenure-track position at Santa Clara University without your support. The process of reading and responding to each other's writing regularly has given me a much richer sense of academic publishing and of how to be a thoughtfully critical reader of another scholar's work. At some level, I think we are able to advance one another's projects in more innovative ways because our research trajectories are so varied. In this group I've experienced genuine feminist collaboration that has meant shared work, not in a mathematical or linear way, but rather in a manner that evaluates and negotiates specific needs at a given moment in time and, further, that is mindful of our whole selves.

In and beyond the assistance we've provided one another with writing, we've also stepped in to help one another through issues like momentary trials in teaching, challenging departmental dynamics, writer's block, and, on occasion, simply managing the guilt of feeling like we're failing our partners or our children because of the stress-inducing demands of our jobs. There's a sense of humanity among the group that is very real and very genuine. I think so often the academy promotes this idea that you are this all-knowing individual—that you are your research, and that you must remain on an isolated island of knowledge and not *need,* let alone *desire,* anyone else. It is profoundly individualist in some ways and working within this truly life-sustaining community of women has enabled me to resist that pull and remain true to myself. It has also made me braver. Working together has empowered me to try new things and to take risks that I may not have otherwise undertaken as a pretenured faculty member.

Dana: Like Sharmila, I think we are fostering a distinct academic community with CASA, one where all of us not only belong but also are essential to a new way of thinking, teaching, writing, and practicing antiracist and anti-imperialist feminisms. This experience of knowledge production as junior faculty has been revolutionary for me because our work together has demonstrated the power of collective knowledge production.[16] My best work has arisen out of CASA's engagements because not only does our sharing agitate against the isolation and individualism of academic work but also our dialogue has allowed a creative, and at times magical, convergence of our areas of expertise and approaches. In fact, our work together has shown me a more politicized transdisciplinarity in action; I can actually see how our practice of knowledge production has not been blinded by our commitment to the goals of our individual disciplines or careers but instead has transcended this because of our collective desire to practice antiracist and anti-imperialist feminisms in our teaching, research, and activist/community engagement.

I have also been struck by the organic emergence of informal norms that have arisen, in part, out of our feminist check-ins, which explore our whole beings rather than only our "ideas" or our individual selves as academics focused on career-oriented goals. So, for example, when we offer critical feedback on one another's research, we offer feedback on what this piece of work could offer to a range of domains—to critical teaching, to community-based scholarship, to scholar-activism, and to pushing different intellectual agendas. We do not offer critique based on narrow conceptions of what a discipline wants or what a journal article should look like or on what niche a new book should fill. Rather, we think more widely about the author's intellectual and activist vision and therefore we can offer more dynamic feedback. Another significant informal norm is our commitment to seeing one another as embedded in wider communities than academia and to help facilitate these relationships as *foundational* to our survival in the imperial university. This kind of enrichment deters the imperial university taking over our lives.

Molly: This conversation makes me think about how impossible it is to be a feminist antiracist scholar as an *individual.* So we have to really confront and think about how to get around, and even challenge, the competitive individualism that pervades the academy and that, I'm sorry to say, many feminist academics have embraced. This is a masculinist and Eurocentric paradigm, rooted in white supremacist capitalist patriarchy, to use bell hooks's often-cited term.[17] I don't think for a minute, for example, that I obtained my job on qualifications alone. I know those decisions were mediated by many factors, including histories and structures of white supremacy that got me where I am—as a white woman in a tenure-track position at a university.

Challenging this competitive individualism, working to heal one another and ourselves from the very damaging wounds of the imperial university, and creating an antiracist feminist beloved community is something we've been able to do in our work together as a writing group. We have also discovered that, in addition to supporting each other's individual writing projects, we really grow intellectually and personally through collaboration with one another on coauthored projects. This, too, is a way to remake the culture of doing intellectual work: to deflate individualism and to infuse it with curiosity; joy; critical conversations; and love of justice, life, and one another.

Sylvanna: I think it is really hard to put into words what CASA has done for me intellectually and creatively. I feel so nourished by our group and have come to realize that our commitment to one another has only grown stronger over the years. The fact that we have rarely, if ever, had a conversation where all four of us were not involved since 2007 speaks to our profound dedication to one another. As we go through the motions of our academic life, insecurities can seep in. I see it with other junior faculty, but I have not really felt those insecurities ever since CASA formed. I cherish so much that I can share work and ideas with our group before making them public. Since I feel love, comfort, and support in our group, I feel like my ideas are sharper, my writing is better, and I am able to articulate my research agenda in a way that stays true to my principles and politics as an antiracist feminist yet meets the pressures of evaluation I am under as a scholar in a research-1 institution.

We have, in essence, created a peer-mentoring model that is not judgmental in an environment where we are being constantly judged. When I first approached the three of you about forming our group, never in my wildest dreams did I think it would evolve into what it has become today. It is an immeasurable source of support and love that I wish other women faculty could experience. We have built, organically and intentionally, a group entirely oppositional to an academic structure focused on rewarding neoliberal productivity and the establishment of individually based careers, which results in the entrenchment of a politics disconnected from social movements and an investment in being viewed as an "expert." I know for certain that I could not have accomplished alone what I have thus far achieved as part of CASA, and I am so grateful to be on this journey with all of you.

Notes

1. Audre Lorde, *Sister Outsider: Essays and Speeches* (Berkeley: Crossing, 1984).

2. Dana Collins, Sylvanna Falcón, Sharmila Lodhia, and Molly Talcott, "New Directions in Feminism and Human Rights: An Introduction," *International Feminist Journal of Politics* 12, nos. 3–4 (2010): 298–318.

3. Dana Collins, Sylvanna Falcón, Sharmila Lodhia, and Molly Talcott, eds., *New Directions in Feminism and Human Rights* (London: Routledge, 2011).

4. Chela Sandoval, *Methodology of the Oppressed* (Minneapolis: University of Minnesota Press, 2000), 41–65.

5. Kathleen N. Cleaver, "Women, Power, and Revolution," in *Liberation, Imagination, and the Black Panther Party: A New Look at the Panthers and Their Legacy*, ed. Kathleen Cleaver and George Katsiaficas (New York: Routledge, 2001), 124.

6. INCITE! Women of Color against Violence, *The Revolution Will Not Be Funded: Beyond the Non-profit Industrial Complex* (Cambridge: South End, 2009).

7. Noël Sturgeon, *Ecofeminist Natures: Race, Gender, Feminist Theory and Political Action* (New York: Routledge, 1997).

8. Katie Hogan, "Superserviceable Feminism," Minnesota Review, nos. 63–64 (Winter 2005), http://www.theminnesotareview.org/journal/ns6364/iae_ns6364_superserviceablefeminism.shtml.

9. John Muthyala, "Reworlding America: The Globalization of American Studies," *Cultural Critique*, no. 47 (Winter 2001): 91–119.

10. Chandra Talpade Mohanty, *Feminism without Borders: Decolonizing Theory, Practicing Solidarity* (Durham, N.C.: Duke University Press, 2003), 242–45.

11. Irin Carmon, "Shattering Voices from the Military Rape Voices, Verbatim," Jezebel, http://jezebel.com/5766231/the-military-rape-lawsuit-verbatim.

12. bell hooks, *Teaching to Transgress* (New York: Routledge, 1994).

13. Mohanty, *Feminism without Borders.*

14. Chimamanda Adichie, "The Danger of a Single Story" (presented at TED [Technology, Entertainment, Design] Talks, October 2009), http://www.ted.com/talks/chimamanda_adichie_the_danger_of_a_single_story.html.

15. hooks, *Teaching to Transgress,* 12.

16. In May 2012, I received a letter indicating that CSU–Fullerton had awarded me tenure. I participated in the writing of this chapter before receiving this news, and in my writing, I am reflecting upon my six years as an assistant professor, including the support that CASA has given me over these formative years.

17. bell hooks, *Killing Rage: Ending Racism* (New York: Henry Holt, 1996).

11

Citation and Censure

Pinkwashing and the Sexual Politics of Talking about Israel

Jasbir Puar

What follows is an expanded version of a lecture presented at the "Funda-mentalism and Gender" conference at Humboldt University, Germany, on December 4, 2010. The original version of the lecture appeared in *Feminist Legal Studies* and also in *Gender and Fundamentalism,* edited by Ulricke Auga. Since the event detailed here, there have been numerous queer orga-nizing conflicts revolving around Israel/Palestine, including the battle at the New York City Lesbian Gay Bisexual and Transgender Community Center over the use of the term "Israeli Apartheid." Much also has progressed in terms of the development of Palestinian solidarity discourses, the politics of pinkwashing, and antipinkwashing activism; some of those developments are detailed in the endnotes. These debates highlight the importance of fore-grounding the ways that issues of gender and sexuality change, complicate, or nuance how to think about the conflict; they also point to how feminist and queer movements inflect if not alter organizing strategies and struggles. Focusing on the relationship between sexuality and nationalism is also an intervention into the conventional "resistance solidarity" positioning of some left commentators, many of whom continue to think of gender and sexuality as subissues rather than constitutive to the workings of power.

My lecture at Humboldt University was preceded by last-minute accu-satory and offensive communications with the conference-organizing committee, which expressed upset about the title of the talk (originally "Beware Israeli Pinkwashing") and complained that the focus on the Israeli-Palestinian conflict had nothing to do with the conference theme nor my prior work. They stated that they did not understand how my book *Ter-rorist Assemblages: Homonationalism in Queer Times* related to Israel and why I was discussing Israel at all given that, as they understood it, my work focused on feminist and queer critiques of U.S. national/diasporic formation post-9/11. They were exclusively interested in the critique of the Western construction of the Muslim other. They also suggested that the talk was anti-Semitic, based on reading an op-ed I had published in the *Guardian* in July 2010, titled "Israel's Gay Propaganda War." These concerns were communicated just two weeks prior to the conference, even though I had submitted my title and paper information in June of 2010.

One day prior to the start of the conference, the director of the Humboldt Graduate School and also a conference-organizing committee member, Professor Christina von Braun, gave an interview to Alan Posener, a well-known Zionist journalist in Berlin. While Posener is a self-described champion of Muslim rights in Europe, his contributions in the interview with Von Braun reflect one example of the complex ways that anti-Muslim assumptions can be refunctioned and masked within neoliberal discourse. In this interview, von Braun made derogatory comments about my work and person, stating that I had "lost [my] marbles"[1] if I deemed Israel a totalitarian state and claiming that my analysis suffers because it is based on activist work. Von Braun also reiterated the conference committee's statement that my prior work on sexuality and nationalism was quite interesting, but the critique of pinkwashing was unrelated. I withdrew from the conference. After the organizing committee claimed that Posener misstated von Braun's words, and after I requested a public apology, a written retraction from von Braun, and a new moderator, I agreed to give my lecture. The public apology on behalf of the organizing committee was made by Professor Ulrike Auga right before my talk. In January 2011, I received an "apology" from von Braun, which confirmed that she did indeed make those comments in the interview. I am still waiting for the public, written retraction of the article.

This chapter, based on the lecture that I did eventually deliver at Humboldt University, attempts to convey the richness and complexity of a dialogue about the relationship of gay and lesbian sexual rights to the Israel-Palestine conflict. I will do this in three parts: the first part surveys the literature on sexual rights within the Israeli-Palestinian conflict; the second part examines implications of this regional framing of sexual rights for diasporic locations, specifically the United States and Canada, by surveying the Brand Israel campaign; and the third section discusses some of the locational politics of this debate.

A Long History of Homonationalism in Israel?

I have written at length about the political purchase of the production of oppressed homosexuals elsewhere in order to advance U.S. interests and to provide fodder for the evaluation of the sovereign capacities of a nation—what I have called "homonationalism."[2] The force of homonationalism as it operates in Israel is a potent confluence of settler-colonialism and neoliberal economic restructuring that now hails "queer" as productive toward nation building. This history is not necessarily a reflection of any exceptionalist activity on the part of Israel but rather deploys an old tactic intrinsic to colonial occupation—the use of the treatment of women (and now homosexuals) to justify imperialist violence—merged with the contemporary neoliberal accommodation of difference. Given this convergence of settler colonialism and neoliberalism, it actually makes sense that Israel is a "pioneer" of homonationalism.

A growing body of academic scholarship argues that the status of gay and lesbian rights and the politics of Israel and Palestine are inextricably linked or, to quote Gil Z. Hochberg, that the relations between "the politics of homophobia" and "the politics of occupation" are intractable.[3] As Christina von Braun and Ulricke Auga have noted in the introduction of their edited collection, *Gender in Conflicts: Palestine-Israel-Germany*, "In a situation of conflict, societies tend to 'defame' the 'conduct' of women belonging to the other society; they accuse the 'other' women of either sexual libertinism or of sexual narrow-mindedness, both seen as opposed to one's own 'normality.'"[4] While unfortunately this collection does not have any of the numerous examples already brewing of this dynamic as it relates to homosexuality in the region, the cover of the book does have an interesting photo of the Gay Pride March in Jerusalem on Christopher Street Day in 2004, depicting a wall of graffiti with the words "No Pride in Palestine" as the most prominent scrawl legible in English. A concern for how not only women but especially homosexuals have become the symbols of civilizational aptitude—in other words, the biopolitical relationship between gay lesbian queer sexualities and nationalism—has indeed been relevant for some time.

As anthropologist Rebecca L. Stein notes, the rise of the gay equality agenda in Israel is concomitant with the increasing repression of the Israeli state toward Palestinians. She writes, "During the 1990s, Israel's gay communities were being recognized in unprecedented ways in Israeli legal spheres, while changing Israeli policies *vis-a-vis* the occupied territories are creating new forms of un-recognition for its Palestinian population: gay communities were enjoying new forms of social mobility within the nation-state while the literal mobility of Palestinians from the occupied territories was being increasingly curtailed."[5] These gains in the 1990s—what is called "Israel's gay decade"—included protection against workplace discrimination, increasing institutionalization of same-sex partner benefits, and greater inclusion in the Israeli Defense Forces. On the other hand, the 1993 Oslo Accords started strictly delimiting the presence of Palestinian labor pools in Israel and produced increasingly segregated living and working zones, multiplied existing surveillance systems and security checkpoints, and generally reduced the visibility and mobility of Palestinians and contact that they had with Israeli Jews. Renowned Israeli architect Eyal Weizman has done brilliant work on how the Oslo Accords created what he calls "the politics of verticality"—the dividing up of space from a two-dimensional, here-versus-there system to a three-dimensional system of air space, ground space, underground space, sacred space, and checkpoint space that basically tripled the amount of space that could be surveilled, controlled, and fought over.[6] Achille Mbembe has called this a "splintering occupation": multiple separations and provisional boundaries (that shift regularly due to the Jewish settlements and rotating checkpoints) rather than a conclusive division between two territories. (So one question to keep in mind here is, how does this spatial domination affect queer Palestinian organizing?)

Stein asks, "How might one read these two political histories in concert?"[7] This formulation—of the relationship of the rise of gay and lesbian legal rights, as well as popular visibility, that happens in tandem with increasingly xenophobic policies in regards to minority communities within the nation-state and the Others that threaten the borders of the nation-state from outside—is exactly what I have theorized, within the context of the United States as well as some European states, as "homonationalism."[8] In some sense, Jewish studies scholars have been looking at the production of homonationalism as it operates in Israel for quite some time now. Alisa Solomon was among the first to argue that the notion of the progressive status of gays and lesbians Israel has fomented rivalries and divisions between orthodox and secular Israeli Jews. In a 2003 volume titled *Queer Theory and the Jewish Question,* coedited by leading Jewish studies scholars Daniel Boyarin, Daniel Itzkovitz, and Ann Pellegrini, Solomon states, "In today's Israeli culture war, queerness—or at least the tolerance of queerness—has acquired a new rhetorical value for mainstream Zionism: standing against the imposition of fundamentalist religious law, it has come to stand for democratic liberalism."[9] In this formulation, Solomon is clear that queerness has become another ground upon which the cohesion of an Israeli Zionist state is possible; homonationalism here serves to disrupt religious fundamentalist law through mainstream Zionism. A wonderful book by Adi Kuntsman looks at how, within Israeli queer communities, there is a hierarchy between more mainstream Israeli queer Jews and Russian Israeli queers and how the fissures between different factions do not result in equal access to the benefits of gay equality.[10]

Despite these internal contradictions, however, as Amal Amireh notes, "the positive rhetorical function of queerness . . . goes beyond those internal cultural wars (between secular Jews and religious Jews) into the wider culture war between Israelis and Palestinians, where it functions to consolidate a fractured Zionist consensus."[11] As von Braun points out in her recent interview with Alan Posener, this use of gay rights to reiterate the terms of the Israeli-Palestinian conflict—those terms being that Israel is civilized, liberal, and progressive in relation to the backwardness of Palestinian society—is certainly not a new observation (I never claimed that it was "new").[12] What is "new," however, is how these debates are being connected to transnational feminist studies and queer theory. In this regard, I want to laud the publication of a special issue of the *GLQ: A Journal of Lesbian and Gay Studies,* titled "Queer Politics and the Question of Palestine/Israel," edited by Gil Z. Hochberg, which contains fantastic essays that both historicize and contextualize the kinds of discursive and material practices that have been and continue to produce Israel's claim to "gay friendliness" and "gay tolerant" as somehow independent of its repressive politics toward Palestinians.[13] These essays look at the complex codependent intertwining of queerness and nationalism. So, for example, Hochberg analyzes the problematic Israeli patriotism produced through the mourning of the shooting of queer teenagers at the Israeli GLBT Association in August of 2009;[14] Amalia Ziv highlights the work of Black Laundry, a queer group in Israel committed to antioccupation activism;[15] "No Pride in Occupation" is a roundtable discussion among activists, scholars, and activist-scholars in Israel, Palestine, and the diasporas who discuss the complexities of being queer in the region.[16]

The "Pinkwashing" Debate in the Diasporas

Now I want to elaborate upon a series of debates happening transnationally regarding what is widely termed in North American organizing contexts as Israeli Pinkwashing. Jason Ritchie writes, "While the significance of tolerance of homosexuality as a marker of liberal democratic modernity has perhaps declined in recent Israeli political discourse—alongside the decline of Ashkenazi hegemony and the ascendancy of Mizrahi, religious, and ultranationalist politics—that narrative still retains considerable currency in the United States and Europe, where liberal Zionists, especially queer liberal Zionists, frequently deploy it to represent Israel as 'an oasis of liberal tolerance in a reactionary religious backwater.'"[17] (It is thus interesting to note that while Israel continually seeks to align itself culturally and politically with Europe, in the instance of LGBT rights, it discursively locates itself as "the only nation in the Middle East" with such a record.) If it is the case, as Ritchie argues, that the production of the "Israeli gay tolerance/Palestinian homophobia" binary is a recognized discursive tactic of the conflict today, there are multiple reasons for why this debate has now taken hold in diasporic contexts such as the United States and Canada. In part, a critique of the U.S. global War on Terror cannot be so easily separated out from a critique of the Israeli state. Geographer Derek Gregory has written at length about the kinds of post-9/11 foreign policy decisions that aligned even further the United States and Israel in a mutual identification as "victims" of Islamic fundamentalism and united in a fight against the War on Terror. Gregory argues that the Israeli state used 9/11 as a moment to amplify its aggression against the occupied territories and that the United States sanctioned this aggression even as it feared losing their Arab allies in its efforts to rein in al-Qaeda.[18] Further, as von Braun herself confirms in the interview with Posener, Israeli political discourses have indeed been invested in the production of Muslim societies as backward and repressed,[19] contributing in no small part to the discourses of the Muslim Other as the terrorist Other. Therefore, the critique of the U.S. occupation of Iraq and Afghanistan, Islamophobia (both post-9/11 and in its recent rising forms), and Israeli policies toward Palestine are contiguous political positions.

I turn now to the specific diasporic articulations of Israel's "gay-friendly" image: several years ago Israel invested in a large-scale, massively funded Brand Israel campaign, produced by the Israeli Foreign Ministry, to counter its growing reputation as a colonial power. Ranked 185 out of 200 nations in an East West Communications survey in terms of "positive perception," Israel beat Pakistan (186) but not Iran (184). Targeting global cities such as New York, Toronto, and London, the Brand Israel campaign has used events such as film festivals to promote its image as cultured and modern.

One of the most prominent features of the Brand Israel campaign is the marketing of a modern Israel as a gay-friendly Israel. "Stand with US," a self-declared Zionist organization active in the United States, has been quoted in the *Jerusalem Post* as saying, "We decided to improve Israel's image through the gay community in Israel." This "pinkwashing," as it is now commonly termed in activist circles, has currency beyond Israeli gay groups. Within global gay and lesbian organizing circuits, to be gay friendly is to be modern, cosmopolitan, developed, First World, global North, and, most significantly, democratic. Events such as WorldPride 2006, hosted in Jerusalem, and "Out in Israel," held in San Francisco, highlight Israel as a country committed to democratic ideals of freedom for all, including gays and lesbians. It is important to note that homonationalism has scalar movement among local, national, and transnational sites, from the internal contradictions that homonationalism produces within Israel, to the production of Israel as liberal and progressive in relation to the homophobia of Palestine, to the level of global transnational organizing where homonationalism translates—within a liberal telos of progress—into this register as well.

Thus Israeli pinkwashing is a potent method through which the terms of Israeli occupation of Palestine are reiterated—Israel is civilized; Palestinians are barbaric, homophobic, and uncivilized. This discourse has manifold effects: it denies Israeli homophobic oppression of its own gays and lesbians,[20] and it recruits, often unwittingly, gays and lesbians of other countries into a collusion with Israeli violence toward Palestine. In reproducing Orientalist tropes of Palestinian sexual backwardness, it also denies the impact of colonial occupation on the degradation and containment of Palestinian cultural norms and values. Pinkwashing harnesses global gays as a new source of affiliation, recruiting liberal gays into a dirty bargaining of their own safety against the continued oppression of Palestinians, now perforce rebranded as "gay unfriendly." This strategy then also works to elide the presence of Palestinian gay and lesbian organizations—for example, Palestinian Queers for Boycott, Divestment, and Sanctions (PQBDS).

Pinkwashing's effects are being widely contested, especially at gay and lesbian events and despite the censorship of gay and lesbian groups that actively oppose the Israeli occupation. The banning of the phrase "Israeli apartheid" during Pride Week by PRIDE Toronto in 2010, in response to pressure by the city and Israeli lobby groups, effectively barred the group Queers against Israeli Apartheid (QuAIA). However, the ban was rescinded in response to community activism and the twenty-three pride award recipients who returned their prizes in protest of the ban. Frameline's San Francisco LGBT Film Festival faced opposition from Queers Undermining Israeli Terrorism (QUIT), among other groups, for accepting Israeli government sponsorship. In summer 2010, after protests by Palestinian, Arab, Muslim, and other anti-Zionist groups, the U.S. Social Forum in Detroit cancelled a workshop slated to be held by "Stand with Us" on "LGBTQI Liberation in the Middle East," which sought to promote images of Israel as a gay mecca at the expense of Palestinian liberation.

The transnational organizing that is taking place in relation to this issue is very broad and involves many activists and scholars in the United States, Canada, Europe, and Israel/Palestine, and spans from queer of color communities to Palestinian activists, both in and out of Palestine, to diasporic Jews as well as Israeli Jews and Palestinians. Israeli activists such as Dalit Baum have been critical of the Brand Israel campaign as well, reiterating the notion that "the flourishing of gay rights in Israel is being used by the government to divert attention from its gross violation of human rights in the occupied territories."[21] So the constituencies that are involved in these discussions cannot be reduced to a single position; they cannot be summarily dismissed through the reductive accusations of being racist, homophobic, or anti-Semitic; and they cannot be rendered within a Manichean division between right and wrong. And further, all these organizations peaceably participate in this transnational organizing with a respect accorded to the variety of locational, national, and ideological differences among them.

A final twist to the diasporic production of pinkwashing: it is hardly produced by the Brand Israel campaign alone. It is increasingly the case that a stance against Israeli state violence toward Palestinians is advocated and sanctioned but then accompanied by an additional condemnation of Muslim sexual cultures. This has become a standard rhetorical framing produced by liberal supporters of the Palestinian cause.[22] (Note, as another example, the messaging of OutRage!, Britain's premier queer human rights organization, at a Free Palestine rally in London, May 21, 2005: "Israel: Stop persecuting Palestine!" "Palestine: Stop persecuting Queers!") This framing has the effect, however unintended, of analogizing Israeli state oppression of

Palestinians to Palestinian oppression of their gays and lesbians, as if the two were equivalent or contiguous.

It is important to consider how the debate about Israel and Palestine continues to anchor what I have called a homonationalist politics of sexual rights in North America and why this is significant. What is at stake is not a normative decision about whether Israel is gay friendly or whether Palestine and other regions of the Middle East are homophobic. There is no question that Israel's legal record on gay rights suggests a certain notion of liberal "progress"; Palestinian queers who live in the Occupied Territories also articulate how difficult it is to be "openly" gay. But as scholarly literature and political organizing both demonstrate, this is only the beginning of the story. As I have argued elsewhere, the "Woman Question" is now being supplemented with the "Homosexual Question."[23] That is, in the colonial period, the question of how well you treat your women as a determining factor of a nation's capacity for sovereignty has now been appended with the barometer of how well you treat your homosexuals.

How has the homosexual question come to supplement the woman question of the colonial era to modulate arbitration between modernity and tradition, citizen and terrorist, homonational and queer? As elaborated by Partha Chatterjee,[24] this question arose with some force in the decolonization movements in South Asia and elsewhere, whereby the capacity for an emerging postcolonial government to protect native women from oppressive patriarchal cultural practices, marked as tradition, became the barometer by which colonial rule arbitrated political concessions made to the colonized. In other words, we rehearse here Spivak's famous dictum, "white men saving brown women from brown men."[25] This particular triangulation has thus set the stage for an enduring drama between feminists protesting colonial and neocolonial regimes and nationalists who discount the presence and politics of these feminists in their own quests for decolonization. The terms of the women question have been redictated, as feminist scholars have now become the arbiter of other women's modernity—or the modernity of the Other Woman—to reinvoke Spivak for the twenty-first century: white women saving brown women from brown men. Or in terms of the homosexual question, white queers saving brown homosexuals from brown heterosexuals. As these postcolonial scholars have convincingly demonstrated, the production of "homophobia" in a location dealing with epistemological and material violence of colonial occupation, through the use of sexuality to affirm racial and cultural superiority, cannot be considered "cultural" alone but rather, at least in part, a by-product of cultural domination.

Academic Censorship, Anti-Semitism, and Transnational Feminist Alliances

The legacy of postcolonial studies scholar Edward Said's writing and his frustrations with what could be called the secular academic left are instructive in addressing the question of academic censorship and writing and speaking about Palestine in the imperial university. In a memorial to Said in the summer 2006 issue of *Social Text,* which historically has seen itself as reflecting the bastion of the U.S. academic left, focusing on Said's oeuvre as well as his scholarly and political impact, the editors of this special issue, Patrick Deer, Gyan Prakash, and Ella Shohat, trace Said's particular relevance to the foundations of the journal. *Social Text* itself claims it "began its career with Said's work"[26] and published in its inaugural 1979 issue Said's groundbreaking essay "Zionism from a Standpoint of Its Victims," which later became a chapter of *The Question of Palestine.* The editors of the 2006 issue avow, "Such a move at the time, when it was nearly impossible to utter the word 'Palestine' in the public sphere, was vital for the opening up of the debate in leftist academic circles." Two issues later, however, *Social Text* published a rebuttal by Ron Aronson titled "Never Again? Zionism and the Holocaust." Deer, Prakash, and Shohat critically reassessed this response:

> The journal's decision to publish a response that placed the Holocaust at center stage and marginalized the unfolding history of Palestine in the wake of Zionist settlement was indicative of the anxiety, tensions, and contradictions among leftists about the question of Palestine and Israel. The application of anticolonialist and third worldist analytic paradigms to the Middle East has provoked much debate in leftist circles. Scholarly work on the subject, written from within such critical perspectives, has often been deemed "controversial"; its authors, of diverse ethnic or national backgrounds, often end up having to pay a high price professionally and politically. Although not a monolith, *Social Text*'s collective courageously introduced a debate into the heart of the intellectual Left but also manifested a certain ambivalence toward that very decision. In the ensuing years, the journal's editorial focus often reflected this tendency to shy away from addressing Zionism, Palestine, and the Middle East. While Latin

American issues were prominent in the journal's early days, it was
not the case for the Middle East, despite the on-going and devastating U.S. impact on the region.[27]

The editors thus note that the tendency to subsume the plight of Palestinians to the narration of the horrors of the Holocaust and the affective disavowal of U.S. imperial investments and activities in the Middle East are not
bred of Zionist ideologies or positioning alone; rather, they are formative
of intellectual Left circles in the United States, a proclivity that perhaps still
haunts us today. The heralding, as well, of Said's work—with the publication
of *Orientalism*—as "preeminent in postcolonial studies" only served to further reinforce an ambiguous disconnect to and from his work and political
arguments about Palestine. Said's book *Orientalism* went on to become the
foundational urtext of postcolonial studies and concretized the legitimacy of
ethnic studies as well as area studies formations, while *The Question of Palestine* was largely left behind in terms of institutional, intellectual, and political
developments.

In light of this curt history of ambivalence toward Palestine in leftist academic spheres, I want to conclude with some reflections on censorship and
solidarity in relation to the purported "controversy" about my talk in Berlin,
a controversy that might in other locations be simply called "an academic
debate" or even a political disagreement but should not become the basis for
attempts to censor, micromanage, or otherwise vilify someone's work. It is
a controversy that could have easily been avoided, as far as I am concerned,
had open communication happened in a timely and direct fashion instead
of through third parties and interviews with hateful, anti-Muslim reporters.
In general, I have had the good fortune of hearing from many people, in
Europe, all over North America, and in Israel/Palestine, who have enthusi-
astically welcomed this discussion on sexual rights as they function in the
Israeli occupation of Palestine. For those who attempted in various ways to
censor or silence the talk on the basis that, "in the German context," it is anti-
Semitic to be critical of oppressive Israeli state practices toward the Palestinians, it became clear to me that the desires to silence such a debate are, in
fact, the very evidence of the need for this conversation to happen.

I think it is worth thinking about the accusation of anti-Semitism for a
moment from those whom it comes from, those who benefit from this accusation, and what kind of work it does. I agree, along with Judith Butler and
numerous other Jewish intellectuals both inside and outside of Israel, that

292 · JASBIR PUAR

it is crucial to retain a distinction between anti-Semitism, which is a form of racism directed at Jewish peoples that is deeply embedded in biologically deterministic notions of race, and a critique of Israeli state practices (which is *not* the same thing as a stance against the existence of the Israeli state). In fact, the conflation of anti-Semitism with a critique of Israeli state practices is precisely how the definition of Zionism works: through the claim that the state of Israel represents all Jewish peoples everywhere, a geopolitical fantasy and fallacy. Furthermore, it is most important to retain this distinction because otherwise the accusation of anti-Semitism becomes empty, loses its political force, and becomes a blanket alibi for a repression of a complicated conversation around the Israeli-Palestinian conflict.

What I offered in the lecture is not anti-Semitic. I would argue that it is not even a critique of Israeli state practices per se. Rather, it is an analysis of how sexual politics and national politics are irreducibly intertwined with each other and how this works in the particular case of the Israeli-Palestinian conflict. As I have made clear in my work in *Terrorist Assemblages,* this is reflective of a neoliberal phenomenon happening in many national locations; I am thus not "picking" on Israel, as has been voiced by those who differ with me politically. I have not, contrary to the claims of the organizing committee of the conference and in the interview with von Braun, called Israel a totalitarian state. I quote the relevant passage from the *Guardian* piece: "While Israel may blatantly disregard global outrage about its wartime activities, it nonetheless has deep stakes in projecting its image as a liberal society of tolerance, in particular homosexual tolerance. These two tendencies should not be seen as contradictory, rather constitutive of the very mechanisms by which a liberal democracy sanctions its own totalitarian regimes."[28] The fact that this passage keeps being misread as calling the Israeli state totalitarian is a classic symptom of this kind of projection. The difference between a totalitarian state and what Giorgio Agamben calls the "state of exception" is precisely about the way in which liberal democracy and totalitarianism meet at a threshold to excuse liberal democracy from its own rule of law. Agamben has called the post-9/11 period in the United States, where the "writ of habeas corpus" (the right to a fair trial) was suspended for "enemy combatants" despite being on U.S. soil—legitimated in the name of a liberal democracy —as the most extreme state of exception in U.S. history.[29] This is absolutely a different political formation than that of a totalitarian state. What is also striking in the case of Israel-Palestine are the spatial manifestations of the state of exception, whereby the "threshold" that Agamben theorizes ceases to be metaphoric: illegal settlements, checkpoints, segregated highways, and pedestrian zones—the production of new dimensions of space and the intense saturation these spaces (and of life) with regulation and surveillance. This coproduction of space and regulation is rendered possible through discourses of the state of exception and simultaneously is part of, and extends the reach of, these discourses.

We need the term anti-Semitism to mean something other than "critical of Israel," because anti-Semitism still exists. Without this important and hardly semantic distinction, the charge of anti-Semitism becomes a strong projection of the history of the Holocaust onto the bodies of "outsiders" like myself—those not directly interpellated by that history—as a classic form of psychoanalytic disavowal: I accuse you of doing what I am afraid I might be doing myself, what I very much so fear doing, what I don't want to do myself. (Interestingly enough, this projection of the accusation of anti-Semitism onto "others" mirrors the production of migrants in Germany as the prime carriers and transmitters of anti-Semitism; this is not unlike how Muslim immigrants are framed in current culture wars in North America.)

As members of a German society with a history of racial genocide and suppression of dissenting voices and bodies via extermination, perhaps it is worth thinking twice about the kinds of transnational academic feminist alliances that are rendered impossible when the accusation of anti-Semitism is used indiscriminately and when used to censor in the midst of predominantly white Western European academics, a self-identified queer woman of color, and an international speaker for whom a different locational politics is absolutely necessary (and for whom accounting for the "German context" is not exactly her job—otherwise, why bother to invite an international speaker who works in the field of American studies in the first instance?). This triangulation of "outsiders" to act as a lightning rod for divisive debates among progressive allies might indeed be productive in Germany; it may well be that certain conversations are impossible without a third party carrying the charge of anti-Semitism that a melancholic narcissistic attachment to the Holocaust prevents some from acknowledging as their own.[30] But I would want to point out how deeply undermining and damaging it is to transnational feminist and queer academic and activist alliances to use me or any other scholar in this fundamentally antiprogressive and antisolidarity manner. It is, simply stated, a tactic that uses the charge of anti-Semitism not only to mask others' struggles with anti-Semitic tendencies and histories but also as a foil to parochialism—indeed, perhaps to racism and homophobia.

From what I have observed in my limited experience in Germany, the crucial question facing progressives is, can a critique of anti-Muslim racism and critique of anti-Semitism coexist? Is it possible to articulate a critical, progressive stance against anti-Muslim racism without this positioning automatically reduced to being "against Jews" or "anti-Semitic"? It might be worth remembering that the cleavage of Muslims from the category of "Semite" is a historical occurrence in need of deconstruction; at what point did the terms "anti-Muslim" and the phenomenon of "Islamophobia" appear as something separate from anti-Semitism?[31] If a particular "anti-Deutsche position" is critical of the German state for its history of racial genocide during the Holocaust and understands German racism as exceptional, it makes little sense for this very same position to endorse the state practices of yet another not only racist but also apartheid state.

For those who are committed to a critique of anti-Muslim racism and Islamophobia, both here and globally, and yet do not see Israeli state oppression of the Palestinians as part of the production of that racism, that position—this fissuring—is simply untenable for any critical left U.S. politics that stands against the United States and other forms of imperialism. However, this has not always been the case historically in the United States and continues to be tenuous, especially as debate about Israel/Palestine is indeed the site where the contours of academic freedom are being contested and redefined. This is perhaps a locational distinction between the United States and Germany that cannot simply be dismissed as "wrong." I take the locational distinction seriously and without dismissal; I only ask that others do the same.

Notes

1. Alan Posener, "Geschlect als Wissenkategorie," starke-meinungen.de, December 1, 2010, http://starke-meinungen.de/blog/2010/12/01/geschlecht-als-wissenskategorie.

2. Jasbir Puar, *Terrorist Assemblages: Homonationalism in Queer Times* (Durham: Duke University Press, 2007).

3. Gil Z. Hochberg, "Israelis, Palestinians, Queers: Points of Departure," in *GLQ: A Journal of Gay and Lesbian Studies* 16, no. 4 (2010): 510.

4. Ulrike Auga and Christina von Braun, ed., *Gender in Conflicts: Palestine-Israel-Germany* (Berlin: LIT Verlag, 2008).

5. Rebecca L. Stein, "Explosive: Scenes from Israel's Gay Occupation," *GLQ: A Journal of Gay and Lesbian Studies* 16, no. 4 (2010): 521.

6. Eyal Weizman, "The Politics of Verticality," *openDemocracy,* April 23, 2002, http://www.opendemocracy.net/ecology-politicsverticality/article_801.jsp.

7. Stein, "Explosive," 521.

8. Puar, *Terrorist Assemblages.*

9. Alisa Solomon, "Viva la Diva Citizenship: Post-Zionism and Gay Rights," in *Queer Theory and the Jewish Question,* ed. Daniel Boyarin, Daniel Itzkovitz, and Ann Pellegrini (New York: Columbia University Press, 2004), 636.

10. Adi Kuntsman, *Figurations of Violence and Belonging* (New York: Peter Lang, 2009). Although his analysis misreads the relationship between homonationalism and gay rights, see also Aeyal Gross, "Israeli GLBT Politics between Queerness and Homonationalism," *Bullybloggers,* July 3, 2010, http://bullybloggers.wordpress.com/2010/07/03/israeli-glbt-politics-between-queerness-and-homonationalism/.

11. Amal Amireh, "Afterword," in *GLQ: A Journal of Gay and Lesbian Studies* 16, no. 4 (2010): 637.

12. See Posener, "Geschlect als Wissenkategorie."

13. Gil Hochberg, ed., "Queer Politics and the Questions of Palestine/Israel," *GLQ: A Journal of Gay and Lesbian Studies* 16, no. 4 (2010).

14. Hochberg, "Israelis, Palestinians, Queers," 493–94.

15. Amalia Ziv, "Performative Politics in Israeli Queer Anti-Occupation Activism," *GLQ: A Journal of Gay and Lesbian Studies* 16, no. 4 (2010): 537–56.

16. Gil Z. Hochberg, Rima Haneen Maikey, and Samira Saraya, "No Pride in Occupation: A Roundtable Discussion," *GLQ: A Journal of Gay and Lesbian Studies* 16, no. 4 (2010): 599–610.

17. Jason Ritchie, "How Do You Say 'Come Out of the Closet' in Arabic? Queer Activism and the Politics of Visibility in Israel Palestine," *GLQ: A Journal of Gay and Lesbian Studies* 16, no. 4 (2010): 559–60; citing James Kirchick, "Queers for Palestine?," *Advocate,* January 28, 2009, http://www.advocate.com/exclusive_detai_ektid71844.asp.

18. Derek Gregory, "Defiled Cities," *Singapore Journal of Tropical Geography* 24, no. 3 (2003): 307–26.

19. See Posener, "Geschlect als Wissenkategorie."

20. See Gross, "Israeli GLBT Politics"; Kuntsman, *Figurations of Violence and Belonging.*

21. Ziv, "Performative Politics," 537.

22. In January 2009 I signed a petition, or a letter of sorts, written by Teachers against Occupation. It was a letter to Obama (either not yet or just sworn into office) that condemned Israeli actions in Gaza. It noted that Obama was among the first of student supporters of divestment from South Africa while at Occidental College in 1981, quoting him as once having said, "Nobody is suffering more than the Palestinian people." The letter then used language from Obama's website, which at the time

stated, "Our first and incontrovertible commitment in the Middle East must be to the security of Israel," to challenge Obama to put pressure on Israel to withdraw from Gaza. This letter appeared to travel widely in the United States and was signed readily by many academics.

About six months later, I received a response, titled "A Statement of Concern: Calling for Support Regarding Discrimination in the Middle East against Women, Gays, and Lesbians," penned and sent by one Fred Gottheil at the University of Illinois, Urbana-Champaign. The statement goes on to cull evidence from UN agencies, the High Commissioner for Human Rights, academic journals, and NGOs such as Asylum Law and Human Rights Watch on "discrimination against gays and lesbians" in the form of legislation, imprisonment, beheading, the criminalization of sodomy, and the recruitment of guilt-laden homosexuals into suicide bombing squads, along with "gender discrimination," wife beating, honor killing, and genital mutilation. The geographical span is wide: Palestine, Africa, and the Middle East. Despite the diversity of religious affiliations across these regions, the specific practices detailed are all ascribed to Muslims and Islamic belief.

23. Jasbir Puar, "To Be Gay and Racist Is No Anomaly," *The Guardian*, June 2, 2010.

24. Partha Chatterjee, "The Nationalist Resolution of the Women's Question," in *Recasting Women*, ed. Kumkum Sangari and Sudesh Vaid (New Brunswick: Rutgers University Press, 1990), 233–53.

25. Gayatri Spivak, "Can the Subaltern Speak?," in *Marxism and the Interpretation of Culture*, ed. Lawrence Grossberg and Cary Nelson (London: Macmillan, 1988), 271–313.

26. Patrick Deer et al., "Edward Said: A Memorial Issue," *Social Text* 87 (2006): 3.

27. Ibid, 4.

28. Jasbir Puar, "Israel's Gay Propaganda War," *Guardian*, July 1, 2010.

29. Giorgio Agamben, *State of Exception*, trans. Kevin Attell (Chicago: University of Chicago Press, 2005).

30. In his seminal piece "Necropolitics," *Public Culture* 15, no. 1: 11–40, Achille Mbembe points to the problems with Western political theoretical proclivities to centralize the Holocaust as the "state of exception" par excellence, following from both the Foucauldian frame of biopolitics and Agamben (who focuses on the camp), prompting critical interventions by postcolonial theorists. It seems to me that Mbembe calls out continental philosophers who continue to elide the violence of colonial occupations in favor of what appears, at first sight, to be an intellectual proclivity to continually return to the Holocaust, producing fissures between postcolonial, area, and transnational studies and field formations that continually return to Europe as their primary referent point. But is this a purely intellectual, and thus secular, matter, or does this intellectual field fissuring do the work of masking deeply held religious beliefs—or let's say biases—parading as the secular? Following Mbembe's

intervention, it is my contention, or at least a deep suspicion, that so long as the Holocaust remains the dominant trauma of the modern era, the Judeo and the Christian are able to (re)activate an alliance that is built against Islam as a fundamentalist force and does so within the spaces of liberal secular feminist and queer scholarship as well as institutional practices. It appears, at this historical juncture, that the secular is predominantly, if perhaps only, secular in relation to Islam.

31. See Leerom Medovi, "Dogma Line Racism: Islamophobia and the Second Axis of Race," *Social Text* 30, no. 2 (2012): 43–74.

IV

Heresies and Freedoms

12

Within and Against the Imperial University

Reflections on Crossing the Line

Nicholas De Genova

> *Let us compel the war to break in on us, if it must. . . . Let us force it perceptibly to batter in our spiritual walls.*
>
> —Randolph Bourne, "A War Diary"

Wednesday, March 26, 2003. Exactly one week after the commencement of the U.S. invasion of Iraq. At an antiwar teach-in at Columbia University, where I was employed as an untenured assistant professor of anthropology, I celebrated the defeat of the U.S. military in Vietnam as a victory for the cause of human self-determination and unequivocally called for the material and practical defeat of the invasion and occupation of Iraq. Like dozens of other faculty members that night, I had spoken for only about ten minutes. Ten minutes: few words in the great scheme of things—but words well chosen. What I said changed the course of my life and career. In this chapter, for the first time in print, and after more than ten years, I examine my experience of "crossing the line"—transgressing the ordinarily unspoken and unwritten limits, however unstable, of permissible speech—and reflect upon the larger significance of this episode of the suppression of dissent among academic intellectuals within—and against—the imperial university.

Unspeakable Violence, Violence Unspeakable

A few particularly inflammatory phrases from my remarks at the teach-in in 2003 were sufficient for my speech to be promptly catapulted into a media feeding frenzy. This was a moment in our disgraceful history when a toxic politics commanded blind and bellicose faith. George W. Bush's opening salvo in the war against the people of Afghanistan on September 20, 2001, had notoriously provided the occasion for an ultimatum to the world:

"Either you are with us, or you are with the terrorists."[1] The overwhelming and asphyxiating mood in the United States during those first two years of the so-called War on Terror manifested itself—to borrow a phrase from Randolph Bourne, speaking of the raging passion for war in the United States in 1917—as "a chorus so mighty that to be out of it was at first to be disreputable and finally almost obscene."[2] Those who promoted war in Afghanistan and Iraq hungered after the elusive vindication of an illusory heroism: they cloaked themselves in a sanctimonious sense of their own victimization and armored themselves in a delusional "antiterrorist" belief in their own aggressive "self-defense." This is precisely why no repudiation of the Iraq invasion could have hoped to achieve any genuine impact, in my view, unless it was as utterly uncompromising, incorrigible, and indeed as belligerent as the nearly hysterical mania for war that bombarded us relentlessly from every mass-media propaganda outlet. The compulsive desire for war, the furious passion for it, and the veritable bloodlust that had been so cynically cultivated and inflamed in the U.S. populace were nothing less than ghoulish clamor for mass murder, a jingoistic craving for the death of the Enemy.

When I spoke at the Columbia teach-in, therefore, I needed to forcibly confront my audience with the inescapable fact that if it was death that the prowar mob was seeking, then it was death indeed that they would reap. After all the treacherous seductions of the illusion of a sort of military capability so technologically asymmetrical that the United States could perpetrate a war without incurring any serious casualties, I had to hurl back at them a vivid memory of the brute and horrific fact of real carnage. Recalling from recent history another U.S. military intervention—one that commenced with a media spectacle of self-congratulation and then culminated in an excruciatingly humiliating defeat, recorded on videotape and launched into a vertiginous spiral of televised coverage: the invasion of Somalia in 1993—I summoned up the largely suppressed (or perverted) collective memory of the battle of Mogadishu.[3] Following that decisive skirmish, considered to have been the bloodiest single battle for U.S. soldiers since the Vietnam War, jubilant Somali combatants dragged the corpses of occupying U.S. soldiers through the streets of their capital in celebration of their improbable victory. The grisly mass-mediated debacle immediately instigated the retreat of the U.S. military and the failure of the invasion. Here, then, were the real stakes of the U.S. escapade in Iraq. With the hope that the unfolding U.S. war and inevitable occupation might ultimately be met with a veritable anticolonial struggle for Iraqi self-determination—in short, another Vietnam—I proclaimed that I would nonetheless welcome "a million Mogadishus now."

The greater part of my comments, however, had been devoted to providing a historical outline of colonial conquest, genocide, slavery, and imperial warfare as forming the bedrock of U.S. nation-state formation. That same long history, punctuated by U.S. invasions and military occupations, I argued, had likewise been deeply constitutive of a social and political order predicated upon racist violence and oppression. U.S. nationalism and white supremacy have been inextricably linked, historically. I contended that it is necessary, therefore, to repudiate all forms of U.S. patriotism to liberate our political imaginations in order that we might usher in a radically different world, one in which we will not remain the prisoners of U.S. global domination. In this regard, I explicitly confronted the pronounced tendency in the antiwar movement to defensively claim that "peace is patriotic." Peace is not patriotic, I replied—peace is subversive, because peace anticipates a very different world than the one in which we live, a world where the United States would have no place.

With the militaristic fervor at a crescendo, my defeatist provocation became national (and international) headline news. After all, George W. Bush had just delivered his ultimatum to Saddam Hussein and announced the official commencement of the war only one week prior. The larger framework of my remarks was summarily disregarded in favor of a sensationalized, decontextualized mass circulation of the most inflammatory sound bite: the "million Mogadishus" phrase.

The new president of Columbia University, Lee Bollinger, who had just taken up the position that same academic year, was traveling at the time of the teach-in and could have had no specific knowledge of what in fact I had said apart from what was being reported in the mass media. Nonetheless, commenting from afar, Bollinger—who has made his academic career as a scholar of free speech—publicly declared that he was "shocked" and affirmed, referring to my speech, that "this one crosses the line." His reaction was issued as a press release and immediately published on the university's website.[4] In a subsequent iteration, Bollinger declared that he was "appalled" and summarily denounced my comments as "outrageous." Significantly, he added, "Our faculty and students, regardless of their position on the war, have not been silent in their denunciation of [De Genova's] remarks." Thus *regardless of one's position on the war*, faculty and students alike were not-so-subtly instructed by the highest administrative official of the university that both the form and substance of my speech commanded vociferous condemnation; indeed, they were effectively impermissible—I had "crossed the line." Notably, Bollinger had prefaced his judgment of my speech by affirming that "because of the University's tradition of academic freedom," he normally did not comment about statements made by faculty members. Thus he emphasized that the scandal of my speech was expressly not "normal": it was an exception.

Following Bollinger's initial response, the chair of my department (and my immediate administrative superior), Nicholas Dirks, in response to a query from the *National Review*, sent an e-mail reply that was then posted online and also quoted in the *Columbia Spectator*, the student newspaper on campus. Dirks evidently seemed to studiously model his statement on Bollinger's but went still further: "I cherish the principles of freedom of speech and academic freedom. . . . However, I am deeply concerned when the academic obligations of debate and critique are sullied by sentiments that seem profoundly *out of line* with the values and commitments that are fundamental to academic life" (emphasis added). By implication, I could not very well be expected to enjoy the protections of academic freedom if I myself was culpable of "sullying" the very foundations of academic life. By purportedly violating my own obligations, Dirks implied, and by sabotaging the very values that otherwise should uphold the sanctity of that tradition of free inquiry and expression, I had committed an unpardonable transgression. Dirks added that he was "personally appalled" and "repudiated" the offending content of my speech.[5] It is not difficult to discern in these carefully crafted phrases an anticipation on Dirks's part of the not-implausible prospect that he might soon be required to justify my summary termination. Meanwhile, my excommunication from the academic community of debate and critique—at the very least, at Columbia—was progressing with furious rapidity. As Dirks alluded, this was for him less a matter of free speech, academic or otherwise, than a violation of the "values and commitments" that constitute the (normally tacit) boundary of a shared way of (academic) life and thus was deemed to threaten the communal foundations of the university.

Why indeed were these officials of the imperial university not more appalled and outraged by the *real* atrocities that the United States war machine was perpetrating against innocent civilians in Afghanistan and Iraq than the violent imagery I conjured with my words? Bollinger notably concluded his various statements with regretful laments for any undue suffering my words might have inflicted upon the families of "American troops . . . in harm's way," and Dirks expressly repudiated "any statement wishing violence against soldiers or civilians alike." Thus Bollinger explicitly invoked his sympathy for the aggrieved families of the U.S. military participating in the invasion and, with callous disregard for Iraqis, thereby implicitly aligned himself on the side of U.S. nationhood. More ambiguously fashioned as a rejection of "violence" as such, Dirks's comment nonetheless made direct and emphatic reference to the soldiers themselves, not merely their families. But what exactly is the work of soldiers, if not violence? More specifically, what indeed was the express mission of the U.S. soldiers being deployed in Iraq, if not violence and occupation? Was it truly plausible that the invasion, otherwise touted as a campaign of "shock and awe," might be conceivable as anything other than a massive orchestration of disproportionate (imperial) violence? And if U.S. soldiers were indeed, in Bollinger's hackneyed phrase, "in harm's way," weren't the people of Iraq being systematically and mercilessly subjected to immeasurably and incomparably greater harm? Indeed, weren't the "American troops" the very ones inflicting the most devastating harm?

"The Idea of a University": Theory and Practice

If these officers of the imperial university found my rhetoric offensive, weren't they the ones truly at fault for disgracing the values and obligations fundamental to academic life? I refer to their flagrant and instantaneous disregard of the requirement of reasoned discourse and argument—the duty of thoughtful engagement and debate—in favor of outright denunciation. It was a denunciation, moreover, based on no substantive or direct knowledge of what I had said. I repeatedly made efforts to contact Bollinger to meet in person, or at least speak by phone, in order to clarify for him what I had actually said. After all, his telephone line and e-mail account were operating an automated reply that explicitly referred to me by name and passed judgment upon what I was purported to have said. He repeatedly made public statements to the press with regard to me while having never even superficially made my acquaintance.

On the other hand, I was in frequent telephone contact with Dirks, who was my senior colleague and chair of my department, in his capacity as the administrative official directly charged with handling my situation, but similarly he was never once interested in any substantive discussion of anything that I may have said or been alleged to have said. After initially verifying only that I had indeed called for the U.S. military to suffer some woefully large number of "Mogadishus," and asking whether I was at all inclined to make a public apology—and thereby confirming that I was not—his interactions with me became entirely confined to the practicalities surrounding my rather complex and apparently precarious circumstances. Whereas we had previously enjoyed some semblance of collegial rapport, Dirks now assumed a role that was strictly managerial. And he likewise reserved his denunciation of my "appalling" speech exclusively for public consumption. There was no place for dialogue or debate, no considered discourse or reasoned disagreement; my speech was simply "out of line," beyond the pale. I had simply become a "problem" to be managed.

Here, it is useful to situate these dilemmas within their proper sociopolitical context—one that directly concerns the problem of the imperial university, as such. History is also instructive in this regard. In 1917, Columbia University penalized two faculty members, James McKeen Cattell and Henry Wadsworth Longfellow Dana, for their public opposition to World War I with the summary termination of their employment, leading to the resignation of the renowned historian Charles Beard in protest.[6] Responding to these events, in his essay "The Idea of a University," Bourne eloquently noted,

> The university produces learning instead of steel or rubber. . . . As directors in this corporation of learning, trustees seem to regard themselves primarily as guardians of invested capital. They manage as a sacred trust the various bequests, gifts, endowments which have been made to the university by men and women of the same orthodoxies as themselves. Their obligation is to see that the quality of the commodity which the university produces is such as to seem reputable to the class which they represent. . . . the reputation of a university is comparable to the standing of a corporation's securities on the street, the newspapers taking the place of the stock exchange. The real offence of Professors Catell and Dana seems to have been not so much that they were unpatriotic as that they had lowered the prestige of the university in the public mind. . . . No attempt was made to discover whether the newspaper accounts were true. Chatter and rumor were sufficient to convict them. Why? Because on the stock exchange it is by rumor and prejudice that the value of securities is hit, not by evidence. . . . The mischief lies in what people think, not in the actual facts. And for this purpose newspaper chatter is authoritative.[7]

Bourne's critique of the corporate character of the university and its susceptibility to rumor and "bad press" in the World War I era remains equally valid today. Why else would a man such as Bollinger, a scholar of free speech, have no interest whatsoever in the substance of the offending speech beyond the incontrovertibly "authoritative" accounts in the news media? If the press was identifying Columbia with the scandal of "treasonous" speech, what mattered was that this could only do damage to the prestige of the university in the mind of a public that abided by the orthodoxies of the state during wartime.

Uncanny as it may seem, later in 2003, Bollinger himself published an op-ed piece in the *Wall Street Journal* with exactly the same title as Bourne's essay. "With all the pressures toward the closing of our minds that come with conflict in the public arena," Bollinger wrote, "it's not a bad idea to have special communities like universities distinctly dedicated to the open intellect."[8] No, not a bad idea at all. Yet for university officials like Bollinger and Dirks, as for the "trustee autocracy" that Bourne decried generations earlier, what ultimately matters is, precisely, bad publicity. Widely publicized allegations of "sedition" or "economic heresy," which are perceived to diminish the value of the university's commodity and to degrade the institution's corporate credibility and respectability, are deemed infinitely more consequential than sustaining a space of genuinely uninhibited, robust, and wide-open freedom of speech and expression.[9]

My Private Iraq War

In the immediate firestorm of controversy surrounding my remarks, a campaign by wealthy and influential donors to the university's endowment, as well as 104 Republican members of the U.S. House of Representatives and numerous other public officials, demanded that my employment be terminated. Reportedly, the filmmaker Steven Spielberg personally called Dirks to threaten a lawsuit if I were not promptly dispatched from my job. Simultaneously, I was subjected to numerous graphic, aggravated, and repeated death threats—by phone, e-mail, and post—and underwent bewildering disruptions in my ordinary personal and professional life as a result of security considerations.

My home telephone began ringing nonstop from early on the morning of Friday, March 28, when the story broke in the New York City tabloid *Newsday*. The anthropology department office was similarly riddled with enraged inquiries about my whereabouts and hostile denunciations. In addition to contact information for my own and numerous other Columbia offices, my home address and phone number had been posted online—or perhaps had been announced on a talk radio program where the host was inciting people to harass me—and were circulating wildly. Callers to my home number recited my street address and supplied lurid assurances that I would soon be meeting my doom: "We know where you live. We're coming to get you now!" My home telephone was so barraged with harassing calls that it abruptly and inexplicably became inoperative the day after the story first appeared in the news. During those first days, furthermore, television camera crews were camped outside my home, day and night, in SUVs ominously adorned with patriotic bumper stickers and tinted windows. Then police detectives assigned to "investigate" some of the more readily traceable threats to my life assured me that the FBI was also keeping an eye on my case. Those same cops also intimated that there were plans (which never materialized) to hold a hostile demonstration in front of my apartment building. My family and I immediately went into hiding.

My e-mail account was plagued with 25,000 to 30,000 irate, anguished, or harassing messages (including numerous threats of violent retribution). Bollinger later revealed that the telephone lines in his office suffered the same fate and that he also received more than 20,000 e-mails.[10] Indeed, assuming that virtually all his incoming messages sought to demand punitive action against me, an automated response was activated on Bollinger's e-mail account as was an automatic recorded message when anyone called the university switchboard and mentioned my name, reiterating the university president's public denunciation of my speech (while also affirming that it was nonetheless protected by the First Amendment).

On the first morning after our flight into hiding, my partner and I found ourselves having brunch in a cafe with the friend who was hosting us. As if staged for a film, our first day "in hiding" was greeted with the discovery that the woman at the next table was reading a story about me in the Sunday New York Post, including large photos of me that had been reprinted from the Internet. I learned later that, among other things, that Sunday edition of the paper had devoted an editorial to openly promoting the fantasy of a violent reprisal against me for my "seditious" speech: "Where's the Ohio National Guard when you really need it? Seriously? Hey, if a campus crank can wish for personal calamity to befall U.S. forces in Iraq, why not fantasize about a volley of Kent State-style militia musketry rattled off in his general direction?"[11]

After more than a week later, we eventually resumed daily use of our home. However, because so many random strangers had been inspired to describe in graphic detail all the gruesome acts of violence that they desired to inflict upon me (and in some instances, also upon my family), we continued spending the nights in a different "undisclosed" location that had been arranged by the university, until the campus real estate office eventually offered us a new faculty apartment nearly three months later.

During this period, crude handmade flyers with my photo printed on them and designating me an enemy of both the United States and Israel were posted by a Zionist group called the Jewish Defense Organization (JDO) throughout the neighborhood around Columbia. Unbeknownst to me at the time, the JDO was said to have organized a paramilitary training camp somewhere in the Catskill Mountains in upstate New York. They were a splinter faction from the Jewish Defense League and part of the larger Meir Kahane movement, renowned for the assassination of Israeli prime minister Yitzhak Rabin and numerous other murders and bombings. This splinter group's national director, Mordechai Levy, had a history of arrests—for attempted murder, bombings, and other aggravated felonies—as well as a conviction and incarceration for felony assault with a deadly weapon and a guilty plea for the assault of a twelve-year-old boy. The JDO's website, adorned with animated images of automatic weapons, included my photo, home address, and home telephone number, as well as a link to my e-mail and Bollinger's, encouraging its sympathizers to make contact with me directly to share their outrage and otherwise to intensify the campaign to get rid of me, one way or the other.[12]

At the university, the administration arranged for me to be accompanied by campus security officers whenever I went to teach for the remainder of the semester (as the times and locations of my courses were publicly available and indeed had been publicized in a story in the *New York Times*).[13] Students had to show identification and get checked off a registration list in order to enter my classroom. Meanwhile, as I went about my private life, I was occasionally accosted on the street. There were episodes when unexpected and seemingly suspicious incidents around our home sent my family into a panic. Under these utterly unpredictable circumstances, I had taken to carrying weapons with me at all times and continued doing so for a very long time thereafter. I had invited the war home, and it came crashing in upon my whole little world, battering down the fragile semblance of security and privacy that had previously enshrouded my domestic life.

Becoming the Object of Controversy

There were some efforts mobilized to defend my freedom of speech, to support me in the face of such fierce animosity, and to express concern about the perceived failings of my department and the chilling statements of the university administration. A few days after the story broke in the news, my colleague Partha Chatterjee wrote an e-mail on March 31 to the rest of the anthropology department faculty from India, where he was spending the semester, underscoring how crucial it is to guard the university as a very special space protected from the "demands of nationalist politics and patriotic obligation." He encouraged our colleagues to contemplate the importance for us as faculty of being unhindered in our efforts to invite students to engage in the necessary thought experiment of trying to see the U.S. military from the standpoint of its Somali or Iraqi victims. Acknowledging that the scandal surrounding my speech "could have happened to any of us," Chatterjee affirmed unreservedly, "I stand by Nick at this difficult moment." He received rebuttals immediately—likewise by e-mail, copied to the entire faculty (minus myself)—from Rosalind Morris and David Scott, as well as one of the untenured faculty.

Morris, assuming the mantle of self-anointed authority on the De Genova affair (having been the only member of the anthropology faculty present when I spoke at the teach-in), "respectfully" disagreed and assured Chatterjee and the rest of the faculty that my "patently ridiculous" and unnuanced comments "took the form of advocacy" and even exceeded what had been reported in the press.[14] Morris fervently asserted,

> The result of Nick's importunate intervention has been the wholesale denegration [*sic*] of Columbia University's faculty and especially its anti-war activists. It will be months, if not years, before Columbia faculty can speak for progressive causes without being derided for arrogance and accused of encouraging vulgar blood-lust. It has led to death threats against members of this faculty and the abuse of our staff. It has crippled our department, violated its image, and led to the threatened withdrawal of funds and students from our field. I do not hold Nick responsible for the violence of others, and he is not to be

made accountable for the debased mob tactics that he was so perilously close to inviting when he suggested the nobility of fragging.
Nonetheless, we, his colleagues, have yet to receive any acknowledg-
ment of the predicament to which we have also been subject, nor has
the peace movement on campus received from him any expression of
remorse for the damage it suffered . . . this seems a minimal gesture
of goodwill.

In this litany of grievances—whereby I had allegedly instigated a veritable calamity of denigration, derision, abuse, threats, crippling, and violation
upon the department, the university, and "especially its anti-war activists"—
Morris suggested that I had indeed encouraged "vulgar blood-lust" and
came "perilously close to inviting" precisely the sorts of "debased mob tactics" that now the department as whole was suffering. Her conclusion was a
general one: "In these times, care and thought for the consequences for one's
words are . . . necessary. . . . Public discourse is not private speech, and now,
more than ever . . . it behooves scholars to insist on . . . attending to the social
spaces in which our words travel."

David Scott likewise responded directly to Chatterjee, copying the entire
faculty e-mail list. Although he confirmed that he too could "empathize with
the sense of outrage and anger that might have led Nick to make the remarks
he made," he judged that my comments had been "calculated to be inflammatory" and thus insinuated that my speech had been irresponsible:

Precisely BECAUSE the University is to be preserved as a space
for the active cultivation of freedom of speech among faculty and
students it must ALSO insist on the cultivation of responsible
participation (however radical, indeed especially when radical) in
public discourse in the context of the University. This is even more
important in the context of a "teach-in" which is, afterall [sic], in part
a pedagogical exercise. . . . Finally, I'm not sure what you mean when
you say that you "stand by Nick at this difficult moment". I too am
prepared to defend his right to express his views. But I want to insist
that in so far as the occasion is not primarily one of polemic (as in
sloganeering at a street march) but one of reflection even if also one
of advocacy, there must also be a demand for careful expression and
an expectation that a speaker is accountable in some way to the community that shelters such speech.

Scott also specifically objected to my challenge to the preoccupation of the antiwar movement that it appear patriotic (which he agreed was a mistaken tactic). However, he deemed my frontal repudiation of U.S. nationalism to have been "strategically" ill-advised in my speech: "I believe," he contended, "that the anti-war movement ought to refuse to be dragged down that road at all. . . . In my view the anti-war movement must state categorically and repeatedly that talk about 'patriotism' is an obfuscation and underline and elaborate that this is an unjust and imperialist war." In other words, whereas I had explicitly sought to problematize the compulsion to champion opposition to the war as "patriotic" and advocated rejecting that position within the antiwar movement, Scott, although he essentially agreed with my critique, judged that I had been injudicious to address it substantively, because it was not "strategic."[15]

Thus the general reaction of these purported antiwar and anti-imperialist colleagues was that I had violated an unspoken and unwritten code of *responsibility* to which I was "accountable" regarding what is permissible for academics to say in order to not perturb or recklessly endanger what Scott designated "the community that shelters such speech." Sadly, it was precisely these sorts of pronouncements from the self-styled "Left" within the imperial university that most vigilantly sought to police the parameters of propriety and thereby assumed a vanguard role in the repression of genuinely audacious speech. For Morris, "advocacy" itself was beyond the pale, whereas for Scott, there was no room for "polemic," and the task was rather one of "reflection": the academic community should presumptively be "pedagogical," "careful," and circumspect in its demeanor. Indeed, this political imperative within the academic milieu for an aggressively depoliticizing rhetorical "civility" and cautious circumspection were merely the most immediate manifestation of a more pernicious social and political pressure, exerted from all sides, to utterly suppress or at least significantly curtail any expression of unapologetic protest or fearless dissent.

Beyond the resentful and exasperated discussion confined to the internal precincts of my department, other faculty who fashioned themselves as spokespersons for the campus antiwar movement publicly joined the mass-mediated condemnation of my speech. Renowned historian Eric Foner, who had been one of the organizers of the teach-in, in a telephone interview with the *Newsday* journalist who initially broke the story to the public at large, disparaged my comments as "idiotic" and "completely uncalled for."[16] Later in the afternoon on the day the story first broke, Foner was quoted yet again, now on CNN.com (as well as in an interview with the *New York Times*, printed the following day), declaring my statements to have been "reprehensible."[17] Another organizer of the event, political scientist Jean Cohen, credited in the campus newspaper with having first had the idea for the event, effectively denounced me as an "outside agitator": "He and the press have hijacked this teach-in, and I'm very, very angry about it. It was an utterly irresponsible thing to do. And it's not innocent. This was a planned undermining of this teach-in. At the last minute someone couldn't speak, and he just kind of appeared. He ended up on that platform by accident, almost by manipulation." Cohen reportedly said that as soon as it was clear that there was an opening in the program, "[De Genova] was right there, all ready with his speech—which makes me suspicious."[18] Of course, Cohen's wild and paranoid speculations revealed simply that she was in fact utterly ill-informed about the actual circumstances of my participation. (I had indeed been invited by another organizer of the event—my friend and colleague Hamid Dabashi, the person responsible for the panel on which I spoke.) Thus in this climate of jingoistic hostility and professional intimidation, the vast majority of the ostensibly "antiwar" faculty at Columbia, in a desperate effort to recuperate their own credibility and legitimacy, scrambled to distance themselves from me and repudiate what I was purported to have said. Indeed, very few people ever truly knew what I had actually said. It was sufficient that the news media were energetically circulating a few "scandalous" phrases, removed entirely from the larger substance and context of my speech. The desperate attempt to depict me as a veritable "outside agitator" merely verified what was in fact the immediate and irreversible consensus by which I could only be considered an outcast—a de facto untouchable, a persona non grata—within the Columbia "community."

Within those first few days of the eruption of the scandal, likewise on March 31 (the date of all three of the e-mails among the anthropology faculty), at least forty-five PhD students in anthropology petitioned the department's faculty on my behalf. Some of the initiators of this petition were among the foremost organizers of antiwar activism on the Columbia campus. Already well aware and acutely sensitive to the rising hostility among many of the faculty toward me, these students appealed,

> In light of the recent remarks made by President Bollinger, it is crucial to affirm our commitment to Professor De Genova's critical role in the life of our department and university. University life must

be, especially in these times of internationally condemned war and crisis, committed to open and honest debate protected from retribution. Given President Bollinger's public claims to champion free speech and diversity, it is alarming that his statement has foreclosed the possibilities for diversity of opinion and debate in the university. The statement has in effect isolated and endangered this valuable member of our community without carefully engaging with his critical intervention. We believe that it is the role of our department and university to encourage, nurture, and protect critical thinking and political dissent. . . . We therefore call upon the department to resist participating in the distancing of the university from Professor De Genova.

When my classes were cancelled during the first week of the turmoil while I remained in hiding, furthermore, a large group of my students staged a silent protest on campus, sitting in a circle around an empty chair representing my absence, with their own mouths gagged with U.S. flags to symbolically invoke how I had been silenced by the wider campaign of intimidation.

The pressure from students on my behalf provoked the convening of a town hall–style meeting to discuss the controversy within the anthropology department. Remarkably, I was never informed of the event by any member of the faculty and was never invited to participate in the conversation. At the meeting, against the students' demands for a more robust defense of my freedom of speech, several faculty members now publicly and passionately alleged that I had acted irresponsibly and had done unpardonable damage to the reputation of the department. Meanwhile, I was sitting in my office across campus, uninvited and effectively excluded from this department event.

In the following week or two, a letter of solidarity signed by some three hundred academics was delivered to my faculty colleagues in the department as well as the higher administrative officers of the university. This petition declared,

We are . . . concerned about ways in which [Columbia University] may act, officially or implicitly, to punish [Professor De Genova's] exercise of free speech and contravene the principle of academic freedom. At a time when all of our rights to free speech, non-violent association, and legal dissent are under attack, we support Professor De Genova's right to have spoken freely as an invited participant to an open forum. We would like to register our strong opposition to any personal, professional, or legal retaliation that might be directed at him for having made these remarks.[19]

Notably, among many other distinguished scholars, this petition included the signatures of Bertell Ollman (who had an offer of the chairmanship of the Government Department at the University of Maryland rescinded in 1978 due to a controversy over his politics) and Ariel Dorfman (who was driven into exile from Chile by the brutal coup d'état in 1973 that ushered in the Pinochet dictatorship and condemned many of his colleagues to torture and death).

It was only in the aftermath of this pressure from academic colleagues across the United States (and indeed from some other countries as well)—but also only after Bollinger had already declared definitively that I would not be fired in response to the political clamor for my termination—that Dirks, in his capacity as department chair, finally (anonymously) posted an official statement on the departmental website on April 18. Notably, Dirks's official departmental statement was posted unilaterally, in spite of the vociferous desire of the more antagonistic members of the anthropology faulty to draft a collective statement; it declared,

> The department is strongly committed to the principles of the First Amendment and of academic freedom. Professor de Genova will neither be fired nor reprimanded for his statements, which will also have no bearing on periodic academic reviews affecting his employ-ment at Columbia. . . . it must be noted that Professor de Genova's statements do not represent the position of the department. Nor do the remarks of any other individuals stand for the collective views of faculty. The department's affirmation of the rights of all individuals to speak freely in no way binds us to support any particular statements.

Here, indeed, was a rather admirably straightforward statement that cor-rectly affirmed that my speech ought to be seen as comparable to that of anyone else among the department's faculty, both in its putatively free and protected status and in its irreducible singularity.

Affronted all the same by what they deemed in the petitions from stu-dents and fellow academics to be an implicit allegation that they were col-luding with the larger atmosphere of hostility and retaliation, a cohort of my ostensible colleagues, catalyzed in particular by the fervor of Rosalind Morris (accompanied by Nadia Abu-el-Haj, an untenured member of the faculty in Columbia anthropology's sister department at Barnard College), became intensely involved in drafting a more expansive and purportedly substantive response to the petitioners. Eventual signatories predictably included David Scott, as well as Michael Taussig and others. (Not surprisingly, most of the untenured faculty at both Columbia and Barnard were among them.) They contended,

> The petitions make inaccurate and unfair allegations against the Department, and . . . reveal a lack of full knowledge about recent events at Columbia University. . . . [W]e want people to know that our affirmation of Professor De Genova's rights in no way binds us to a statement of support for the content of his remarks. Many individuals have expressed disagreement with Professor De Genova's statements. . . . In this context, we feel it is important that you know the nature of the conversation that has occurred since the Teach-In. . . . In other words, the disagreements with Professor De Genova are various and substantive, but they do not consist in a rejection of his right to dissent. They merely extend such rights to all participants in the debate. . . . We are, moreover, deeply distressed that the intellectual and discursive energies of our colleagues may be dissipated in contests that have no ground in substantiated truths, but that inhabit the realm of rumor. . . . We hope that these statements are read as manifestations of our respect for free speech. We also hope that readers understand why our affirmation of this right cannot become the grounds of our own silencing.

Hence the mobilization of concerned intellectuals to express their solidarity with a colleague who was being subjected to an extraordinary campaign of vilification over his speech was perversely transfigured into an occasion for the alleged "silencing" of some of those who were taking part, to varying degrees, in the vilification.

Although the statement sought to verify and briefly outline the nature of an array of objections to my speech (the details of which I have omitted here),[20] what is supremely duplicitous in this text is that *none* of those expressions of disagreement with my remarks—literally, *no part* of "the conversation that . . . occurred since the Teach-In"—ever involved an actual exchange with me. My ostensible colleagues had made me the *object* of their objections, but I was never once invited into a dialogue or debate of any kind. By issuing a collective statement accompanied by a list of signatories, moreover, this rejoinder performatively presented itself *as if* it were enunciated in the name of the department as a whole (although several prominent members of the faculty had declined to sign). To ensure that their grievances would be noted, the organizers of this effort literally gathered e-mail addresses for every individual petitioner possible and sent out their reply. For many of the recipients, this statement served merely to confirm their worst fears.

Throughout these days and weeks after the story broke, I was hounded constantly by the television, radio, and print news media. My remarks became a favorite *bête noir* for the full rogues' gallery of right-wing pundits on television, radio, and the Internet. I was even invited to a live debate with Newt Gingrich and Sean Hannity, which they proposed to hold at the Columbia University Law School. In this context of intense adversity, with the barrage of harassment and death threats unabated, even after the initial two or three weeks, I was eager to have a more full representation of my point of view heard. I therefore granted an interview to the seemingly stodgy *Chronicle of Higher Education*, whose editors then ran the piece—without my knowledge or consent—under a headline nominating me "The Most Hated Professor in America" (April 18, 2003). Hence the widest public forum for news and discussion within the U.S. academy broadcasted a rather sensationalist confirmation that, within the imperial university, some forms of dissent could only be deemed anathema, indeed loathsome.

Becoming an Object of Toleration

In the variety of adverse reactions of my colleagues and administrative overseers, there was a rather telling consistency in their obligatory declarations that they, *of course*, "defended" my First Amendment right to free speech. Beneath this liberal pretension and their apparent confidence in the unquestionable fixity of that supposed "right," one nonetheless detects the persistent trace of a very palpable anxiety about the extent to which such civil liberties were in any sense secure or reliable in the prevailing political climate of securitarianism under the War on Terror's official "state of emergency." Moreover, inasmuch as these commentators (from Bollinger down through Morris, Scott, and the sundry signatories of the statement in response to the petitioners) were unanimous about my speech being "protected," they routinely affirmed that I was "within my rights" to say whatever I wanted. My speech, therefore, was strictly *lawful* (that is to say, not criminal), even if it was morally repugnant or politically reckless. My speech, then, was rendered an object of their *toleration*: it was something to be "tolerated," not because it was in any sense "deserving," but because affording it such grudging tolerance was a necessary evil in the self-interest of preserving the presumable "rights" or liberties that these colleagues felt to be endangered even for themselves.

Within this liberal framework, of course, the form of repercussion would not be the prohibitory mode of censorship but rather the *inhibitory* mode imposed through *censure*. In other words, insofar as I was untenured, a cacophony of denunciation was meant to effectively silence me through an injunction to *self*-censorship. My structural position ordinarily ought to have ensured that I inhabited a condition of sustained and protracted vulnerability to the punitive professional recrimination of an eventual denial of promotion and tenure. When I violated the tacit terms of that academic covenant—which pervasively encourages scholars to speak and write in disguised, Aesopian, obfuscatory language and exalts the exchange value of apparently sophisticated esoteric complexity—the penalty was not overt official sanction but instead a concerted silencing that could be enforced only through the multifarious manifestations of political disapprobation and professional disregard. During the six years after the teach-in that I remained employed there, I was never again invited to speak publicly at Columbia— about neither my scholarship nor my politics—except by students. I had been summarily made into a pariah in my home institution.

Two months after the controversy over my speech erupted, Bollinger addressed the families of graduating students in his commencement address. Predictably, he framed his remarks with the obligatory gesture toward the future and the prospective careers that awaited the young people who were celebrating the completion of their educational experience at Columbia. Bollinger explicitly signaled the salience of the events of September 11, 2001, for this generation, and he unreservedly upheld the notion of U.S. global hegemony as their special collective responsibility:

> What is the New World to look like, with the United States as the dominant military, economic, and cultural power on the planet? As a society, we are just beginning to feel our way into this New World. . . . What are our responsibilities? What should be the character of our

relationships with the other parts of the world? . . . These are the
kinds of future-shaping questions that confronted the early graduates
of Columbia, like Hamilton, Jay, and Livingston, who had to figure
out the Declaration of Independence and the Constitution, and this
is the magnitude of the questions now confronting you, and us.

Given the recent (and still fresh) scandal surrounding my remarks, furthermore, Bollinger also invoked the dilemmas of free speech, with recourse to a
rather revealing analogy, which I quote here at length:

Eight decades ago, in 1918, five Russian aliens living in New York City
were arrested for distributing leaflets praising the Russian Revolution, denouncing President Woodrow Wilson for military actions in
the First World War, and calling for a general strike among workers,
especially workers at munitions plants. The case became a landmark
in the development of our principle of freedom of speech because of
a famous opinion by Justice Oliver Wendell Holmes, Jr. Holmes had
no sympathy for the speakers, whom he called "poor and puny ano-
nymities," or their message, which he called a "creed of ignorance and
immaturity." But he argued that our Constitution has a "theory"
and that theory is that "the ultimate good desired is better reached
by free trade in ideas—that the best test of truth is the power of the
thought to get itself accepted in the competition of the market. . . ."
This means that the First Amendment should protect speech until
the point at which it "so imminently threaten[s] interference with the
lawful and pressing purposes . . . that an immediate check is required
to save the country."
But there is, and was, another view. A well-known law professor,
John Wigmore, challenged Holmes. The nation was at war, he said,
the outcome was uncertain, soldiers were dying, and munitions were
critical. Holmes was "blind to the crisis—blind to the lasting needs
of the fighter in the field, blind to the straining toil of the workers at
home, obtuse to the fearful situation which then obsessed the whole
mind and heart of the country." Here we have, he said, a "misplaced
reverence" for freedom of speech at the expense of our proper
concern for fellow citizens. And, so, to him the "moral right of the
majority to enter upon the war imports the moral right to secure

success by suppressing public agitation against the completion of the struggle."

Holmes, in fact, was on the losing side of this decision, but his dissenting views carried the day with history—with history, that is, up to now. The feelings we have that I have called familial, and that live in an extended orbit . . . including the soldiers who fight on the nation's behalf, often clash with the seemingly abstract values and principles we also embrace for social and other purposes. That was true one hundred years ago; it is true today; and it will still be true one hundred years from now. I believe Holmes had it right (although I prefer different reasons), and Wigmore did not. But that is not my point. My point is that now and in the future we will need, as much as ever and perhaps even more so, to bear in mind the underlying sources of the tensions we feel in difficult issues, to bear in mind how those before us resolved them, and to bear in mind that some hard questions never will and really never should disappear.[21]

Thus Bollinger sought to defend his position yet again, this time by assuming the posture of the pedagogue. By implication, he seemed to reaffirm with this analogy that the message of one Nicholas De Genova—an untenured assistant professor and, as such, indisputably a "poor and puny anonymity"—was one of "ignorance and immaturity." But the immediate passions of the moment, the quasi-primordial ("familial") feelings that many might extend so far as to encompass the nation's soldiers, had to be tempered by the established wisdom acquired with the long view of history: the "seemingly abstract values" of free speech and a "free trade in ideas . . . in the competition of the market" had to be protected in order to ensure "the ultimate good." These were "hard questions" and "difficult issues," Bollinger acknowledged, but he reminded his audience on this auspicious occasion that he had Oliver Wendell Holmes and the Constitution on his side.

The Imperial University: Autonomy as "Self-Policing"

This sort of self-congratulatory justification on Bollinger's part for his refusal to buckle under the tempestuous pressures of the political moment, however, was hardly the genuine and devout commitment to the freedom of speech and expression, *as such*, that it pretended to be. There was always another unspoken dimension. Shortly before Bollinger's speech to the commencement audience, the outgoing provost of Columbia, Jonathan Cole, gave a lecture on "Defending the Idea of the University in Troubled Times" (May 9, 2003), published thereafter as an essay on "defending the university post-9/11." Long esteemed as a stalwart liberal champion of academic freedom, Cole contended explicitly that "we, in defending the idea of the university, must educate the public about why we defend the faculty whose ideas offend many people." His reasoning was quite simply that those who would seek to enforce the majority opinion did not adequately comprehend that they are merely the "current beneficiaries of a predominant point of view" and that "the tables can turn quickly." Moreover, in Cole's estimation, there was a special significance to the scandal surrounding my speech. Not only did it involve a dramatically greater sheer *quantity* of adverse reaction from the general public and alumni in the form of irate e-mails, letters, and phone calls than other comparable controversies, but it also signaled a qualitative shift. The De Genova case was "important," Cole clarified, "because the type of protest took on a different character." Citing the petition from 104 U.S. congressmen demanding my dismissal, he explained, "It is deeply troubling that nearly a quarter of the members of the House of Representatives should have such a profound misunderstanding of the basic principles governing a university—in particular, the process of self-policing through application of organized skepticism that actually worked at Columbia in this case through the criticism of his speech by colleagues."[22] Cole contended that my remarks were "immediately—*immediately*—criticized as totally inappropriate by other distinguished faculty members who took part in the teach-in" (emphasis in original), and presumably it is this that he sought to depict as "organized skepticism" and robust criticism. In fact, "immediately" (i.e., during the teach-in), there was virtually no real substantive intellectual engagement or debate, merely a few very brief remarks taking exception to particular details of my speech. Be that as it may, however, the more crucial proposition here concerns what Cole had to say about "the basic principles governing a university." In this regard, he explicitly quoted the petition from Congress that noted that I had "not yet earned the promise of lifetime academic employment," namely, *tenure*. Thus what was "deeply troubling" for Cole was that so many elected officials seemed oblivious to, or irreverent toward, the fact that universities have their own internal mechanisms for "self-policing."

Indeed, it is the tenure process that serves as the most decisive disciplinary technology within academia. Cole seemed to insinuate that the bombastic sort of opportunistic meddling in the internal governance of the university, instigated by J. D. Hayworth and his Republican cohort in Congress, was an affront to basic democratic protocols with respect to academic freedom of thought and expression. We have our own ways of dealing with the likes of Nicholas De Genova, thank you, Cole seemed to reply. We can police our own ideological parameters quite efficiently enough without your clumsy and ham-fisted intrusions into the sanctity of the scholarly precinct.

For his part, Hayworth understood well enough how the imperial university works. In his original letter to Bollinger (dated April 1, 2003) urging that I be fired, Hayworth nevertheless dutifully invoked "a deep appreciation for America's tradition of academic freedom." Subsequently, however, he repeatedly clarified his position that there was indeed nothing "academic" about my intervention at the teach-in and it therefore did not deserve the protection of academic freedom: according to Hayworth, "it was hate speech, pure and simple." And while he admitted that I had a "right" to speak however I might, he contended that I did not enjoy any comparable right to employment at a prestigious university. Two weeks after initiating his campaign to have me terminated, following Bollinger's official rebuke, Hayworth derisively affirmed his sense that Columbia's officialdom was merely "[hiding] behind the highfalutin principle of 'academic freedom' and the First Amendment," insisting that for such "nutty professors" as the "mouthy" Nicholas De Genova, academic freedom was truly the last refuge of "seditious" scoundrels. More important, however, Hayworth smugly proclaimed, "I predict that when the time is right, Nicholas De Genova will be quietly denied tenure."[23]

This, after all, is almost precisely what happened. A few years after the events, when the scandal had long subsided, Columbia quietly denied me promotion in 2007 and preempted the possibility of my being considered for tenure review.[24] In the letter officially notifying me of the senior anthropology faculty's decision, the portion concerning the putative basis for the verdict reads, "It is the [tenured faculty]'s judgment that, while you have a noteworthy record of teaching and service, you have been sufficiently productive in terms of your record of publication, and you have begun to achieve outside recognition for your work, there remain substantive reservations about your scholarship. In particular, with the focus on your singly-authored book, the [tenured faculty] concluded that this did not demonstrate the high level of scholarly achievement necessary for tenure at Columbia, which is the chief criterion for promotion to Associate Professor." Notably, the singly authored book specified in the letter—one of three scholarly books that I published during the four years following the 2003 teach-in—had won two awards and was a finalist for another. Just one year after the scandal, Dirks, formerly chair of the Department of Anthropology, had been appointed executive vice president of arts and sciences at Columbia. Bollinger, for his part, went on to heavy-handedly preside over one public free speech controversy after another.

Intellectual Freedom . . . or Scandal as a Way of Life

Here, it is instructive to recall the poignant remarks of Edward Said, the Palestinian scholar who, until his death in September 2003, was indisputably Columbia's most eminent professor. Speaking in particular of universities in the Arab world, Said depicted a bleak scenario for intellectual freedom whenever the demands of nationalist politics prevailed in academia: "Alas, political conformity rather than academic excellence was often made to serve as a criterion for promotion and appointment, with the general result that timidity, a studious lack of imagination, and careful conservatism came to rule intellectual practice. Moreover, because the general atmosphere . . . has become both conspiratorial and, I am sorry to say, repressive—all in the name of national security—nationalism in the university has come to represent not freedom but accommodation, not brilliance and daring but caution and fear, not the advancement of knowledge but self-preservation."[25] Said originally delivered these remarks in South Africa in the immediate aftermath of the fall of apartheid as a cautionary tale. He was specifically concerned to identify the pitfalls of a nationalist consensus that might foreclose the possibility of free, open-ended, and critical inquiry in scholarly life. "If the academy is to be a place for the realization not of the nation but of the intellect—and that, I think, is the academy's reason for being," he asserted, "then the intellect must not be coercively held in thrall to the authority of the national identity."[26] Paradoxically, these insights may finally prove to have become even more pertinent in the imperial metropole than in those fledgling states that have variously sought to institutionalize their "national liberation" in the wake of decolonization and postcolonial sovereignty. For if every nationalism is truly a stultifying foreclosure of our imaginative political horizons, the cruel and decadent imperial national chauvinism of the United States is surely more invested than any other in suppressing any radical alternatives to the existing world order, which the U.S. nation-state has itself largely produced and seeks to continue to dominate.

At the height of the controversy over my speech, amid the mad scramble to rebuke and delegitimize me, it was Edward Said—for me, a very esteemed and precious senior colleague—who summoned me to his home to offer his support and counsel. At the time, Professor Said was nearing the end of a very long battle with leukemia and the repeated torment that resulted from its medical treatment with chemotherapy. I did not know Edward very well, but we had collaborated as part of a very small circle of Columbia professors operating as the Faculty Committee on Palestine, which had launched a campaign in fall 2002 for the divestment of Columbia University funds from firms doing business with the Israeli military. It had been Bollinger's very first baldly political act as the university's president to denounce our efforts: he had lambasted the analogy between the Israeli occupation of Palestine with South African apartheid as "offensive and grotesque."[27] A few months later, during the ongoing media firestorm over my antiwar speech, sitting in his parlor, Edward was deeply alarmed to learn that I had granted an interview to the *Chronicle of Higher Education* (which had not yet appeared in print). He was convinced that it would only serve to do more damage. (When the interview was published, the *Chronicle* unmistakably proved Edward's words to have been prophetic.) He imparted to me a most valuable and profoundly memorable lesson: "*Never* talk to the press!" Edward had earned this sage insight through hard personal experience (particularly when he was pilloried in the media for symbolically throwing a stone across the Israeli border with Lebanon). Edward's words will always remain with me as a lasting gift. He understood, as I was quickly learning, that it did not matter what I might say now any more than it mattered what I had said in the first place. The society of the spectacle in which we live is one in which the mass media opportunistically exploit, feed upon, and systematically distort every instance of scandal as an end in itself.[28] Thus the news media can never provide a genuine forum or platform for the substantive articulation or clarification of any complex intellectual, ethical, or political position, particularly any that radically disrupts or seeks to subvert the dominant order of society.

I had publicly dared to follow through the logical implications of my opposition to the invasion by explicitly affirming what for me was the only sound conclusion—that one must actually endorse the defeat of the imperialist aggressor, the United States. My remarks had been intended as an intervention into the vital debates within the antiwar movement in the United

States, beginning on my own campus. What ensued was something that no one had anticipated. In that spectacular context of unrelenting and unforgiving publicity, if university faculty across the United States had not been adequately forewarned by the Columbia president's initial insinuation that I was culpable of an unpardonable kind of extremism and had committed a sort of rhetorical treason, there followed countless subsequent verifications that my career and my life itself were imperiled as a consequence. As many of my department's international graduate students argued in my defense, my position was indeed the virtually unanimous and uncontroversial position of the *global* antiwar movement outside of the United States. It was only scandalous—indeed, unpardonable and intolerable—within the imperial university of the United States. Ironically, in his scholarly work on British colonialism in India, Dirks himself has written, "No imperial ambition can ever be unencumbered by scandal. Indeed, scandal is what empire is all about."[29]

Notes

1. George W. Bush, "Address to a Joint Session of Congress and the American People," White House Office of the Press Secretary, September 20, 2001, http://georgewbush-whitehouse.archives.gov/news/releases/2001/09/20010920-8.html.

2. Randolph S. Bourne, "The War and the Intellectuals," in *War and the Intellectuals: Collected Essays, 1915–1919* (Indianapolis, Ind.: Hackett, 1999), 4.

3. By the perversion of collective historical memory with regard to the Battle of Mogadishu, I refer of course to the nationalist revision of those events in the Hollywood film *Black Hawk Down* (2001). Remarkably, historical consciousness of what had actually happened in Somalia just one decade earlier tended to be so shallow that news reports routinely, indeed ubiquitously, framed my remarks with explicit reference to the cinematic representation of the real events. By 2003, the mythologized Hollywood version had evidently acquired a more enduring truth and significance.

4. Lee Bollinger, press statement released March 29, 2003, and posted on the Columbia University website as "President Bollinger's Statement on Recent Comments by Assistant Professor De Genova," http://www.columbia.edu/cu/news/03/03/statement_Genova.html.

5. Nicholas Dirks, e-mail reply to the *National Review*, as reproduced online and partially quoted in Margaret Hunt Gram, "De Genova Teach-In Comments Spark Fury: Bollinger, Professors Denounce His Call for 'a Million Mogadishus,'" *Columbia Spectator*, March 31, 2003, http://media.www.columbiaspectator.com/media/storage/

paper865/news/2003/03/31/News/De.Genova.TeachIn.Comments.Spark.Fury
-2036920.shtml.

6. See "Quits Columbia; Assails Trustees," *New York Times*, October 9, 1917,
http://query.nytimes.com/mem/archive-free/pdf?res=FB071FFA3A5F157A93CBA
9178BD95F438185F9. See also the derisive editorial "Columbia's Deliverance," *New
York Times*, October 10, 1917, http://query.nytimes.com/mem/archive-free/pdf?res
=9807E2DA113BE03ABC4852DFB667838C609EDE.

7. Randolph S. Bourne, "The Idea of a University," in *War and the Intellectuals:
Collected Essays, 1915–1919* (Indianapolis, Ind.: Hackett, 1999), 152–53.

8. Lee C. Bollinger, "The Idea of a University," *Wall Street Journal*, October 15, 2003,
http://www.columbia.edu/cu/president/docs/communications/2003-2004/031015
-idea-of-a-university.html.

9. Bourne, "The Idea of a University," 154; I allude to Bollinger's book, *Uninhibited, Robust, and Wide-Open: A Free Press for a New Century* (New York: Oxford
University Press, 2010).

10. Lee C. Bollinger, "Academic Freedom and the Scholarly Temperament" (Benjamin N. Cardozo lecture), *The Record of the Association of the Bar of the City of New
York* 60, no. 2 (2005): 328.

11. "Columbia ♥ Hate," *New York Post*, March 30, 2003, http://www.unitedjerusa-
lem.org/index2.asfp?id=268648&Date=3/30/2003.

12. For background, see generally the Wikipedia entries on Levy (http://
en.wikipedia.org/wiki/Mordechai_Levy) and the JDO (http://en.wikipedia.org/wiki/
Jewish_Defense_Organization). This was merely one example among many of a
conflation of my opposition to the Iraq invasion with comments that I had made in
April 2002 at a public rally at Columbia in support of the people of Palestine. Those
pro-Palestinian remarks had originally become the object of a much smaller scandal
instigated by coverage in the *New York Post* but were later revisited frequently in denunciations of my opposition to the Iraq War.

13. *New York Times* readers were informed of the Columbia University building
and room number as well as the day of the week that my undergraduate course met;
see Dan Barry, "For a Future Soldier, Life on a Liberal Campus Can Be a Battle,"
New York Times, April 2, 2003, B13, http://www.nytimes.com/2003/04/02/nyregion/
nation-war-war-home-for-future-soldier-life-liberal-campus-can-be-battle.html
?pagewanted=2.

14. An editorial in the student-run campus newspaper, the *Columbia Spectator*, had similarly made the charge that the teach-in was to be faulted for conflating "teaching" with "advocacy." In a letter to the editor (dated March 28, printed March 31, 2003, alongside my own letter responding to the coverage of my
speech), Eric Foner, a professor of history and one of the event's organizers, responded sarcastically that the editors needed to consult "a resource they seem

not to have previously encountered—the dictionary." Supplying a definition of the term *teach-in*, Foner affirmed that the essence of such an event was precisely "the combination of education and advocacy." Morris would appear to have fallen into the same misconception. See http://www.columbiaspectator.com/2003/03/31/letters-editorprofessor-qualifies-quotation-article-and-addresses-criticism.

15. In an editorial comment (dated May 2003), opening an issue of the academic journal that he founded, Scott states that "we live today, wherever we live, in a fundamental 'state of emergency'" characterized by "an ominous global project . . . taking shape with ferocious speed"; David Scott, "Editorial Comment: Our Times," *Small Axe*, no. 14 (September 2003): v. One is left to wonder what indeed Scott would consider to be appropriate as a response to an "emergency." Of course, writing in a small-circulation academic publication does afford some rhetorical license. In an essay in a later issue of the same journal, Scott writes, "We live in Dark Times. They do not favor forbearance, they do not shelter generosity, they do not encourage receptivity. They are, rather, obdurate times . . . that seem to require a new routine of silencing and assimilation, a new regime of prostration, submission, and humiliation. . . . But Dark Times . . . need people who can give us illumination—and calls them forth into the public realm. . . . They are people whose vocation of dissent enables us to glimpse some possibility in ourselves and in others hitherto obscured by the priority we give to the solace of a good night's rest"; David Scott, "Stuart Hall's Ethics," *Small Axe*, no. 17 (March 2005): 2. It is regrettable that my own vocation of dissent—whatever its shortcomings—which propelled me nonetheless irreversibly into the public realm during these dark times, never met with Scott's forbearance, generosity, or receptivity.

16. Ron Howell, "Columbia Professor Calls for 'a Million Mogadishus,'" *Newsday*, March 28, 2003; reprinted by the *Sikh Times*, http://www.sikhtimes.com/news_032703b.html.

17. Tamar Lewin, "At Columbia, Call for Death of U.S. Forces Is Denounced," *New York Times*, March 29, 2003, http://www.nytimes.com/2003/03/29/education/29PROF.html?ex=1049605200&en=b2571f49df0e2981&ei=5062&partner=GOOGLE.

18. Gram, "De Genova Teach-In Comments Spark Fury."

19. The petition was publicized online on the website of Historians against the War, on a page concerning "Civil Liberties and Academic Freedom"; full text available at http://www.historiansagainstwar.org/freedom/genova.html.

20. For considerations of length, I have opted to omit these details. A fuller discussion will appear in my forthcoming book, *Crossing the Line: A Memoir of Free Speech during Wartime*. Notably, these various objections and criticisms of my comments were apparently based entirely on the news media reportage or Morris's representations of my speech.

21. Lee Bollinger, "2003 Commencement Address," Columbia University, May

21, 2003, http://www.columbia.edu/cu/president/docs/communications/2002-2003/030521-commencement.html.

22. Jonathan R. Cole, "The Patriot Act on Campus: Defending the University Post-9/11," *Boston Review*, Summer 2003, http://bostonreview.net/BR28.3/cole.html.

23. J. D. Hayworth, "Mouthy Professor Should Be Fired," *Arizona Republic*, April 14, 2003, http://www.azcentral.com/arizonarepublic/opinions/articles/2003/04/14/20030414hayworth14.html.

24. Tenure at Columbia operates on a seven-year model, whereby there is a fifth-year review at which one may be promoted to associate professor (without tenure)—or terminated with no prospect that an ensuing legal dispute could ever result directly in a granting of tenure.

25. Edward W. Said, "Identity, Authority, and Freedom: The Potentate and the Traveler," *Transition* 54 (1991): 4–18.

26. Ibid., 13.

27. Telis Demos, "Bollinger Dismisses Faculty Petition for Israel Divestment," *Columbia Spectator*, November 8, 2002, http://www.columbiaspectator.com/2002/11/08/bollinger-dismisses-faculty-petition-israel-divestment.

28. See Guy Debord, *The Society of the Spectacle* (1967; repr. New York: Zone Books, 1995). For a fuller discussion of the so-called War on Terror in terms of the society of the spectacle, see Nicholas De Genova, "Spectacle of Terror, Spectacle of Security," in *Accumulating Insecurity: Violence and Dispossession in the Making of Everyday Life*, ed. Shelley Feldman, Charles Geisler, and Gayatri Menon (Athens: University of Georgia Press, 2011), 141–65. For a fuller discussion of the Debord's original theorization of this concept, see Nicholas De Genova, "Alien Powers: Deportable Labor and the Spectacle of Security," in *The Contested Politics of Mobility: Borderzones and Irregularity*, ed. Vicki Squire (London: Routledge, 2011), 91–115.

29. Nicholas Dirks, *The Scandal of Empire: India and the Creation of Imperial Britain* (Cambridge: Harvard University Press, 2006), 35.

13

Teaching by Candlelight

Vijay Prashad

A few years after 9/11, my dean called me for a meeting.[1] It was a pleasant enough day, a little chilly and overcast but nothing dramatic. I walked across the beautiful campus of the private liberal arts college where I teach in Connecticut. Along the way, I greeted and was greeted by students, staff, and other faculty. My geniality felt a little forced, because I was anxious about what awaited me at my walk's end. The dean and I had a fractious relationship, although it was neither personally unpleasant nor professionally threatening. This time, the dean's call had been brief and the summons immediate. His expression was grave. I sat in one of the plush chairs in an office that seemed unusually empty of the books that normally clutter the shelves of an academic room. He was polite, and he asked how I had been. Then he told me that he had received a few letters that accused me of being a communist and an agent of foreign powers. He laid out the facts in the letters and then leaned toward me, touched my wrist, and asked if the college could do anything to ensure my safety.

I was shocked. Not by the letters, for those are now frequent. My e-mail, answering machine, and mailbox are familiar with the bile of different kinds of hateful political forces. There is even a website that asks for my head—nothing tops that. What surprised me was the dean's reaction: he could care less about the actual allegations and was simply worried about my well-being. As I walked back to my office in a daze, I thought about my position of privilege. The letters that came to the dean were filled with poor English grammar, misspellings, and outrageous accusations. They could not be taken seriously in themselves, particularly when they were being hurled at a tenured professor at a private college. Of course, the same dean, before 9/11, challenged my right to teach a course on Marx, but on this score, he was upright. The braying of the multitude, even if correct, could not assail the comfortable position of the tenured professor. My academic and political freedom trumped their prejudices.

330 · VIJAY PRASHAD

Still, the idea of the "campus radical," the domesticated rabble rouser who provides the academy with its illusion of ideological diversity, concerned me. As long as the radical is in a minority, as long as the radical is unable to drive campus culture, nothing is threatened. To consider the problem of "academic freedom" and the recent assaults on individual faculty members on the terrain of their right to assert certain opinions, without an analysis of how many of us get away with what we do and say or even get our views promoted, is insufficient. Shouldn't we at least be asking who gets to even hear our views or afford to sit in our classes? Campus democracy needs to be understood on a far greater canvas than in the terms of "academic freedom." We have to be alert to the fact that it is this narrowed notion of democracy (academic freedom) that allows our intellectual institutions to get away with a great deal of undemocratic activity.

A few years ago, I came upon a survey that helped me widen the way I understand campus democracy. It comes from two social scientists (Harvard University's Neil Goss and George Mason University's Solon Simmons). Their survey of a thousand U.S. residents, conducted for the American Association of University Professors (AAUP), shows that twice the number of those asked have confidence in the U.S. academy over the White House.[2] Despite the assaults on the academy by the right wing, the public's faith in the major academic institutions remains. They have not entirely bought the view that higher education is compromised by its liberalism or radicalism. It helped of course that George W. Bush had such a low standing, so the comparison at that time might not be fair (I wonder what people would say now, with Barack Obama in the Oval Office). When asked to name the biggest problem facing higher education, a plurality (42.8 percent) pointed to "the high cost of college tuition," while 17 percent worried about "binge drinking by college students." Only a small number focused on the issue of "political bias in the classroom" (8.2 percent) and "incompetent professors" (5 percent).[3] Add the latter together and you get more people worried about campus larceny and debauchery than about either political indoctrination or incompetence.

The question of affordability of higher education is salient to any discussion of academic freedom. A survey from 2000 of 850 U.S. residents found that less than a tenth of adults who enjoy a family income of between $30,000 and $75,000 believe that college education is affordable. Those who make less than $30,000 fear that their children won't be able to go to college, and those who make more than $75,000 also have their misgivings about college costs.[4]

A 2005 study by the College Board found that both public and private colleges are increasingly unaffordable to all U.S. residents, but of course among the lowest income earners and wealth holders, the burden is greatest (at public two-year colleges, cost of attendance sucks up more than a third of the family income for those in the lowest family income quartile).[5] These high prices come at a time when the buying power of family incomes has declined and when outright grants given to those who need it have been replaced by merit-driven (public and private) loans. Yet there seems to be no letup in the desire of young people to go to college (in October 2005, almost 70 percent of high school graduates went to some kind of college).[6]

The credit crunch since 2007 and its attendant financial crisis have simply deepened a problem that had already revealed itself. The cost of college tuition has risen from 23 percent of median annual incomes in 2001 to 38 percent in 2010, following a longer-term trend of college cost increases (since 1983, the average cost of college rose by three times the rate of inflation). Colleges can no longer afford to provide generous financial aid packages. A Bain & Company and Sterling Partners study looked at the books of U.S. colleges and found the following: "Institutions have become overleveraged. Their long-term debt is increasing at an average rate of approximately 12 percent per year, and their average annual interest expense is growing at almost twice the rate of their instruction-related expense. In addition to growing debt, administrative and student services costs are growing faster than instructional costs. And fixed costs and overhead consume a growing share of the pie."[7] To pay for these inflated costs, students and parents have been taking out vast amounts of debt. This money has been borrowed from private lenders and the government. Private money dropped from $20 billion just before the recession to $6 billion in 2011. Most students cannot afford to pay tuition. Most colleges cannot afford to give financial aid to all their students. Therefore, students who want to go to college have to carry loans and go into debt. It is this tendency that has driven the amount of student debt to over $1 trillion greater than the volume of credit card debt.

Campuses, therefore, are now home to students whose families and whose own labor is taxed highly to pay for their education. The increased level of student indebtedness and the pressure to work during college years structure the experiences of students during their college years. A U.S. congressional study found that by the 1990s, when the stock market boomed and the good times rolled for the well-off, college debt spiraled out of control. Between 1992 and 1999, annual borrowing for students at four-year public colleges rose by 65 percent, from $1,800 to $3,000. This meant that the average debt for a four-year cycle rose in this period to $15,000. With this burden, the congressional study noted, "students from low income families are often unable to support loans after graduation."[8]

If this is the case at public schools, it is not dissimilar at private schools (the cutback in federal aid to public schools is now matched by the decline in stock market–held endowments at most private schools). Three-quarters of students work, and most of them do so not to support their excesses but to get by; the time spent on the job adversely affects their grades.[9] Among working-class students, the problem is acute. A large number (29 percent) work more than thirty-five hours a week, and of them a majority (53 percent) fail to graduate.[10]

College degrees still provide a boost to the earning power of workers. Young people are driven to college by a desire to learn and by the knowledge that today's college degree is worth the price of yesterday's high school diploma. This flow is unchecked, and it is what makes the higher education market inelastic. Prices skyrocket, and the customers continue to throng at the door. There is little choice when the job offerings are fewer. As jobless growth overcomes the economy, and as nontradable services are the only boom sector in the U.S. job market, the anxiety about getting paid after laying out a large investment increases. The pressure on students to curtail their imagination during their college years is immense. Find a major that guarantees a good job and spend your time on campus doing as many internships as possible to grease your way into the narrowest of doorways that lead to corporate success. For the neoliberal academy, this is the student's stairway to heaven.

The freedom of the student to enjoy the world of ideas and to seek solutions to planetary problems and opportunities is narrowed. Where is the space for the students to enjoy the ideological and intellectual freedom necessary for critical thought and expression? All the talk about a common core curriculum for a liberal student body is anachronistic and unaware of the neoliberal reality that tears into the students' ability to think outside their indebtedness. This is not to say that our students are always worried about debt and unable to be creative and bold with their ideas. Rather, the problem of debt in the context of jobless growth inhibits all but the most intellectually driven students, and this debt consciousness contributes to the nihilism felt by many toward our social institutions (the binge drinking is a symptom of the problem, not a problem sui generis).

What does all this have to do with academic freedom? The debate over the political commitments and views of the faculty is a red herring. It ignores the academy's main problem with contemporary higher education: the tendency for higher education to become increasingly vocational and less intellectual. This is not the fault of the student or of television or other such cultural shifts alone, but it is the necessary consequence of the way "education" has become one more capital input into the worker commodity. The freedom of our students to think is not encroached upon by this or that individual faculty member but by increased costs for higher education, a lack of federal support for these costs, and the fears of joblessness and indebtedness associated with both these high costs and the decreased number of lucrative careers in the offing. Helen Lowery of Boston University put it bluntly, "I really want to work in advocacy law," she told the *Christian Science Monitor*, "but from a practical perspective that's not going to happen. I just won't be able to pay back my loans."[11] No wonder the survey found a plurality worried more about college tuition than about the academic freedom of the faculty. The freedom to think is encroached upon by the encumbrances of money. Lowrey worried about this before the current financial crisis. It is worse now.

A previous president of my college had the indelicacy to use current corporate jargon when speaking to the faculty. I learnt from him the term "blue skying" (thinking outside material constraints), and he once tried to get me to go with him on a fund-raising junket to Europe ("Wheels-up time is 9 a.m.," he said in tune with my mumbled demur). He wore corporate blue suits and walked around with a posse of vice presidents, all dressed in corporate livery, each brandishing a folder. They looked like a militia, strolling around the campus, measuring the fat, eagerly, hungrily cutting, cutting, cutting—and yet, spending, spending, spending on noncurricular hardware. It is a tribute to the public university that this president, whose spending spree at my private colleges, was hauled up when he presided over not one but two public universities. Quite forthright, he would defend his private spending as the bait to draw in large donations at the same time as he cut essential budgets on the academic side.

Nothing about this president and his gang is unique. They are now part of the normal fabric of U.S. higher education. Indeed, the campus is no longer an "ivory tower" or a "city on the hill." It more closely resembles that other major culture-creating institution: the U.S. corporation. Income inequality (between the president and the janitor) is stark, but this is only the most vulgar instance of the convergence of academic and corporate cultures. The assault on campus unions that try to provide a living wage for the workers, on graduate student unions that try to get a wage for indentured teachers, on adjuncts who enjoy no security of tenure, and so on *teaches* our students that the corporate free market culture is acceptable and that it is rational. As Paul Lauter wrote in 2002, "The free market ideology being taught at US universities has to do with winning the hearts and minds of young Americans to the fantasy that their interests are at one with those of [corporate] executives. Such lessons are reinforced within the multiplying classrooms devoted to promoting enterprise, marginalizing labor, submerging the realities of social-class disparity, and above all, promoting the underlying ideological tenet of free market capitalism: individualism."[12]

Elsewhere, Lauter argues that what the university *teaches* in its very structure is the culture of the dominant classes: the president is ensured a sweet retirement package while the faculty is left with bleak options; a university is lauded for its biomedical discoveries as the population that surrounds it suffers from medical ills untreated for lack of health insurance and a health care infrastructure; a college pays its "adjunct" teaching staff far below a reasonable wage and justifies this based on pleasant sounding terms like "flex time"; and the university extends its dominion over the neighborhood through gentrification and eminent domain.[13] This culture of the dominant class is a culture of hierarchy. Those who are in the right schools are able to aspire to upward mobility, while others can still hope for something better than their origins. Debt becomes the necessary price to pay for the rewards of a system that is already on display on the campus.

Higher education and K–12 are one of the five major sites for the reproduction of U.S. culture (the others being the state, the military, the corporation [including the media], and religious institutions). Because the academy trains young minds when they are at their most vulnerable, the stakes at this site are immense. That such a large section of the U.S. public goes through the higher education system makes management of this site so central to the worries of the dominant class. To compound these objective fears are the nature of the personnel who staff higher education. An unpredictable fragment of the "new class," the professional and managerial sector, staffs the academy. Cultural critic Michael Denning suggests that this fragment of the "new class" betrays ambivalence between the flanks of capital and labor. Such uncertainty by the cultural authors of so powerful an institution makes the stakes of social control "very great indeed."[14]

Since the late nineteenth century, the "new class" within the academy has periodically faced disciplinary pressures from the dominant class. There is a continuous line of suppression that runs from the expulsion of Populist social scientists in the 1890s to the current assault on critical intellectuals. This struggle is over the immense cultural resources of the academy and how they are deployed for the intellectual and ethical reproduction of the population. Two influential and articulate groups produce in different measures and in separate registers the assault on the "new class." In 1953, the philosopher Sidney Hook called the first group the "cultural vigilantes," among whom he included "political demagogues in *both* political parties, religious fundamentalists in both Catholic and Protestant denominations, and some zealots and marginal types in some patriotic organizations. To these must be added certain lobbyists and advertisers who wish to discount the principles of democratic socialism, the New Deal, the Welfare State . . . because the economic and social interests they represent would be adversely affected were these principles carried out."[15] Sociologically, Hook's description fits our time, with characters like David Horowitz and his now eponymous center fitting the bill of the "zealots and marginal types," while his enablers, such as former Colorado governor Bill Owens (Republican) and former Colorado state senator Bob Hagedorn (Democrat), donning the robes of the "political demagogues." The cultural vigilantes draw on a widespread discontent with class hierarchy by painting the institutions of higher education as bastions of elitism; this is their unique ability to draw on mass sentiment and distort popular disgust at hierarchy against this petty bourgeois fragment rather than against bourgeois society and capitalism in general. Many intellectuals do us no favors by adopting the mandarin robes of high culture and setting us apart from the lives and labors of working people. Most of our anxiety about the assault on the "new class" is derived from the populism of the cultural vigilantes and on their proximity to sections of state power. For politicians, the cry against radicals in the ivory tower is a much cheaper way to ally mass concern over the inability of many to pay for college than it is to actually create meaningful public policy that opens the doors of higher education to everyone. David Horowitz, for instance, has no plan to address the escalation of costs and tuition. It is far easier for the vigilantes to bemoan elitism and radicalism than actually address the core apprehensions of the public. And because of their ability to influence populist lawmakers who also have no agenda for popular discontent apart from symbolic issues, they are able to make mayhem at public institutions (such as for Ward Churchill at the

University of Colorado and Kevin Barrett at the University of Wisconsin). Part of the assault seems calculated with the desire to bash public institutions and to promote the free market private model favored by the political demagogues. My liberal New England private college is only temporarily afloat; the hard rocks of financial distress call out like the sirens as we drift toward them inexorably.[16]

The second group, to upend Sidney Hook, comprises the sanctimonious liberals. These are the guardians of higher education who invoke high-minded principles such as "academic freedom" when it suits them and to protect those whom it deems worthy at a certain time. During the McCarthy era, when the vigilantes raised the question of the loyalty of the faculty, it was the liberals who fired them or edged them out on the basis of "academic freedom." An exemplary case comes to us from the University of Washington. On January 22, 1949, the university fired three professors for their relationship with the Communist Party. Dr. Raymond B. Allen, the university's president, defended the action as one that did not abridge the policy of "academic freedom." On the contrary, the removal of the Communists would only strengthen the principle. Communists, Allen wrote a few months later, are not free because they are enslaved "to immutable dogma and to a clandestine organization masquerading as a political party." By joining the legal Communist Party, or being affiliated to it in any way, the teacher has "abdicated control over intellectual life." The classroom, Allen wrote, is a "chapel of democracy," and so the only teacher who can be allowed into this chapel must be a "free seeker after truth." Indeed, "as the priests of the temple of education, members of the teaching profession have a sacred duty to remove from their ranks the false and robot prophets of Communism or any other doctrine of slavery that seeks to be in, but never of, our traditions of freedom."[17] Hook, who became the leading advocate of anticommunism in the academy, sinisterly wrote of the need for "ethical hygiene" to expunge the profession of Communists.[18]

Allen and other university presidents produced a high-minded defense of their assault on certain academics.[19] Their point is simple: to be worthy of the protections of "academic freedom," the faculty member must be an open-minded seeker of the truth and not a dogmatic adherent to received wisdom. Such a principle, of course, immediately excludes anyone who has a religious faith and whose views are mediated through clerical institutions. Because the principle appeared so shallow, the philosopher Willis Moore wrote, "Whatever the ostensible goal of the early stages of this restrictive movement, its later intent was the achievement of a settled conservative orthodoxy in the political, economic, and general social opinion of America." The onslaught within the culture industries (including the academy), Moore continued, is designed to undermine "the more humane, idealistic and internationalistic tendencies of the past few decades."[20]

Academic freedom, as Allen bluntly put it, is only to be granted to the intellectual who adopts a solitary pursuit of truth. Anyone who is associated with any organized political change has, by this logic, abdicated his or her intellectual suspicion: the moment you close analysis and act, you have ceased to enjoy the protections of academic freedom. But even this is a selective use of a principle, because it does not apply, as I suggested earlier, to those who strive for change based on certain theological or even political principles (such as anticommunism). Moore, less enamored by liberal anticommunism, indicates that the crusade on campus was against ideologies and movements that fostered antisystemic change. "Free thinkers" are welcomed if they are gadflies who do not pose a challenge to the system, or if, despite their own political predilections, they worked in the arena of the sciences (where expertise shielded them from the aggression of the political commissars).[21]

Our liberal institutions operate with a general adherence to a concept of academic freedom that is borrowed from John Stuart Mills's 1859 *On Liberty*, where the utilitarian and East India Company official argued that contrary opinions are important, not for themselves, but because they enable society to check its truths and to ensure that social norms are not in error. We tolerate the campus radical as long as he or she is simply a foil for the correctness of liberal precepts and as long as he or she does not indulge in any attempt to move a transformative political agenda on the campus culture. This impoverished idea of freedom is valuable for a class society that sees a critique of itself as manageable as its Other, as long as it is constrained. Allen's vulgar statements are not far from the generosity of Mill.

These are not arcane ideas. A majority of those surveyed by the AAUP in 2006 (62.6 percent) said it was acceptable for the university to "dismiss professors who join radical political organizations like the communist party." A small number of people (57 percent) felt that "there's no room in the university for professors who defend the actions of Islamic militants." In this same pool, a majority (61.5 percent) said it was acceptable for a professor to oppose the Iraq War and to "express anti-war views in the classroom."[22] The same dean that worried for my safety challenged my right to teach a

Marxist class on *Capital*, because, in his words, "that book is responsible for genocide" (and what about the Bible?). On August 6, 2012, the California legislature passed HR 35 ("Relative to Anti-Semitism"), which defined any criticism of Israel as "anti-Semitism" and thereby banned such criticism on pain of censure in state-funded educational institutions. As the late writer Alexander Cockburn put it, "Anti-Semitism has become like a flit gun to squirt at every inconvenient fly on the window pane." Anti-Semite, Islamic militant, Communist—once the tar brush of gentility paints such words on the door of a faculty member, regardless of their actual opinions, the game is over for that person.

It is a sign of our times that the academic left has taken to the principle of academic freedom, not only to defend it against the opportunistic assault of the political right, but also as a shelter for our opinions. What happened to Ward Churchill and what happens to countless faculty who, for example, take the side of campus workers, attempt to explain U.S. imperialism's blowback, or fight against the indignity of campus culture for so-called minorities is to be expected. The academic left cannot rely on institutional protection for our adversarial positions, but then again, being embattled and disorganized, this is to be anticipated. When we take positions that challenge the status quo ideology and institutions, particularly in a time of endless war, we have to find some means to defend our right to those positions. Given the prejudice of academic freedom to protect our individual right to speak, we tend to coast into that safe harbor. This becomes more convenient than defending our right to an opinion based on the social force of the ideas—a defense that is not covered by the institutionally validated horizon of academic freedom. Our political weakness has resulted in agoraphobia. The struggle over "academic freedom," as it is generally constituted, is more than that of a principle, but it is over ideas. The principle is against the creation of the very social force that would allow our ideas to have cultural valence. That is what makes its defense insufficient.

Alongside a defense of academic freedom, affirmative action, and other such liberal principles, it is imperative that teachers push for a genuine campus democracy. This includes all that we already do, such as give support for the creation of a culture of solidarity over a culture of hierarchy on campus. Unions, collaborative work among students, and enriched intellectual debates over contentious issues: all these are fundamental. But none of these are sufficient without the insistence that higher education be a free public good (alongside free preschool). The debate over affirmative action, for instance, is impoverished because all sides accept the neoclassical assumption that educational access is a matter of scarcity and resource allocation. Since there are not enough seats, the colleges have to make some choices of whom to accept. But what if there were enough seats nationwide for all those who wanted to go to college and what if no one had to compete with anyone else for grants? Colleges would still have to choose their own student body based on a variety of contested factors, but at the very least the applicants would not be barred from entry into campus because of a lack of space. In other words, racism and antiracism are not solved by the displacement of neoclassical constraints, but the debate over prejudice will be healthier if it does not occlude the structural problems of scarcity driven by capitalism, which is itself inherently profit-centered and social Darwinist. If students could come to college on tax money, it would allow them to spend time on ideas and to depart into the world without the albatross of student debt. Their freedom would be greatly enhanced by such a measure.

The call for free higher education is not at all idealistic or utopian. Of the main advanced industrial countries (the twenty-four OECD states), in only three do public funds cover less than half the costs for college (Japan, South Korea, and the United States). In most of these states, government money accounts for between 70 percent and 90 percent of college costs (Austria, Czech Republic, Denmark, France, Germany, Hungary, Iceland, Ireland, Italy, Mexico, Netherlands, Norway, Portugal, Spain, Sweden, and Turkey). The governments of Australia, Canada, and the United Kingdom contribute between 55 percent and 70 percent of the college bills.[23] As the Labor Institute's Sharon Szymanski found, "the tuition and fees at all public degree granting institutions is approximately $24.7 billion. This is a relatively small amount, equal to approximately 1.3 percent of current federal budgets."[24] A readjustment of military expenditure or corporate tax breaks could easily account for this money. The $25 billion is a small proportion of the cost of the wars ($8 trillion since 9/11) and of corporate tax breaks (of which, deferral on foreign income is by itself $1 trillion). The cost of higher education is a fraction of the $1.35 trillion to $3 trillion, which is the range of the cost of the Bush and Obama tax cuts—so much hidden money, so much enforced austerity. Instead, colleges raise their fees and tuition and make higher education increasingly undemocratic. The campaign for free higher education needs traction, and it needs to be combined with the struggles for affirmative action and for academic freedom.[25] In these scoundrel times, we need more of some things, less of others: more imagination, more resources, and more solidarity; less vigilantism, less militarism, and less hierarchy.

Notes

Thanks to Malini Johar Schueller and Ashley Dawson for their persistent patience; Paul Lauter for reading this chapter (which draws on many of his ideas); Amitava Kumar for getting me to think seriously about our profession in the first instance and for a close read of this chapter; Preston Smith for introducing me to the Campaign for Free Higher Education; the work of Cary Nelson, Evan Watkins, Marc Bousquet, and the people at *Workplace: A Journal for Academic Labor* on the vocationalization of the university; and to Elisabeth Armstrong for pushing me in directions I didn't even know existed. This chapter developed out of a keynote address to the Society of American Law Teachers Conference on "Academic Freedom and Teaching Activism in the Post 9/11 World," Suffolk University Law School, Boston, Massachusetts, September 9, 2006. Thanks to Tayyab Mahmud and Eileen Kaufman for their generosity. The essay was first published in *Social Text* in spring 2007. It has been revised for this volume.

1. That dean is now gone and so is the president who appears later in the chapter. I now work under a new dean and president, both of whom are aware of the dialectic that constrains and drives academic work in our age.

2. Neil Gross and Solon Simmons, "Americans' Views of Political Bias in the Academy and Academic Freedom" (working paper, May 22, 2006), 4. This study was commissioned by the American Association of University Professors and it can be downloaded from their website.

3. Gross and Simmons, "Americans' Views of Political Bias," 10–11.

4. S. O. Ikenberry and T. W. Hartle, *Taking Stock: How Americans Judge Quality, Affordability and Leadership at U.S. Colleges and Universities* (Washington, DC: American Council on Education, 2001), 34–35; Laura W. Perna and Chungyan Li, "College Affordability: Implications for College Opportunity," *NASFAA Journal of Student Financial Aid* 36 (2006): 8.

5. College Board, *Trends in College Pricing* (Washington, DC: College Board, 2005), quoted in Perna and Li, "College Affordability," 17.

6. Bureau of Labor Statistics, *College Enrollment and Work Activity of High School Graduates* (Washington, DC: Author, 2006).

7. Jeff Denneen and Tom Dretler, *The Financially Sustainable University* (Boston: Bain and Sterling Partners, 2012), 3.

8. Advisory Committee on Student Financial Assistance, *Empty Promises: The Myth of College Access in America: A Report of the Advisory Committee on Student Financial Assistance* (Washington, DC: Author, 2002), 11–13.

9. Ibid., 11; Tracey King and Ellynne Bannon, *At What Cost? The Price That*

Working Students Pay for a College Education (Washington, DC: Public Interest Research Group, 2002), 2–3.

10. Advisory Committee on Student Financial Assistance, *Access Denied: Restoring the Nation's Commitment to Equal Educational Opportunity* (Washington, DC: Author, 2001), 11.

11. Chris Gaylord, "For Graduates, Student Loans Turn into an Albatross," *Christian Science Monitor*, May 17, 2006; Janet Kidd Stewart covers the parents' point of view in "College's Major Dilemma: For Love or Money," *Chicago Tribune*, November 6, 2005.

12. Paul Lauter, "From Adelphi to Enron," *Academe* 88 (2002).

13. Paul Lauter, "Content, Culture, Character," *Works and Days 41/42* 21 (2003).

14. Michael Denning, *Culture in the Age of Three Worlds* (London: Verso, 2004), 134.

15. Sidney Hook, *Heresy, Yes, Conspiracy, No* (New York: John Day, 1953), 11.

16. This is the view of James F. Jones Jr., "To Reweave the Helices: Trinity's DNA by Our Two Hundredth Birthday. A White Paper Written for the Faculty Retreat" (Hartford: Trinity College, 2011).

17. Raymond B. Allen, "Communists Should Not Teach in American Colleges," *Educational Forum* 13, no. 4 (May 1949). The context of the story is well summarized in Ellen W. Schrecker, *No Ivory Tower: McCarthyism and the Universities* (New York: Oxford University Press, 1986), 94–112.

18. Schrecker, *No Ivory Tower*, 107.

19. For a range of views, mostly in favor of curtailment of communists, see Benjamin Fine, "Majority of College Presidents Are Opposed to Keeping Communists on their Staffs," *New York Times*, January 30, 1949.

20. Willis Moore, "Causal Factors in the Current Attack on Education," *AAUP Bulletin* 41 (1955): 623–24.

21. These are the views of Noam Chomsky, R. C. Lewontin, and Ray Siever, collected in *The Cold War and the University: Toward an Intellectual History of the Postwar Years* (New York: New Press, 1997).

22. Gross and Simmons, "Americans' Views of Political Bias," 14.

23. Sharon Szymanski, "Free for All: Free Tuition at All Public Colleges and Universities for Students Who Meet Admission Standards" (working paper, Debs-Jones-Douglass Institute, Labor Institute, and PACE member, New York City, Local 1–149, 2002), 29.

24. Szymanski, "Free for All," 29.

25. Information on the campaign is available at http://www.freehighered.org. For an excellent call for free higher education, see Preston Smith II and Sharon Szymanski, "Why Political Scientists Should Support Free Public Higher Education," *PS: Political Science and Politics*, October 2003, 699–703.

14

UCOP versus R. Dominguez: The FBI Interview

A One-Act Play á la Jean Genet

Ricardo Dominguez

Almost five years ago, Electronic Disturbance Theater (EDT) 2.0/b.a.n.g. lab released the first iteration of the Transborder Immigrant Tool (TBT), a mobile-phone technology that provides poetry to immigrants crossing the U.S.–Mexico border while leading them to water caches in the Southern California desert. In 2010, the project caused a firestorm of controversy on the American political scene, and the artists of EDT/b.a.n.g. lab were investigated by three Republican congressmen and the University of California, San Diego (UCSD), where Ricardo Dominguez, cofounder of EDT (with Brett Stalbaum) and principal investigator of b.a.n.g. lab, is an associate professor in the visual arts department.

TBT was already under investigation starting on January 11, 2010, by UCSD (this included the entire group of artists working on it: Brett Stalbaum, Micha Cardenas, Dr. Amy Sara Carroll [University of Michigan], and Elle Mehrmand). Then Ricardo Dominguez came under investigation for the virtual sit-in performance against the University of California Office of the President (UCOP) on March 4 (against students' fees in the UC system and the dismantling of educational support for K–12 across California). That was then followed by an investigation by the FBI Office of Cybercrimes. The FBI was seeking to frame the performance as a federal violation, a cybercrime, based on UCOP stating that they lost $5,600 because of the disturbance. It is important to know that the cost had to be over $5,000 for it to be a crime, so UCOP tacked on $600 to push the performance into cybercrime territory.

UCSD and UC students, faculty, and labor unions joined national and international groups and organizations to protest the investigations, and the attempt to de-tenure Dominguez, via protest marches, petitions, and letters of support. A letter of support was sent by the UC Multi-Campus Research

Group (MRG) in International Performance and Culture to Mark Yudof, president of the UC system on Wednesday, April 7, 2010:

Letter from Core Members of the UC MRG in
International Culture and Performance

Dear President Yudof, Chancellor Fox, SVC Drake,
and other concerned parties:

We, the members of the UC Multi-Campus Research Group in International Performance and Culture, write in support of Ricardo Dominguez (Associate Professor, Visual Arts, UCSD) and his collaborators at b.a.n.g. lab. We have recently heard disturbing news about Professor Dominguez's tenure being placed under review in response to several of his recent research and performance projects, and we are deeply concerned about such developments. Professor Dominguez is an internationally renowned performance artist and researcher whose work has been curated and anthologized in a wide range of venues; he is known as an exemplary artist, scholar, and teacher, and we count ourselves fortunate to have him as a colleague within the UC system. We write to provide some disciplinary context for his work, which we hope will encourage you to abandon any potential efforts to revoke his tenure.

We understand the projects in question to be:

(1) Professor Dominguez's participation in the inter-institutional project "Transborder Immigrant Tool"; and

(2) Professor Dominguez's participation in a virtual sit-in on the UCOP web site as part of the collective actions taken on March 4, 2010 in response to the current crises facing public higher education in California.

The Transborder Immigrant Tool is an innovative project that cross-cuts the technology and the arts. Using low-cost and recycled mobile phones loaded with mapping software, the project aims to reduce deaths and serious illnesses for those traveling through California's deserts. Although this project has been met with some controversy in the press, we see this work as being imminently ethical and, perhaps just as importantly, a serious and innovative extension of precedents in performance research that have similarly aimed to pose questions about structural inequality, citizenship and civility, and humanitarianism—questions that have occupied many different performance traditions through the 20th and 21st centuries, if not earlier. Dominguez's work, in this regard, is both part of a longer disciplinary tradition in the visual arts and, importantly for the UC, an innovative and forward-thinking extension of these queries to the problems and conditions that define our contemporary age.

It is also important to note, despite sensationalist media reports to the contrary, that the Transborder Immigrant Tool has not as yet been used by anyone unaffiliated with b.a.n.g. lab. It is still in development, with input from non-profit border organizations and the Border Patrol. We understand that UCSD has received complaints from several members of the US Congress who have unfortunately been misinformed about the project's scope, and who are attempting to intervene into the practice of academic and artistic freedom. As scholars and artists who have chosen to work in the context of a public institution in the interest of the "greater good," we find such interventions from political representatives into university research projects to be offensive, unethical, and in breach of their responsibilities as elected leaders.

We also understand that information about Professor Dominguez's work with the Transborder Immigrant Tool has been included with all of his professional reviews at UCSD, only now (after the receipt of letters from members of Congress) to be investigated. We are deeply concerned that what might, in other disciplines, be called the "results" of a research project could be used retroactively to question that project's basis. We trust that you, too, will respect the necessary integrity of scholarly and artistic research by refusing to bend to political pressure and by continuing to support the vibrant, innovative, forward-thinking, and ethical research program of Professor Dominguez and b.a.n.g. lab.

The March 4 "Virtual Sit-In" on the UCOP.edu website, similarly, represents an innovative approach to political action and civil disobedience. It is not, as some reports have attempted to assert, the equivalent of a "Distributed Denial of Service" (DDOS) attack, for several reasons: First, unlike all DDOS attacks, a virtual sit-in is transparent. This means that all participants actively accept the terms of the sit in; the creators of the sit-in are openly identified; and only computers used by specific individuals are involved. (DDOS attacks, on the other hand, use anonymous software programs and filters to disguise the creators and participants.)

Second, like "real world" (embodied) sit-ins, a virtual sit-in is part of a broader set of cultural and political actions directed toward a specific, non-essential site with a specific message in mind. It is also limited in time and scope, precisely like a performance, with a set beginning and ending. The purpose of a virtual sit-in is to participate in a broader collective social action (in this case, March 4), transparently, in the interest of conveying the sentiments of a collective social body.

Finally, given the primary purpose of public universities, we would hope that the UC would welcome the critical questions raised by a virtual sit-in about collectivity, about accessibility, about the important role universities play in technological and artistic innovation in a time when these cherished values are so severely under threat by diminishing state support. We see the March 4 virtual sit-in as an important extension of the many other collective actions engaged on March 4, pedagogically as well as artistically instructive.

In short: Ricardo Dominguez is at the very vanguard of performance art traditions, and we count ourselves extremely fortunate to count him as a colleague. His international reputation as an innovative artist and scholar strengthens the UC's position as a leader in the fields of theater/performance and the visual arts. We trust that the values of academic and artistic freedom that define the university's role in public service will convince you to abandon attempts to revoke his tenure.

Sincerely,

Patrick Anderson
Assistant Professor Department of Communication
Affiliated Faculty
Critical Gender Studies
Affiliated Faculty, Ethnic Studies
University of California, San Diego
9500 Gilman Drive #0503
La Jolla, CA 92093-0503

Prelude

(*Black screen. Soft whispers that build into a chorus-gone-chora*):

Dear All,

Yudof has responded (with a long list of cc's, excluding Ricardo) to the letter of support for Ricardo from the MRG in International Performance and Culture. The MRG letter was used as the basis for the online petition (which currently has nearly 2,500 endorsements). I'm attaching his response below. It seems clear that the virtual sit-in/Denial of Service distinction is going to be key in this "investigation"; to that end, I wonder if some of us might start working on developing a different view of the legal, aesthetic, and scholarly precedents than the strict constructionist interpretation of policy that the administration will no doubt champion. We might, for example, strategically deploy literalism to confront literalism itself: e.g. in the policy cited by Yudof (below), how do we measure "excessive strain" and "interference" in the context of pedagogy, activism designed to promote public education, and artistic endeavors, all of which are presumably in line with university goals (and thus not "interference") and of a scale in line with other March 4 activities (and thus not "excessive"); and/or: how might a virtual sit-in actually promote access to (and thus not "impede availability of") "university communications services" for students studying civil disobedience? I unfortunately cannot make this Wednesday's meeting (I teach Wednesday evenings), but I'd be happy to work on this with others during other times.

Patrick Anderson

(*The screen goes black*).

Scene One

(*The light turns on slowly; we are in middle of a high-tech incubator*).
(*FBI agents confront Ricardo Dominguez, who is walking out of his office at CALIT2/UCSD on September 17, 2010, at 11:00 a.m. They are wearing heavy fur-lined coats, hats, and holding small placards that say, "We are your friends." They interview Dominguez.*)

FBI: No, no, stay. Do not move. We know you are an artist. We like having you around. As for new media art, we are all for it! (*They* *keep their hats and coats on and bow to a copy of* Mirror of Production *and slowly kiss its footnotes.*)

UCOP: (*Runs into the office and slams the door and grabs one of the FBI agent's hands*). Put your hand here. (*Places the agent's hand on a UCOP server.*) We are all tense. We are all wrought up. We knew you were on your way, which meant we were in danger. We waited for you all a-tremble in the shadows . . . while perfuming our server. . . . Oh! Do you want to hold our server?

FBI: (*The FBI agents smile and hum for little while until UCOP feels better. Then they begin to speak while pretending to hit an invisible tennis ball back and forth.*) I am Special Agent Todd Walbridge. I spend most of my life here: 9797 Aero Drive San Diego, CA 92123. I like to use my phone. Please call me any time you would like to. We have an operator on call 24/7: Phone 858-565-1255. Or you can always fax us. We like a good fax: 858-499-7356. (*The second FBI agent speaks.*) Hi! I am FBI Special Agent Edward O. Cabral from the Cyber Investigation Division and you can reach me at the same phone number, and you can also fax at the same number as well. Can we give you our cards? They are really nice. Oh, are you recording us?

Ricardo: (*Trying to eat his lunch while watching* Glee *on his smarty phone.*) No. Are you recording me?

FBI: (*They are both speaking rather loudly into their watches.*) No. Well, sometimes. But we are definitely not recording this conversation now.

Ricardo: (*Still trying to eat his lunch and still watching* Glee.) You should both speak to the NSA research lab right above me. They're working on new forms of warrantless wireless capture systems—so I can't guarantee that the NSA is not listening to us.

FBI: (*Smile at one another and continue to play tennis.*)

UCOP: (*Pops up and points at Ricardo Dominguez.*) Well, yes or no, is there a simulation happening here. . . . ?

Ricardo: (*Still trying to eat his lunch and still watching Glee.*) Well, yes and no. A "minor simulation" that feels very "real" in a social technological sense of effective affects within and without our current postcontemporary networks.

FBI: (*Stop playing tennis and sit down. UCOP plops down on the lap of FBI Agent Todd.*) We just want to obey our superior and respond to the complaint by UCOP. And try to understand the true nature of the issues. What really is the case? Did you or didn't you take down the UCOP website?

Ricardo: (*Stops watching* Glee.) Are you going to charge me with a crime and arrest me right now? Do I need to ask you for a search warrant? Should I contact my lawyers right now? Should new media art be something nice to look at? Should most people on the planet just be named Bob? It would make identification issues much easier.

FBI: (*They take out notepads and pencils. UCOP has now fallen asleep.*) No. We would just like to know more about your art and research. We are thinking of taking classes here at UCSD. Tell us about your research, Professor Dominguez.

Ricardo: (*Picks up an essay by Dr. Jill Lane, New York University, titled "Digital Zapatistas," and reads.*) "Ricardo Dominguez, co-founder of the Electronic Disturbance Theater (EDT), notes the range of metaphors that have until now informed our imagination of cybernetic space: 'frontier, castle, real estate, rhizome, hive, matrix, virus, network'. Because cyberspace is by definition a discursive space, the imposition of any one metaphor has a performative effect on the cyberreality it describes, turning cyberspace into the domain of private ownership, or frontier outposts, or rhizomatic community. 'Each map,' says Dominguez, 'creates a different line of flight, a different form of security, and a different pocket of resistance'. Each map enables and effaces certain kinds of travel and their attendant social infrastructure: ports of entry and exit, laws of access, and rights of passage." (*TDR* 47, no. 2 [Summer 2003]: 129–44. Posted Online March 13, 2006.)

FBI: (*Looking at a copy of the* Orestia *by Aeschylus.*) Has UCSD or UCOP ever attempted to end your art practice or research at any point between 2005 and 2010?

Ricardo: (*Pointing to a picture of himself and President Mark G. Yudof standing together in front of a local carousel.*) No. Never. I have received full support, funding, and awards, and I have earned tenure in part for this work and it is the core reason that I was hired. I was hired to expand the language and practice of electronic civil disobedience, hacktivism, tactical disturbances, the performative matrix, and the development of new media aesthetics and practices under the sign of the post-contemporary-as-research.

FBI: (*Each handing Dominguez's FBI file to the other and weighing it in their hands.*) You seem to be doing a good job developing your research and your art practice. You know we both participated in a number of sit-ins as students. (*They both make the Black Power fist.*) We never imagined any space like this then. We mean this type of art? Or art research. Is it art? (*They both cup their hands and whisper.*) Did you know the UCOP site went down because of your artwork?

Ricardo: (*He puts on a lab coat with a CALIT2 logo on it.*) No. In the decade-plus of doing these performances, no website has ever gone down because of our EDT gestures. Some became very slow when trying to respond to specific questions, such as, "404 File Not Found_Democracy?" on this UCOP server. Some governments, corporations, and social groups have imagined that their sites went down. Since the nature of the gesture is virtual—or what we have named a "minor simulation"—and calls forth a social drama/social conversation about the nature of new media, new media art, and collective social expression in the twenty-first century, the design of contestational art forms in a distributed age—not about taking down websites.

UCOP: (*UCOP wakes up and holds its server above its head.*)

Core Members of the UC MRG in International Culture and Performance

Dear Core Members:

Thank you for your e-mail of April 7 sending your statement of support of Professor Ricardo Dominguez on our San Diego campus. I am pleased to know that you hold Professor Dominguez in high regard. As I hope you will understand, I cannot comment on any pending investigation, given rights to privacy, but I can say that the University is committed to supporting its faculty members and their academic freedom. I am confident that Chancellor Fox and her staff, working with the faculty, will address these issues without intervention from the Office of the President. That said, I do want to respond to your comments about protections for a "virtual sit-in" on the UCOP Web site. UC's Electronic Communications Policy (http://www.ucop.edu/ucophome/policies/ec/),

Section III (see p. 8) covers allowable use of our electronic systems and reads as follows:

D. Allowable Uses. 7. Interference. University electronic communications resources shall not be used for purposes that could reasonably be expected to cause excessive strain on any electronic communications resources, or to cause interference with others' use of electronic communications resources. Users of electronic communications services shall not: (i) send or forward chain letters or their equivalents in other services; (ii) "spam," that is, exploit electronic communications systems for purposes beyond their intended scope to amplify the widespread distribution of unsolicited electronic messages; (iii) "letter-bomb," that is, send an extremely large message or send multiple electronic messages to one or more recipients and so interfere with the recipients' use of electronic communications systems and services; or (iv) intentionally engage in other practices such as "denial of service attacks" that impede the availability of electronic communications services.

Our Chief Information Officer, David Ernst, is charged with investigating whether the participation in a "virtual sit-in" that degraded service to our user community violated this policy and, if so, what the consequences should be. Although I am sympathetic to the need for free expression in pursuit of new artistic directions, neither the First Amendment nor Academic Freedom, in my view, protects substantial and material interference with ongoing educational and related activities. One of the great challenges we currently face is to convince a wider California public that they should support the University of California strongly even during times of financial stress for the state. I hope you agree that our tradition of viewpoint-neutral application of policies governing professional conduct by faculty and staff is one of the great strengths we rely on to demonstrate our commitment to the public good. I appreciate your taking the time to write with your concerns.

With best wishes, I am sincerely yours,

Mark G. Yudof, President

cc: Chancellor Marye Anne Fox

Provost Lawrence Pitts

Executive Vice President Nathan Brostrom
Vice President Steven Beckwith
Chief Information Officer David Ernst
General Counsel Charles Robinson
Deputy General Counsel David Birnbaum

(*UCOP walks out of the Ricardo Dominguez's office at CALIT2, mumbling about "zombie botnets" and having to find a new condo for President Yudof after he wrecked the last one.*)

FBI: (*They take out calculators and tap out numbers rapidly.*) Professor Dominguez, do you know that UCOP is saying that they lost $5,600 in server time and systems administration technical cost and repairs? And do you know anything above $5,000 U.S. dollars is a federal offense?

Ricardo: (*Now Skyping with members of the Coyotech research group working in Chiapas, Mexico.*) I find UCOP's server going down surprising, since in the world of postcontemporary digital culture, First World infrastructure is about developing greater levels of robust capabilities. Systems now are built for millions of hits an hour—if not more. Also, I would like to see how UCOP is coming up with this cost figure, since it sounds to me that the technical administration team working on UCOP's servers should be held responsible for not keeping the server up to current standards. In the world of postcontemporary digital culture, infrastructure is about greater levels of robust capabilities. Systems now are built to accept millions of hits an hour—if not more.

(*Ricardo Dominguez puts on 4-D glasses and stares at the new Mayan technology app in development.*)

I do not think that UCOP is seeking to investigate me and b.a.n.g. lab's research at CALIT2 because its servers went down. I think it has to do with the UCOP's own sense of fragility after the explosion of racist incidents at UCSD before March 4 and the major strikes and actions on March 4 against the student fee hikes at UCSD and across the state. It seems to me that I am the target of their personal anxieties over the mess that they made of the great system of public education. Besides, I was hired to do this research; I was not hired to teach what is already well known and

accepted as new media art but to present new and edgy formations of art and knowledge.

FBI: (*Looking at the UCSD police report on Ricardo Dominguez.*) We
understand that this gesture was not a botnet or cracking gesture.
(*They point to the HTML and JavaScript from the March 4, 2010,
ECD performance.*) What does this HTML code for the 404 files
do?

Ricardo: (*Having some coffee from a cup with a Mayan symbol on it,
a symbol that represents the "politics of the question."*) That is the
code for 404 files. They have mentioned it to you already. They are
part of the poetics of the gesture—the code requests questions of
the authorized database of the UCOP server that focus on what
data do not contain—about what is missing in the database.

FBI: (*Taking out two photographs of Brett Stalbaum and Micha Cardenas walking in the Anza-Borrego State Park, testing the Transborder Immigrant Tool.*) Were Brett Stalbaum and Micha Cardenas
involved in the March 4 gesture?

Ricardo: (*Now grading student projects from his Electronic Civil Disobedience: Theory and Practice class.*) No. Only my students and I
developed, installed, and performed the code for the gesture. It is
a class that I have taught every year since 2005, and it always ends
with a gesture similar to this one.

FBI: (*Closing the UCSD police report and lighting up their cigars.*)
We will probably not move forward beyond this interview. But
you should be aware that you have violated U.S. Code 1030 (Title
18>Part 1>Chapter 47>1030 Sections 1 and 5). (*They just sit smil-
ing, humming, and smoking cigars.*)

Ricardo: (*Coughing.*) I really need to move on with my day gentle-
men. If you have no further questions?

FBI: (*They put on their fur hats and walk out very slowly.*) Goodbye,
Professor Dominguez. We hope that we will never have to see you
again, but it is not really up to us. (*They stop and peek back into
the office.*) We never thought of art in this way. Just fascinating.

(*Scene ends. Fade to black.*)

P.S. The FBI investigation ended on April 10, 2011. No charges were ever
made against Professor Ricardo Dominguez, any of his students, or b.a.n.g.
lab researchers.

Acknowledgments

This book has come to fruition after a long journey, as many edited books do, but in this case our efforts to publish a volume about the imperial university constantly reminded us of the very challenges and crises of work in the academy we were trying to explore and document. It was not easy to try to publish an edited book critical of the U.S. academy at a moment when academic publishing itself has become such a difficult endeavor. So we are deeply grateful to our editor, Richard Morrison, at the University of Minnesota Press for his enthusiastic support, thoughtful advice, and creative suggestions. If it were not for his principled vision, this book would never have seen the light of day and these stories from the trenches of academic wars would not have appeared in print. We also wish to thank Erin Warholm-Wohlenhaus for her editorial assistance and for shepherding this project to publication. We would also like to thank Mabel Kyinn, Scripps College '16, for her meticulous help with formatting some of the chapters, especially in a very short period of time.

The contributors to this book are among those scholars and activists who inspired us to embark on this project. It is their courage and incisive critique that compelled us to persist with making sure that this book would be published. We thank them for their patience, diligence, and brilliance.

Sunaina wishes to thank her colleagues at UC Davis, particularly in the Department of Asian American Studies as well as others, for their consistent intellectual and political support and for their solidarity in moments of campus repression and crisis. She is also grateful to the students and faculty at UC Davis who continue to mobilize to democratize the university, in the face of all kinds of pepper spraying. Since this project grew out of an intellectual and political conversation and partnership, Sunaina wants to thank Piya for her warmth, dogged persistence, supportiveness, and personal concern shown not just to her but to all the contributors of this book, not to mention her impressive integrity as a feminist scholar. It seems fitting that a book that grew out of our collaboration on an antiwar statement of solidarity was being finalized as we found out that we were both targeted, along with several South Asian feminist and postcolonial studies scholars in the United States, by right-wing Hindu nationalist activists for our public opposition to state-sanctioned anti-Muslim massacres and political repression in India as well as our criticism of Israeli state violence. This campaign of intimidation reminded us of the urgency of this book's call for wider antiwar and antiracist solidarity in the imperial university.

Piya would like to thank all those friends, colleagues, and students who stood by her during a difficult transition in 2012 when she left her job at UC Riverside after eighteen years of service to join Scripps College—an experience that brought to the fore, with a sharp and sad irony, some of the tensions articulated in this collection. She is deeply grateful for the wisdom and presence of her baba, her first and greatest teacher. Piya would also like to give her deepest thanks to Sunaina, whose tenacity, compassion, and extraordinary editorial acumen really set a very high bar and also demonstrated how scholarly rigor, ethical solidarity, and friendship can be forged through such a project—which began with a simple but passionate discussion on a park bench in Oakland about the costs of "success" in the academy. Finally, Piya is deeply grateful for the hospitality and solidarity of new and old friends in both of these quite different sites of the U.S. academy in which she has worked—a public university and a private liberal arts college. Like Sunaina, she continues to be inspired by the verve, courage, and smarts of so many students who—in their struggles for democracy, transparency, and justice within their educational institutions—have become her finest teachers.

Contributors

Thomas Abowd teaches in the departments of anthropology and Arabic studies at Tufts University. He is the author of the forthcoming book *Colonial Jerusalem: The Spatial Imaginary in a Divided City*. He was awarded a Fulbright Fellowship to do research in Jerusalem, Palestine, in 2012.

Victor Bascara is associate professor in the Department of Asian American Studies at UCLA. He is the author of *Model-Minority Imperialism*. His ongoing research projects include an examination of the dynamics of isolationism and U.S. imperialism in the interwar period (1919–1941) and a study of post-1975 refugee culture in Asian Pacific America.

Piya Chatterjee is Backstrand chair and professor in the Department of Feminist, Gender and Sexuality Studies at Scripps College. She is author of *A Time for Tea: Women, Labor, and Post/Colonial Politics on an Indian Plantation* and coeditor of *States of Trauma: Gender and Violence in South Asia*.

Dana Collins is associate professor of sociology at California State University, Fullerton. She has been conducting critical ethnographic research in the Philippines since 1999 following gay-led gentrification, sexual labor, and the production of gay urban spaces. She is working on a book on this research titled *Laboring Districts, Pleasuring Sites: Sexuality and Place-Making in the Urban Philippines*.

Nicholas De Genova has taught anthropology and Latino studies at Columbia and Stanford Universities. He is author of *Working the Boundaries: Race, Space, and "Illegality" in Mexican Chicago*, coauthor of *Latino Crossings: Mexicans, Puerto Ricans, and the Politics of Race and Citizenship*, editor of *Racial Transformations: Latinos and Asians Remaking the United States*, and coeditor of *The Deportation Regime: Sovereignty, Space, and the Freedom of Movement*.

Ricardo Dominguez is associate professor at University of California, San Diego, in the visual arts department, a Hellman Fellow, and principal/principle investigator at CALIT2 (http://bang.calit2.net). He is cofounder of the Electronic Disturbance Theater, which developed virtual sit-in technologies in 1998 in solidarity with the Zapatista communities in Chiapas, Mexico, and for which he collectively produced the award-winning Transborder Immigrant Tool, a GPS cellphone net tool to aid safe crossing of the U.S.–Mexico border.

Sylvanna Falcón is assistant professor of Latin American and Latino/a studies at the University of California, Santa Cruz. Her book in progress is about antiracist feminist activism at the United Nations. She is coeditor of *New Directions in Feminism and Human Rights* (2011) and serves on the editorial collective of Societies without Borders: Human Rights and the Social Sciences.

Farah Godrej is associate professor of political science at the University of California, Riverside. She is the author of *Cosmopolitan Political Thought: Method, Practice, Discipline* (2011).

Roberto González is professor of anthropology at San Jose State University. He is author of *Zapotec Science: Farming and Food in the Northern Sierra of Oaxaca; Anthropologists in the Public Sphere: Speaking Out on War, Peace, and American Power; American Counterinsurgency: Human Science and the Human Terrain;* and *Militarizing Culture: Essays on the Warfare State.*

Alexis Pauline Gumbs is a queer black troublemaker with a PhD in English, African and African American studies, and women and gender studies from Duke University. Gumbs is author of a collection of poems, *101 Things That Are Not True about the Most Famous Black Women Alive,* and coeditor of the forthcoming *This Bridge Called My Baby.*

Sharmila Lodhia is assistant professor of women's and gender studies at Santa Clara University. She is coeditor of *New Directions in Feminisms and Human Rights* (2011).

Sunaina Maira is professor of Asian American studies at the University of California, Davis. She is author of *Desis in the House: Indian American Youth Culture in New York City.* She coedited *Youthscapes: The Popular, the*

National, the Global and *Contours of the Heart: South Asians Map North America*, which won the American Book Award in 1997. Her most recent book is *Missing: Youth, Citizenship, and Empire after 9/11.*

Julia Oparah (formerly Sudbury) is professor and chair of ethnic studies at Mills College. She is author of *Other Kinds of Dreams: Black Women's Organisations and the Politics of Transformation*, editor of *Global Lockdown: Race, Gender, and the Prison-Industrial Complex,* and coeditor of *Outsiders Within: Writing on Transracial Adoption* and *Color of Violence: The Incite! Anthology.* She is a cofounder of Critical Resistance, a national organization that aims to dismantle the prison-industrial complex.

Vijay Prashad is the George and Martha Kellner chair in South Asian history and professor of international studies at Trinity College. He is the author of fourteen books, most recently *Arab Spring, Libyan Winter* and *Uncle Swami: South Asians in America Today.* His book *The Darker Nations: A People's History of the Third World* was selected by the Asian American Writers' Workshop as the best nonfiction book of 2008.

Jasbir Puar is associate professor of women's and gender studies at Rutgers University. She is the author of *Terrorist Assemblages: Homonationalism in Queer Times*, which won the 2007 Cultural Studies Book Award from the Association for Asian American Studies. Her edited volumes include a special issue of *GLQ* titled "Queer Tourism: Geographies of Globalization" and a volume of *Society and Space* titled "Sexuality and Space."

Laura Pulido is professor in the Department of American Studies and Ethnicity at the University of Southern California. Her latest book is *A People's Guide to L.A.,* which she coauthored with Laura Barraclough and Wendy Cheng.

Ana Clarissa Rojas Durazo is assistant professor in the Department of Women's, Gender and Sexuality Studies studies at California State University, Long Beach. She coedited *Color of Violence: The INCITE Anthology.*

Steven Salaita is associate professor of English at Virginia Tech. He is author of *Anti-Arab Racism in the USA*; *The Holy Land in Transit: Colonialism and the Quest for Canaan*; *Arab American Literary Fictions, Cultures, and*

Politics; and *The Uncultured Wars: Arabs, Muslims, and the Poverty of Liberal Thought.*

Molly Talcott is assistant professor of sociology at California State University, Los Angeles. She is coeditor of *New Directions in Feminisms and Human Rights* (2011).

Index

Note: The italicized f following page numbers refers to figures.

AAUP. *See* American Association of University Professors

Abowd, Thomas, 9, 10, 22, 24, 26, 28, 29, 31, 33, 36, 217

academia, 220, 222–23, 227, 230, 276, 278, 304, 305; contradictory space of, 262–63, 263–68; corporatization of, 110; ethical/methodological conformity in, 220; feminist collaboration and, 261; liberation of, 116–17; militarization of, 20, 102, 115; politics in, 225, 266; prisonization of, 20, 115; responsibility in, 218; revolution and, 266

Academic Bill of Rights, 25

academic containment, 13, 21–30, 48n48; logic of, 23, 28, 29, 34, 43

academic freedom, 6, 22, 23, 33, 37–38, 48n48, 88, 183, 229, 304, 321, 322, 327n19, 329, 330, 333, 336, 337, 345, 346, 351; boundaries of, 38, 41; crises of, 5, 12; defense of, 36, 338; discourse of, 8, 41; erosion of, 93–94, 97n35; higher education and, 339; holy grail of, 34–35, 36–37, 40, 42, 43; ideals of, 39, 40, 231; language/spirit of, 229; principle of, 35, 37, 38, 41, 42, 43, 338; teaching/learning and, 263–68

academic-military-industrial complex, 18, 19, 42, 101, 190, 191–92, 209

academic-military-prison-industrial complex (Academic-MPIC), 19, 20, 99, 117, 191; unmasking, 108–15

academic repression, resistance to, 19–20, 35, 41, 42

academics, 22, 37; individualism of, 100; political, 40, 221; politics/grassroots movements and, 267; progressive, 116–17; Zionist, 223

academy, 7, 17, 261; colonial, 232; cultural resources of, 335; imperialism and, 99; neoliberal, 6, 99–102, 332; postcarceral, 20, 115–17; privatization of, 264; professionalization of, 35; repression within, 19

accountability, 150, 153, 247, 254, 257, 311

ACTA. *See* American Council of Trustees and Alumni

activism, 4, 120n42, 100, 108, 172, 175, 176, 185n2, 218, 229, 262, 347; academy and, 266; anti-Israeli state violence, 226; antioccupation, 285; antipinkwashing, 281; antiprison, 105, 109, 206; antiwar, 93, 204, 310, 311, 313; anti-Zionist, 169, 171, 288; community, 173, 288; human rights, 173–74; scholar, 261, 277

ADL. *See* Anti-Defamation League

affirmative action, 26, 147, 156, 167n37, 338, 339

Agamben, Giorgio, 292–93, 296n30

Agee, Phillip, 89

Agozino, Biko, 113

Ajami, Fouad, 222
Akom, Antwi, 191
Al-Arian, Sami, 10, 28
Alexander, M. Jacqui, 239, 250
Alfred, Taiaiake, 230
Ali, Ayaan Hirsi, 28
Allen, Raymond B., 336, 337
al-Qaeda, 89, 105, 235n14, 286
Althusser, Louis, 61, 75n23
American Anthropological Association, 15
American Association of Collegiate Registrars and Admissions Officers (AACRAO), 56
American Association of University Professors (AAUP), 37, 40, 50n90, 330, 337, 340; academic freedom and, 35, 36, 38, 41; boycotts and, 39, 50n94; founding of, 15; report by, 23
American Council of Trustees and Alumni (ACTA), 11, 21, 25, 45n13, 46n33
American-Israel Political Action Committee (AIPAC), 174
American Jews for a Just Peace, 176
American Psychological Association, 19
Anderson, Warwick, 64
ANSWER, 31
anticommunism, 336, 337
Anti-Defamation League (ADL), 31, 32, 171, 172, 174
anti-imperialism, 22, 29, 60, 263, 265, 266, 267, 275, 312
antiracism, 24, 33, 264, 267, 269, 271, 339
antiracist feminist scholars, 265, 266–67, 270–71, 277, 278; challenges for, 264; research question for, 266
anti-Semitism, 32, 171, 174, 180, 224, 282, 288, 290–94, 338; accusation of, 291–92, 293; boycotts/divestment and,

29; claims of, 176, 181, 183, 184, 293; criticism of Israel and, 292–93
antiwar movement, 9, 18, 24, 28, 104, 204, 206, 312, 324, 325
apartheid, 39, 40, 41, 169, 172, 267, 294; Israel and, 31, 175, 183, 281, 287–88; South African, 174, 175, 253, 324
"Apologies to All the People in Lebanon" (Jordan), 257
Arab Spring, 127
Arendt, Hannah, 17, 46–47n33
Are Prisons Obsolete?, 190
Arizona Prison Moratorium Coalition (APMC), 105–6, 108
Arizona State Legislature 15–112, 99, 117n2
Army Specialized Training Programs (ASTPs), 16
Association for the Study of the Middle East (ASMEA), 222
Association of American Universities, Gates at, 93
Aswad, Barbara, 184
Auga, Ulricke, 281, 282, 283
authority, 133, 232; challenging, 135, 161

Bain & Company, study by, 331
Bakke v. Regents of UC (1978), 77n45
b.a.n.g. lab, 345
Banker's Dozen, 138
Barceló, Rusty, 190, 210n9
Barghouti, Marwan, 119n25
Barghouti, Omar, 40, 42
Barnard College, 228, 316
Barrow, Clyde, 36
Bascara, Victor, 14, 45n15
Baum, Dalit, 288
BDS. See Boycott, Divestment, and Sanctions
Beard, Charles, 35, 306
becoming, process of, 238–39
Becoming Black, 239, 254

Behar, Moshe, 170

behavior: control experiments, 112; disruptive, 132–33, 135, 202; heterosexual, 205; nonviolent, 135; political, 36

Bell, Derrick, 65

Benitez, Francisco, 54, 55, 72, 73, 76n29

Best, Steven, 41

"Beware Israeli Pinkwashing" (Puar), 281

Bin Laden, assassination of, 105–6

Birgenau, Robert, 132

Birnbaum, David, 352

Birzeit University, 5, 39

black: becoming, 255; being, 254–55

black English, 30, 237, 238, 256; first rule of, 248; learning, 251, 252; police brutality and, 251–54; teaching, 253–54

black feminists, queer poetics of, 34

Black Laundry, 285

Black Panther Party, 242, 265–66

Black Power, 23, 350

Blackwell, Maylei, 193, 200, 213n59

Bloom, Allan, 23

Board of Regents (UC), budget crisis and, 1

Board of Trustees (USC), 149

Boas, Franz, 15

Boggs, Grace Lee, 267

Bollinger, Lee, 303, 304, 305, 308, 309, 319, 320, 323; academic freedom and, 322; BDS and, 174; de Genova and, 313–14, 315, 317, 318; Israeli human rights/civil liberties organizations and, 174–75; trustee autocracy and, 307

Bourne, Randolph, 301, 302, 307

Bowker, Albert, 243

Boycott, Divestment, and Sanctions (BDS), 31, 170, 174, 177, 185n1; growth of, 172, 173, 184; nonviolent

movement and, 169; student initiative and, 175

boycotts, 48n63, 50n90, 50n94; academic, 29, 39, 40, 170; cultural, 48n63, 170

Brand Israel campaign, 282, 286, 287, 288

Brooklyn College, 10, 173; boycott at, 29

Brown, Nathan, 130, 132

Brown v. Board of Education (1954), 64, 65, 66

budget crisis, 1, 25, 263

budget cuts, 101, 125, 126, 128, 197

Bureau of Indian Affairs, 16

Bureau of Insular Affairs, 58

Bush, George W., 222, 303, 330, 339; Afghan War and, 301–2; executions and, 105

Butler, Judith, 38, 40, 291; BDS and, 173; USACBI and, 170

California Institute of Technology, 13, 148

California Prison Industry Authority, 274

California State Assembly resolution HR 35, 32

California State University, Fullerton, 269, 279n16

California State University, Long Beach (CSU–Long Beach), 200, 203, 206, 207; Chicanas at, 192, 193, 205; Chicano studies at, 188, 194–95, 201, 204, 213n59; heteromasculinist politics at, 198; opening of, 196; psychological abuse within, 197

California State University, Los Angeles (CSU–Los Angeles), 274

CALIT2, 347, 350, 352

Campaign for Free Higher Education, 340

"Campaign for the University of Southern California," 148
Campus Watch, 25, 92, 180, 224
capital, 17, 108; corporate, 19, 156; private, 139, 141
Capital, 338
capitalism, 15, 69, 240, 242, 264; antiracist/feminist critiques of, 34; corporate/militarized, 13; neoliberal, 5, 7, 10, 20, 26, 28, 42
carcerality, 21, 42, 111, 114, 115, 190
Cardenas, Micha, 343, 353
Carter, Jimmy, 170, 172, 179
CASA. *See* Collective of Antiracist-Feminist Scholar Activists
CCA. *See* Corrections Corporation of America
CCNY. *See* City College of New York
censorship, 6, 10–11, 33–34, 37, 265, 290–94, 318
Centers for Academic Excellence, 86, 91
Charter Act (1813), 13th Resolution of, 68
Chatterjee, Partha, 289, 310, 311
Chican@s, 200; queer, 188, 195, 196, 198, 202, 205, 206, 207, 208–9; trans, 198, 208–9
Chican@ studies, 187, 188, 191, 289; and Chicano studies compared, 210n2; ethnic studies and, 189–90
Chicana Feminisms Conference, 192, 203, 204
Chicana feminists, 196, 203, 204; Mexican/Chicano nationalisms and, 199; as threat, 197
Chicanas, 188, 198, 199, 201, 202, 208–9; attacks on, 195, 197; core courses and, 195; tenure and, 196, 197; violence against, 204, 206, 207
Chicana studies, 24, 146, 196, 197
Chicano movement, 193, 194, 199, 200, 201, 204, 205; Chicano Manifesto

of, 199; Chicano studies and, 196; politics and, 198, 213n59; victimization of, 206
Chicanos: attacks by, 198; colonial sex/gender dominance and, 200; queer, 195; threat to, 204
Chicano studies, 24, 146, 198–99, 201, 214n60; academic work and, 203; and Chican@ studies compared, 210n2; Chicano movement and, 196; decolonizing, 202–7; ethnic studies and, 193, 209; exile from, 187–88; heteropatriarchal, 188, 194–98, 207, 208, 209, 210n2; lesbians/jotos and, 205–6; tenure and, 197; victimization of, 206
Chicano Studies: Genesis of a Discipline, 194
Chingón politics, 198, 206
Chomsky, Noam, 17, 32
Christianity, 268; education and, 75n23
Christian Science Monitor, Lowery and, 333
Chronicle of Higher Education, 317, 324
Churchill, Ward, 10, 335–36, 338
CIA, 80, 82, 84, 86, 90, 91–92, 93; al-Qaeda and, 89; assassination plots by, 92; history of, 87; IC Centers and, 88; intelligence simulation exercise by, 79; Nasr kidnapping and, 89; scientific research and, 17, 89
citizenship, 5, 11, 22, 30, 65, 192, 193, 344; education and, 54, 62, 63, 65; intellectual, 220; military culture and, 90; multicultural, 33; patriotic, 21
City College of New York (CCNY), 15, 16, 243, 244
City University of New York (CUNY), 25, 238, 242; admissions policy at, 243–44; minorities at, 241, 243

civil disobedience, 4, 129–30, 134, 135, 138, 345, 347; electronic, 349; non-violent, 25, 132

civility, 17, 29, 33, 59, 344; academic, 28; rhetorical, 312; Western, 189

civilization, 21, 24, 55, 61, 83; education and, 14

civil liberties, 137, 173, 317, 327n19; Israeli, 174–75

civil rights, 32–33, 190, 192, 202

Civil Rights Act (1964), 32, 162, 193

civil rights movement, 9, 18, 25, 243, 244

class, 231, 264, 270, 335; pedagogy of, 7; politics of, 21; privileges of, 9; race and, 272

classism, 263, 265

class wars, culture wars as, 25

Cleaver, Kathleen: Black Panther Party and, 265–66

Closing of the American Mind, The, 23

Clover, Joshua, 129–30, 139

Coalition Provisional Authority, 107

Cockburn, Alexander, 338

Cohen, Jean, 313

Cohn-Haddow Center for Jewish Studies, 177

COINTELPRO, 22, 23, 92

Cold War, 6, 17, 18, 19, 22, 23, 55; defense industry of, 129

Cole, Jonathan, 321

collaboration, 34, 167n39, 242, 250, 262, 277, 338; feminist, 261, 276

Collective of Antiracist-Feminist Scholar Activists (CASA), 34, 263, 279n16; formation of, 261–62; knowledge production and, 275–78

college costs, government money for/by country, 339

College of Ethnic Studies, 191, 193

College of Hawai'i, 58, 69

College of Police Science (CUNY), 238, 245

colonialism, 5, 9, 24, 34, 40, 189, 230, 275, 325; academic, 191, 194; institutions of, 55, 60; legacy of, 245–46; racial/sexual politics of, 196; settler, 7, 10, 30, 31, 33, 41, 43, 118n7, 240, 283; slavery and, 272

colonization, 28, 67, 72, 199, 229, 272; battles of, 188; Israeli, 170, 203; narratives of, 269; Zionist, 233

colony, as laboratory, 63–66

Columbia Spectator, 304, 326n14

Columbia University, 170, 225, 228, 303, 309, 319, 326n12, 326n13; BDS and, 175; controversy at, 244, 306, 307, 308, 310–17; divestment and, 174, 324; politics at, 318; teach-in at, 301, 302, 311; tenure at, 321, 322, 328n24

Committee for Tenure Justice (CTJ), 153–54, 161

Committee on the Exercise of the Inalienable Rights of the Palestinian People (CEIRPP), 119n24

Communist Party, 23, 36, 336, 338

composition, 33, 245; police, 248–49

Conciencia Femenil (ConFem), 202–7

Congress of Racial Equality (CORE), 242, 244

COPS. See College of Police Science

Córdova, Teresa: quote of, 187

Cornell University, 100

Corporate university, 126; tenure process at, 153–61

Correctional Service of Canada, 112

Corrections Corporation of America (CCA), 102, 110, 118n8

Council of UC Faculty Associations, 129

crime, 110, 113, 190; racialized fear of, 103, 104

criminalization, 100, 127, 137–39, 140, 257; legal, 138, 139; rhetoric of, 131–37

criminal justice, 111, 112, 113, 114

crisis, 22, 268; continuities and, 11–13

critical ethnic studies (CES), 9, 146

Critical Resistance, 103

CSU–Long Beach. *See* California State University, Long Beach

CTJ. *See* Committee for Tenure Justice

cultural capital, 9, 275

culturalism, neoliberal, 4, 226

cultural studies, 8, 25

cultural supremacy, 12, 13, 14, 290

cultural vigilantes, 37, 335

culture, 68, 163n10, 268; academic, 267, 334; campus, 337, 338; department, 202; digital, 352; freezing, 200, 205; high, 335; homosexual, 206; institutional, 148; material, 54; military, 90; national, 7, 21, 68; political, 151; popular, 72; victimization of, 206; white, 270; youth, 9

culture wars, 7, 11, 13, 21, 24, 25, 26, 28, 29, 34, 221; as class wars, 25; university, 224

CUNY. *See* City University of New York

curriculum, 59, 268, 269; Anglophone/ American literature, 67; development of, 18, 20, 83, 248

cybercrime, 343

Cyber Investigation Division, 348

Dabashi, Hamid, 313

Daily 49er, 204

Dalrymple, Louis, 60, 61, 63

Davis, Angela, 23, 103, 170, 190

Davis, Mike: prison-industrial complex and, 103

Davis, Nira Yuval, 272

Davis Dozen, criminal charges against, 4

death penalty, 105

Debord, Guy, 328n28

debt, 332; credit card, 214n68, 313, 331; student, 4, 12, 126, 214n68, 130, 331, 334

Declaration of Independence, 319

Declaration of Principles on Academic Freedom and Academic Tenure, 37

decolonial projects, 198, 202, 207

decolonization, 5, 18, 55, 57, 61, 209, 323; movements, 289; Palestinian, 234n5; politics of, 189; potential of, 196; process of, 11

Deer, Patrick: on Aronson rebuttal, 290–91

"Defending the Idea of the University in Troubled Times" (Cole), 321

defense industry, 17, 129

Defense Intelligence Agency (DIA), 79, 82, 85, 89

De Genova, Nicholas, 9, 19, 26, 29, 33, 34, 36, 37, 40, 41, 43, 315, 320; academic repression and, 35; Bollinger and, 313–14; criticism of, 303, 310–11, 316; tenure and, 322

democracy, 5, 7, 11, 30; campus, 39, 330; cooperation and, 233

denial of Service distinction, 347

Denning, Michael: capital/labor and, 334

Department of Corrections and Rehabilitation (California), 114

Department of Defense, 19, 93, 183; research funding by, 13; research universities and, 17–18

Department of Higher Education, Chicano studies and, 193

Department of Homeland Security, 82, 130, 242

Department of Women's Studies (UCR), 1

Dewey, John, 15, 17, 46n33
DIA. *See* Defense Intelligence Agency
"Digital Zapatistas" (Lane), 349
Director of National Intelligence (DNI), 79, 82, 84, 86, 87, 93; IC Centers and, 81, 88, 91, 92
Dirks, Nicholas, 306, 315, 323; on scandal/empire, 325; termination and, 304; trustee autocracy and, 307
discipline, 112, 238, 241–43
discourse, 8, 37, 41, 54, 56, 67, 305; academic, 13, 291; colonial, 219; dominant, 270; educational, 14; imperial, 60; liberal, 137, 266; neoliberal, 282
discrimination, 26, 152, 167n36, 173; anti-Jewish, 181; anti-Palestinian, 183; class, 265; dismantling, 264; evidence of, 155–56; gender, 155, 162, 165n25, 265, 296n22; Israeli, 177; racial, 31, 32, 155, 265; religious, 31; tenure review and, 154, 159, 160; transparency and, 157; workplace, 284
disinvestment, 128; neoliberal, 25, 126, 139
dissent, 13, 21, 87–88, 301, 312, 327n15; academic, 18, 22, 37; class politics and, 22; cost of, 130; criminalization of, 107, 125, 132, 136, 137, 140; engaging in, 12, 43, 140–41; nonviolent, 129; privatization and, 131; scholarly, 6, 19–20; suppressing, 108, 139, 140, 191
diversity, 37, 71, 162, 192, 314, 330; college, 154, 155; educational importance of, 65; faculty, 160, 167n36; intelligence agencies and, 88; language of, 26; multiculturalist pedagogy of, 190; racial/ethnic/gender, 70, 151, 162
divestment, 29, 116, 125; call for, 50n90, 174, 175, 178

DNI. *See* Director of National Intelligence
dominance, 189; challenging, 11, 29; economic, 7, 10; global, 19, 303; military, 7; political, 7, 10; sex/gender, 200
dominant class, 335; higher education and, 334
Dominguez, Ricardo, 34, 36, 42, 43, 347, 348, 352, 353; culture of solidarity and, 39; EDT and, 343, 349; FBI file for, 350; interview of, 50n91; investigation of, 41, 343; performance art traditions and, 346; TBT and, 345; virtual sit-in and, 344
Dorfman, Ariel, 315
DuBois, W. E. B., 254, 255
"Dump Farallon" campaign, 102

Eagleton, Terry, 68
East India Company, 337
economic crisis, 130, 145, 241
economic development, 107, 109, 116, 126
economics, neoliberal, 233, 283
EDT. *See* Electronic Disturbance Theater
EDT/b.a.n.g. lab, 343
education, 9, 71, 81, 84–85, 94, 274; access to, 126, 241; Christianity and, 75n23; citizenship and, 54, 62, 63, 65; civilization and, 14; cost of, 130; democratizing influence of, 65, 126; empire and, 63, 69; freedom and, 275; imperial discourse and, 60; incarceration and, 109, 251; labor market and, 55–56; neoliberal disinvestment in, 25; right to, 3, 40; role of, 61, 63; socialization of, 18; state/local government and, 65; tax money for, 117; transformative/ solidarity-building

education (*continued*)
moments in, 273; vulnerability
in, 269. *See also* higher education;
public education
educational apparatus, 59, 60, 64, 66
educational reform, 57–63, 64, 68
"Education Not Incarceration" campaign, 109
Ehrlich, Ken, 138, 139
Eisenhower, Dwight: military-industrial
complex and, 17, 103, 190
Electronic Communications Policy, 350
Electronic Disturbance Theater (EDT),
41, 343, 349, 350
El-Haj, Nadia Abu, 29, 228, 316
Ely, Robert T., 47–48n48
empire, 59, 62; contradictions of, 57;
cultural lexicon of, 192; education
and, 63, 69; epistemologies of, 189–
93; nation and, 73; resisting, 101
enemy combatants, 104, 106
English, 237; remedial, 241; teaching,
243
English literature, 68, 71
Enlightenment, 30, 63, 67
Enloe, Cynthia, 208, 272
Equal Employment Opportunity Commission, 162
equality, 38, 63, 183, 285
ethics, 15, 221, 232, 335
ethnic cleansing, 177, 179
ethnic studies, 18, 23, 25, 28, 30, 101,
193–95, 230, 267, 291; assessment
of, 193–94; attacks on, 9, 102, 188,
197; Chican@ studies and, 189–90;
Chicano studies and, 193, 209; incorporation of, 24
ethnopoetics, 239–40
Eurocentrism, 229, 268, 269
Evans, Linda, 103, 118n16

exceptionalism, 24, 104, 268, 283;
American, 6, 272; Israeli, 32, 33, 224

faculty, 145; Chicana, 167n36, 198, 199;
criminalization of, 139; Mexican-
American/Chicano/a, 167n36; queer,
154; women of color, 154, 161, 266
faculty governance, 146, 148, 149, 150, 160
Fadli, Meriam, 81
Falcón, Sylvanna, 9, 11, 27, 29, 31, 34
Falk, Richard, 170
Fanon, Franz, 254–55
Farallon Capital Management, 102
FBI, 20, 22, 41, 79, 80, 81, 82, 86, 93, 108,
185n6, 308, 347–48, 349, 350, 352;
history of, 87; IC Centers and, 88;
interviews by, 27, 50n91; investigation by, 353; makeover of, 91; public
safety and, 27; surveillance by, 5, 23,
92
Feldman, Jonathan, 47n34
feminisms, 28, 37, 281, 297n30; academic, 267; antiracist, 261, 276; Chican@,
207; Chicana, 187, 188, 196, 197, 198,
199, 201, 202, 203, 204, 209; superserviceable, 34, 267; transnational,
250, 261, 267, 271, 290–94; women of
color, 198–202
Feminist Legal Studies, 281
feminists, 264; Chican@, 198, 206;
Chicana, 199, 204, 206, 209; queer/
trans/mujeres, 187
feminist studies, 8, 25, 30, 224, 271, 285
Feminist Writing Group (FWG), 261
Ferguson, Roderick, 207, 212n30; ethnic
studies and, 18, 193–94
Filipino in America, A, 59–60
financial crisis, 9, 331, 333, 336
Finkelstein, Norman, 10, 217, 228
First Amendment, 38, 308, 315, 317, 319,
322, 351

Flores-Ortiz, Yvette, 200

Foner, Eric, 312–13, 326n14

foreign policy, 6, 29, 264, 269

Foucault, Michel, 114

Fox, Marye Anne, 344, 350, 351

Frameline, film festival of, 288

freedom, 13, 30, 34, 40, 192; education and, 275; political, 38, 329

Freedom Center, 25

freedom of expression, 8, 22, 38, 134, 183, 304, 307, 320, 322, 351

Freedom of Information Act, 92

freedom of speech, 4, 5, 303, 304, 307, 310, 311, 314, 316, 317, 319, 320, 323

freedom of thought, 322, 333, 337

Freeman, Samuel, 87, 88, 92

free market model, 26, 334, 336

Free Palestine rally, 288

Fulbright, William, 17, 190; learning from, 91–95

Fulbright Fellowship, 94

funding, 10, 13, 82, 87–88, 109; corporate, 84, 94, 101, 102, 116; military, 19, 84

GABRIELA, 267

Gandhi, Mohandas, 59

Gates, Henry Louis, Jr., 227

Gates, Robert, 93, 235n16, 272

gay/lesbian groups, 33; censorship of, 287; Israeli, 283–84; Palestinian oppression of, 289

Gay Pride March, 283

gay rights, 172, 283, 289; homonationalism and, 295n10; Israeli-Palestinian conflict and, 282, 285

Gaza, 295n22; Israeli attack on, 4, 9, 31, 32, 173, 177, 227

Geller, Pamela, 48n64

gender, 29, 30, 34, 210n2, 231, 264; anxieties around, 270; criminalized, 205; liberal ideology of, 7; nonconformity, 102, 201; policing, 100; politics of, 21, 24, 140; sexuality and, 281

Gender and Fundamentalism, 281

Gender in Conflicts: Palestine-Israel-Germany, 283

gender-responsive strategies (GRS), 114

gender studies, 9, 28, 267

genocide, 10, 30, 43, 190, 246, 303

Gilmore, Ruth Wilson, 103, 106, 163n5

Gingrich, Newt, 317

Ginsberg, Terri, 10, 228

Giroux, Henri, 46n31, 46n33, 110; imperial university and, 190; patriotic correctness and, 21

Gitlin, Todd, 24, 225, 226, 227

Glissant, Edouard, 250; counterpoetic approach and, 242; ethnopoetics and, 239–40; racism and, 241; on subject/object, 249

globalization, 13, 26, 73, 103, 108, 110; critiques of, 269, 270, 271; Israeli-Palestinian conflict and, 263; neo-liberal, 58, 116; readings of, 45n15; resisting, 101

Glover, Clifford, 245, 247, 249, 251, 252

GLQ: A Journal of Lesbian and Gay Studies, 285

goals, 71, 82, 100; career-oriented, 277; political, 261; university, 347

Godrej, Farah, 10, 12, 19, 24, 25, 27, 42

Goldberg, David Theo, 137

González, Roberto, 13, 15, 17, 19, 20

Goode, Michael, 251

Goss, Neil, 330

"Got Intelligence?" camp, 91

Gottheil, Fred, 296n22

Graduate and Professional Student Senate (USC), 149

Graeber, David, 10

graffiti, 55, 283; photo of, 53

Gramsci, Antonio, 43, 203
Gratz v. Bollinger (2003), 77n45
Grenada, 238; invasion of, 33, 242, 249, 250
Groves, Leslie, 16
Guantanamo, 28, 103
Guardian, 282, 292
Gumbs, Alexis, 9, 12, 21, 23, 31, 33, 34, 42; ethnic studies and, 18; police English and, 30
Gusterson, Hugh, 84–85

Hamilton, Alexander, 319
Hampshire College, divestment and, 174
Hannity, Sean, 317
Hardt, Michael, 192
Harlem University, 244
Harmon Family Foundation for an Academy of Polymathic Study, 163n8
Harvard University, 62, 80, 147, 185n2; tenure and, 158
health care, 110; disinvestment in, 128; tax money for, 117
heteronormativity, 34, 207
heteropatriarchy, 188, 194, 196, 197, 201, 202, 204, 205, 206–7, 208, 209, 264; Chicano, 198, 203; feminist betrayal of, 203
heterosexism, 210n2, 265
"Heterosexualism and the Colonial/Modern Gender System" (Lugones), 201
higher education, 13, 27, 60, 90, 100, 108, 109, 145, 162n4, 166n31, 189, 265, 333; academic freedom and, 339; access to, 6, 117; affordability of, 330; crises for, 344; cultural vigilantes and, 335; culture of, 146, 147, 334; culture wars on, 25; democratization of, 116; dismantling of, 9, 42, 116; economy of, 158; exclusion from,
4, 146; as free public good, 338–39; funding for, 82, 84, 94, 101, 109; inelastic market for, 332; infrastructure of, 59; knowledge production in, 56; liberalism/radicalism and, 330; minority/immigrant studies and, 25; mission of, 11, 30; myth of, 229; normal fabric of, 333–34; prisons and, 99, 102, 110; privatization of, 4, 6, 101; restructuring, 145; transformation and, 100. *See also* education
Higher Education Act (1965), 193
Hijas de Cuauhtemoc, 203, 204
Hillel, 172, 173, 176, 177
Historians against the War, 327n19
Hochberg, Gil Z., 283, 285
Hollinger, David, 23
Holmes, Oliver Wendell, Jr., 319, 320
Holmesburg Prison, 112
Holocaust, 290, 291, 293, 294, 296–97n30
homeland, narratives of, 269
homeland security, 27, 111
homonationalism, 28, 33, 287, 295n10; history of, 283–85; queers and, 289; religious fundamentalist law and, 285; Zionism and, 285
homophobia, 33, 42, 264, 283, 288, 289, 293; Israeli, 287; Palestinian, 286, 287
homosexuality, 34, 283, 289, 292; culture and, 206; liberal democratic modernity and, 286
honor killings, 33, 296n22
hooks, bell, 273, 275
Horowitz, David, 25, 26, 28, 37, 48n63, 224, 335
House Intelligence Committee, 80
House of Representatives, 207, 321
humanitarianism, 7, 28, 31, 345
human rights, 40, 173–75, 190, 192; institutionalization of, 262; queer, 288

human rights abuses, 31, 86, 288; Israeli, 169, 170, 171, 172, 174–75, 176, 177, 178, 182; Palestinian, 101

Human Rights Watch, 296n22

Huntington, Samuel, 83

Hussein, Saddam, 106, 107, 303

hypermasculinity, 201, 206

hypernationalism, 35, 226

IBM, prison labor and, 103

IC Center. See Intelligence Community Center of Academic Excellence

ICSP. See "Intelligence Community Scholarship Program"

ideals, 39, 40, 218; corporate, 231; political, 55

"Idea of a University, The" (Beard), 306

identity, 248, 269, 349; gender, 201, 270; national, 7, 323; political, 24, 230

IFjP. See International Feminist Journal of Politics

IGKNU. See Integrated Global Knowledge and Understanding Collaboration

Ignatiev, Noel, 116

"I Have a Dream" speech (King), 67

Illinois American Association of University Professors (AAUP), 166n32

immigration, 9, 111, 270

imperial cartographies, 13, 14–21, 57–63

imperialism, 30–31, 43, 59, 73, 233, 246, 251, 254, 324; academy and, 99; blowback by, 338; core issues of, 8; critiques of, 34, 270; educational mission and, 60; forms of, 294; geopolitics of, 8; high, 57; internalized, 239; Israeli, 238, 242, 256, 257; left discourse on, 270; nationalism and, 6; participating in, 240; political, 12; prisons and, 105; racism and, 6, 7; state formation and, 6; struggle against, 42; subjugation/violence and, 7; support for, 242; U.S., 264, 269, 270; warfare and, 6

imperial networks, thickening of, 72–73

imperial projects, 24, 55, 56

imperial university, 5–8, 100, 169, 269, 271, 306, 312, 317, 320–23; academic censorship and, 290; as contact zone, 55, 66; critical interrogations of, 108; decolonizing, 43; dissent against, 301; idea of, 54–57; international law and, 172; logics of, 266; solidarity within, 257; state of exception and, 11; struggle within, 263, 277; uses of, 54–57; War on Terror and, 11

incarceration, 104, 111, 115; education and, 109, 251; increase in, 113; racialized use of, 103, 114

indigenous peoples, 5, 27, 189, 240

individualism, 38, 334; competitive, 261, 267, 277

inequality, 111; income, 126, 333–34; racial/class, 26, 128; socioeconomic, 128; structural, 156, 195, 344

Ines, Doroteo, 59–60, 63, 64, 75n17, 76n31

Institute for Policy and Economic Development, 82

institutions: building, 58, 194; culture-creating, 333; private, 145; undemocratic activity of, 330

Integrated Global Knowledge and Understanding Collaboration (IGKNU), 87

intellectual freedom, 40, 117, 323–25, 332

intelligence, 17; domestic, 82; international, 82; military, 15, 18; outsourcing, 129; recruiting, 83–85 intelligence community, 20, 79, 80, 83, 85, 87, 90, 91, 92; diversity and, 21, 88; minorities and, 82; support for, 93

Intelligence Community Center of Academic Excellence (IC Center), 15, 79–80, 82, 93, 94; academic freedom and, 88; critical thinking skills at, 89; deception by, 91–92; development of, 81, 83; DNI and, 81, 88, 91, 92; funds from, 87–88; intelligence community and, 91; learning about, 85–87; locations of, 80; marketplace of ideas and, 85; name change for, 87; scholarship/travel and, 83–84; student participation in, 80, 90

"Intelligence Community Scholarship Program" (ICSP), 84

Intelligence Reform and Terrorism Prevention Act, 80

intelligence training, 79, 83, 84; students of color and, 20–21

International Feminist Journal of Politics (*IFjP*), 262

International Spy Museum, 79

intervention, 8, 272

Iranian Revolution (1978–1979), 27

Iraqi Ministry of Justice, 107

Iraq War, 301, 302; opposition to, 307–10, 326n12, 337Irvine 11, criminalization of, 4

Islam, 16, 26

Islamic Jihad, 31

Islamic militants, 22, 337, 338

Islamophobia, 26, 29, 286, 294

Israeli Defense Forces, 137, 284

Israeli GLBT Association, 285

Israeli National Police and Security Agency, 108

Israeli-Palestinian conflict, 26, 31, 218, 235n14, 281, 292; gay rights and, 282, 285; globalization and, 263

Israel: Peace not Apartheid, 179

Jay, John, 319

JC Penney, prison labor and, 103

Jenin refugee camp, massacre at, 178

Jerusalem Post, on Israeli gay community, 287

Jewish Defense League, 309

Jewish Defense Organization (JDO), 309

Jewish Federation, 172, 176

Jewish Voice for Peace, 31, 173, 176

Jews against the Occupation, 173

John Jay College of Criminal Justice, 245, 247, 248

John Jay College of Political Science, Black English at, 237

Jordan, June, 30, 239, 240; anti-imperialist critiques and, 33; black English and, 248, 251–54; poem by, 255–56; teaching by, 237, 238, 241, 242, 243, 254

Jordan, Reggie: death of, 253, 256

Jordan, Willie: paper by, 253

Journal of Academic Freedom, 50n94

JROTC, military culture and, 90

justice, 38, 162, 220; building, 209, 230; criminal, 111, 112, 113, 114; racial, 109; restorative, 111; retributive, 106; social, 262, 273

Kahane, Meir, 309

Ka Palapala, 53, 66; photo from, 70

Katehi, Linda, 132

Kelley, Robin, 170

Kennedy, Edward, 111–12

Kerr, Clark, 54, 56, 68, 73

Khalidi, Rashid, 28

Khan Bani Sa'ad prison, 107

Kimball, Roger, 23

King, Martin Luther, Jr., 67

Kingston Penitentiary for Women (P4W), 112

Kinzer, Stephen, 89

Klein, Mark, 89

Klingman, Albert, 112, 190–91

Knapp, Adeline, 61, 62, 63

knowledge, 12, 102, 222; advancement of, 203, 323; cartographies of, 18; repression of, 6

knowledge production, 10, 21, 35, 56, 191, 205; collective process of, 275–78; social relations of, 111; warcraft and, 18

Kohl, Helmut, 238

Kovel, Joel, 10, 217, 228

Kuntsman, Adi, 285

labor, 10, 9, 55–56, 60, 334; academic, 41; Asian immigrant, 49n79; intellectual, 233; prison, 103, 274; sexual, 248; studies, 224; women's, 208

Labor Institute, 339

Lane, Jill, 349

Las Rebeldes, 202–7

Latin@s, 196, 201, 202, 207

Latinos, 97n19, 200

Latino studies, 208, 214n60

Lauter, Paul, 334

La Voz de Aztlán, 206

law, 140; criminalization and, 137–39; international, 101, 172, 174

law enforcement, 25, 81, 111, 127, 131, 132, 211n20, 244–45; harassment by, 205; theory, 64. See also police

leadership, 86, 125, 126, 127, 130, 132–33, 134, 136; Chicana, 204; male, 201

lesbians, 205–6

Levine, Mark, 131

Levy, Mordechai, 309

Lewis, Bernard, 222

Lewontin, R. C., 16

"LGBTQI Liberation in the Middle East," 288

LGBT rights, 286

liberal arts, 71, 101

liberal education, 54, 60, 65, 67, 101; concept of, 59; goals of, 71

liberalism, 13, 178–82, 330

liberal principles, defense of, 338–39

liberal progressives, 24, 41

Lieberman, Joseph: ACTA and, 11

literary analysis, political, 219, 221

Lloyd, David, 164n15

loans: merit-driven, 331; student, 214n68, 333

Lorde, Audre, 30, 239, 248, 251, 253, 258n1, 258n2; anti-imperialist critiques and, 33; black English and, 237; COPS and, 245; dialogics of race and, 254; differences and, 261; poetic and, 246, 257; power and, 246–47; racism/sexism and, 246; on revolution, 250; rhetoric and, 247, 249; student protests and, 242; teaching by, 237, 238, 241, 242, 243, 245, 246, 247

Lorde, Jonathan, 247

Los Arcos, 86

Lott, Eric, 226

Lovejoy, Arthur, 15

Lowery, Helen, 333

Luce, Henry, 58, 69

Lugones, María, 201

Mackinnon, Catharine, 272

MADRE, 238

Makiya, Kanan, 222

MALCS Institute, 190

malinchista refrain, 198–202, 205

Malintzín Tenepal, 199

Mandela, Nelson, 175

Manifest Destiny, 7, 30

manifest knowledge, 13, 30–34, 43

Manji, Irshad, 28

Marcos, Imelda, 73

Marshall, Thurgood, 77n44

Martí, José, 189

Martin, Leah, 81

Martinez, Betita, 200, 206

Marx, Karl, 329

Masri, Khaled el, 90

Massad, Joseph, 28, 228

mass incarceration, 102, 104, 108, 111, 114; as economic motor, 103; higher education and, 99, 110; sustaining, 115; technologies of, 99; understanding of, 106

Mbembe, Achille, 284, 296–97n30

McCarthy era, 17, 22, 33, 35, 36, 38, 50n91, 336

McCoy, Alfred, 64

McFate, Montgomery, 46n19

McIntosh, Carl, 193

McIntosh, Peggy, 270

McKinley, William, 63

McLaren, Peter, 41

MEChA, 87, 88, 203, 206

media art, 347–48

Medical Apartheid: The Dark History of Medical Experimentation on Black Americans from Colonial Times to the Present, 190

medical experimentation, prisoners and, 111–12, 190

Mehrmand, Elle, 343

Meister, Bob, 129

Meredith, James, 77n45

Mexican American studies, 167n36; eradication of, 99–100, 117n2

Middle East Forum, 227

Middle East studies, 8, 26, 227

Middle East Studies Association (MESA), 222

migration, 60, 274; criminality of, 190; forced, 240; narratives of, 269

militancy, 27, 170, 206

militarism, 5, 10, 21, 24, 43, 103, 116, 191, 340; American, 232; culture of, 105; demands of, 55; Israeli, 227; prisons and, 104–8; scientific research and, 16, 17; struggle against, 29, 101, 266; university and, 6

militarization, 17, 21, 66, 127–31, 134–35, 136, 264; campus, 129, 130, 192; logic of, 125; strategies of, 140

military-industrial complex, 94, 104, 110; academia and, 101, 102; prison-industrial complex and, 105, 190; warning about, 17, 103

military-prison-industrial complex (MPIC), 19, 21, 43, 105, 107, 110

military science, 13, 14, 19

Mills, John Stuart, 37, 337

Minerva Consortium, 19, 93

Mirror of Production, 348

MIT, 13, 47n35; CIA and, 17; gender discrimination and, 162

Mogadishu, 302, 303, 306, 325n3

Mohanty, Chandra Talpade, 250, 271, 273

Monitor, The, 86

Moore, Henry, 16

Moore, Willis, 336, 337

moral issues, 24, 68, 129, 135, 136, 220, 227, 232

Morris, Rosalind, 312, 315, 317, 326–27n14; de Genova and, 310–11

MPIC. *See* military-prison-industrial complex

Mulholland, Joseph P., 244

Multi-Campus Research Group (MRG) in International Performance and Culture, 343–44, 347, 350

multiculturalism, 4, 23, 24, 26, 32, 33, 66, 80, 220, 224

Muslim Student Association, 31
Muslim student organizations, 27, 31
Muslim youth, 5, 27–28

Nanlal-Rankoe, Margo, 10
"Narratives: In the Tradition of Black Women" (Clarke), 257
National Association of Scholars, 224
National Defense Authorization Act (2012), 27, 137
National Defense Education Act (1958), 81
National Endowment for the Arts, 183
National Endowment for the Humanities, 183
nationalism, 5, 6, 11, 13, 15, 28, 68, 303, 323; Afro-Caribbean, 240; Chicano, 198, 199, 200; gay lesbian queer sexualities and, 283; liberal, 226; Mexican, 199; queerness and, 285; repudiation of, 312; right-wing, 29; science and, 56, 68; sexuality and, 281
National Labor Relations Act, 185n5
National Review, 224, 304
national security, 12, 19, 27, 105, 108, 272, 323
National Security Agency (NSA), 82, 89
nation building, 6, 30, 60, 76n31
Nation of Islam, 235n16
nation-state, 7, 21–22, 30, 63, 303, 323; Other and, 284
Negri, Antonio, 192
Nelson, Cary, 37, 41, 50n94
neocolonialism, 20, 57, 189
neoconservatives, 25, 26, 37
neoliberalism, 55, 57, 59, 71, 73, 125, 267; conceptual baggage of, 141; dissent against, 108; geopolitics and, 12; logic of, 139, 140; marketplace of

ideas and, 242; militarized violence and, 272; settler colonialism and, 283
neoliberal state, 127, 139, 141; legal power of, 137–38; War on Terror and, 137
Network of Concerned Anthropologists, 15, 19
"Never Again? Zionism and the Holocaust" (Aronson), 290
New Directions in Feminism and Human Rights, 262
New Disciplines Project, 93
Newfield, Christopher, 25, 126, 145
New Jewel movement, 250
New Republic, The, 224
Newsday, 307, 312
New York City Council, 173
New York City Lesbian Gay Bisexual and Transgender Community Center, 281
New York Civil Liberties Union (NYCLU), 242
New York Police Department, 241, 244; colonizing function of, 246, 248
New York Post, 308, 326n12
New York Times, 89, 250, 309, 313, 326n13; Gates in, 235n16; Horowitz ad in, 48n63; Jordan in, 255–56
NietoGomez, Anna, 193, 194, 200, 201, 203
Nikias, Max, 148, 163n8, 163n10
NLRB v. J. Weingarten, Inc. (1975), 180, 185n5
nobody, becoming, 237–38
"Nobody Mean More to Me than You and the Future Life of Willie Jordan" (Jordan), 238, 251, 252
Nocella, Anthony, II, 41
nonviolence, 128, 133, 136

Norfolk State University, 81, 83; IC
  Center at, 80
normatization, 15, 19, 220
North Atlantic Treaty Organization
  (NATO), protesting, 264, 265
Not with Our Money—Students Stop
  Prisons-for-Profit, 110
*No University Is an Island: Saving Aca-
  demic Freedom,* 41
NSA, 89, 91, 92, 348

Obama, Barack, 28, 42, 84, 295n22,
  296n22, 339
objectivity, 221, 229, 231, 264; myth of,
  230, 232; suprapolitical, 222
occupation, 3–5, 11, 28, 41, 72, 104, 264,
  302, 305; colonial, 106, 289; freedom
  from, 40; illegal, 31; Israeli, 170, 172;
  legacy of, 107; military, 5, 13, 40,
  101, 170, 171, 172, 303; overseas, 5–6;
  Palestinian, 171, 208, 242, 256, 291,
  324; politics of, 283; prisons and,
  106; university and, 6; violence of, 9;
  zones of, 43
occupied territories, 174, 283, 284, 286,
  288, 289
Occupy/Decolonize UC Davis, 3, 4
Occupy movement, 3, 12, 27, 34, 43,
  108, 117, 127, 128, 129, 172; clamping
  down on, 4, 131; slogans of, 5
Occupy Oakland, 132
OED. *See* Office of Equity and Diversity
Office of Cybernetics (FBI), 343
Office of Equal Opportunity (WSU),
  180, 181
Office of Equity and Diversity (OED),
  155–56, 202; report by, 156–57; support
  from, 197; tenure outcomes and, 159
Ohio National Guard, 308
On Liberty, 337

Oparah, Julia, 9, 11, 12, 13, 20, 31, 42;
  countercarceral politics and, 21, 190;
  dangerous complicities and, 19
"Open Admissions Experiment"
  (CUNY), 243
oppression, 31, 241, 251, 264, 303
Oren, Michael, 227
Orestia, 349
Orientalism, 64, 219, 221
Oslo Accords (1993), 171, 172, 284
Other, 14, 16, 18, 24, 268, 274, 289, 337;
  Arab/Muslim, 269, 282, 286; nation-
  state and, 284
"Out in Israel" (event), 287
OutRage!, 288
outsiders, 8–11, 293
Overthrow, 89

pacification, 55, 56, 62
Palestine question, censorship of, 33–34
Palestine solidarity, 4, 176, 185n2, 206,
  281; rise/fall/rise of, 170–75
Palestine Solidarity Committee, 171
Palestinian, becoming, 238, 240, 254–57
Palestinian Academic and Cultural Boy-
  cott of Israel (PACBI), 40
Palestinian Intifada, 27, 170, 171, 172, 173
Palestinian liberation, 217, 220, 234n5,
  225, 288
Palestinian Liberation Organization
  (PLO), 171, 256
Palestinian Queers for Boycott, Divest-
  ment, and Sanctions (PQBDS), 287
Palestinians, 172, 173, 219, 227, 237;
  academic boycotts and, 39; deaths
  of, 257; human rights for, 31; Israeli
  policies towards, 177, 283; killings of,
  177, 256; mobility of, 284; oppression of, 283, 291; war crimes against,
  100

Palestinian territories, occupation of, 100, 169, 174

Palimpsests, 238–39, 241

Palmer Raids, 15

patriarchy, 106, 204, 263, 275

PATRIOT (Provide Appropriate Tools Required to Intercept and Obstruct Terrorism) Act, 27, 93, 129, 137

patriotic correctness, 21, 109

patriotism, 11, 12, 21, 225, 226, 303, 312; debates about, 5; intellectual, 227; Israeli, 285; liberal, 225; Zionism and, 203

Pat Roberts Intelligence Scholarship Program (PRISP), 84, 92, 93, 94

pedagogies, 7, 11, 59, 116, 190, 238, 242, 248, 257, 263, 347; anti-imperialist, 271; antiracist feminist, 265; censorship of, 13; critical, 37, 262, 275–78; empowering, 273–75; feminist, 34; responsible, 232

Pedagogies of Crossing, 239

penal dependency, dismantling, 115–17

Pennsylvania Medical School, 112

pepper spraying, 3, 4, 12, 128, 130

performance, 2, 344, 346, 350

Philippine Women's University (PWU), 54, 72, 73, 76n29

pinkwashing, 33, 281, 286–90

Pinochet, Augusto, 315

Pipes, Daniel, 180, 224

Pitts, Lawrence, 351

Plan de Santa Bárbara, 212n42

Plessy v. Ferguson (1896), 64

poetic: becoming, 239–41; distinguishing, 246–48

poetics, 238, 239, 254, 257; queer, 34; transnational, 240

Poetics of Relation, 239

poetry, 239, 241, 254

police, 211n20, 239; becoming, 241–43; militarized, 127, 128, 132, 134; racist, 245

police brutality, 25, 30, 130, 243; black English and, 251–54

police composition, imperative sentence and, 248–49

police English, 30, 248

policing, 6, 8, 29, 32, 64, 113, 191; outsourcing, 129; racialized, 108

political, 222, 229–30, 231; in academic promotion, 228; polemical and, 219

political action, 221–23, 345, 346

politicization, 25, 222, 226

politics, 7, 15, 17, 38, 223, 232, 255, 318, 338; academics and, 225, 267; administration and, 36; anti-imperialist, 269; antiwar, 104; class, 22, 140; colonial, 188, 205; countercarceral, 190; feminist, 188, 268; feminist Chican@, 188; labor, 9; Middle East, 183; national, 292; nationalist, 310; queer, 188; racial, 24, 140; scholarship and, 229; sexual, 24, 201, 206, 292; social movement and, 278; subjectivities and, 268–72; Zionist, 185n2, 235n16

Posener, Alan: interview by, 282, 285, 286

Post, Robert: on academic freedom, 37–38

postcolonial studies, 26, 230, 291

Postethnic America: Beyond Multiculturalism, 23

power, 2, 6, 18, 58, 225; Chicana, 195; economic, 19; exercise of, 231; imperial, 107, 234n14; institutional, 263; legal, 137–38; militarized, 12; plenary, 58; police, 191; question of, 246–47; soft, 7; state, 227, 229, 231

"Power" (Lorde), 238, 246, 249, 258n1, 274

Prakash, Gyan, 290–91

Prashad, Vijay, 9, 12, 20, 32, 34, 36, 39; cultural vigilantes and, 37; freedom/justice/equality and, 38

Price, David, 15, 92

PRIDE, 288

prison-industrial complex, 102–4, 106, 107, 108, 109, 110, 111, 115, 275; changes for, 113–14; military-industrial complex and, 105, 190; transnational, 99

prison industry, 21, 104, 106; divesting from, 116; emergence of, 102–3; growth of, 102, 103, 110–11, 114; private, 107, 110

prisoners, 113; exploitation of, 190–91; increase in, 113; medical experimentation and, 111–12, 190; women, 114

prisons, 116; civilian, 104; economic development and, 107; expanding, 109; higher education and, 102, 110; imperialism and, 103, 105, 106; militarism and, 104–8; private, 102, 110; as source of data, 111; university and, 190

PRISP. See Pat Roberts Intelligence Scholarship Program

privacy, 157, 158–59, 310, 350

privatization, 10, 102, 110, 126, 140, 146, 264; neoliberal, 28, 141; protesting, 25, 127, 129–30, 131, 138, 139, 145; systemic, 125, 127

progressives, 39, 116, 171, 224

Project Camelot, 18, 47n38

promotion, 218, 219–20, 229, 267, 318; denial of, 10; faculty controlled, 145; scholarship and, 234

protestors, 1–2, 3, 12, 129, 132–33, 137; confrontation with, 127, 133, 134–35, 136; inequities and, 128; safety/security and, 134

protests, 2, 3, 18, 19, 127; anti-imperialist, 206; antiwar, 35, 206; criminalization of, 138; instances of, 135–36; military-academy nexus and, 181–89; response to, 135; strategies for, 32; student, 242

Puar, Jasbir, 28, 29, 31, 32, 33–34

public education, 1, 131, 136, 263, 264, 332, 352; accessibility of, 130; advocating for, 126; democratizing, 162n4; disinvestment in, 125, 139–40; dismantling of, 9, 12; prisonization/militarization of, 109. See also education

public services, disinvestment in, 128, 139

public spaces, 254, 264; occupation of, 128, 131

public universities, 56, 266; corporatization of, 25; heteropatriarchal racialized symmetries and, 194; primary purpose of, 346; privatization of, 6, 25, 129; restructuring, 12, 145

Pulido, Laura, 9, 22, 23, 26, 36

Punch, 60

PWU. *See* Philippine Women's University

Queens College: SEEK and, 244; sit-ins at, 243

queerness, 249, 285

"Queer Politics and the Question of Palestine/Israel" (Hochberg), 285

queers, 24, 33, 201, 204, 254, 264, 283; criminalized, 205; homonationalism and, 289; Israeli, 285; Palestinian, 284, 289

Queers against Israeli Apartheid (QuAIA), 288

queers of color, 288, 293

queer studies, 8, 25, 28, 30, 101, 281, 285

Queers Undermining Israeli Terrorism (QUIT), 288

Queer Theory and the Jewish Question, 284
Question of Palestine, The, 290, 291

Rabin, Yitzhak, 171, 309
race, 14, 23, 67, 231, 254, 264; anxieties
    around, 270; class and, 272; deter-
    ministic notions of, 292; dialogics of,
    254; pedagogy of, 7; politics of, 21
"Race and the Urban Situation"
    (course), 246
racial counting, process of, 160
racial genocide, 293
racial hierarchy, 14–15, 270
racialization, 29, 30, 61, 243
racial management, 70–71, 155, 156
racism, 9, 29, 31, 32, 42, 100, 180, 181,
    182, 183, 185n6, 238, 241, 245, 246,
    247, 250, 263, 264, 274, 275, 288,
    292, 293; anti-Arab, 177; anti-
    Muslim, 33, 294; charges of, 155;
    Chicana feminists and, 204; coun-
    tering, 204, 265, 266; imperial, 6, 30;
    institutional, 175–78; neoclassical
    constraints and, 339; structural, 156;
    university, 195
radicalism, 23, 26, 42, 56, 226, 330, 335
Ramadan, Tariq, 217
Ramlal-Nankoe, Margo, 217
rape, as weapon of war, 272
Rapp-Coudert Committee, 15
Raza, 206
Readings, Bill, 14, 21, 42, 43, 45n15
Reagan, Ronald, 23
Reclaim UC (blog), 133, 137
relation, 238, 249–51
"Relative to Anti-Semitism" (HR 35), 338
religion, 7, 21, 68
Rendón, Armando, 198, 199
Reorder of Things: The University and Its

Pedagogies of Minority Difference,
    The, 193–94
repression, 6, 12, 15, 20, 37; domestic,
    8; militarized, 206; protest and, 19;
    resisting, 101
research, 14, 18, 217, 262, 275, 276,
    277, 278, 344; circulation of, 228;
    controversial, 229; groundbreaking,
    230; humanistic, 232; moral issues
    and, 232; political, 203; scholarship
    and, 219; scientific, 16; socialization
    of, 18; social justice-oriented, 265;
    substandard, 220
Reserve Officer Training Corps
    (ROTC), 84
resistance, 71, 101, 136, 196, 281; anti-
    colonial, 199; dilemma about, 20;
    heteromasculinist, 199; spirit of, 187
resources, 56, 339, 340; cultural, 335;
    redistribution of, 234–35n14
responsibility, 65, 226, 232, 233, 250;
    collective, 318–19; scholarly, 218;
    unwritten code of, 312
Rich, Adrienne, 258n2
Right to Education campaign, 5
"Rise of English, The" (Eagleton), 68
Riverside County Sheriff's Department,
    2, 129
Riverside Police Department, 2, 129
Robinson, William, 32, 228
Robinson-Edley report, 134, 135
Rockefeller, Nelson: drug laws and, 241
Rockefeller Conference Center, 39
Rojas, Clarissa, 9, 10, 18, 23, 24, 43
Rosaldo, Renato, 208
Rumsfeld, Donald, 272

Sabeel, 173
Sabra refugee camp, massacre at, 256
safety, 12, 134, 329; public, 27, 136–37, 140

Said, Edward W., 64, 221–22, 290; Faculty Committee of Palestine and, 324; intellectual freedom and, 323; on orientalism, 189

Said, Wadie, 10

Salaita, Steven, 10, 22, 24, 26, 29, 31, 32, 33, 36, 40

San Antonio Express-News, 88

Sandoval, Chela, 264

San Francisco LGBT Film Festival, 288

San Francisco State University (SFSU), 187, 197, 207; Chicano/a studies at, 196; Latina students at, 191

Schecter, Ellen, 23, 35

scholarship, 8, 11, 14, 31, 83–84, 203, 220, 222, 228; activist, 10; anti-American, 12; anti-imperial, 81; antiracist, 100; anti-Zionist, 230; censorship of, 13; contemporary, 227; ethics of, 229; justice-oriented, 232; leftist, 81; marginalizing, 22; nonobjective, 230; nonpolitical, 222; political, 218, 221, 229; promotion and, 234; public, 10; queer, 297n30; research and, 219; responsible, 221, 229

"School Begins" cartoons (*Punch*), 60

School of the Americas, 18, 87

school-to-prison pipeline, 109

Schultz, Dagmar, 258n2

science, 14, 94; military research and, 13; nationalism and, 56, 68; technology and, 17

Scott, David, 310, 311, 312, 317, 327n15

Scott, Joan, 39

Search for Education, Elevation and Knowledge (SEEK), 241, 244

security, 23, 137, 192, 243, 307, 310; campus, 130; divesting from, 110, 116; national/global, 129

security forces, resistance by, 130–31

"security studies" program, 183–84

SEEK. *See* Search for Education, Elevation and Knowledge

segregation, 32, 40, 65, 77n44, 284, 293

self-determination, 34, 40, 223, 233, 249–50, 303

self-interest, 251, 266, 318

self-policing, 320–23

Seligman Report (AAUP), 23, 35

Sen, Amartya, 73

Senghor, Leopold, 254

Senior Hiring Initiative, 150

September 11th, 18, 28, 33, 79, 82, 104, 191, 318, 329; crisis of repression and, 6; response to, 105

settler colonialism, 10, 30, 31, 33, 41, 43, 118n7, 240; foundational mythologies of, 7; neoliberalism and, 283

sexism, 42, 197, 200, 246, 264, 274, 287; challenging, 199, 265, 266; structural, 156

sexual harassment, 182, 202, 203

sexuality, 7, 34, 231, 270; gay lesbian queer, 283; gender and, 281; nationalism and, 281; social scientific knowledge of, 205

sexual rights, 34, 291; homonationalist politics of, 289

SFSU. *See* San Francisco State University

Shakespeare, William, 68, 71 72

Shatila refugee camp, massacre at, 256

Shea, Thomas, 245, 246, 247–48, 249, 251

Shipper, Jody, 165n27, 165n29

Shohat, Ella, 290–91

Shrecker, Ellen W., 35

Simmons, Solon, 330

Sister Outsider, 250

Sisters Supporting Sisters in South Africa (SISA), 238, 258n2 sit-ins, 243, 344; virtual, 343, 345–46, 347, 350

SJP. *See* Students for Justice in Palestine

Slaughter, Anne-Marie, 127

slavery, 66, 115, 272, 303

Smith, Andrea, 116, 201, 230

Smith, Linda Tuhiwai, 230

social control, 156, 334

social death, 30, 193, 248

social disorder, 113, 241

social mobility, 109, 126

social movements, 18, 207, 267, 275; anti-imperialist, 106; institutions and, 194; politics and, 278; racial-/ethnic-based, 189

social norms, 28, 37, 337

social order, 189, 196, 303

social problems, 103, 115, 312

social science, 18, 19, 94, 164n17

Social Text, 290, 340

Society of American Law Teachers Conference, 340

Sociologists without Borders, 267

Soden, Dennis: on intelligence community, 82

Sodexho Alliance, CCA and, 110

Soldatenko, Michael, 194

solidarity, 8–11, 39, 170, 255, 257, 273, 340; building, 274; campaign for, 181; feminist, 9, 33; pedagogy of, 257; queer, 33

Solomon, Alisa, 284, 285

Soto, Sandy, 197

space, 56; contradictory, 262–63, 263–68; coproduction of, 293; public, 128, 131, 254, 264

Spanish-American War (1898), 58, 61, 62

Special Operations Research Office (SORO), 18

speech: freedom of, 4, 5, 303, 304, 307, 310, 311, 314, 316, 317, 319, 320, 323; offending, 306, 307, 308

Spielberg, Steven, 307

spy agencies, 79–80, 84, 89; minority youth and, 91; universities and, 94–95

Spy Camp, 79, 80, 83, 91

Stalbaum, Brett, 343, 353

Stamps Family Charitable Foundation, 163n8

"Stand with Us," 227, 288

Stanford University, 13, 15, 80

State Normal School, 72

State University of New York (SUNY): black English and, 237, 238; Jordan and, 251, 252; people of color and, 241

Stein, Rebecca L., 283, 284

stereotypes, 20, 137, 200

Sterling Partners, study by, 331

Stokes Program, 92, 93

Stop Islamicization of America campaign, 48n64

Student Bill of Rights, 25

Students for Academic Freedom, 26, 37, 48n56

Students for Justice in Palestine (SJP), 4, 31, 32

subjectivities: Chicana, 188, 212n42; hypermasculinist, 204; imperial, 192; political issues and, 268–72; queer, 188

subordination, 63, 111

Summer Intelligence Seminars, 83, 91

Summers, Larry, 172, 185n3

SUNY. *See* State University of New York

surveillance, 23, 27, 29, 42, 99, 103, 104, 293; culture of, 109; domestic, 92; post-9/11, 5, 6; racialized, 100, 108

Taft, William Howard, 63

Talcott, Molly, 9

Taraki, Lisa, 39–40, 42

Taussig, Michael, 316

TBT. *See* Transborder Immigrant Tool

Teachers against Occupation, 295n22

teaching, 237, 262, 275, 276

teach-ins, 301, 302, 310, 311, 312, 313

Technion Institute, 100, 101

technology, 17, 64, 110; detention, 108, 113; disciplinary, 321–22; heteropatriarchal, 199

Tempest, The, 72

tenure, 10, 22, 167n37, 218, 219, 265, 267, 271, 318, 334, 343; advancing, 262; Chicano/a, 196, 197; denial of, 10, 151–52, 154, 157, 159, 161, 162, 232, 344, 346; disciplinary technology and, 321–22; faculty controlled, 145; granting of, 152, 153, 160, 328n24; success rate for, 159; women of color and, 151–52, 154, 160, 208; Zionists and, 232

Tenure Bill of Rights, 157, 158, 161

Tenured Radicals: How Politics has Corrupted Our Higher Education, 23

Tenure Forum, flyer from, 153*f*

tenure process, 164n17, 165–66n30, 166n33, 167n37, 217, 219–20; challenges to, 162; at corporate university, 153–61; discrimination in, 154; openness in, 158; problems with, 151–53, 154, 156; racial/gender bias in, 155; transparency in, 157, 162; at USC, 146, 150–53

terrorism, 29, 27, 179, 185n6, 243; fighting, 137, 266; Israeli, 183; Palestinian, 171

Terrorist Assemblages: Homonationalism in Queer Times, 281, 292

terrorists, 286, 302; deportation of, 28; detention of, 104, 137

Third World Liberation Front Strike, 193

Thirteenth Amendment, 115

Thompson, Reagan, 81

toleration, object of, 317–20

torture, 135, 315; Israeli, 175, 179

Transborder Immigrant Tool (TBT), 41, 343, 344, 345, 353

Trinity University, 79; IC Center at, 80, 81; Spy Camp at, 83, 91

Truman, Harry S., 23

Tucson Unified District, Mexican American studies program and, 117n2

tuition hikes, 1, 25, 125, 128, 130, 330, 339

Tutu, Desmond, 170, 173, 174, 175

Tydings-McDuffie Act (1934), 60, 75n17

UCAPT. *See* University Committee on Academic Promotion and Tenure

UCAPT Manual, 161, 167n37

UCB. *See* University of California, Berkeley

UC Davis. *See* University of California, Davis

UC Irvine. *See* University of California, Irvine

UCLA. *See* University of California, Los Angeles

UCOP. *See* University of California Office of the President

UCR. *See* University of California, Riverside

UCSD. *See* University of California, San Diego

UCSF. *See* University of California, San Francisco

UC Southern Branch, 72

UH. *See* University of Hawai'i

UMAS. *See* United Mexican American Students

Undergraduate Student Government (USC), 149

"Unfairallon" campaign, 102

United Mexican American Students
(UMAS), 194, 201, 203, 206, 213n59
United Nations, 190; Israeli occupation
and, 118n7
United Nations Office at Geneva
(UNOG), CEIRPP of, 119n24
United Nations World Conference
against Racism (WCAR), 263
university: clichés about, 54; colonial
interests and, 191; conservatism of,
56; culture of, 148, 209; democratizing, 55; discourse of, 67; as gathering
place, 71; heteropatriarchal ordering
of, 208; idea of, 305–7; neoliberal, 10,
25, 28, 139; as policing institution,
253; postimperial, 67, 72–73; privatization of, 9, 28, 138; radicalism of,
56; self-conceptions of, 66
University Committee on Academic
Promotion and Tenure (UCAPT),
155, 157, 158, 159, 166n32, 167n37
University of California (UC): budget
crisis for, 25; demonstrations and,
131; leadership of, 125, 126, 127, 132–
33, 136; privatization of, 125, 126, 127,
128–29, 140; regents, 128–29; support
for, 71, 351
University of California, Berkeley
(UCB), 3, 13, 80; divestment and,
174; leadership, 130; police, 130;
protests at, 128
University of California, Davis (UC
Davis), 77n45, 130; Chicano/a studies at, 196; pepper spraying at, 3–4;
protests at, 128; U.S. Bank and, 138
University of California, Irvine (UC
Irvine), Israeli ambassador at, 4
University of California, Los Angeles
(UCLA), 68, 138, 162n4; Shakespeare
course at, 72; and UPR compared,
71–72; USC and, 147

University of California, Riverside
(UCR): leadership, 133, 134; penalties for, 4; protests at, 128, 133–34,
139
University of California, San Diego
(UCSD), 41, 50n91, 343, 345, 347,
349, 353; Compton Cookout and,
192; racist incidents at, 352
University of California, San Francisco
(UCSF), Genentech Hall at, 191–92
University of California, Santa Barbara,
190, 228
University of California, Santa Cruz,
129, 187, 262
University of California Office of the
President (UCOP), 142n8, 348, 349,
352, 353; travel advisory by, 130;
virtual sit-in at, 343, 344, 345; web
site of, 350
University of Chicago, 16, 80
University of Hawai'i (UH), 54, 55, 58;
discourse of, 56; female students at,
70f; founding of, 57, 69; history of,
69; literary studies, 66–71
University of Hawai'i (UH)-Manoa,
founding of, 71
University of Maryland, College Park,
315; IC Center at, 80
University of Michigan, 170, 171
University of Mississippi, Meredith and,
77n45
University of Puerto Rico (UPR), 54, 55,
58; discourse of, 56; English department at, 72; founding of, 57; graffiti
at, 53f; history of, 69; literary studies
at, 66–71; Shakespeare course at, 72;
and UCLA compared, 71–72
University of Southern California (USC),
59; academic prestige for, 145, 146, 147,
148; administrative structure of, 148–
50; culture of, 151, 154, 161, 163n10;

education (*continued*)
  faculty University of Southern
  California diversity at, 160, 167n36;
  fund-raising by, 149; improvements at,
  148–49; opportunities/privileges at, 145;
  private status of, 146, 147; racial/eth-
  nic/gender diversity at, 151, 162; racial
  management and, 155; tenure process
  at, 146, 150–53, 154, 157, 158, 161, 164n17,
  165–66n30; UCLA and, 147
University of Texas, El Paso, IC Center
  at, 80, 82
University of Texas, Pan American
  (UTPA): DNI and, 86; exploitation
  of, 88; "Got Intelligence?" camp and,
  91; IC Center at, 80, 85, 86, 87, 88
University of the Philippines (UP), 54,
  55, 58; discourse of, 56; history of,
  57, 69; literary studies at, 66–71
University of Washington, 36, 336; IC
  Center at, 80
University of Wisconsin, Milwaukee:
  symposium at, 239
University of Wisconsin, Whitewater:
  tenure/promotion at, 217
UP. *See* University of the Philippines
UPR. *See* University of Puerto Rico
U.S. Army Corps of Engineers, prisons
  and, 107
U.S. Bank, UC Davis and, 138
U.S. Campaign for the Academic and Cul-
  tural Boycott of Israel (USACBI), 170
U.S. Campaign to End the Occupation,
  173
U.S. Code 1030, 353
U.S. Social Forum, cancellation of, 288
U.S. Supreme Court, 64, 66, 180
USC. *See* University of Southern
  California
Uses of the University, The, 54
USS *Thomas,* 61, 63

UTPA. *See* University of Texas, Pan
  American

value, 9; abstract, 320; cultural, 64, 66,
  71
Vatos Locos Party, 192
Vice-Provost Task Force on Graduate
  Education (USC), 150
Victoria's Secret, prison labor and, 103
Vietnam War, 94, 203, 207, 301, 302,
  303; Chicanos and, 204; protesting,
  206
vigilantism, 336, 340
violence, 42, 134, 135, 199, 239, 249,
  274, 289, 304, 305, 308; antiqueer/
  antitrans, 192; campus, 189, 244;
  colonial, 189, 204; culture of, 272;
  epistemic, 115; gendered, 271, 272;
  genocidal, 30; heteropatriarchal, 192,
  195–98; imperial, 191, 209, 283, 305;
  institutional, 187; intracommunity,
  209; Israeli, 257; militarized, 128,
  272; misogynous, 196; physical, 115;
  police, 191, 244, 245, 253; public
  safety and, 136–37; racial, 192, 196,
  238, 303; responding with, 133; sexual, 206, 271, 272; state, 3, 10, 30–31,
  101, 227; structural, 25; transforming, 202; unspeakable, 301–5, 309;
  against women, 106, 203, 206, 208
Violent Radicalization and Homegrown
  Terrorism Act (HR 1955), 93
Virginia Tech: IC Center at, 80; tenure
  at, 217
Viswanathan, Gauri, 68–69
"Voices of the Children" workshop, 251
Von Braun, Christina, 283, 292; interview of, 282, 285, 286

Walker, Alice, 170
Wallerstein, Immanuel, 18

Wall Street Journal, Bollinger in, 307

Walzer, Michael, 226, 227

war, 7, 9, 11, 30, 41, 42; academic, 13; challenging, 5–6; of conquest, 56; imperialist, 6, 303, 312; nation making and, 30; occupation and, 106; state formation and, 6

war crimes, 173, 178

War on Drugs, 104, 140, 192, 274

War on Terror, 6, 16, 19, 27, 92, 106, 140, 192, 206, 207, 208, 242, 286, 302; culture war on, 26; frontlines of, 13; imperial university and, 11; neoliberal state and, 137; state of emergency and, 317

War Relocation Authority, 16

Warrior, Robert, 230

Washington, Harriet, 190–91

Washington Post, 89, 250; on IC Centers, 80–81

Waters, Roger, 170

Wayne State University (WSU): Arab world and, 176; BDS and, 175; discrimination/harassment at, 173; divestment and, 175, 178; IC Center at, 80; as imperial university, 183–84; institutional racism and, 175–78; Palestinians and, 172; political firestorm at, 176

Weekly Standard, 224

Weizman, Eyal, 284

White, Tim, 134, 136

whiteness: blackness and, 255; as privilege, 270

white supremacy, 43, 198, 277

Wigmore, John, 319, 320

Wilson, James Q., 113

Wilson, Woodrow, 319

"Woman Question," 289

women of color, 165n25, 261; sexual violence against, 206; tenure and, 151–52, 154, 208; working-class, 214n68; writing by, 198

women's studies, 9, 18, 23, 28, 245, 267

Workplace: A Journal for Academic Labor, 340

World War I, 15, 306, 307, 319

Wright, Michelle, 239, 254, 255

writing, 8, 198, 217, 261, 262

writ of habeas corpus, enemy combatants and, 292

WSU. *See* Wayne State University

Wynter, Sylvia, 238–39, 255, 256; ethnopoetics and, 239–40; racism and, 241; sociopoetics and, 240

Yale University, 80; "Dump Farallon" campaign and, 102; U.S. Special Forces training center at, 98n37

Young, Iris Marion, 233

Yudof, Mark G., 4, 134, 138, 344, 347, 349, 351, 352

Zionism, 181, 218, 219, 220, 224, 227, 228, 284, 287, 290; commitment to, 230, 232; criticism of, 31; definition of, 292; homonationalism and, 285; normative status for, 225; patriotism and, 203; versions of, 223; xenophobic, 185n2

"Zionism from a Standpoint of Its Victims" (Said), 290

Zionists, 26, 28, 29, 170, 171, 172, 173, 174, 177, 179, 180, 182, 183, 223, 224, 226, 227, 228, 233, 291; human rights and, 31; liberal queer, 286; political and, 229–30; right-wing, 176; tenure decisions; and, 232; traditionalist, 230